Second Edition

WOMEN, POLITICS, AND AMERICAN SOCIETY

Nancy E. McGlen
Niagara University

Karen O'Connor
American University

Prentice Hall, Upper Saddle River, New Jersey 07458

Library of Congress Cataloging-in-Publication Data

McGlen, Nancy E., (date)
    Women, politics, and American society / Nancy E. McGlen, Karen
    O'Connor. — 2nd ed.
        p.   cm.
    Includes index.
    ISBN 0-13-639097-8
    1. Women's rights—United States.   2. Women in politics—United
States.   I. O'Connor, Karen, (date).
HQ1236.5.U6M394   1998
305.42'0973—dc21   97-31497
                                                                    CIP

Editor-in-Chief: Nancy Roberts
Assistant Editor: Nicole Signoretti
Editorial Assistant: Kathryn Sheehan
Director of Production and Manufacturing: Barbara Kittle
Managing Editor: Ann Marie McCarthy
Production Liaison: Fran Russello
Project Manager: Linda B. Pawelchak
Manufacturing Manager: Nick Sklitsis
Prepress and Manufacturing Buyer: Bob Anderson
Cover Director: Jayne Conte
Cover Design: Wendy Alling Judy
Cover Art: "Friends"/Diana Ong/Superstock, Inc.
Electronic Art Creation: Asterisk Group, Inc.
Marketing Manager: Chris DeJohn
Copy Editing: Lynn Buckingham
Proofreading: Nancy Menges

This book was set in 10/12 Palatino by Stratford Publishing Services
and was printed and bound by Courier Companies, Inc.
The cover was printed by Phoenix Color Corp.

Printed in the United States of America
10   9   8   7   6   5   4   3   2   1

ISBN 0-13-639097-8

Prentice-Hall International (UK) Limited, *London*
Prentice-Hall of Australia Pty. Limited, *Sydney*
Prentice-Hall Canada Inc., *Toronto*
Prentice-Hall Hispanoamericana, S.A., *Mexico*
Prentice-Hall of India Private Limited, *New Delhi*
Prentice-Hall of Japan, Inc., *Tokyo*
Simon & Schuster Asia Pte. Ltd., *Singapore*
Editora Prentice-Hall do Brasil, Ltda., *Rio de Janeiro*

Contents

2   WOMEN'S POLITICAL PARTICIPATION   60

PART II   EMPLOYMENT AND EDUCATIONAL RIGHTS AND REALITIES

 # Preface

We have worked together for more than twenty years and have lived through many of the changes chronicled in this book. We also have experienced these changes through the eyes of our students, who seem to get younger every year. It is they we must first thank for keeping our interests in women and politics alive. While the study of women, politics, and American society can indeed be frustrating, the enthusiasm and interest of our students have kept the subject matter from becoming too depressing, even during the 1980s, a time that some argue saw gains in women's rights begin to disappear.

In this text we try to share our enthusiasm for the study of women and politics. It is our experience that many people are woefully unaware of the battles that many heroic women and women's organizations have fought since the 1800s to garner basic, fundamental rights. This book addresses women and politics in American society by combining historical and topical approaches with a focus on political rights, education and employment, and familial and reproductive rights.

We hope we offer our readers a more comprehensive understanding of where women are today in America, the battles they have fought, and what changes still need to be made before full equality can be reached. We hope that this book produces as many questions as it answers and motivates readers to pursue subjects of particular interest in greater detail.

We would like to thank our colleagues in the Women's Caucus for Political Science and the Organized Women and Politics Section for always being there to support research of this nature: Judy Baer, Meredith Reid Sarkees, Denise Baer, and Sue Carroll. Thanks also go to the following reviewers: Anne N. Costain, University of Colorado; Lauren Holland, University of Utah; Emily Stoper, California State University; Laura R. Woliver, University of South Carolina; and Sarah Slavin, Buffalo State College.

The librarians at the State University of New York at Buffalo and Niagara University were especially helpful.

Many women's organizations and research institutes—including the Center for American Women and Politics, the Institute of Social Research at the University of Michigan, the National Women's Political Caucus, the National Organization for Women, Concerned Women for America, EMILY's List, the Ms. Foundation, the Congressional Caucus for Women's Issues, RENEW, and the Reproductive Freedom Project of the American Civil Liberties Union—provided us with valuable information. We would also like to acknowledge the Inter-University Consortium for Political and Social Research, the Louis Harris Association, and the Roper Organization for survey data and summaries used throughout the book.

We would like to express our appreciation to Bernadette Nye, now at American University; Maria Bevacqua and Noah Messing, both former students at Emory University; Heather Pearce at Niagara University; and Jess Waters, Graham Barron, and Sarah Brewer at American University for their research assistance and help. We never would have gotten this manuscript to Prentice Hall without them.

And, finally, we would like to thank our families.

Nancy E. McGlen
Karen O'Connor

Introduction: Women's Movements in America

Women's efforts to gain political, economic, and social equality in America are as old as the United States itself. As early as March 31, 1776, Abigail Adams wrote to her husband, John, who was in attendance at the Continental Congress:

> In the new Code of Laws . . . I desire you would Remember the Ladies, and be more generous and favourable to them than your ancestors. Do not put such unlimited power into the hands of the Husbands. Remember all Men would be tyrants if they could. If particular care and attention is not paid to the Laidies [*sic*] we are determined to foment a Rebelion [*sic*], and will not hold ourselves bound by any Laws in which we have no voice, or Representation.[1]

The rebellion predicted by Abigail Adams, however, did not begin for more than half a century.

In 1848, a woman's rights convention was held in Seneca Falls, a small town in central New York. Present at that meeting were many women who soon were to become leaders of what we call the first woman's movement, including Elizabeth Cady Stanton and Lucretia Mott. Today these women are most remembered for their efforts to secure female suffrage; in 1848, however, their goals were much broader in scope.

At the Seneca Falls Convention, a Declaration of Sentiments modeled after the U.S. Declaration of Independence was drawn up by attendees.[2] Later, at the same meeting, a series of resolutions calling for the abolition of legal, economic, and social discrimination against women was passed. Twelve days later a larger meeting was held in Rochester, New York. At that meeting, which was presided over by a woman (a controversial move at the time), an even more revolutionary set of resolutions was drafted. Both documents reflected these women's dissatisfaction with contemporary moral codes, divorce and criminal laws, and the limited opportunities for women to obtain an education, participate in the church, and enter careers in medicine, law, and politics. While the agenda of rights for women set forth at these conventions has been expanded over the years, women today continue to work toward many of the goals first publicly enunciated at Seneca Falls.

Since 1848, however, the pursuit of women's rights has been intermittent. There have been periods of high activity, when pressure for reforms has been keen. Most often these phases have been followed by years of little visible or public organized effort. In the pages to follow, we focus on three high points of activity when definable women's rights movements existed: (1) the early woman's movement (1848–1875), (2) the suffrage movement (1890–1925), and (3) the women's rights movement (1966–present). We examine these three periods of women's rights activity by detailing the rise and development of each movement, its philosophy, and its accomplishments in three issue areas: (1) politics; (2) education and employment; and (3) personal rights, including those within the family and those dealing with reproductive freedom.

Where appropriate, we trace the development and activities of organizations or social movements that arose to oppose these women's movements' efforts for expanded rights. We also examine the nature of the movements themselves and why they developed when they did. Thus, we pay particular attention to factors that social movement theorists consider important to the rise or development of social movements: (1) an organizational base and organizational support that includes government support and the presence of preexisting groups upon which to build, (2) the availability of leaders or organizers (who often have experience in other groups), (3) the existence of communications networks to facilitate expansion of a movement, and (4) the role of crises (or what we term *critical mobilizing events*) to foster or even to reinvigorate a movement. Also key to our discussion is an examination of the kinds of rights sought by women in the various women's rights movements. It is our contention that those movements that sought rights that could be termed by some as *public goods,** which by definition are available to all and therefore often threatening to many, are less likely to succeed. Movements seeking public goods, which often are viewed by some as public bads, are more likely to encounter strong opposition than movements whose goals are more limited.

To facilitate our analysis of the development of women's rights—and the role that organized women's groups have played in the achievement of those rights—this book is divided into three parts: Part I—Political Rights and Realities, Part II—Employment and Educational Rights and Realities, and Part III—Familial and Reproductive Rights and Realities. The first chapter of each section describes the political efforts undertaken to obtain various

---

*Political scientists generally define *public goods* as "necessarily shared goods" or ones that once provided to a single member of any group cannot be denied or withheld from others in the group whether or not they contributed to its attainment. An example of a public good would be the proposed equal rights amendment, which was defeated in 1982. Had it been ratified, equal rights would have been guaranteed to *all* women, whether or not they personally favored the amendment.

rights. Because these endeavors were strongly influenced by the particular characteristics of each women's rights movement, as well as by a number of other political and social factors, we attempt to show how these several factors interacted to affect the successes of each movement. The second chapter of each section then focuses on the social changes still needed to obtain the conditions necessary for the full exercise of rights. The transformation of public opinion, especially that of women, toward women's participation in each area is of special interest. This is followed by a discussion of how hard-fought-for rights have been translated into realities and what legal and social barriers remain to the achievement of full equality for women.

While we have divided "rights" into three general areas, they often overlap. Efforts to achieve success in one area have often affected progress in others. Changes in social institutions that allow for the fuller exercise of political rights, for example, have often influenced participation in the economic or social spheres. This has been particularly true of women's role within the family. Changes in marital age, number of children, and other aspects of family life have important ramifications on political and economic participation.

Perhaps most importantly we cannot ignore the fact that only women give birth, which has permeated their efforts to seek expanded rights. Assumptions about women's child-rearing capabilities as well as their "motherhood" duties are a common theme that has linked debates concerning political, employment, and educational rights.

Women in the United States clearly have made major legal, political, and social advances since 1848 and especially in the past thirty years. Yet much remains to be accomplished. The so-called Nannygate debacle that occurred early in the first Clinton administration, when charges were made that only female and not male nominees for Cabinet positions were asked about their child-care or other household arrangements, is but one example of the problems that continue to plague women in their effort to reach the full equality first demanded at Seneca Falls. A 1993 United Nations report estimated that it would take nearly one thousand years for women to gain the same political and economic clout as men.[3] We hope that as you read the pages to follow you will gain a fuller appreciation of the activities of those who have gone before you, learn what changes still need to occur, and be inspired to carry on the mission.

AN OVERVIEW OF WOMEN'S RIGHTS MOVEMENT ACTIVITY

The Early Woman's Movement (1848–1875)

During much of the early nineteenth century, a prime topic of discussion and of women's writings was women's proper role in society. Nevertheless, no organized activity for women's rights occurred. In the 1840s, as an outgrowth of religious revivalism, however, both men and women were encouraged to work for those less fortunate than themselves. The temperance and abolition movements, both developed by followers of revivalism, attracted large numbers of supporters. Women were initially assigned minor roles in these efforts, and the battle over their right to take action in "political causes" was often heated. Nevertheless, women eventually took an active and vocal role, especially within the more liberal branch of the antislavery movement headed by William Lloyd Garrison. Garrison, the editor of *The Liberator*, a leading abolitionist newspaper, theorized that the rights of blacks and women to vote and otherwise participate in government followed from the position that all men and women were created equal. Thus, both groups possessed the same inalienable rights to life, liberty, and the pursuit of happiness.

This view fostered the formation of numerous local and national female antislavery societies in the mid-1800s. These organizations brought women together for the first time and gave them the opportunity to develop leadership and political skills.

One of the first women to speak out publicly was Maria W. Stewart, a writer for Garrison's *Liberator*, who gave a series of four public addresses in Boston. At a time when public speaking for women was a rarity—except at Quaker meetings—Stewart's speeches were even more notable because she was African American.[4] Actions of women including Stewart and the Grimké sisters of South Carolina, Sarah and Angelina, who first gained their fame as abolitionists, earned for other women the right to speak out on political issues. The social code that made it unladylike for women to speak in public was "bent" to accommodate the perceived need for action against a horrible evil—slavery.

Participation in the antislavery movement helped to spark women's recognition that they, as a *class*, were subjected to discrimination. More specifically, in 1840, Lucretia Mott and Elizabeth Cady Stanton accompanied their husbands to a meeting of the World Anti-Slavery Society in London, England. After their long and arduous trip, the women were denied the right to participate in the meeting. A lengthy and vehement debate by the assembled delegates ensued. In the end, Mott and Stanton were told to take seats in the balcony because, as *women*, they could not participate in the meeting. This stinging rejection led them to realize that their position in society was not much better than that of the slaves they were working to set free. Mott and Stanton immediately resolved to call a convention of women to petition for their rights. Both women had families to raise, so it was not until eight years later that they convened a meeting in Stanton's hometown of Seneca Falls, New York, believing that the time was opportune to press for additional rights.

Friendships among other women active in the abolitionist cause produced a set of linkages, which with the aid of abolitionist newspapers and annual conventions served as a communications network of sorts for the fledgling woman's movement until after the Civil War. No independent national women's rights organizations, however, were formed until the late

1860s. In 1869, after a disagreement over endorsement of the Fifteenth Amendment occurred, two rival organizations, the National Woman Suffrage Association (NWSA) and the American Woman Suffrage Association (AWSA), were founded. From that time through the mid-1870s, women's groups lobbied for a variety of reforms advocated at Seneca Falls. Generally, they focused on woman suffrage, but their efforts were to no avail, as no state added women to its list of eligible voters during that period. Women's work for expanded rights, including suffrage, was grounded in their belief that "the gender hierarchy of male dominance and female submission was not natural but arbitrary."[5] Their anger at the unfairness of this system often came through loud and clear. Not surprisingly then, as women continued to press for women's rights during the next few decades, they met with little success. Their views were simply seen by many as too radical.

The Suffrage Movement (1890–1925)

In 1890, after years of limited activity, NWSA and AWSA were merged to create the National American Woman Suffrage Association (NAWSA) with Susan B. Anthony, a longtime close friend of Elizabeth Cady Stanton, at its helm. Anthony, in fact, had founded NWSA along with Stanton.[6]

We date the beginning of the suffrage movement as 1890, but other social trends also helped to foster the second push for equality. Both the temperance and progressive movements were instrumental to the development of the suffrage movement in the late nineteenth and early twentieth centuries. The Woman's Christian Temperance Union (WCTU), whose primary focus was the abolition of liquor, was founded in 1874 and promoted woman suffrage as early as 1879. Its phenomenal growth to more than 200,000 members by the early 1900s helped a large number of women to perceive the need for suffrage.[7] In the North and West, the Progressive Era gave birth to the settlement house movement, the National Consumers' League (NCL), and the Women's Trade Union League (WTUL). Both organizations were made up largely of white, middle-class women who sought to improve the working conditions of less fortunate children and women. Eventually, many women active in these organizations came to see the ballot as a prerequisite for their success. They claimed the vote would allow women to reform society, a task that they, as women, were particularly well suited to do.

This ideology clearly buttressed these women's limited demand for the vote. Most supporters of suffrage were avowedly content with their roles as mothers and wives. In fact, their position and the logic used to support it were the ideology of the earlier movement in reverse. While Stanton, the intellectual leader of the woman's movement, had claimed that motherhood and marriage were only *incidental roles* for women with respect to any claim for rights, leaders of the suffrage movement viewed motherhood and marriage as an *important basis* for the right to vote.

The existence of strong women's organizations, especially the WCTU, helped to spread this idea to women who had been untouched or unconvinced by women's rights advocates of the earlier era. In particular, the WCTU was especially effective in the South, where it was able to cloak the "radical" vote idea under the rubric of temperance. Thus, the WCTU was responsible for organizing women in a region that had previously seen few women's organizations.

The temperance and progressive movements also provided training for suffrage leaders. For example, two later presidents of NAWSA came to the suffrage movement via their activities in the temperance movement. Indeed, an interlocking directorate of sorts developed between the various reform groups and the NAWSA, as depicted in Table I–1.

Social Movement Connections

The period from 1820 to 1850 saw the development of several religious, moral, and social reform movements including the temperance movement, the abolition movement, and the woman's rights movement. These movements were largely centered in the Northeast. Central New York State was an area of particularly intense activity.

Historian Alice Rossi has argued that this proliferation of social causes can be traced to the economic instability of the period and the region, as the United States began to shift from an agricultural land-based economy to an industrial society.[a] These economic changes seriously challenged traditional values. Entrepreneurial skills and money—not land or family heritage—now determined status in the new economy. To compensate for their inability or unwillingness to join the new capitalist culture, many middle-class women and men were drawn to social causes that emphasized betterment of the community. The personal ties forged among the women who participated in these efforts formed the basis for their combined attempt to reform the role of women in society. As Table I–1 indicates, these various reform movements were supported by leading women's rights advocates of the nineteenth century.

[a]Alice S. Rossi, ed., *The Feminist Papers: From Adams to de Beauvoir* (New York: Columbia University Press, 1973).

The progressive and temperance movements alone, however, probably would have been insufficient to produce an effective women's movement were it not for the development of a large organizational base of women that came from the tremendous growth of women's clubs in the 1880s and 1890s. White middle-class women, freed from many domestic tasks by the development of many labor-saving devices, devoted some of their extra time to participation in self-improvement groups such as reading societies or book clubs, as they are called in some communities today.[8] An important club movement also began among well-educated and affluent African American women,

TABLE I–1 Social Movement Connections

Women's Rights/Suffrage Advocate (Year of birth)	Religious Revivalism	Temperance	Moral Reform	Abolition	Peace	Settlement House/National Consumers' League
Sarah Grimké (1792)	X	X	X	X	X	
Lucretia Mott (1793)	X	X	X	X	X	
Angelina Grimké (1805)	X	X	X	X	X	
Elizabeth Cady Stanton (1815)		X		X	X	
Lucy Stone (1818)		X		X		
Susan B. Anthony (1820)		X	X			
Anna Howard Shaw (1847)		X				
Alice Stone Blackwell (1857)		X		X	X	X
Florence Kelley (1859)				X	X	X
Carrie Chapman Catt (1859)					X	
Jane Addams (1860)				X	X	X

Note: All women listed, except for Lucretia Mott and the Grimké sisters, were officers of the National American Woman Suffrage Association.

Source: Adapted from Alice S. Rossi, ed., *The Feminist Papers: From Adams to de Beauvoir* (New York: Columbia University Press, 1973).

who often joined these clubs for companionship and self-improvement. But, unlike most white women, African American women also saw these groups as a way of alleviating racial injustice and underscoring their own religiosity and character.

When women in these clubs became involved in social causes, they quickly realized their own inferior political position. Thus, in 1914, the immense General Federation of Women's Clubs (GFWC) decided to support the suffrage movement, which added the organizational strength necessary for a successful social movement. Other organizations of professional, university, and even working women also began to support woman suffrage and became affiliated with NAWSA. The result was a powerful movement that was able to mount what Carrie Chapman Catt called a Winning Plan to coordinate the efforts of thousands of women to lobby for the vote.

By 1920, this alliance was able to secure passage of the Nineteenth Amendment, which gave women the right to vote. The fragile coalition that made up the suffrage movement soon disintegrated, however, when its diverse constituent groups could no longer agree on a new postsuffrage agenda.[9]

The Women's Rights Movement (1966–Present)

After the demise of the suffrage movement, there was little organized protest activity by women for women until the 1960s. What we call the women's rights movement, which began in the 1960s, had two distinct personas reflecting the origins, leadership, and goals of each branch. What we term here as the *younger* branch of the women's rights movement was far more radical in its orientation than what we term the *older* branch of the movement as originally personified by the National Organization for Women (NOW) and its more traditional, rights-oriented strategies and demands.* Today, however, most would agree that the distinction between the two branches no longer clearly exists. Many of the goals of the younger branch have been incorporated into those of the older branch *or* have become smaller special interest movements, such as the battered women's, domestic violence, rape, or feminist health clinic movements, or have become subsumed in the broader women's rights movement.[10]

The Younger Branch. Initially most women active in the younger branch of the movement were involved with other protest movements. In the early 1960s, many women working in the civil rights movement, a significant number of whom were college students or recent graduates, began to sense that men in these organizations failed to value women's contributions. Like Stanton and Mott more than a century before, they came to see their position as analogous to the blacks for whom they were seeking expanded rights. Around the same time this recognition began to occur, civil rights groups such as the Southern Christian Leadership Council (SCLC), the Congress of Racial Equality (CORE), and the Student Non-Violent Coordinating Committee (SNCC) were organized. As some of these organizations entered a "Black Power" phase, they drove most white activists into other movements, especially the growing leftist student antiwar movement. There, too, women experienced sexism. At a 1965 meeting of Students for a Democratic Society (SDS), for example, "catcalls, storms of ridicule and verbal abuse"[11] were hurled at women who broached the women's issue. When a women's rights plank was introduced at the next annual SDS meeting, its sponsors "were

---

*Various authors use different terms to describe not only the overarching movement that we call the women's rights movement but also the initial strains of this movement. Zillah R. Eisenstein, *The Radical Future of Liberal Feminism* (Boston: Northeastern University Press, 1993), for example, labels this movement *liberal feminism.* Jo Freeman, *The Politics of Women's Liberation* (New York: Longman, 1975) was the first to delineate the younger and older branches of the movement. Sarah M. Evans, *Born for Liberty: A History of Women in America* (New York: Free Press, 1989), 270–91, calls what we term the younger branch the *women's liberation movement,* and our women's rights movement, the *new feminist movement.* See also Cynthia Harrison, *On Account of Sex: The Politics of Women's Issues 1945–1968* (Berkeley: University of California Press, 1988), and Nancy F. Cott, *The Grounding of Modern Feminism* (New Haven, Conn.: Yale University Press, 1987). And Flora Davis, *Moving the Mountain: The Women's Movement in America Since 1960* (New York: Simon & Schuster, 1991) delineates several names and strains within what we term the *younger branch.* See also Alice Echols, *Daring to Be Bad: Radical Feminism in America, 1967–1975* (Minneapolis: University of Minnesota Press, 1989); Judith Evans, *Feminist Theory Today: An Introduction to the Political Theories of Second Wave Feminism* (Beverly Hills, Calif.: Sage Publications, 1996); Stacey Young, *Changing the Wor(l)d: Discourse, Politics and the Feminist Movement* (Boston: Routledge, 1997); and Imelda Whelehan, *Modern Feminist Thought: From the Second Wave to Post-Feminism* (New York: New York University Press, 1995).

Rethinking the Roots of the Current Women's Rights Movement

Until recently, most scholars have traced the dawn of the current women's rights movement to several factors including publication of Betty Friedan's *The Feminine Mystique* in 1963. Her account of how she surveyed her Smith classmates for their fifteen-year college reunion and how their boredom and dissatisfaction provided the spark of recognition that led her to write her own book is being challenged, somewhat ironically, by a Smith professor of American Studies. Daniel Horowitz argues that Friedan's works represent a "reinvention of herself."[a] He notes that Friedan was a politically conscious editor in chief of the college paper and then, after graduation, a writer of articles and pamphlets for several "left-wing" news services and papers.[b] Horowitz, and a growing number of feminist historians, now believe that "we've been wrong to separate the turbulent '60s from the supposedly complacent 1950s."[c] He and others now argue that the roots of Friedan's ideas, as well as those of American feminism, can be traced directly back to American radicalism. This is a connection that some fear, believing that conservatives will attempt to brand feminists as communists.[d] Still Horowitz's argument is an interesting one that many feminists are now exploring.

[a]Daniel Horowitz, "Rethinking Betty Friedan and *The Feminine Mystique:* Labor Union Radicalism and Feminism in Cold War America," *American Quarterly* (March 1996): 1–42.

[b]Ibid.

[c]Quoted in Karen Winkler, "Relooking at the Roots of Feminism," *The Chronicle of Higher Education,* April 12, 1996, A10.

[d]Ibid., A16.

---

pelted with tomatoes and thrown out of the convention."[12] And a similar situation occurred the next year at the National Conference for a New Politics. When two women, Jo Freeman and Shulamith Firestone, both former civil rights activists, demanded that the convention address issues of sexism, they were patted on the head and told to "calm down, little girl."[13] The conference then decided not to deal with these women's "trivial complaints."[14] Freeman left to found a radical women's group in Chicago; Firestone did the same in New York City.

Subsequently, often without knowledge of what was happening in other areas of the country, women began to hold meetings in cities across the United States. This new idea of women's liberation was spread mainly through the existing infrastructure and communications network of the student movement and counterculture. SDS women and those from other New Left groups, in particular, were well suited to the task of organizing the women's groups that sprung up in many parts of the country. The development of a new form of organization, the consciousness-raising group, allowed these women to spread ideas, especially the notion that the problems they experienced were not the result of individual failures or situations, but instead had roots in the dominant culture and thus were common to all women.

Since the early to mid-1970s, these local groups and their progeny have played an important role in establishing feminist women's health care centers, rape crisis centers,[15] shelters for battered women, and even feminist women's bookstores. They have also sought to work with more traditional groups within the system, and after a period of relative quiet, many reemerged to play key roles in the pro-choice arena. In fact, the specter of major limitations on abortion rights that emerged in the 1980s may have brought about the same kind of merger in diverse women's groups that occurred in 1890, when NWSA and AWSA merged to become the National American Woman Suffrage Association.[16]

The Older Branch.   The United States has long been a nation of joiners. At least since the 1890s, many national organizations were composed largely of women. After 1920, however, few of those organizations were politically active for women's rights. Nevertheless, some groups, most notably the National League of Women Voters (LWV), the National Federation of Business and Professional Women's Clubs (BPW), and the National Council of Negro Women (NCNW), had long been pursuing improvement in women's status in the legislative arena. These groups provided a potential leadership base for a social movement, but they needed to be galvanized to act.

Several events occurred to motivate these women's groups to action. The civil rights movement and the resultant awareness of rights, along with the publication of Friedan's *The Feminine Mystique* in 1963, helped to disseminate the idea of group oppression to women across the United States.[17] Also occurring in 1963 was the issuance of a report by John F. Kennedy's newly created President's Commission on the Status of Women. This report, *American Woman*, documented in great detail the extent of discrimination against women in all areas of life. Following JFK's lead, the governors of all fifty states established state commissions on the status of women. These commissions soon began to issue their own state reports on women's status.

The "event" that finally mobilized some women on the president's commission to take action was the Equal Employment Opportunity Commission's (EEOC) failure to enforce provisions of the 1964 Civil Rights Act, which prohibits sex discrimination in employment. In 1966, at the Third National Conference of Commissions on the Status of Women, attendees learned that conference bylaws prohibited them from passing a resolution demanding that the EEOC treat sex discrimination complaints seriously. Thus, several of the women present decided to form an independent pressure group—the National Organization for Women (NOW). Most of NOW's original members had served on the president's commission, and its leadership was drawn almost exclusively from the commission's ranks.

The Feminist Label

Historian Nancy F. Cott tells us the term *feminist* entered the English language sometime around 1910. Then, as now, it meant a "complete social revolution" in the roles of women. Cott explains that early feminism had "two dominating ideas: the emancipation of woman both as a human-being and as a sex-being."[a] Its goals were the elimination of all barriers that prevented women from achieving complete development as individuals. More radical in its demands than the suffrage movement, it attracted only a few of the youngest and most educated women of its day. It persisted organizationally as the National Woman's Party, with its demand for complete constitutional equality of women and men (see Chapter 1).

The premises of modern-day feminism are traceable to its roots in early feminism. Three main tenets of this philosophy continue today.

1. Women should be the equal of men. No gender is superior.
2. Women's roles and status are a product of the social structure and thus changeable.
3. Women are self-identified as a social group; thus they are positioned to act "as a group" to change their status.[b]

Cott claims that both early and modern feminism contain paradoxes, emphasizing sexual equality but sexual differences, individual freedoms but collective action, unity but diversity among women, and gender consciousness but elimination of gender roles.

The word *feminist* continues to mean very different things to many different people. In 1988, only 42 percent of all women polled had a "somewhat or very favorable" feeling toward feminists. Only two years later, 69 percent reported "somewhat or very favorable" feelings toward "the women's movement." Moreover, 33 percent said they considered themselves to be a "feminist."[c] By 1995, 41 percent of the women polled in a national survey conducted by the Feminist Majority Foundation said they considered themselves to be "feminists."[d] When the dictionary definition of feminism—"someone who supports political, economic, and social equality for women"—was read to respondents, 67 percent labeled themselves as feminists (45 percent) or strong feminists (22 percent). Education and income, two closely related factors, are strongly associated with a woman's willingness to label herself a "strong feminist" as illustrated in Table I–2.

[a]Nancy F. Cott, *The Grounding of Modern Feminism* (New Haven, Conn.: Yale University Press, 1987).

[b]Ibid.

[c]Surveys by the Center for Political Studies of the Institute for Social Research, University of Michigan, November 7, 1990–January 26, 1991.

[d]Women's Equality Poll, 1995. The Roper Center. *Public Opinion Online*, June 23, 1995.

TABLE I–2 Women's Responses to the Question: "Are You a Strong Feminist?"

Women Responding "Yes"

All Women Who Voted	Women Who Voted, by Education		Women Who Voted, by Income		Women Who Voted, by Age	
14%	<H.S. grad.	8%	<$15,000	10%	18–29	17%
	H.S. grad.	7%	$15,000–29,999	12%	30–44	18%
	Some college	13%	$30,000–49,999	15%	45–59	4%
	College grad.	18%	$50,000–99,999	19%	60+	7%
	Postgrad.	32%	$100,000+	31%		

Source: The Public Perspective, Nov./Dec. 1991, 93.

Unlike founders of the younger branch, these women were well trained as leaders, but there were few organizers among them. Not surprisingly then, NOW's initial growth was slow. Additionally, other women's rights organizations were formed after NOW, often because of some disagreement with NOW over tactics. The formation of many of these new organizations, as well as the increasing political activity of existing women's groups, often was fostered by women connected with NOW or the various state commissions on the status of women. Thus, little new ground was broken in terms of reaching beyond these organizational bases until 1970. Indeed, the movement might have failed when the limits of this base were reached had it not been for widespread free publicity.

This came early in 1970 when the national media finally began to focus on the women's rights movement. The *New York Times, Newsweek, New York* magazine, and the national television networks all devoted time or space to women's issues.[18] According to Jo Freeman, "The cumulative impact of the series of stories was tremendous. Within the short space of a few months the movement went from a struggling new idea to a national phenomenon."[19] When NOW organized a strike to commemorate the fiftieth anniversary of the ratification of the Nineteenth Amendment, extensive reporting of the event further helped to familiarize millions of American women with the existence of the women's movement. Practically overnight, NOW's membership burgeoned as its ideas were carried to a nationwide audience. The publication of *Ms.* magazine in 1972 and the fanfare surrounding it also spread the word of the new movement even further as it provided a communications network for isolated women around the country.

NOW's push for the equal rights amendment (ERA) and the quick support it garnered from most other women's groups provided the necessary cohesion to cement and focus the new movement. NOW pushed for an ERA believing that passage of an amendment was the easiest way to bring about a guarantee of equality. Prior to 1971, the U.S. Supreme Court had declined to find that women were protected from state discrimination by the equal protection clause of the Fourteenth Amendment. Even if the Court interpreted the Fourteenth Amendment to protect women from some forms of discrimination, without a specific constitutional guarantee of equality, women might always be less than full citizens under the law. Thus, final passage of the ERA in both Houses of Congress in 1972 provided an emotional high to movement activists who turned their energies to ratification by the states.[20]

The media attention that aided development of the older branch, however, also contributed to the development of a countermovement. By the mid-1970s, some women came to perceive additional rights for women as a threat to their way of life. The proposed ERA and the legalization of abortion that occurred in 1973 with the Supreme Court's decision in *Roe v. Wade* were viewed as particularly ominous changes (see Chapter 5). Using the organizational base of fundamentalist religious groups and other conservative political organizations, prominent conservative Republican Phyllis Schlafly and others created a countermovement that effectively blocked passage of the ERA. Schlafly's Eagle Forum was initially devoted to stopping passage of the ERA. More recently, the Eagle Forum as well as Concerned Women for America (CWA), founded by Beverly LeHaye, have effectively mobilized to stop passage of many bills supported by the liberal women's rights movement, including, until 1993, passage of the Family and Medical Leave Act.

These two rival women's movements continue to go head to head most notably in the area of reproductive freedom rights. Prior to 1989, lacking the single unifying factor of an equal rights amendment, the current women's rights movement appeared to be in disarray. On July 3, 1989, however, the U.S. Supreme Court issued its opinion in *Webster v. Reproductive Health Services* (see Chapter 5). A few weeks before the decision, pro-choice supporters, galvanized by the threat of the Court's overruling of *Roe v. Wade,* organized a march of more than half a million people—the largest ever to occur up to that time in Washington, D.C. The Court's decision has clearly spurred women's rights supporters to action.[21]

The Clarence Thomas hearings also galvanized liberal women's rights supporters. In 1991, many women around the nation sat aghast watching their televisions as the all-male and all-white Senate Judiciary Committee questioned African American Anita Hill for hours during the hearing on the appointment of Clarence Thomas to the U.S. Supreme Court.[22] Initially, his appointment to the bench had been fought by women's rights groups that believed that he would provide the fifth and deciding vote to overrule *Roe v. Wade.* It was then learned that while Thomas headed the EEOC—the federal agency charged with investigating claims of sex discrimination *including* sexual harassment—one of his young assistants believed she had been the object of Thomas's improper sexual behavior. As white male senator after white male senator questioned law professor Anita Hill's veracity, mental stability, and morals, many white women around the country were outraged while

Women's Views on the Changing Roles of Women

In 1970, as the women's rights movement was just gaining some visibility, the Virginia Slims Company commissioned the Roper Center to conduct a public opinion poll to gauge the views of women toward the new movement. It continues to poll Americans periodically. As Table I–3 reveals, Roper found that less than a majority (40 percent) of women in those early years favored efforts to "strengthen or change women's status in society." By 1989, 77 percent of the women interviewed favored an improvement in the status of women, and only a handful (12 percent) opposed such efforts. By 1996, however, that percentage remained virtually unchanged at 78 percent.

By the late 1980s, most women believed women's roles would and should continue to change. Most women (58 percent) reported that they believed these changes would occur "as a matter of course without any organized effort on the part of women."[a] Only 37 percent indicated an organized women's movement was needed to work for further improvements for women. Moreover, of those who thought a women's movement was needed in the 1990s, almost half believed there should be some changes in the emphasis of the movement, with most favoring more of a focus on economic (equal pay) and career (equal opportunities) issues. This ambivalence about organized efforts to help women is nothing new. In 1970, only 34 percent of all women reported that they believed that the organizations designed to improve women's status were helpful.

In *Backlash: The Undeclared War on American Women*, reporter Susan Faludi argues that the 1980s witnessed a "backlash" by politicians and the media against the advances toward equality recently made by women.[b] She cites examples such as the popularity of the movies *Fatal Attraction* and *Overboard*, both of which shared a "get the woman/bitch" theme, and blaming the women's movement for the rise in heart disease and suicide rates among career women.[c] The efforts of the 105th Congress to roll back affirmative action for women and to restrict abortion rights, and even the current frequent criticisms of Hillary Rodham Clinton, can be viewed—in Faludi's terms—as efforts to stifle advances of women in society and politics.

[a]Specific wording used in Virginia Slims poll. All statistics derived from Virginia Slims poll conducted by the Roper Center.

[b]Susan Faludi, *Backlash: The Undeclared War on American Women* (New York: Doubleday, 1991).

[c]Ibid., 38.

black women struggled to cope with this public battle.[23] Said Melba Joyce Bird, director of African American Studies at the University of Michigan–Flint, "Black women are still expected to . . . endure indignities simply because to reveal the truth about the devils in the camp would be an embarrassment for the race."[24]

It was clear to many women, regardless of race, that most of the members of the all-male Judiciary Committee "just didn't get it." Many women

TABLE I-3 Views on Women's Status in Society

Question: Do You Favor or Oppose Most of the Efforts to Strengthen and Change Women's Status in Society Today?

	Favor (%)	Oppose (%)
1970	40	42
1972	48	36
1974	57	25
1980	64	24
1985	73	17
1989	77	12
1996	78	10

Source: The Roper Center at the University of Connecticut. *Public Opinion Online,* April 11, 1996.

decided on the spot to run for public office; others decided to get involved in politics. Adding to this outrage were gaffes made by Vice President Dan Quayle, such as attacking a fictional television character (the unmarried Murphy Brown) for choosing to have a child. (Pro-choice advocates were quick to point out that Murphy was in a no-win situation with the Bush administration, which strongly opposed abortion for *any* reason except situations that endangered the life of the mother.) Quayle denounced Brown as a symbol of the decaying family. This added fuel to the fire of women who were looking for change and who were angry at twelve years of Republican administrations. Many were especially angry when Republicans used the theme of a return to family values as their 1992 presidential nominating convention mantra at the same time President Bush vetoed the Family and Medical Leave Act.[25]

Many argue that these revitalized women, and the reenergized women's rights movement, contributed to the election of the largest number of women ever in the U.S. House and Senate in 1992. Yet, in 1994, women stayed home from the polls (see Chapter 2) and Republicans took control of both houses of Congress. Although Bill Clinton, a president who calls himself a "feminist," was reelected in 1996, women's gains continue to come under attack. It may take another Anita Hill/Clarence Thomas debacle, or passage of unpopular abortion restrictions, to reengage the women who made such a difference in 1992. While many advances toward the goals first enunciated in Seneca Falls nearly 150 years ago have occurred, many remain unmet. These unmet goals and the strategies and changes needed to meet them are the focus of the remainder of this book.

NOTES

1. H. L. Butterfield, Mark Friedlaender, and Mary-Jo Kline, eds., *The Book of Abigail and John: Selected Letters of the Adams Family, 1762–1784* (Cambridge, Mass., and London: Harvard University Press, 1975), 121, quoted from a letter dated March 31, 1776.
2. A complete text of the Declaration of Sentiments can be found at "created equal," http://www.rochester.edu/SBA/declare.html
3. "Sexual Equality 1,000 Years Off?" *Atlanta Journal and Constitution*, February 5, 1993, 1.
4. See "Maria W. Miller Stewart" in Edward T. James, ed., *Notable American Women*, vol. 3 (Cambridge, Mass.: The Belknap Press of Harvard University, 1971), 377–78.
5. Nancy F. Cott, *The Grounding of Modern Feminism* (New Haven, Conn.: Yale University Press, 1987), 18.
6. See generally, Lois W. Banner, *Women in Modern America: A Brief History*, 3rd ed. (New York: Harcourt Brace, 1994). See also, Suzanne M. Marilley, *Woman Suffrage and the Origins of Liberal Feminism in the United States, 1820–1920* (Cambridge, Mass.: Harvard University Press, 1997).
7. Janet Zollinger Giele, *Two Paths to Women's Equality: Temperance, Suffrage, and the Origins of Modern Feminism* (Old Tappan, N.J.: Twayne, 1995).
8. Karen J. Blair, *The Clubwoman as Feminist: The Womanhood Redefined, 1868–1914* (New York: Holmes & Meier, 1980).
9. Sara Hunter Graham, *Woman Suffrage and the New Democracy* (Baton Rouge: Louisiana State University, 1996).
10. See, for example, Flora Davis, *Moving the Mountain: The Women's Movement in America since 1960* (New York: Simon & Schuster, 1991), who argues that the distinction disappeared in the mid-1970s.
11. Quoted in Judith Hole and Ellen Levine, *Rebirth of Feminism* (New York: Quadrangle Books, 1971), 112.
12. Ibid.
13. Ibid., 113–14.
14. Quoted in ibid., 113–14.
15. Maria Bevacqua, "Rape on the Public Agenda: Feminist Consciousness and the Politics of Sexual Assault" (Ph.D. diss., Emory University, 1997).
16. Myra Marx Ferree and Patricia Yancey Martin, eds., *Feminist Organizations: Harvest of the New Women's Movement* (Philadelphia: Temple University Press, 1995). But see Nancy Whittier, *Feminist Generations: The Persistence of the Radical Women's Movement* (Philadelphia: Temple University Press, 1995).
17. Betty Friedan, *The Feminine Mystique* (New York: Norton, 1963).
18. See a history of NOW at http://www.now.org/history/history.html and Toni Carabillo's, *The Feminist Chronicles 1953–1993* at http://www.feminist.org/research/chronicles/chronicl.html
19. Jo Freeman, *The Politics of Women's Liberation* (New York: Longman, 1975), 150.
20. Jane Mansbridge, *Why We Lost the ERA* (Chicago: University of Chicago Press, 1986).
21. Karen O'Connor, *No Neutral Ground: Abortion Politics in an Age of Absolutes* (Boulder, Colo.: Westview Press, 1996).
22. For accounts of the Clarence Thomas hearings, see Jill Meyer and Jill Abramson, *Strange Justice: The Selling of Clarence Thomas* (New York: Houghton Mifflin, 1994), and Timothy M. Phelps and Helen Winter-Mintz, *Capitol Games: Clarence Thomas, Anita Hill, and the Story of a Supreme Court Nomination* (New York: Hyperion, 1995).
23. See Toni Morrison, *Race-Ing Justice, En-Gendering Power: Essays on Anita Hill, Clarence Thomas, and the Construction of Reality* (New York: Pantheon, 1992), and Anita Hill and Emma Coleman Jordan, eds., *Race, Gender and Power in America: The Legacy of the Hill-Thomas Hearings* (New York: Oxford University Press, 1995).
24. Quoted in Ronald Dworkin, "One Year Later, the Debate Goes On," *New York Times*, October 25, 1992, 1.
25. Myra Marx Ferree and Beth B. Hess, eds., *Controversy and Coalition: The New Feminist Movement* (Old Tappan, N.J.: Twayne, 1994), and Sheila Tobias, *Faces of Feminism: An Activist's Reflections on the Women's Movement* (Boulder, Colo.: Westview, 1997).

PART I

POLITICAL RIGHTS AND REALITIES

As early as 1875, the U.S. Supreme Court confirmed that American women were citizens of the United States, but the Court also held that citizenship did not include a basic political right—suffrage. It took Congress and the states an additional forty-five years to ratify a constitutional amendment guaranteeing women the right to vote.

Today, few laws bar women's participation in the political arena, but vestiges of past barriers remain. Cultural and social attitudes continue to impede women's exercise of political rights. These extralegal barriers affect the composition of state and national legislative bodies. Only 11.2 percent of the lawmakers in the 105th Congress are women, and the sexual composition of other legislative and judicial bodies is only slightly more representative.

The ability of a women's movement to gain supporters and ultimately to achieve its goals often has hinged on the public's perception of the rights sought. During the suffrage movement, for example, opponents often characterized the franchise as something that would affect both men and women negatively. Thus, a critical element in achieving the vote was the suffrage leaders' ability to counter these arguments by stressing the limited nature of voting rights for women and by emphasizing potential benefits to society.

Some efforts for expanded political rights have been successful without producing strong countermovements, especially when the goals sought have not appeared to pose any significant threat to the political or social order. In the mid-1800s, for example, when few gave the suffrage cause much chance of victory, no significant antisuffrage movement developed. Likewise, in the 1970s, women in the younger branch of the women's rights movement received only token opposition to one of their goals—replacement of the present political system—largely because of the remote possibility of their success. During the same period, however, the proposed equal rights amendment drew fierce opposition, and its supporters were not able to counter its opponents in enough states to gain ratification. Clearly, the nature and implications of the political rights sought and the probability of victory have often been critical parts of the battle.

The battle for rights and the ensuing problems of implementing those rights are the topics of the next two chapters. Chapter 1 discusses women's attempts to gain access to the political arena and to gain equal rights in general. Chapter 2 then examines the impact of altering those political rights and examines how, why, and to what extent women have participated in the political process since the early 1900s. Finally, remaining barriers to the attainment of a full and equal civic role for women are discussed.

The Struggle for Political Rights

At the time of the Seneca Falls Convention in 1848, suffrage was a radical idea. In fact, a resolution supporting expanding the "elective franchise" to women received only a bare majority of votes. Given that convention attendees were more liberal than most, it becomes easier to understand why many long, hard years of organizing, petitioning, and educating both the public and government officials were necessary before suffrage was finally attained by constitutional amendment in 1920. In 1923, after that victory, some women sought fuller rights for women through the addition of another amendment to the U.S. Constitution—the equal rights amendment (ERA). As we shall see, that effort was not nearly as successful as the more simple demand for the vote. During the battle for ERA ratification, some women's groups continued to pursue expanded political opportunities for women. After the ERA's defeat in 1982, even more women turned their energies in that direction. High on their list of priorities was the election and appointment of women to public office. But to understand the underrepresentation of women in politics, the history of efforts to obtain the right to vote and equal rights under the Constitution must first be understood.

THE WOMAN'S RIGHTS MOVEMENT AND THE BALLOT

The women who attended the Seneca Falls Convention were primarily concerned with securing greater economic and social rights. In fact, at least initially, the right to vote was only a secondary concern. Lucretia Mott, in particular, feared that a demand for the franchise would make women look "ridiculous" and urged her sisters to "go slowly."[1] In spite of her caution, however, the ballot was demanded on the basis of the belief that women were first and foremost individuals and citizens and deserved not only the same economic and social rights but also the same political rights as men. Paraphrasing the Declaration of Independence, women at the Seneca Falls Convention proclaimed: "We hold these truths to be self-evident: that all men *and women* are created equal; that they are endowed by their Creator with certain inalienable rights; that among these are life, liberty, and the pursuit of happiness"[2] (emphasis added).

Involvement in the abolition effort led many leaders of the woman's movement to see the issues of slavery and women's rights as intimately linked. Most believed that once society accepted the concept of individual rights as embodied in the Declaration of Independence as the rationale for freeing and enfranchising slaves, suffrage logically would be extended to women, regardless of color. Although Elizabeth Cady Stanton and Lucretia Mott's logic may have been correct, their estimation of the public's reaction to woman suffrage was not. Woman's movement leaders failed to realize that their demands for female suffrage directly challenged socially determined role divisions between men and women. And because demands for female suffrage often were coupled with calls for more controversial changes in women's status, many came to link suffrage with the reform of other issues including divorce, education for women, or child custody. This was in spite of the fact that the New Jersey Constitution of 1775 granted all inhabitants worth "50 pounds a year" the right to vote. Election officials allowed propertied women to vote, and New Jersey and its women citizens apparently suffered no long-lasting dire consequences.

Prior to the Civil War, woman's rights activists chose not to form a national association to press for greater rights. Rather, they continued to rely largely on abolitionist associations to spread their ideas. Northern and midwestern organizational activity was limited to little more than yearly conventions to address women's common problems and to discuss strategy to obtain the vote. Often announcements of these meetings were carried in abolitionist newspapers as well as in women's magazines. In addition to these conventions, petition campaigns—a tactic regularly employed by abolitionist-based female antislavery societies—were used to demand suffrage in some states. These petition campaigns presented the signatures of men and women supporting a particular issue to legislators. While they sometimes resulted in positive legislative change involving property or material rights, petition campaigns failed to produce any state constitutional suffrage amendments.

With the advent of the Civil War, even these minimally independent efforts for women's rights were abandoned as many women focused their energies on the war effort and the campaign for an antislavery amendment. Fully expecting women's rights to be granted simultaneously with Negro rights, Susan B. Anthony and Elizabeth Cady Stanton, among others, helped to form the National Women's Loyal League (NWLL) to work for an amendment to end slavery.

Hopes for granting simultaneous rights to blacks and women were soon dashed. Republican politicians, the major proponents of abolition, feared that support for woman suffrage would doom the chances for ratification of an amendment enfranchising Negroes. To ensure that their party would be "rewarded" with the votes of two million southern Negro males, the Republican-controlled Congress opted not to mix the two issues.

Many abolitionist men also turned a deaf ear to the call for woman suffrage. In 1866, for example, the American Anti-Slavery Society rejected appeals to unite the two causes, prompting women to form a new abolitionist organization with men who supported female suffrage. The stated purpose of the new American Equal Rights Association (AERA) was universal suffrage for blacks and women.

The Civil War Amendments

Even AERA, however, soon abandoned woman suffrage when it supported the proposed Fourteenth Amendment to the U.S. Constitution. When a majority of its members agreed that "Now is the Negro's hour," Stanton, Anthony, and their followers were furious. They were particulary incensed by AERA's support of text contained in the Fourteenth Amendment, which introduced the word *male* into the U.S. Constitution for the first time.[3] Not only did Stanton and Anthony argue that women should be included in any attempt to secure fuller rights for Negroes, who had been freed from slavery with passage of the Thirteenth Amendment in 1865, but they also voiced fears that this clause would necessitate yet another constitutional amendment before women could vote in national elections. Even though they felt betrayed by AERA's support of the Fourteenth Amendment, Stanton, Anthony, and other supporters of woman suffrage were not yet ready to sever their ties with the organization they had helped to found.

The event that finally caused Stanton and Anthony to leave AERA was its support of the proposed Fifteenth Amendment, which called for giving Negro males the right to vote. The then-controversial amendment read, "The right of citizens of the United States to vote shall not be denied or abridged by the United States or by any State on account of race, color, or previous condition of servitude." Feverish attempts to have the word *sex* included proved futile, as women once again were told that the rights of Negro men must come first.

Interestingly, until passage of the Fifteenth Amendment, woman's movement leaders believed that the question of voter qualifications was a matter for the individual states. With enactment of the Fifteenth Amendment, however, it became clear that an amendment to the U.S. Constitution would in all likelihood be necessary before women could vote in national elections.[4]

New Groups Founded

Faced with the apparent need to alter their strategy, which had sought suffrage legislation on a state-by-state basis, and abandoned by AERA, which had failed to support a proposal to call for a woman suffrage amendment, Stanton and Anthony founded the National Woman Suffrage Association (NWSA) in 1869. NWSA dedicated itself to the joint causes of securing greater rights for women in *all* spheres of life—especially in education, work, marriage, and the family—and securing a national constitutional amendment to enfranchise women.

Later that year, Lucy Stone, who had remained a member of AERA, founded the more conservative American Woman Suffrage Association (AWSA), which stressed the feasibility of a state-by-state route to woman suffrage. In AWSA's pursuit of that lone goal, it tried to avoid association with controversial issues that could cloud the suffrage issue.

Unlike NWSA, whose leaders had few dealings with abolitionists, AWSA leaders continued to expect that abolitionists and Republicans would adopt their cause as soon as the issue of Negro rights was resolved. This hope and the strategies adopted to support it (the state-by-state route, for example, was proposed to leave the federal arena open for debate on Negro suffrage) were counter to everything Stanton and Anthony believed. AWSA's organizational structure was also fragmented. Composed of official state delegations and strong local affiliates, AWSA required that new members be sponsored by at least two existing members.

NWSA's far more informal structure reflected Stanton's and Anthony's more liberal beliefs. Because they believed that a federal amendment was preferable to AWSA's state-by-state approach, NWSA initially made little effort to establish a state or local associational structure. This failure often resulted in the loss of potential members. State woman's rights associations often affiliated with AWSA because their participation appeared more appreciated there and their efforts, seemingly, could have greater impact.

Only gradually did Anthony and Stanton realize that, unlike abolitionists who faced few problems in convincing slaves of their oppressed status, many women were completely satisfied without the vote. Thus, shortly after ratification of the Fifteenth Amendment, Stanton, Anthony, and NWSA began a concerted effort to organize more women. Reaching out beyond the abolitionist movement, they attempted to attract the support of women they had met during the Civil War. Those who belonged to the National Women's Loyal League (NWLL) or those who volunteered in hospitals or collected money to buy much-needed medical supplies for the war effort were early targets of their organizing efforts. These largely middle-class women had not previously been active in politics or in the abolitionist movement. Stanton and Anthony also sought to gain sympathizers from those women who were members of the short-lived postwar Working Woman's Association (WWA). WWA members, as wage earners, also had not been involved in any women's rights activity previously. Women from both groups, however, were considerably more conservative about the position of women in society than either Anthony or Stanton. Consequently, efforts to attract these women eventually led to a considerable toning down of NWSA's radical demands for divorce reform and equal rights and to an increasingly narrow focus on suffrage. However, before it toned down its rhetoric, NWSA's image as an organization dedicated to altering society was fairly well established.

Woman Suffrage and the Fourteenth Amendment

Aware of its image problems, NWSA attempted to "conservatize" and to narrow its goals. For example, Francis Minor was a prominent attorney whose wife, Virginia, was the president of the Missouri Woman Suffrage Association (MWSA) and a close friend of Anthony. In 1869, he wrote persuasively about his belief that women, as citizens, were entitled to vote under the existing provisions of the Fourteenth Amendment. Minor believed that if his theory was used as the basis for litigation challenging the disenfranchisement of women, demands for suffrage would be perceived as much less frivolous.

Minor's ideas were widely publicized by NWSA leaders. Along with an explanatory letter from Minor, they were published in two consecutive issues of *The Revolution,* a newspaper founded by Anthony and Stanton to publicize the movement. The impetus for a concerted effort to test the logic of Minor's argument, however, did not arise until January 1871 when Victoria Woodhull, a controversial figure herself, made a presentation to Congress. Using arguments very similar to those posited by Minor, she urged legislators to pass enabling legislation to give women the right to vote under the newly enacted Fourteenth Amendment.[5]

When Woodhull chose to address Congress on the opening day of NWSA's 1871 annual convention, her actions attracted considerable public attention. As editor of a controversial newspaper, she was an open advocate of "free love" and was reported to be living with a man who was not her husband. In spite of her reputation, NWSA leaders invited Woodhull to repeat her remarks later that day when their meeting opened.

Woodhull's appearance had mixed benefits for NWSA. On the negative side, NWSA's alliance with Woodhull caused some members of the press to ridicule the organization openly and to link NWSA and suffrage with declining moral standards. Numerous articles and cartoons were printed depicting Woodhull and those in favor of votes for women as "free lovers." In response, the more conservative AWSA, trying hard to preserve its own public image, quickly passed the following resolution in an effort to disassociate itself from NWSA and free love:

> Resolved . . . That the claim of woman to participate in making the laws she is required to obey, and to equality of rights in all directions, has nothing to do with special social theories, and the recent attempts in this city and elsewhere to

associate the woman suffrage cause with the doctrines of free love, and to hold it responsible for the crimes and follies of individuals, is an outrage upon common sense and decency, and a slander upon the virtue and intelligence of the women of America.[6]

Sometimes more astute than NWSA leaders, AWSA leaders recognized that linkages between suffrage and more radical issues, particularly those as controversial as free love, would damn their cause.

On the positive side, the "Woodhull Convention" infused NWSA members with a new sense of purpose and generated some favorable publicity along with the bad. The *Washington Republic*, for example, described the annual meeting as follows:

It was thus a convention with a new idea.... indicating healthy life in the movement. The consequence was that the cause of woman's enfranchisement made a new, sudden, and profound impression in Washington.[7]

Litigating for the Franchise. Francis Minor quickly moved to seize upon the enthusiasm that Woodhull's remarks inspired and to counter any adverse publicity that Woodhull brought to NWSA. He urged that test cases quickly be brought to determine if the courts would obviate the need for additional legislative action. A number of legal scholars and judges had publicly agreed with Minor's arguments. More importantly, the chief justice of the United States, Salmon Portland Chase, offered his belief that it would be wise for women to test the parameters of the Constitution to determine if they were enfranchised by its provisions.

While this change in strategy was met with great excitement, it appears that NWSA leaders did not actually expect a favorable decision from the courts. The leaders clearly anticipated a strong written dissent from the chief justice and believed that his opinion could be used as a means to educate and to inform the public on the issue of woman suffrage.[8] In essence, litigation was attempted to convince the public that female suffrage was not a passing fad or something evil. Indeed, the need for enlightened and favorable discussion of woman suffrage was particularly acute. The Woodhull affair had tarnished both suffrage and NWSA's image.

Litigation was viewed by NWSA leaders as a conventional tactic to focus serious national attention on suffrage. Only one of the three major test cases brought by NWSA members, however, was given a full hearing by the U.S. Supreme Court. Fittingly, it involved Virginia Minor. In *Minor v. Happersett* (1875),[9] Minor, with her husband, Francis as coplaintiff (as a married woman she had no right to sue in her own name), sued a St. Louis voter registrar after he refused to allow her to register to vote. Francis Minor claimed that his wife's rights under the Fourteenth Amendment were violated because she was denied "the privileges and immunities of citizenship, chief among which is the elective franchise." This argument was rejected by the Missouri courts, and the Minors appealed their case to the U.S. Supreme

Court. In 1875, a unanimous Court upheld the Missouri court's determination. Writing for the Court, the new chief justice, Morrison R. Waite (Chase died in 1873), maintained that suffrage was *not* a right of citizenship.

After the *Minor* decision, NWSA turned to more commonly used modes of political activity. The unanimous decision in *Minor* made it clear that a real victory in the courts would not be forthcoming any time in the near future. To litigate further would only destroy any credibility NWSA had established. Its leaders, therefore, refocused their efforts on obtaining a constitutional amendment.

Toward a Constitutional Amendment

While NWSA viewed litigation as important, it never really abandoned its drive for a constitutional amendment. From 1868 to 1875, its leaders made many attempts to have a female suffrage amendment added to the Constitution. In the 1870s, for example, NWSA members testified before Congress in support of a bill that would have given women in the District of Columbia the right to vote. Their efforts were of no avail, even on that limited level.

NWSA also continued to use other avenues to advocate its goals. By necessity, many of its efforts were aimed at education. NWSA leaders realized that the public as well as elected officials needed to be better informed on the question of suffrage and its actual potential consequences before suffrage could be attained.

This strategy of education and agitation can be traced to the exposure of several woman's rights leaders to Garrisonian abolitionism. William Lloyd Garrison had previously argued that to bring about social and legal change one must first change ideas. So, in addition to testifying before congressional committees on the necessity of a woman suffrage amendment, NWSA leaders staged a number of what today would be called "media events." For example, as late as July 4, 1876, at the U.S. Centennial celebration in Philadelphia, Anthony led a delegation of women onto the platform where assorted dignitaries were assembled. She handed a woman's rights declaration to the chair of the event and then turned and marched out of the hall with other women who handed out copies of the document to the startled audience. Once outside, the women mounted another platform and read the Declaration on the Rights of Women to the large crowd assembled in Independence Square. They demanded, among other things, the inclusion of women on juries and the end of taxation without representation.[10]

In these as well as other efforts, AWSA members never joined NWSA. Indeed, AWSA continued to take every precaution to distance itself from its more radical sister and even chose a different strategy to obtain the vote. While NWSA pursued its quest for a national suffrage amendment, AWSA persisted in its attempts to change state constitutions. Neither organization, however, made many inroads after 1875. Suffrage had been sufficiently complicated by

NWSA's advocacy of other goals to produce considerable antisuffrage reaction in the public, even though no strong opposition group arose.

The Antisuffrage Movement

Woman suffrage had many detractors. Arguments against it were numerous. Some critics argued that the Bible counseled the exclusion of women from politics. Antisuffrage forces relied heavily on the book of Genesis and the writings of St. Paul to maintain that God created separate spheres for men and women—men's place was out in the world, which included politics, whereas women's proper place was in the home, away from politics. Suffrage opponents further argued that women's "natural roles" were those of wife and mother. Thus, any change in this natural order would destroy society. Others claimed there was no need for suffrage because a woman's husband would fully protect her rights. They argued that if women got the vote, the only result would be to set wife against husband, which would result in the destruction of the family. In the first U.S. Senate debate on the question of woman suffrage, Senator George H. Williams summarized many of these arguments:

> It has been said that "the hand that rocked the cradle ruled the world," . . . by their elevated social position, [women] can exercise more influence upon public affairs than they could coerce by the use of the ballot. When God married our first parents in the garden . . . they were made bone of one bone and flesh of one flesh; and the whole theory of government and society proceeds upon the assumption that their interests are one. . . . The woman . . . who undertakes by the use of some independent political power to contend and fight against man, displays a spirit which would, if able, convert all the now harmonious elements of society into a state of war, and make every home a hell on earth.[11]

These or similar sentiments probably were shared by most men and women in the 1860s. Public opinion, including that of most women, was generally negative, and more often than not, hostile, toward expanded political rights for women. These negative attitudes were exacerbated by the advocacy of controversial ideas by some woman's movement members. Most people viewed notions of divorce reform and free love with horror. The reluctance of the Republican Party to support woman suffrage foreclosed the possibility of a quick, national solution. NWSA's weak organizational structure, which was limited to a loose national leadership group with few actual members, made any mass uprising to demand the vote impossible. These factors, along with the creation of rival groups in 1869, and the movement's limited source of potential supporters, help explain the minimal headway made toward suffrage. It was not until reconciliation occurred between NWSA and AWSA in 1890 that a new source of supporters was made available, and significant progress toward attaining the ballot was made.

THE SUFFRAGE MOVEMENT:
THE QUEST FOR THE VOTE CONTINUES

In 1890, largely on account of the efforts of Alice Stone Blackwell, Lucy Stone's only daughter, NWSA and AWSA joined forces to become the National American Woman Suffrage Association (NAWSA).[12] To that time, efforts to secure the ballot had borne little fruit, although the territory of Wyoming enacted a suffrage law in 1869. Numerous suffrage campaigns in the states, however, met with failure. The state campaigns suffered from poor organization, a limited number of women who supported suffrage efforts, and a lack of more general popular support. In addition, state suffrage campaigns often faced stiff opposition from liquor interests, which feared that temperance-minded suffrage workers would vote for Prohibition—the banning of the sale of alcoholic beverages. Clearly, additional respectability and organization were necessary before women would receive the vote. Even though these changes ultimately occurred, the result was a radically altered women's movement. In fact, the transformation was so great that by 1890 a new movement, called the suffrage movement, emerged.

Constituent Groups

In ideology, NAWSA more closely resembled the more conservative AWSA, whose philosophy slowly became dominant. Although some of the broader goals earlier espoused by NWSA had been achieved—greater educational opportunities for women, for example—many others, including significant divorce reform, trade unionism, and the legalization of prostitution, were dropped by NAWSA in favor of a single cause—woman suffrage.

The chances for success of a new movement spearheaded by NAWSA were aided by a variety of factors. First, thousands of previously unorganized, more conservative women were mobilized.[13] This process began in the 1870s with the founding and subsequent marked growth of the Woman's Christian Temperance Union (WCTU). The WCTU's prime goal was abolition of the liquor trade. But, under the able leadership of Frances Willard, the former dean of the Women's College of Northwestern University, it became a leading advocate of woman suffrage. Willard convinced WCTU members that suffrage was a necessary antecedent to attaining prohibition. She was eventually able to bring many of WCTU's 176,000-plus members, most of whom were traditional, religious women, into the suffrage cause. The WCTU's endorsement of suffrage was particularly important in the South, where it found support with religious fundamentalists. Of course, many southern women held strong biases against the specter of African American voters—male or female. The influx of WCTU members into the suffrage movement further exacerbated the rightward, conservative drift of NAWSA, as WCTU leaders began to become powerful forces in the new suffrage movement.

The Woman's Christian Temperance Union and Woman Suffrage

The campaign to eliminate the sale and consumption of alcohol in the nineteenth and early twentieth centuries was one of the first major political efforts undertaken by women acting independently of men. This drive was spearheaded by the Woman's Christian Temperance Union (WCTU). At a peak membership of 176,000, the WCTU was the largest women's organization ever to exist up to that time. (To put this in perspective, in 1997 NOW claimed 250,000 members; Concerned Women for America, 600,000.) The WCTU was able to restrict the sale of liquor in many communities, and for a limited time, the whole nation, after it lobbied successfully for passage of the Eighteenth (Prohibition) Amendment.

Women linked temperance to family issues. Some men wasted money on liquor, while their wives and children went hungry. Some women also associated domestic violence and sexual assaults with drinking liquor.

Attempts to link the WCTU and woman suffrage were at first resisted by temperance leaders, but under the leadership of Frances Willard the two movements were entwined. Elected president of the WCTU in 1879 on a prosuffrage platform, Willard argued that prohibition would come only if women could vote for it. Willard did not stop with the vote. Under her leadership, the WCTU endorsed a number of reform causes ranging from the creation of kindergartens to campaigning for more comfortable clothing for women. The result was to bring these issues, and especially the campaign for the vote, to the attention of a large group of relatively conservative middle-class women. In the Midwest, the association between the two causes was strongest, and campaigns for the vote relied heavily on local chapters of the WCTU. Of course, from the perspective of the liquor industry, the tie between the WCTU and woman suffrage meant that both causes were legitimate targets. Fearful that Willard was right and that giving women the vote would bring about the end to the liquor traffic, the industry pumped thousands of dollars (a lot of money at the time) into the antisuffrage effort. Thus, the ties between the WCTU and the woman suffrage movement were a mixed blessing, drawing supporters who might not have originally favored suffrage but also mobilizing a well-financed foe.[a]

[a] For more on the WCTU, see Janet Zollinger Giele, *Two Paths to Women's Equality: Temperance, Suffrage, and the Origins of Modern Feminism* (Old Tappan, N.J.: Twayne, 1995).

The growth of what is termed the club movement—so dubbed because so many middle-class women joined a variety of self-improvement clubs in the 1880s and 1890s—was a second factor assisting the development of the suffrage movement. In 1888, for example, Susan B. Anthony, recognizing the possible political usefulness of these clubs for the suffrage cause, helped to create an alliance called the National Council for Women. An even larger and more powerful umbrella association, the General Federation of Women's Clubs (GFWC), claimed a membership of more than two million by 1910.

In general, two types of clubs were affiliated with GFWC. The first type consisted of self-improvement groups, such as book clubs. These groups tended to attract white, educated, married, middle-class women. Confined to the home for most of the day, these women sought female companionship and intellectual stimulation to fill their leisure time. The second and more important type, however, consisted of the civic and department clubs that sprang from and were a part of the progressive movement. Most of the civic clubs were organized to improve municipal services and to bring about government reform, whereas the department clubs promoted specific issues such as abolition of child labor or improved conditions for working women.[14]

African American women, too, had their own groups. By 1916, the National Association of Colored Women, founded in 1896, had twenty-eight state federations and a membership of more than 50,000. Its first president, Mary Church Terrell, was appointed to the District of Columbia school board in 1895, becoming the first African American woman in the country to hold such a position. The association sponsored Mother's Congresses and Mother's Clubs to foster teaching of home skills to poorer women. It also lobbied for improvements in public education and was at the forefront of the battle against lynching.[15]

Within these progressive organizations, many women came to recognize their inferior political status and the need for the ballot. Without the ballot, they saw little chance to enact government reform or legislation to improve the status of working women or children. Thus, like WCTU members, many club women and those allied with the progressive movement became active in the suffrage cause, even though the GFWC did not formally endorse woman suffrage until 1914.

Like temperance workers, these new supporters of woman suffrage were fairly conservative. Many believed that a woman's proper place was in the home. Indeed, many chose to do club work rather than to seek employment outside of the home because club activities allowed them to pursue what they viewed as their more important domestic duties. They viewed progressivism and efforts to secure unadulterated foods, child labor laws, and better government as merely extensions of their traditional roles of wife and mother. Even those who joined the National Consumers' League (NCL), a progressive association formed to improve working conditions for women and children, were in basic agreement with the idea that a woman's "sphere" was the home. Although the NCL and other groups fought for improved factory conditions, they did so to make certain that poor women would be able to be better mothers and homemakers.

Educated Suffrage. These women were undeniably considerably more conservative than those in the first movement, but their conservatism was in many ways merely a reflection of the ideological changes that most members

Ida B. Wells and the Club Movement

Ida B. Wells was born in 1862 in Mississippi of slave parents. She was educated at a freedman's high school during Reconstruction. At the age of fourteen, after the death of both parents, she lied about her age to secure a teaching position in a rural school. Later she moved to Memphis where she taught in the city's Negro school system while she pursued her education at Fisk University. While a student there, she refused to give up her seat on a train to take a seat in the coach reserved for colored passengers and was forcibly removed. Undaunted, she sued the Chesapeake & Ohio Railroad and won her case in the state circuit court. Although the decision was overturned by the Tennessee Supreme Court in 1887, she actually challenged the segregated train system nine years before the U.S. Supreme Court decided *Plessey v. Ferguson* (1896).[a]

Wells's courage brought her to the attention of the leader of the Negro Press Association. He urged her to use her talents to write for small Negro-owned papers. Her court case and her repeated articles criticizing the inadequate education given to Negro children led the school board to fire her, so she then turned all of her energies to writing.

After three of her friends were lynched in 1892, she became a one-woman crusade against lynching. She founded antilynching societies and conducted in-depth analyses of lynchings in the South. She also was a member of a delegation that visited President William McKinley in 1898 to demand that federal action be taken to stop lynchings.

Wells married a Chicago lawyer in 1895. Her interest in the welfare of Negroes led her to found Negro women's clubs and the first Negro woman suffrage association. As president of the Ida B. Wells Club of Chicago, she worked to provide kindergartens and music instruction for the community. She also founded the Negro Fellowship League, which included a social center and a reading room that could be used to help assimilate the thousands of African Americans who were leaving the South and settling in Chicago. She also worked with national suffrage leaders including Jane Addams of Hull House and participated in the 1913 suffrage march on Washington, D.C., and the 1916 women's demonstration at the Republican National Convention to demand the inclusion of a suffrage plank in the platform.

Wells died in Chicago at age sixty-nine. In 1940, the city dedicated the Ida B. Wells Housing Project to honor her many achievements on behalf of African Americans and all Chicagoans.[b]

[a]163 U.S. 537 (1896).

[b]For more information on Wells, see Alfreda M. Duster, ed., *Crusade for Justice: The Autobiograpy of Ida B. Wells* (Chicago: University of Chicago Press, 1970/1991).

of their social class had undergone since the Civil War. The post-bellum era spawned several trends and changes that altered the native-born, white, middle-class view of democracy and politics. In the South, newly freed slaves and northern carpetbaggers helped to produce the turmoil and corruption of Reconstruction. In the North, waves of immigrants crowded into urban areas where their votes often formed the backbone of powerful and corrupt political machines. The West also had its fair share of political machines. In view of this seemingly nationwide political corruption, many came to believe that certain elements in society (blacks and immigrants) should be kept out of politics or, at least, that only the "better" elements of society should be in positions of political control. The notion that all humankind was endowed with inalienable, natural political rights quickly gave way to the idea of "political capacity" or "educated suffrage." These phrases were used to describe the philosophy that only those who had the ability to participate should have the right to do so. Antisuffrage forces, in fact, began to voice the opinion that adding women to the list of voters would only increase the number of "poor, ignorant, and immoral" elements, thus outnumbering the "patrician, intelligent, and impeccably proper" voters.[16]

NAWSA members and leaders also were often unwilling to associate suffrage with what some termed *the colored problem.* In 1898, Mary Church Terrell spoke at NAWSA's annual meeting and urged the convention to pass a resolution urging that "suitable accommodation" be created on trains. As one African American delegate put it, "educated colored women should not be hindered from working for the improvement and moral elevation of their less fortunate sisters."[17] Traveling for suffrage and self-improvement was intolerable for African American activists who were barred from sitting in all but the worst cars of passenger trains.

Southern women in attendance strongly objected to the resolution. To assuage this important source of support, Susan B. Anthony told the convention that it was beyond the scope of NAWSA's charge to pass "resolutions against railroad corporations or anybody else."[18]

These examples of political expediency and political strategy exacerbated the breach between black women and the predominately white suffrage movement.

Suffragists proclaimed that they had the necessary "capacity" to exercise the franchise and defended their ability on two grounds. First, they reasoned that *as women* they had special contributions to make to the more efficient and honest running of government. Second, they argued that their capacity rested in their membership in that segment of society best suited to participate—the native-born, white, middle class. NAWSA's arguments and actions were often racist in nature as it tried to build support in the South.

One version of NAWSA's first line of reasoning was that women were inherently less corruptible and less influenced by partisan loyalties. Its leaders argued that women would become an important bloc of voters in passing progressive legislation and in defeating political machines. Suffragists even asserted that the moral nature of women would mean a reduced likelihood that the nation would go to war if women were allowed to vote.

A closely related position was that women had a duty to bring their expertise into the legislative process. Their status as homemakers and mothers became the prime reason for giving women the ballot. While motherhood was an important argument for suffrage, the belief of many of its proponents that middle-class, native-born women would be better voters by virtue of their social status was often carried to extremes. Taking on racist overtones, some maintained, for example, that the votes of native-born, white women could be used to outweigh those of African Americans in the South or immigrants in the North. Others, including Stanton, called for the imposition of literacy or educational qualifications to reduce the number of immigrant and black voters.[19] As late as 1919, in denying the membership application of an African American women's organization, NAWSA justified its action, noting that if it welcomed black women, supportive votes of southern Democrats in Congress would be jeopardized.

There is, however, ample evidence that more than simple political expediency was also present. Racism and nativism were also evident. In 1893, for example, the following resolution was passed by NAWSA:

> *Resolved,* that without expressing any opinion on the proper qualifications for voting, we call attention to the significant facts that in every state there are more women who can read and write than all Negro voters; more white women who can read and write than all foreign voters; so that the enfranchisement of such women would settle the vexed question of rule by illiteracy, whether of home-grown or foreign-born production.[20]

Given these kinds of statements, it is surprising that women like Ida B. Wells or groups like the National Association of Colored Women had anything to do with NAWSA. NAWSA was not only racist but also politically conservative in nature. For example, NAWSA initially attempted to secure the vote on a state-by-state strategy and did not work for a national constitutional amendment. This tactic was adopted, at least in part, so as not to offend southern women and/or politicians who were wedded to the notion of states' rights. NAWSA's organizational structure was consistent with its pursuit of the state strategy. Like AWSA, it was composed of state organizations with a loose national leadership, at least until 1915. In fact, to gain greater southern support, in 1903 it even adopted its own states' rights plank allowing each state to set its own membership standards, thereby allowing southern affiliates to exclude black women.[21]

Suffrage Flounders. These policies virtually guaranteed state organizational autonomy but did little to help women actually win the vote on the state level. While there were some early suffrage victories in Colorado (1893) and Idaho (1896), after Wyoming (1890) and Utah (1896) entered the Union as suffrage states, no other states joined the suffrage column until 1910.[22] Although tremendous efforts were expended on state suffrage campaigns (noted historian Eleanor Flexner cites 480 efforts in thirty-three states, seventeen actual referendum votes, but only two victories from 1870 to 1910), these efforts went largely unrewarded.[23] It became increasingly clear to NAWSA that it could never win adoption of woman suffrage provisions in every state constitution.

Reasons for suffragists' failure to win victories along the East Coast in particular were numerous. First, NAWSA leaders were often ineffective, providing little direction for suffrage supporters. NAWSA had no national headquarters; the hometown of each NAWSA president became the organization's temporary base of operations. It also had a series of weak presidents; and without national direction, state associations floundered. Moreover, states where suffrage campaigns were launched were chosen in a haphazard fashion that often led to needless expenditures of time and energy on lost causes.

NAWSA also faced an increasingly sophisticated, well-organized, and well-financed opposition. Suffrage victories in Washington (1910) and California (1911), and in Arizona, Kansas, and Oregon in 1912, convinced opponents that the issue was alive and well. Liquor interests and political machines, sometimes financed by big business, began impressive antisuffrage campaigns that often were combined with voting fraud. Opposition to suffrage was so widespread in the South that chances for success there seemed particularly slim. In 1915, organized opposition contributed to the defeat of a suffrage referendum in four states in a period of but a few weeks. These defeats and recognition of the growing organization of antisuffrage forces finally led NAWSA leaders to recognize the need for a new strategy. Although the election of Carrie Chapman Catt as NAWSA president in late 1915 facilitated change, a new strategy was being tried even before she reorganized NAWSA.

Toward a National Amendment

In late 1912, the NAWSA board appointed Alice Paul, who had worked with the more militant British suffragettes, to its Congressional Committee. She quickly infused new life into the committee and immediately began to tap and build existing support for a *national* constitutional suffrage amendment. Within a few months, Paul was able to organize more than five thousand women to parade through the streets of Washington, D.C., for suffrage the day before Woodrow Wilson's presidential inauguration. Marchers dressed in white, some even on horseback, slowly made their way down Pennsylvania Avenue, where they encountered antagonism from some spectators. Although NAWSA had obtained a parade permit, when a riot ensued as mobs of spectators turned on the women, police offered the marchers no assistance. Many other citizens who watched the parade were outraged about the absence of protection for females. This sense of outrage at the violence directed at women, plus the very size of the parade that was staged at a time when all eyes were on the U.S. capital, resulted in a spectacular media event that brought incalculable press attention to the suffrage movement. Capitalizing on this free, favorable publicity, the committee launched a national woman suffrage petition drive and began to send regular delegations to see President Wilson to press for a national solution.

Paul, sensing momentum and believing in a national strategy, formed a new organization, the Congressional Union, in April 1913, to work exclusively for a national amendment. Although she remained chair of the NAWSA Congressional Committee, a break with the larger organization was inevitable. At the NAWSA convention in 1913, Paul's insistence that a federal amendment be the sole target of suffrage forces was at odds with the beliefs of most NAWSA leaders, who continued to cling to the state-by-state approach. Not surprisingly, Paul was removed as chair of the Congressional Committee.

After her fall from grace with NAWSA, Paul devoted her full energies to the Congressional Union. Following the lead of British suffragettes, the Congressional Union began to hold the party in power responsible for failure to pass a suffrage bill, a tactic also strongly opposed by NAWSA. In 1914, union members actively campaigned against congressional candidates of the Democratic Party, which had failed to endorse woman suffrage. All the while, the union, later called the National Woman's Party (NWP), pressed Congress for an amendment to the U.S. Constitution. Its effort resulted, at least, in a renewed interest in a suffrage amendment, a proposal that had been nearly dormant for more than twenty years. Like NAWSA, it also used racist appeals, particularly in the South where it tried to appease fears that a constitutional amendment would complicate what it called "the race problem."[24]

A Winning Plan. Many of NAWSA's own members, excited by the Congressional Union's enthusiasm and focus, pressed its leaders to work more actively for a constitutional amendment. Carrie Chapman Catt needed little convincing. After decisive state referenda defeats in 1916, she devised what was called a Winning Plan; its object was to direct all NAWSA's resources and cooperating organizations toward the goal of achieving a woman suffrage amendment to the U.S. Constitution by 1922. A key component of the plan was national coordination whereby *all* state associational activity was to be geared toward the single goal of an amendment to the U.S. Constitution.[25]

Catt's Winning Plan was quite detailed. Associations in suffrage states were to pressure their legislators to request that Congress pass a constitutional amendment. Additionally, national officers handpicked states for new campaigns where passage of state amendments was seen as feasible. Other state associations were to direct their efforts toward presidential suffrage or voting rights for women in party primaries in states that allowed state legislatures to make those changes. Catt believed that it was critical "to keep so much 'suffrage noise' going all over the country that neither the enemy nor friends will discover where the real battle is."[26] To keep the battle national in scope, Catt targeted southern and northern states for intense activity to break the spirit of suffrage opponents. To speed up the process even more, Catt planned to have support for the suffrage amendment included in both party platforms by 1920 to facilitate state ratification by 1922.

While World War I, like the Civil War before it, diverted much of the suffrage leaders' energies, Catt wisely insisted, unlike Stanton and Anthony earlier, that suffrage work continue to come first and that NAWSA continue to follow her plan. Slowly the Winning Plan began to produce results. The antisuffrage "solid South" was cracked in March 1917 when women in Arkansas won the right to vote in state primary elections. In addition, several legislatures enacted presidential suffrage laws. And in the same year, New York voters approved the addition of a suffrage amendment to their state constitution.

These events resulted in the enfranchisement of more women, but strong opposition in the U.S. Senate prevented proponents from securing the two-thirds majority required for a constitutional amendment. Southern senators stood firmly against the amendment and were joined by others from New England and some eastern states. Opposition was justified on the rationale of states' rights, but many women, particularly those in southern suffrage associations, rejected this claim. Southern senators, for example, supported a Prohibition amendment and were not upset by the national government's intrusion into that area. In fact, southern proponents believed that the true motive of Senate opponents was a combination of resistance to any change in women's roles and fear of what female suffrage might do to the lucrative cotton industry in the South and Northeast. Manufacturers there relied heavily on female workers, child workers, and oppressed black workers. Senate suffrage opponents believed that manufacturers' cheap labor resources would be threatened if the amendment passed and women voters used their ballot strength to secure enactment of equal pay and/or factory inspection laws.

Recognizing that changes had to be made in the composition of the U.S. Senate before passage of the suffrage amendment could become a reality, NAWSA leaders launched a campaign to defeat their opponents who stood for reelection in 1918. The political clout of the suffragists produced the defeat of two powerful opponents of the amendment. When this show of force was coupled with the addition of several more states into the suffrage column—South Dakota, Michigan, Oklahoma, Iowa, Minnesota, Missouri, Ohio, Wisconsin, and Maine—quick passage of the Nineteenth Amendment was virtually assured.

Meeting in a special session in the spring of 1919, first the House of Representatives and then the Senate passed the suffrage amendment. Ratification by the necessary thirty-six states was completed in 1920, and the first national election with full woman suffrage occurred in November of that year. In spite of the Nineteenth Amendment, black women in the South were still effectively disenfranchised by a variety of practices that kept most African Americans—male or female—from voting.

Suffrage Not Enough—The Beginning of the End

Women in NAWSA, its constituent groups, and the NWP celebrated the ratification of the Nineteenth Amendment, or the Susan B. Anthony amendment, as it was sometimes called. The Anthony amendment, however, did
not appease the desire of the NWP for full equality. Its leaders, in fact,
quickly turned their energies toward the passage of an amendment to ban *all*
discrimination based on sex. Their view of women's roles, however, differed
from that held by most women. Even a majority of suffragists wanted no further changes made in women's status. Their single agreed-upon goal had
been suffrage. Once suffrage was secured, the base of the suffrage movement
quickly began to disintegrate.

Without another common issue or set of issues to unite them, the many
and varied women's groups that had made possible the passage of the Nineteenth Amendment began to go their separate ways. Some suffrage leaders
tried to counter this phenomenon by starting new organizations. Some members of NAWSA founded the National League of Women Voters (LWV) in
1919 to work to educate female voters concerning the elective and legislative
processes. Other, more radical women, such as Catt, became involved in the
growing movements for peace, birth control, or equal rights. These efforts
aside, many felt powerless to stop fractionalization of the movement. Even
while state ratification of the Anthony amendment was pending, Anna
Howard Shaw, a past NAWSA president, lamented, "I am sorry for you
young women who have to carry on the work in the next ten years, for suffrage was a symbol, and now you have lost your symbol. There is nothing for
women to rally round."[27]

The Women's Joint Congressional Committee. Some suffrage leaders,
particularly those active in the newly formed LWV, believed that there was a
chance to save the movement. They sensed that most participants in the suffrage movement were issue oriented and that their continued involvement in
the political process could be had if the right kind of association could be
formed. Therefore, the LWV moved to create an umbrella-type organization
composed of a variety of women's groups previously active in the suffrage
cause. The Women's Joint Congressional Committee (WJCC) was established
in late 1920 to identify and to lobby for the enactment of national legislation
of concern to women. With fourteen sponsoring organizations and a total
membership of ten million, WJCC quickly moved to become a clearinghouse
for women's issues and to avoid duplication of effort among its constituent
groups.

WJCC, however, soon fell into disarray. Initially it was able to mobilize
its constituent groups to pressure Congress effectively for enactment of citizenship and prenatal care legislation for women. But controversy over goals
and the growing recognition of legislators that women *did not* vote as a bloc
led to an immediate decline in its power over Congress. Also contributing to

its decreasing prestige was the widely publicized disagreement that occurred among women's groups over the prospect of an equal rights amendment.[28]

The NWP and the Equal Rights Amendment. Writing about the early 1920s, noted historian William H. Chafe commented, "No issue divided women's organizations more than the Equal Rights Amendment to the Constitution."[29] As first submitted to the Congress in December 1923 by Daniel Anthony (R-Kans.), Susan B. Anthony's nephew, the proposed amendment read, "Men and women shall have equal rights throughout the United States and every place subject to its jurisdiction."

The NWP's support of the amendment immediately split the already faltering suffrage movement into two distinct coalitions: (1) "hard-core feminists" and (2) "social feminists." NWP leaders, as spokespersons for hard-core feminists, rejected pleas from WJCC social feminists to work for causes such as peace, birth control, and social reform. Instead, they saw these efforts as diverting their energies from the ultimate goal—equality—and thus a waste of time. The powerful National Consumers' League, in particular, found itself forced to take a public stand against the amendment because of the clear indications that the ERA, as written, would negate all protective labor legislation for women—legislation that the NCL believed imperative to the health and well-being of female workers.

The division among women over the ERA continued into the 1930s, although no real women's rights movement was evident. Nevertheless, in 1940, the Republican Party added support of the amendment to its platform.[30]

Largely because of the NWP's continued pressure, some form of an ERA was introduced in at least one house of Congress every session between 1923 and 1971. The House of Representatives held hearings on the proposed amendment in 1948 but failed to do so again until 1971. In contrast, the Senate held hearings in several sessions, and in 1950 and 1953 it passed the proposed amendment. Reflecting the hard-core/social feminist split, however, on both of those occasions the Senate version included a rider guaranteeing that protective legislation for women would not be affected.

Unlike many social feminists, the NWP continued to insist that women, like blacks, had to be guaranteed equality in all spheres and that such change could not come about easily without a specific constitutional amendment. But the NWP was clearly more radical than most other women's groups. Thus, it was not until the development of the current women's rights movement that passage of an equal rights amendment came close to reality.

THE DRIVE FOR WOMEN'S POLITICAL RIGHTS

Initially, women's rights groups gave little thought to expanded political rights per se, although they clearly shared the goal of greater representation of women in government. For example, in one of the National Organization for Women's (NOW) first letters to prospective members, its purpose was explained:

> . . . to initiate or support action, nationally or in any part of this nation, by individuals or organizations, to break through the silken curtain of prejudice and discrimination against women *in government* . . . the *political parties,* the *judiciary* . . . and in every field of importance in American society[31] (emphasis added).

These women saw that the civil rights movement had been able to make impressive changes in the status of African Americans—now they wanted similar progress for women.

Nowhere among NOW's specific goals enunciated at its first national meeting was a specific call for additional political rights. This absence is largely attributable to the fact that by 1967 the political inequalities experienced by women were quite different from those encountered by leaders of the early woman's and suffrage movements. While a variety of laws and practices kept women out of jobs or hampered their abilities for advancement in the 1960s, women enjoyed most basic political rights. Consequently, NOW and other older-branch groups devoted most of their early efforts to alleviating discrimination in the economic, educational, and social spheres, where problems were more immediate, and to the passage of the equal rights amendment. Many NOW members, as well as other supporters of women's rights, believed that once equality came in those spheres, especially through passage of an ERA, fewer of their efforts would have to be directed at blatant types of discrimination (because such practices would be unconstitutional), freeing them to work toward their goal of greater representation of women in government.

Women Seek Rights through Litigation

While most women's rights activists lobbied for an equal rights amendment, some groups, realizing the successes that the National Association for the Advancement of Colored People (NAACP) had in securing additional rights for blacks through the courts, began to explore the feasibility of a litigation strategy designed to seek a more expansive judicial interpretation of the scope of the Fourteenth Amendment. Although prior forays into the courts such as the *Minor* case in 1875 and others as recently as 1948 had ended unfavorably,[a] some believed that the times had changed enough for the justices (or some of the justices) to recognize that sex-based differential treatment of women was unconstitutional.

The Fourteenth Amendment protects all U.S. citizens from state action that violates equal protection of the laws. Early on, the Supreme Court decided that certain rights were entitled to a heightened standard of review. When fundamental rights such as First Amendment freedoms or suspect classifications such as race are involved, the Court uses a heightened standard of review called strict scrutiny to determine the constitutional validity of the challenged laws. In legal terms, this means that if a statute or governmental practice makes a classification based on race, for example, the statute is presumed to be unconstitutional unless the state can provide "compelling affirmative justifications"—that is, unless the state can prove the law is necessary to accomplish a permissible goal. During the 1960s and into the 1970s, the Court routinely struck down as unconstitutional statutes that discriminated on the basis of race.

Many believed that the status of women and the climate for change were sufficiently positive to convince even a conservative Court that some change in its interpretation of the Fourteenth Amendment was necessary. The first group to seek the elevation of statutory classification based on gender to a suspect classification status (thus entitling it to strict scrutiny) was the American Civil Liberties Union (ACLU). Its first women's rights case was *Reed v. Reed* (1971).[b] Ruth Bader Ginsburg, a member of the ACLU board who in 1993 became the second woman to serve on the U.S. Supreme Court, argued the case before the Supreme Court. Her enthusiasm and interest in the expansion of women's rights via constitutional interpretation led the ACLU to found the Women's Rights Project (WRP).

At issue in *Reed v. Reed* was the constitutionality of an Idaho statute that required that males be preferred to females as administrators of estates for those who die intestate (without a will). The National Federation of Business and Professional Women, the National Organization for Women, and the Women's Equity Action League all filed amicus curiae briefs urging the Court to interpret the Fourteenth Amendment to prohibit discrimination against women as well as African Americans.

Reed v. Reed turned the tide in terms of constitutional litigation. While the Court did not rule that sex was a suspect classification, it concluded that the equal protection clause of the Fourteenth Amendment prohibited unreasonable classifications based on sex. Two years later, in another WRP case, *Frontiero v. Richardson* (1973),[c] the Court fell one justice short of elevating gender to a suspect classification. Finally, in 1976, after a series of cases had been brought to it by Ginsburg and other women's rights lawyers, the Court ruled that sex-discrimination complaints would be judged by a new, judicially created intermediate standard of review a step below strict scrutiny. In *Craig v. Boren* (1976),[d] the owner of the Honk 'n' Holler Restaurant in Stillwater, Oklahoma, and Craig, a male under age twenty-one, challenged the constitutionality of the state law that prohibited the sale of 3.2 percent beer to males under the age of twenty-one and to females under the age of eighteen. The state introduced a considerable amount of evidence in support of the statute, including the following:

> Eighteen- to twenty-year-old males were more likely to be arrested for driving under the influence than were females of the same age.
>
> Youths aged seventeen to twenty-one are more likely to be injured or to die in alcohol-related traffic accidents, with males exceeding females.
>
> Young men were more inclined than females to drink and drive.

The Supreme Court found that this information was "too tenuous" to support the legislation. In coming to this conclusion, the justices carved out a new two-tiered "test" to be used in examining claims of sex discrimination. According to the Court, "[T]o withstand constitutional challenge, . . . classifications by gender must serve important governmental objectives and must be substantially related to achievement to those objectives." As *Craig* demonstrates, men, too, can use the Fourteenth Amendment to fight gender-based discrimination. Since 1976, the Court has applied that intermediate standard to most claims involving gender that it has heard. Thus, the following kinds of practices have been found to violate the Fourteenth Amendment:

Single-sex public nursing schools[e]

Laws that consider males adults at age twenty-one but females at age eighteen[f]

Laws that allow women but not men to receive alimony[g]

State supported all-male military academies[h]

In contrast, the Court has upheld the following governmental practices and laws:

Draft registration provisions for males only[i]

Statutory rape laws that apply only to female victims[j]

The level of review used by the Court is crucial. Clearly, a statute that excluded blacks from a draft registration would be unconstitutional. But, because gender is not subject to the same higher standard of review that is used in racial discrimination cases, the exclusion of women from the requirements of the Military Selective Service Act was ruled permissible because the government policy was considered to serve "important governmental objectives."

One can perhaps better understand, then, why women's rights activists continue to argue that until the passage of an equal rights amendment women will never come close to enjoying the same rights as men. An amendment would automatically raise the level of scrutiny that the Court applies, although there is concern about how "equal" would be applied to situations of gender difference such as maternity.[k]

[a]*Goessaert v. Cleary,* 335 U.S. 464 (1948).

[b]404 U.S. 71 (1971).

[c]411 U.S. 677 (1973).

[d]429 U.S. 190 (1976).

[e]*Mississippi University for Women v. Hogan,* 458 U.S. 718 (1982).

[f]*Stanton v. Stanton,* 421 U.S. 7 (1975).

[g]*Orr v. Orr,* 440 U.S. 268 (1979).

[h]*U.S. v. Virginia,* 116 S.Ct. 2264 (1996).

[i]*Rostker v. Goldberg,* 453 U.S. 57 (1981).

[j]*Michael M. v. Superior Court of Sonoma County,* 450 U.S. 464 (1981).

[k]See Laura Woliver, "The Equal Rights Amendment and the Limits of Legal Reform," *Polity* 21 (Fall 1988): 183–200.

Source: Adapted from Karen O'Connor and Larry J. Sabato, *American Government: Continuity and Change* (Boston: Allyn & Bacon, 1997), 209–10.

Women in the younger branch were even less interested in expanded political rights per se. Two factors largely account for their lack of participation. Most in the younger branch either rejected the political system as corrupt or believed that the end of women's oppression would not come about through participation in or alteration of the political system. Some, for example, believed that women's oppression was traceable to racism, capitalism, imperialism, the patriarchal system, or some combination of those factors. Hence, women's inferior status could be remedied only when these systems were overthrown and replaced by a new political order.

Some in the younger branch argued that an end to oppression and discrimination against women in the political arena would come only after sex-role stereotypes and their supporting structures (traditional courtship and sexual double standards, the traditional family, etc.) were abolished. Other women maintained (and continue to do so) that the patriarchal, social, and political systems as well as the capitalist economic system must be overthrown before women will be free. While some in the younger branch called for the "full participation [of women] in the decision-making processes and positions of our political, economic, and social institutions,"[32] the focus of most of these small groups was largely on the raising of individual women's consciousness as a prelude to social and hence political revolution and/or providing limited help to local women in specific issue areas. Moreover, when these groups mobilized to act, they usually did so at the local level. Their activist work in rape crisis centers, battered women's shelters, and health clinics, for example, empowered these women at the *local* level.[33]

While often disagreeing on the focus, both branches of the movement agreed that changes had to be made in the political or legal system. It was the more conventional route to change—the addition of a constitutional amendment guaranteeing equality of rights to all women—however, that became the first major rallying point for change.[34]

The President's Commission on the Status of Women and NOW

In 1961, President John F. Kennedy created the President's Commission on the Status of Women. The commission was created in large part as a payback for a political debt to the women who had worked so hard for his election. Those supporters were outraged when President Kennedy appointed few women to major governmental positions. To appease these women, and some say to avoid the question of the ERA, which he opposed, Kennedy established the commission with former activist First Lady Eleanor Roosevelt as its chair.[35]

In June 1963, the commission's report, *American Woman*, recommended increased appointment of women to important political positions. The sole advocate of the ERA on the commission, Marguerite Rawalt, persuaded other commission members to temper their rejection of the need for an ERA.

Eleanor Roosevelt

Hillary Rodham Clinton is not the first First Lady to have played an active role in government as part of her husband's administration. Nor is she the first one to be criticized for it. In fact, Rodham Clinton once told reporters that she has often dealt with the criticisms hurled at her by "having conversations . . . in [her] head with Mrs. Roosevelt." Those conversations have "been one of the saving graces that I have hung on to for dear life," Rodham Clinton told an audience at a fund-raiser for the Eleanor Roosevelt Monument Fund.[a] Later, however, when Bob Woodward's book on the Clinton White House reported that "sacred psychologist" Jean Houston taught Rodham Clinton to communicate with spirits, the First Lady was criticized for trying to communicate with Roosevelt.[b]

Hillary Rodham Clinton, who has read extensively about other first ladies, is constantly compared to Eleanor Roosevelt. Both pressed their husbands to appoint women to the Cabinet. (Frances Perkins, appointed by Franklin Roosevelt in 1932, was the first female cabinet member in the United States.) Whereas critics continually blame Rodham Clinton's role as head of the President's Health Care Reform Task Force for its failure, FDR's secretary of the interior told Eleanor Roosevelt to "stick to her knitting and keep out of the affairs connected to my department."[c]

Eleanor Roosevelt was always interested in the poor and underprivileged. After graduation from high school, she was a settlement house volunteer and soon joined the National Consumers' League, where she worked with Florence Kelley.

After her marriage, she devoted most of her time to raising her children. Then, in 1920 she became active in the new League of Women Voters and coordinated its legislative program. In 1922, she joined the liberal Women's Trade Union League (see Chapter 3).

In addition to pushing for Frances Perkins's appointment, she also lobbied for the appointment of other women, especially to posts in the Women's Bureau. As First Lady, like Rodham Clinton, Eleanor Roosevelt wrote regular syndicated newspaper and magazine articles to push her progressive ideas. She served on the Board of the NAACP and, as vice chair of its legal fund, raised money to lay the groundwork for *Brown v. Board of Education*. She continued her work for civil rights and women's rights after her husband's death. Her last public position was as chair of the first President's Commission on the Status of Women, a job she held until her death in late 1962.

[a]Quoted in Ann Gowen, "Eleanor and Me; Hillary Tells of 'Talks' with Powerful First Lady," *Washington Times,* February 23, 1993, E-1.

[b]Kenneth L. Woodward et al., "Soul Searching," *Newsweek,* July 8, 1996, 33.

[c]Gowen, "Eleanor and Me," E-1.

Thus, the commission report "concluded that a constitutional amendment need not *now* be sought," paving the way for a possible future recommendation to the contrary.[36]

Five years later, however, many women's groups still did not greet the concepts embodied in the amendment with enthusiasm. In fact, when NOW endorsed the ERA in 1967, some of its members resigned in protest, voicing fears similar to those noted earlier by social feminists and many existing women's groups: The proposed amendment would negate protective labor legislation.

Later in 1967, Martha Griffiths (D-Mich.), one of the few women in the House of Representatives, used a discharge petition to force the amendment out of the House Judiciary Committee. It had been blocked there since 1948 by its powerful committee chair, Emanuel Celler (D-N.Y.). After extensive hearings, on August 10, 1970, the full House had its first occasion ever to vote for the ERA. After eloquent presentations by female representatives, it passed on a vote of 350 to 15.

A somewhat different pattern emerged in the Senate. In May 1970, prior to the House vote, the Senate Subcommittee on Constitutional Amendments held hearings. Several representatives from the AFL-CIO testified in opposition to the amendment. No women's groups spoke out against it. A similar pattern emerged when new hearings were held by the full Senate Judiciary Committee, after the House vote. Most of those who testified, including the John Birch Society, the AFL-CIO, and the National Council of Catholic Women, spoke against the amendment. Senator Sam Ervin (D-N.C.) proposed a rider that prohibited the drafting of women into the armed forces. It also contained language limiting the ERA's effect on protective legislation such as maximum-hour laws; initially his amendment had substantial support.

In 1970, the Citizens Advisory Council on the Status of Women (which replaced the President's Commission on the Status of Women) reported to President Richard M. Nixon its belief that an amendment was necessary, thus rejecting the earlier recommendation of the original commission. Included in its report was a legal analysis of the ERA's impact on protective legislation that concluded that when benefits were given to women, they would be extended to men. That report gave impetus to the tremendous effort that was launched by myriad women's organizations, culminating in a Senate vote of 84 to 8 for the ERA on March 22, 1972.

The Proposed Equal Rights Amendment

Section 1　Equality of rights under the law shall not be denied or abridged by the United States or by any State on account of sex.

Section 2　The Congress shall have the power to enforce, by appropriate legislation, the provisions of this article.

Section 3　This amendment shall take effect two years after the date of ratification.

The Ratification Effort

General agreement existed about how the ERA would affect political, educational, and employment opportunities. Controversy over its impact on family relations, especially divorce, alimony, and child support laws, and the specter of military service for women should there be another draft, were present from the beginning.

In fact, once the ERA was sent to the states for their approval, the real battle over its ratification began in earnest. Initially, ratification seemed a virtual certainty. Supreme Court rulings striking down most protective legislation as unlawful under the Civil Rights Act of 1964 (see Chapter 3) helped to bring into the ERA camp most of the social feminist and labor groups that had initially opposed it. Even some women in the younger branch who saw little to be gained from a constitutional change supported the amendment, perceiving it to be a symbol and a possible tool to facilitate the acquisition of additional rights. Additionally, public opinion polls revealed growing national support for the ERA.

Between March 1972 and January 1973, twenty-eight states quickly moved to ratify the amendment, prompting Martha Griffiths to predict confidently in March 1973, "ERA will be a part of the Constitution before the year's out."[37] These early victories, however, were not an indication of an easy road ahead. States that failed to ratify the amendment, especially in the South, often had political cultures resistant to innovative legislation or expanded women's rights. Additionally, many ERA supporters failed to recognize growing grass-roots opposition.

During the drive for the Nineteenth Amendment, NAWSA acted as an umbrella organization and as *the* single major representative of prosuffrage forces. NAWSA also had strong state and local affiliates upon which to rely once the ratification effort turned from the national to the state level. In contrast, the women's rights movement had no spokesperson, no Winning Plan, and few state affiliates. These deficiencies became increasingly grave in the wake of growing and well-organized state and local opposition. Weak or nonexistent state organization was particularly critical given that Congress attached a seven-year time limit for ratification of the amendment.

ERA—The First Stage (1972–1977). During this stage, NOW, the LWV, and the National Federation of Business and Professional Women's Clubs (BPW) sponsored letter and telegram campaigns, provided expert testimony, and supported pro-ERA candidates. State groups were reactive and were created or mobilized only in response to anti-ERA activity. While pro-ERA groups defeated some state legislators who opposed ratification, only five states ratified the ERA after 1973.[38]

During this period, BPW funded a study that recommended that women's rights groups band together to form a more organized and well-financed national headquarters to coordinate state campaigns and solicit money. In addition to being among its earliest supporters, BPW played a key role in funding the movement for the ERA, billing its members $1.50 per year for support of the ratification effort. Its financial and political resources allowed BPW to be an instrumental force in seeing the ERA through Congress. It also was a leading force in bringing together key organizations in ERAmerica in January 1976, in an attempt to orchestrate states' efforts to get the needed legislative support at that level. But ERAmerica, which relied on member organizations for help, soon turned out to be relatively poor and powerless. Thus, without a strong national coordinating organization, actions to ratify the ERA relied almost exclusively on the efforts of individual groups, particularly NOW, BPW, and LWV, as well as ad hoc coalitions. Not only did each of these groups pursue different strategies, but all sought to become the leader in the ratification effort.

ERA—The Second Stage (1977–1979). In 1977, NOW adopted different tactics "which marked the ascendancy of NOW as the leading proponent of the ERA."[39] Its rise to the forefront was triggered by the adoption of two campaigns. First, NOW called for an economic boycott of states where ratification had not yet occurred. Generally, this boycott took the form of having large national associations cancel or threaten to cancel conventions scheduled in cities located in unratified states. Even the American Political Science Association voted not to hold its annual meeting in Chicago, Illinois, a state where ratification had not occurred, after extensive lobbying by women in the Women's Caucus for Political Science. Second, given the impending deadline for ratification—March 1979—a resolution to extend that deadline an additional seven years was introduced in Congress at the urging of numerous women's groups. In addition, these groups, as suffragists had done before, sponsored a march on Washington, D.C., that attracted more than 100,000 participants. Many dressed in white as suffragists had done long before in their quest for the Nineteenth Amendment. These well-planned efforts ultimately led Congress to approve a thirty-nine-month extension period for ratification over the strong objections of amendment opponents.

Both of these strategies were national in nature and quite unlike the Winning Plan devised earlier by Carrie Chapman Catt. In fact, the then-president of NOW, Eleanor Smeal (later head of the Fund for a Feminist Majority), justified the necessity of a national campaign saying that "this is an unratified country. We communicate as a nation . . . our states are economically interdependent [and] [o]ur opposition is national."[40] This kind of determination to pursue a national strategy in the wake of growing anti-ERA and New Right strength in nonratified states' legislatures is noteworthy given that the amendment could not be ratified without the approval of those states.

Anti-ERA forces were best mobilized at the state level. Drawing women from the organizational bases of the conservative wing of the Republican Party, fundamentalist churches in the South, and a reenergized antiabortion movement (see Chapter 5), Phyllis Schlafly effectively organized STOP ERA, which led the fight against ratification of the amendment. Schlafly, the editor of the conservative monthly *Phyllis Schlafly Report* and a former speech writer for Senator Barry Goldwater (R-Ariz.), laid the groundwork for an anti-ERA movement as early as 1967.[41]

Schlafly was a master at grass-roots mobilization, which was a key factor in defeating the ERA at the state level. Schlafly and the Eagle Forum, a group she founded in 1975 to fight ratification, lobbied state legislators in key states, while pro-amendment forces continued to work largely on the national level.

Building on her conservative base, Schlafly became the symbol of the anti-ERA movement as she effectively argued that the amendment would mean:

1. Private schools would have to be coed;
2. All sports, including contact sports, would be coed;
3. All persons would pay the same income tax regardless of their income;
4. Abortions would be government-funded;
5. Homosexuals could be schoolteachers;
6. Women would be forced into combat;
7. Men could refuse to support their wives;
8. A woman's right to her home and support of her children could be denied;
9. Homosexual marriages would be legal; and
10. Homosexuals would be allowed to adopt children.[42]

Other ERA opponents argued that it would legalize unisex toilets and pornography.[43] The ambiguity surrounding the ERA encouraged many to view it as a threat to the status quo. As the ERA was portrayed by its opponents, the traditional family, the institution of marriage, and the right of a wife to be supported by her husband would be jeopardized by ratification. Phyllis Schlafly, in answer to the question of who would profit from the ERA, wrote in an often reprinted quotation, "Women will lose, families will lose, society will lose."[44]

ERA—The Third Stage (1979–1982). In spite of the apparent success of STOP ERA's *state* efforts and public perception problems, in late 1979 NOW fully devoted itself to implementation of a new *national* plan of action. By 1982, NOW was receiving more than $1 million a month for ERA ratification and had formed several political action committees (PACs) to elect pro-ERA candidates. It also used a variety of other traditional and nontraditional strategies. For example, "ERA missionaries" went door to door seeking support in unratified states, and pro-ERA entertainers went on television to gain support and publicity. A variety of forms of protest also occurred. For example, some women chained themselves to Republican headquarters, while others conducted hunger strikes or performed acts of vandalism.

These tactics came too late and generally occurred at the wrong level of government. Even in states such as Illinois, which were the targets of massive pro-ERA efforts, few votes were changed. The amendment was finally defeated on June 30, 1982, when the time period for ratification expired. The lack of a coordinated effective effort, however, was probably just one of several factors that contributed to the ERA's defeat. In fact, had it not been for the activities of anti-ERA groups with their close ties to state legislators and corporate interests, the amendment's chances of passage would have been far greater.[45] By the early 1980s, however, the political tide in the nation had turned. Conservative Ronald Reagan was elected president in 1980, and a backlash against many gains by women was soon to begin.[46]

The Aftermath of the ERA Ratification Effort: Women's Groups Mobilize for Expanded Political Opportunities

When the ERA was not ratified, NOW chose to continue to press for the amendment at least in part because ERA direct-mail solicitations stimulated donations. But, many other groups sought to focus their efforts elsewhere. Many turned their energies toward preservation of abortion rights that were under attack from conservatives and the Reagan administration (see Chapter 5). Others concentrated on litigation to press the courts for expanded constitutional rights for women. Without an ERA guaranteeing women's equality under the U.S. Constitution, women were forced to look for statutory remedies to prevent discrimination. We explore many of these efforts in Chapter 3.

A Woman for Vice President—the Women's Rights Movement, the Gender Gap, and Party Politics

In 1984, Geraldine Ferraro became the first woman to be nominated by a major party for the position of vice president of the United States. The selection of Ferraro by Walter Mondale was the result of a campaign by the women's rights movement to place a woman on the Democratic Party ticket. The leaders of this effort believed a woman would make the Democratic Party victorious, but in November the election results indicated Ferraro had little impact on the choice of voters.[a]

The triggering factor for the nomination of Ferraro, or a woman vice presidential candidate, was the gender gap, a difference in the voting behavior of men and women.[b] The gender gap first attracted public attention in 1980 when women were markedly less likely than men to vote for Ronald Reagan (56 percent of men but only 47 percent of women voted for Reagan in 1980). Many women activists believed this gender gap could be expanded in 1984 if the Democratic Party nominated a woman for vice president. Bella Abzug, a founder of NOW and then a member of Congress (D-N.Y.), for example, writing in a November 1983 editorial, pressed the case for a woman vice president, noting that her group, Women's Presidential Project, had been researching this possibility since 1982.

Button from Geraldine Ferraro's 1984 campaign for the vice presidency.

Eleanor Smeal, a former NOW president, formed the Gender Gap Action Campaign. It promoted the idea of a woman vice president in full-page ads in the *New York Times*. Under the presidency of Judy Goldsmith, NOW was also active throughout the 1983–1984 period in urging Democrats to nominate a woman. In July 1984, Democratic presidential candidate Walter Mondale tapped Geraldine Ferraro, a three-term member of the House of Representatives, to be his running mate, hoping that a woman vice-presidential candidate would help the Democrats unseat Ronald Reagan.

The high point of the Ferraro campaign may have been her acceptance speech at the Democratic National Convention. The floor of the convention was crowded with women delegates and alternates who wept, cheered, and shouted "Gerry" at this new milestone for women. But the moment was not to last. Within a few weeks, the debate over Ferraro's own finances and those of her husband had slowed the momentum Mondale's campaign got from her selection. Antiabortion forces also targeted Ferraro's pro-choice position. Writing later, Ferraro summarized her reaction to the campaign: "I wasn't prepared for the depth of the fury, the bigotry, and the sexism my candidacy . . . would unleash."[c]

Studies by academics and surveys by pollsters found that most voters reacted favorably to Ferraro, but stereotypes about a woman's ability to be president, especially her ability to manage foreign affairs, persisted. Less than enthusiastic evaluations of Ferraro were most common among white men and Southerners. In November, when the final votes were counted, the gender gap persisted but a majority of men and women voted for Ronald Reagan (62 percent of men and 56 percent of women).[d] Most commentators, in analyzing the election results, believed that Ferraro's impact on the final result, like that of most vice-presidential candidates, had been minimal.[e]

[a]Kathleen A. Frankovic, "The 1984 Election: The Irrelevance of the Campaign," *PS,* Winter 1985, 39-47.
[b]Carol Mueller, *The Politics of the Gender Gap* (Beverly Hills, Calif: Sage, 1988).
[c]Quoted in *Newsweek,* October 7, 1985, 60.
[d]Frankovic, "The 1984 Election," 39–47.
[e]Ibid.

Former vice-presidential candidate Geraldine Ferraro is fond of telling female audiences, "If you don't run, you can't win."[47] Sentiments like these led to the creation of several groups to encourage women to do just that, as well as to provide support for those who chose to run. Some women opted to work within the existing two-party structure. And both parties, but especially the Democratic Party, took measures to encourage women to participate and even run for office. For example, the Women's Council of the Democratic Senatorial Campaign Committee gave $1.5 million to the ten Democratic women who ran for the Senate in 1992. Some groups, most notably the National Women's Political Caucus (NWPC), the Coalition for Women's Appointments, the Fund for a Feminist Majority, and Black Women Organized for Action, were founded with the electoral process as their primary target. Other women's organizations, including the League of Women Voters, the American Association of University Women, and NOW, also began to focus their energies on the enhanced political participation of women in electoral politics. And, in response to campaign law reform that occurred in the early 1970s, a variety of women's PACs, including the Women's Campaign Fund, EMILY's List, and WISH List, became important sources of financial support for women candidates.

The National Women's Political Caucus (NWPC)

Founded in 1971, the NWPC is a national, grass-roots organization dedicated to increasing the number of feminist women elected at all levels of government.[48] Its founders included leaders of many major women's organizations, among them Gloria Steinem, Bella Abzug, and Betty Friedan. Rep. Shirley Chisholm (D-N.Y.), another founder, was elected to Congress in 1968 and actually ran in the New York State Democratic presidential primary in 1972. (Although she lost, Chisholm received 151.5 votes on the first ballot at the 1972 Democratic Convention, becoming the first African American woman to run for president.) LaDonna Harris, a Comanche Indian, was also a founder of the NWPC. (The first congressional wife ever to testify before Congress,

Harris later ran for vice president of the United States on the Citizens Party ticket.)

NWPC goals include increasing support for women candidates and reforming party structures to assure equitable representation for women. The organization also publicizes women's issues when they are at stake in elections, monitors the selection of women delegates to party conventions, and holds regional training sessions for women candidates and campaign workers throughout the United States. NWPC is unique in its multipartisan base. To accommodate the needs of its members and to fulfill its commitment to increased representation in the political parties, however, it maintains special Democratic and Republican task forces.

Since its creation, NWPC has had a noticeable impact on Democratic Party rules, in particular. At the 1976 Democratic National Convention, it led the move for a written guarantee that women would constitute 50 percent of the delegates at the 1980 convention. To prevent an embarrassing floor fight, soon-to-be-nominated candidate Jimmy Carter met with women's rights leaders to reach a compromise. The resultant "deal" involved Carter's promise to appoint women to high-ranking positions in his administration should he be elected. Other parts of the compromise included provisions in the party rules that mandated that "future conventions shall promote equal division between delegate men and delegate women"[49] and required the Democratic National Committee (DNC) to encourage the state parties to adopt rules to effectuate this goal. In 1978, the DNC actually passed a resolution that required that 50 percent of the future convention delegates be women.

The NWPC has had only limited success in securing feminist reforms within the Republican Party. The different levels of progress in the two parties may be due, in part, to the more conservative nature of the Republican Party and the fact that NWPC is composed of a sizeable percentage of women who identify themselves as liberal Democrats.

Since 1976, the NWPC has been at the forefront of efforts to increase the number of women appointed to high-ranking, policy-making federal jobs. It convenes the Coalition for Women's Appointments, composed of representatives from more than seventy women's and public interest groups, to identify qualified female candidates, collect and forward their résumés to the White House, and then lobby for their appointment. The appointments coalition forwarded the names of many eventual nominees to the Carter, Bush, and Clinton administrations. The coalition and NWPC also work with the Federation of Women Judicial Lawyers Screening Panel and NOW to identify qualified women for the federal bench.

The Feminist Majority Foundation

The Fund for a Feminist Majority was created in 1987 by Peg Yorkin, a prominent feminist producer and philanthropist, and Eleanor Smeal, a former

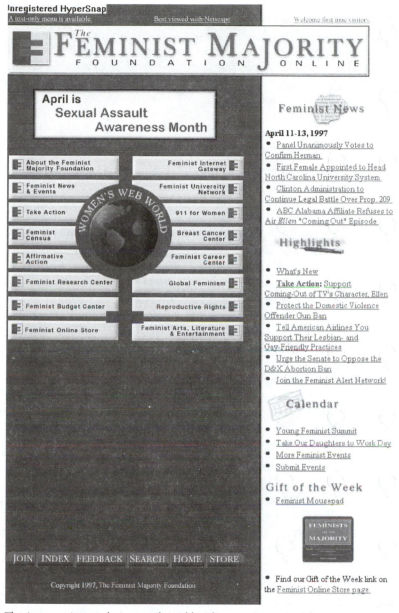

A text-only menu is available.   Best viewed with Netscape   Welcome first time visitors

The FEMINIST MAJORITY
FOUNDATION ONLINE

**April is
Sexual Assault
Awareness Month**

WOMEN'S WEB WORLD

- About the Feminist Majority Foundation
- Feminist News & Events
- Take Action
- Feminist Census
- Affirmative Aotion
- Feminist Research Center
- Feminist Budget Center
- Feminist Online Store

- Feminist Internet Gateway
- Feminist University Network
- 911 for Women
- Breast Cancer Center
- Feminist Career Center
- Global Feminism
- Reproductive Rights
- Feminist Arts, Literature & Entertainment

JOIN   INDEX   FEEDBACK   SEARCH   HOME   STORE

Copyright 1997, The Feminist Majority Foundation

Feminist News

April 11-13, 1997

- Panel Unanimously Votes to Confirm Herman
- First Female Appointed to Head North Carolina University System
- Clinton Administration to Continue Legal Battle Over Prop. 209
- ABC Alabama Affiliate Refuses to Air *Ellen* "Coming Out" Episode

Highlights

- What's New
- **Take Action:** Support Coming-Out of TV's Character, *Ellen*
- Protect the Domestic Violence Offender Gun Ban
- Tell American Airlines You Support Their Lesbian- and Gay-Friendly Practices
- Urge the Senate to Oppose the D&X Abortion Ban
- Join the Feminist Alert Network!

Calendar

- Young Feminist Summit
- Take Our Daughters to Work Day
- More Feminist Events
- Submit Events

Gift of the Week
- Feminist Mousepad

FEMINISTS
and the
MAJORITY

- Find our Gift of the Week link on the Feminist Online Store page

The Internet is now being exploited by diverse women's rights groups to build coalitions and spread the feminist message. "On line organizing is a very powerful tool," says Fund for a Feminist Majority's Ellie Smeal (a former president of NOW). "Women are outnumbered on the Internet and we want to change those numbers" (quoted in Julia Duin, "Liberal Feminists Network on Net," *Washington Times,* February 3, 1996, A4). As its homepage reveals, the Fund for a Feminist Majority provides links to a wide array of sources of interest to women. (Copyright 1997, The Feminist Majority Foundation. Reproduced with permission.)

president of NOW, who had guided that organization through much of the ERA ratification effort. One of the Feminist Majority's major activities is its nationwide campaign to recruit more women to run for political office. It also provides a much-needed source of feminist news and links to other feminist organizations in addition to providing Web page links to many less well financed women's organizations.[50]

League of Women Voters

The League of Women Voters was one of the original members of the Women's Joint Congressional Committee. It soon, however, abandoned its support of women's issues, preferring to call itself "a citizen's group rather than a women's organization."[51] It did not endorse the ERA until the early 1970s and only truly came to feminist activism in the 1990s. At that time, it took the lead in efforts to lobby for passage of the National Voter Registration Act (the Motor Voter Law). After women voters stayed home in droves in 1994, the League, in combination with its efforts to implement the Motor Voter Law, also launched what it termed a comprehensive Election 96 Campaign.[52] Its central focus was getting out the vote, with a goal of achieving 85 percent registration and turnout rates. It worked in conjunction with the *Ladies Home Journal* magazine throughout 1996 to highlight issues of women's political participation and its consequences.

The League specifically targeted racial and ethnic minorities and eighteen- to twenty-four-year-olds in its Get Out the Vote effort, partnering itself with MTV's Rock the Vote, which was begun by MTV before the 1992 elections to educate and motivate young voters.

The American Association of University Women

Although the American Association of University Women (AAUW) was formed in 1881 to help women find jobs and network in business, it recently became more extensively involved in politics in the wake of the 1994 elections that resulted in a conservative Republican-controlled Congress. It saw this Congress as "threaten[ing] to devastate every initiative that AAUW had worked for [for] decades."[53] Thus, it launched the AAUW Voter Education Campaign in July 1995. This campaign was divided into two parts. The first consisted of an organized nationwide fax campaign and e-mail network to inform women on how issues before Congress affected their lives: "Biweekly Get the Facts alerts were produced in partnership with 43 organizations in a nonpartisan, issue-based coalition, the Women's Network for Change."[54] The second part of its campaign was a get-out-the-vote effort designed to organize AAUW members to encourage *drop off voters*—those who voted in 1992 but stayed home in 1994—to go to the polls in 1996. Members used phone banks to call nearly one million women in fifty key congressional districts.

National Organization for Women

After the defeat of the ERA, NOW "began to focus less on trying to influence men in power and more on electing feminists to replace them."[55] In 1992, it joined the chorus of women's organizations seeking more women in elective office with its Elect Women for a Change campaign.

NOW also supports gender equity in political appointments and is a member of the Coalition for Women's Appointments. On the state level, NOW has also targeted the appointment of more women. "Gender balance" on boards and commissions continues to be a goal of state NOW chapters especially in states that require governors' appointments to be divided equally between the sexes.[56]

Women's PACs

As a result of changes in the national campaign finance laws, in 1974, it became possible for organizations to create political action committees (PACs) to raise money for candidates running for public office. In response, several women's organizations, including NOW, BPW, and NWPC, created PACs in the 1970s, although they generally supported both women and men candidates. The exception was the Women's Campaign Fund, which was organized in 1974 with the express purpose of contributing solely to the campaigns of women candidates.

During the 1980s, new PACs for women candidates or candidates supporting women's issues were established almost every year, but these groups were generally small and underfunded. By 1989, there were thirty-three PACs that gave money primarily to women candidates. According to the Center for the American Woman and Politics (CAWP), in 1988, seventeen of those PACs gave more than $1.1 million to 464 candidates. The big breakthrough year for PACs supporting women candidates came in 1992. Not only were twelve new PACs founded, raising the total number of PACs supporting only or mainly women candidates to more than forty, but the contributions to those PACs skyrocketed. Collectively, PACs contributed nearly $12 million to women candidates running for public office in the fall elections. This represented almost a quadrupling of these groups' donations from 1990. Women's groups' PAC contributions, in fact, rose 314 percent from 1990. Phyllis Schlafly's Eagle Forum had the greatest gain among conservative PACs, increasing by 198 percent to $148,000. On the liberal side, the now disbanded Hollywood Women's Political Committee posted the largest increase to $278,500.[57] In 1996, the top three women's PACs—EMILY's List, the Women's Campaign Fund, and the Concerned Women for America PAC—contributed more than $17 million.[58]

The Women's Campaign Fund. The Women's Campaign Fund (WCF) was the first national, nonpartisan PAC dedicated "to the election of pro-choice women to public office."[59] Since its creation, it has provided financial support to 1,500 pro-choice Democratic, Republican, and independent candidates for public office at all levels of government, from city and county seats to the U.S. Congress. In 1996, the WCF contributed $2.4 million to candidates it endorsed. In addition to providing campaign support, since 1994, the fund has run "Making It to the Top" seminars to provide women officeholders with nonpartisan training for career advancement. Along with the NWPC and many other pro-choice organizations, it tried to highlight and advance the pro-choice position at both political parties' national conventions.

NOW/PAC and NOW Equality PAC. In 1977, NOW created two PACs to put individual contributions together to fund the candidacies of feminists. NOW members may contribute to NOW/PAC, which supports candidates for national election. NOW Equality PAC fills up the political pipeline by supporting women candidates at the state and local levels. The Equality PAC is not regulated by federal law. NOW/PAC claims to be the only "women's rights PAC that bases its endorsements on a broad feminist agenda" including pay equity, welfare reform, and a vast range of economic issues.[60] Like the Women's Campaign Fund, NOW's two PACs allow it to endorse Republican, Democratic, and independent women at all levels of government, believing that "lower level offices serve as a pipeline to the highest levels of office."[61] NOW prides itself on endorsing strong feminists "in ways that defy conventional political wisdom."[62] NOW/PAC, for example, was an early supporter of Cynthia McKinney, who was deemed "too young, too liberal and, with her cornrow hairstyle, too black to win."[63] With NOW/PAC support, McKinney won in 1992, 1994, and even in 1996, when her district was dramatically redrawn in a way that excluded a large proportion of black voters. Said Carol Moseley-Braun (D-Ill.) of her own campaign, "Without [NOW] there would be no Carol, candidate for the Senate."[64] NOW/PAC raised over $200,000 in 1996.[65]

EMILY's List. The largest of the women's PACs is EMILY's List ("Early Money Is Like Yeast—It Makes the Dough Rise"), which was founded in 1985 to support viable, pro-choice Democratic women running in congressional and gubernatorial races. Its goal is to raise money early on in the election cycle so as to put more women in elective office. It tries to do this by putting them on its "list" and encouraging its members to support endorsed women. Each election cycle, members of EMILY's List agree to contribute no less than $100 to at least two of the recommended candidates on the list. (It costs $100 to become a member of EMILY's List.) Unlike other PACs, whose boards decide how members' contributions are to be spent, EMILY's List members write their checks to the candidates of their choice. They are then bundled together and sent directly to the candidate by EMILY's List. Since 1988,

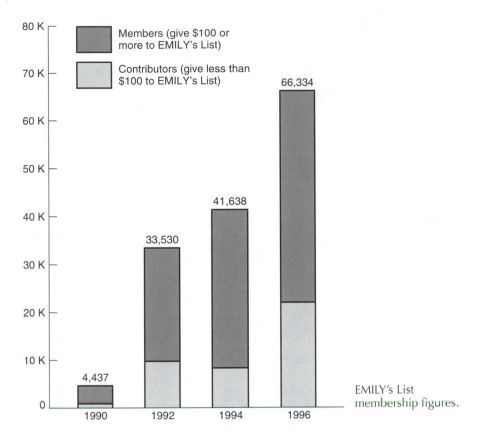

EMILY's List membership figures.

EMILY's List has been the largest financial resource for women candidates. It also supported House candidates for the first time that year.

Aware that money was not enough, EMILY's List's leaders recognized the tremendous opportunity presented by the reapportionment of the House of Representatives that was to take place in 1990. To prepare to seize that opportunity, in 1989 EMILY's List held a debriefing conference for the candidates it supported in 1988 and published "Campaigning in a Different Voice," a study of gender-related issues faced by female candidates for the House. Soon after, in 1990, it commissioned a national poll on the choice issue and how it affects female Democratic candidates. It also worked with the National Committee for an Effective Congress, using the committee's huge computer capacity to identify likely new congressional seats for 1992. Representatives from EMILY's List met with pro-choice Democratic women to brief them on ways to keep abreast of the potential district boundary changes and to suggest ways to keep their districts winnable. It also made an extensive search for viable candidates. Its efforts were key to women's successes in 1992. EMILY's List raised more than $6.2 million that year, which it donated to the campaigns of fifty-five women candidates, making it the largest PAC supporting congressional candidates—male or female.[66] Most of the women elected in the "Year of the Woman" were supported by EMILY's List.

EMILY's List also provides professional training for candidates and their staffs, conducts surveys and issue research, and helps with campaign message development.[67] In 1996, like many other women's organizations, EMILY's List tried to mobilize women voters to vote for pro-choice female candidates. Its WOMEN VOTE project raised more than $3 million to use to turn out additional pro-choice women voters. It also contributed an additional $12 million directly to candidates in 1996.[68]

The WISH List. The success of these liberal women's PACs led to the creation of WISH List (Women in the Senate and House) in late 1991. Like EMILY's List, viable candidates for the Senate, House, and governorships are recommended to members who send their checks directly to the group, where they are bundled. It supports Republican pro-choice women, including New Jersey Governor Christine Todd Whitman and Senator Kay Bailey Hutchinson (R-Tex.). In 1992, it raised more than $400,000 from its 1,500 members. In 1994, it contributed $370,000 to forty candidates, including the only newly elected pro-choice Republican woman elected that year.[69]

RENEW. The Republican Network to Elect Women (RENEW) is among the newest of women's political action committees. It was founded in 1993 to recruit, train, and help support Republican women candidates in local, state, and national elections.[70] It supports Republican women candidates without regard to their position on abortion.

CONCLUSION

Women have made tremendous strides since they first gathered in 1848 in Seneca Falls hesitant to demand the vote. It took two eras of women's movement activity to win the franchise and much longer to move toward parity in the political process.

Once the Nineteenth Amendment was ratified, women's groups were divided over what goals to pursue. Social feminists wanted to continue their work for protective legislation, a goal that was in direct odds with the NWP's major goal—the addition of an equal rights amendment to the Constitution. While the NWP worked hard for passage of the ERA, it was not until the rise of the current women's rights movement that it looked like an ERA might become a reality. But pro-amendment forces failed to learn from the lessons of history: Their failure to mobilize at the state level in the face of well-organized opposition stymied their efforts.

The period 1970–1982—years critical to the development of the current women's rights movement—was one of intense mobilization and growth, but most efforts were concentrated on the ratification of the ERA. Some groups such as the NWPC, however, remained focused on women's access to the political process. Women's organizations' continued efforts allowed women's PACs, especially EMILY's List, to take advantage of the unique circumstances present in the 1992 election cycle—open seats caused by reapportionment, congressional scandals, a revitalized women's rights movement motivated by a fear of losing access to abortion rights, and women's anger at the Senate Judiciary Committee's treatment of Anita Hill during the Clarence Thomas hearings. All of these unique factors combined to make 1992 the "Year of the Woman." The 1994 midterm elections were not kind to progressive women. Women's groups then stepped up their efforts, and again record numbers of women joined legislative bodies all over the United States, often encouraged and aided every step of the way by women and women's groups.

NOTES

1. Quoted in Eleanor Flexner, *Century of Struggle* (New York: Atheneum, 1974), 76.
2. Elizabeth Cady Stanton, Susan B. Anthony, and Matilda Joslyn Gage, eds., *History of Woman Suffrage*, vol. 1, 1848–1861 (Rochester, N.Y.: Charles Mann, 1881), 70–71.
3. The critical section of the amendment reads:
    Section 2 . . . or in any way abridged, except for participation in rebellion, or other crime, the basis of representation therein shall be reduced in the proportion which the number of such *male* citizens shall bear to the whole number of *male* citizens twenty-one years of age in such State (emphasis added).
4. Ellen Carol DuBois, *Feminism and Suffrage: The Emergence of an Independent Women's Movement in America, 1848–1869* (Ithaca, N.Y.: Cornell University Press, 1978).
5. This legislation would have been easier for proponents to secure. A constitutional amendment requires a two-thirds majority vote; enabling legislation requires but a simple majority.
6. Elizabeth Cady Stanton, Susan B. Anthony, and Matilda Joslyn Gage, eds., *History of Woman Suffrage*, vol. 2 (New York: Fowler & Wells, 1882), 810–11.
7. Reprinted in ibid., 441–42.
8. Much of this discussion comes from Karen O'Connor, *Women's Organizations' Use of the Courts* (Lexington, Mass.: Lexington Books, 1980), chap. 3.
9. 88 U.S. 162 (1875).
10. For the full text of the Declaration of Rights, see Mari Jo Buhle and Paul Buhle, *The Concise History of Woman Suffrage* (Urbana: University of Illinois Press, 1978), 297–303.
11. *Congressional Globe*, 39th Cong., 2d sess., 1867, pt. 1: 56.
12. Sara Hunter Graham, *Woman Suffrage and the New Democracy* (New Haven, Conn.: Yale University Press, 1996).
13. See Nancy F. Cott, *The Grounding of Modern Feminism* (New Haven, Conn.: Yale University Press, 1987), for an excellent account of the constituent groups and their diverse philosophies.
14. See generally, Karen J. Blair, *The Club Woman as Feminist* (New York: Holmes and Meier, 1980).
15. See Pat McKissack and Frederick McKissack, *Mary Church Terrell: Leader for Equality* (Springfield, N.J.: Enslow, 1991).
16. See Aileen Kraditor, *The Ideas of the Woman Suffrage Movement, 1890–1920* (New York: Columbia University Press, 1965; Anchor Books, 1971), 20.
17. Quoted in Judith Papachristou, *Women Together* (New York: Knopf, 1976), 142–43.
18. Ibid., 143.
19. Graham, *Woman Suffrage*, 21–25.

20. Quoted in Papacristou, *Women Together,* 100.
21. Graham, *Woman Suffrage.*
22. Flexner, *Century of Struggle,* 222.
23. Ibid.
24. For more about the NWP see Doris Stevens, *Jailed for Freedom: The Story of the Militant American Suffragist Movement* (New York: Schocken, 1976), and Christine A. Lunardini, *From Equal Suffrage to Equal Rights: Alice Paul and the National Woman's Party, 1910–1928* (New York: New York University Press, 1986).
25. William H. Chafe, *The Paradox of Change: American Women in the 20th Century* (New York: Oxford University Press, 1991), 18–21.
26. Flexner, *Century of Struggle,* 281.
27. See Mary Carroll, "Wanted—A New Feminism: An Interview with Emily Newell Blair," *Independent Woman,* December 9, 1930, 499, for a discussion of Shaw's concerns.
28. Chafe, *The Paradox of Change.*
29. William H. Chafe, *The American Woman: Her Changing Social, Economic, and Political Role, 1920–1970* (New York: Oxford University Press, 1972), 112. See also Susan Ware, *Beyond Suffrage: Women in the New Deal* (Cambridge: Harvard University Press, 1987), and Kristi Anderson, *After Suffrage: Women in Partisan and Electoral Politics Before the New Deal* (Chicago: University of Chicago Press, 1996).
30. Janet K. Boles, *The Politics of the Equal Rights Amendment: Conflict and the Decision Process* (New York: Longman, 1991).
31. Quoted in Papachristou, *Women Together,* 220.
32. "Chicago Women Form Liberation Group," pamphlet reproduced in ibid., 229.
33. For more about women at the local level see, Laura Woliver, *From Outrage to Action: The Politics of Grassroots Dissent* (Urbana: University of Illinois Press, 1993).
34. Anne N. Costain, *Inviting Women's Rebellion: A Political Process Interpretation of the Women's Movement* (Baltimore: Johns Hopkins University Press, 1992).
35. For an excellent discussion of the founding of NOW and the creation of the commission, see Toni Carabillo, *The Feminist Chronicles—Part 1a* (http://www.feminist.org./research/chronicles/part1a.html).
36. Groups supporting the proposed amendment during this period included the National Federation of Business and Professional Women's Clubs and the National Association of Women Lawyers. See Catherine East, "The First Stage: ERA in Washington, 1961–1972," *Women's Political Times,* September 1982, 7.
37. Quoted in Carol Felsenthal, *The Sweetheart of the Silent Majority* (Garden City, N.Y.: Doubleday, 1981), 235.
38. Much of this discussion comes from Janet Boles, "Building Support for the ERA: A Case of 'Too Much Too Late,'" *PS* 15, Fall 1982: 572–77. See also Jane Mansbridge, *Why We Lost the ERA* (Chicago: University of Chicago Press, 1986).
39. Boles, "Building Support," 574.
40. Quoted in "Organizations Supporting Equal Rights Amendment," *National NOW Times,* May 13, 1980, 14–15.
41. Felsenthal, *The Sweetheart.*
42. List derived from Felsenthal, *The Sweetheart.* See also, Pamela Johnston Conover and Virginia Gray, *Feminism and the New Right: Conflict Over the American Family* (New York: Praeger, 1983); Boles, *The Politics of the Equal Rights Amendment;* Suzanne Crowell, "Four Days in Houston—Watershed for Women's Rights," *Civil Rights Digest* 10, Winter 1978: 3–13; and Mansbridge, *Why We Lost the ERA.*
43. John Hebers, "Equal Rights Amendment Is Mired in Confused and Emotional Debate," *New York Times,* May 28, 1978, 1, 44. See also Rex E. Lee, *A Lawyer Looks at the ERA* (Provo, Utah: Brigham Young University Press, 1980).
44. *Phyllis Schlafly Report,* July 1975, 4.
45. See Mansbridge, *Why We Lost the ERA,* 295–96, for a discussion of the role that numerous insurance companies played in the defeat of the ERA, which would have brought with it unisex insurance rates. See also Mary Frances Berry, *Why ERA Failed: Politics, Women's Rights and the Amending Process of the Constitution* (Bloomington: Indiana University Press, 1988).
46. Susan Faludi, *Backlash: The Undeclared War Against Women* (New York: Crown, 1991).
47. Geraldine Ferraro, speech delivered at Women and the Constitution: A Bicentennial Perspective, Colony Square Hotel, Atlanta, Georgia, February 11, 1988.

48. National Women's Political Caucus at http://feminist.com/nwpc.htm
49. See http://feminist.com/nwpc.htm
50. See http://www.feminist.org/home.html
51. Leila J. Rupp and Verta Taylor, *Survival in the Doldrums: The American Women's Rights Movement, 1945 to the 1960s* (New York: Oxford University Press, 1987), 49.
52. http://lwv.org/~lwvus/eleccamp.html
53. Get the Facts at http://www.aauw.org/5000/votedini.html#j4
54. Ibid.
55. http://www.now.org/nnt/05-96/nowpac.html
56. Jane Gross, "At NOW Convention, Goal Is Putting More Women in Office," *New York Times*, July 1, 1990, A1.
57. Glenn R. Simpson, "Study: PAC Spending Jumps 18% in 1992," *Roll Call*, June 3, 1993. NEXIS.
58. See the Federal Election Commission report at http://www.fec.gov/finance/pacdisye.htm
59. Women's Campaign Fund mimeo (no date).
60. NOW PAC's Election Report. http://www.now.org/pac/facts.html
61. Ibid.
62. Ibid.
63. Ibid.
64. Ibid.
65. "PAC Fundraising at 18 Months," *Political Finance and Lobby Reporter*, September 25, 1996. NEXIS.
66. See the Federal Election Commission report at http://www.fec.gov/finance/pacdisye.htm
67. "EMILY's List: The Facts," http://www.irsociety.com/ertukel3.html
68. Ibid.
69. Jamae Jafari and Sheryl Henderson, "EMILY's List Spells Success," Gannet News Service, February 22, 1993. NEXIS.
70. For more on RENEW see http://members.aol.com/gorenew/ index.html

Women's Political Participation

To the dismay of suffrage leaders, the removal of legal barriers to political participation failed to result in equality between the sexes in the political arena. African American women, poor white women, and recently immigrated women often were denied the right to vote and participate in politics because of practices such as poll taxes and unfairly administered literacy tests. It appears, however, that one of the most significant factors that kept many women from exercising their political rights was the existence of negative cultural attitudes about women engaging in political activity. Historically, these attitudes have led to voter resistance toward women candidates and an unwillingness on the part of women to get involved in the political process. Cultural attitudes toward and restrictions on women's political activity have also resulted in other barriers to women's full political equality: the lack of preparation of women for political activity and outright sex discrimination by party leaders and government officials. While these barriers and the attitudes that underlie them have diminished over time, other system-specific problems continue to prevent women from achieving parity with men in the political arena.

CULTURAL ATTITUDES ABOUT THE POLITICAL PARTICIPATION OF WOMEN

Our knowledge of societal attitudes toward women's political participation both before and shortly after 1920 is scant. In the 1930s, the first nationwide opinion polls revealed that public attitudes toward the participation of women in politics were decidedly negative. At a time when only a handful of women held public office, 60 percent of all citizens polled rejected the idea that "we need more women in politics."[1] This aversion to the involvement of women in politics was particularly strong with respect to elective office. More than half of those surveyed were opposed to women serving as governors or senators. When asked in 1937 about their willingness to vote for a qualified woman for president, only 27 percent of all men and 40 percent of all women polled answered affirmatively.

Biases against political activity by women continued. In 1946, for example, an astounding 88 percent of all men and 87 percent of all women polled responded that the office of mayor "should nearly always be held by a man." In 1949, almost half of those polled reported that they would not vote for a woman for president even if she was qualified for the office and nominated by the party for which they regularly voted. These negative attitudes did not extend to all areas of political activity. Nearly half of all respondents to a 1946 survey favored a woman over a man as head of a Red Cross chapter or president of a Parent-Teacher Association. Community activity was and still is often considered to be an extension of a woman's primary roles of mother and homemaker. These kinds of activities were not even considered politics in the late nineteenth century because women did them; politics was understood to be party politics and was restricted to men.[2]

Polls conducted in the 1950s and 1960s found only small changes in attitudes toward women in politics. Most respondents continued to agree that women could or should take part in school affairs, but more than 40 percent of those interviewed in 1955, 1963, and 1969 responded that they would not vote for a woman for president.

Impact of the Current Women's Rights Movement on Political Rights and Political Participation

Public support for women's participation in politics increased considerably by the late 1960s. E. M. Schreiber attributes this change to the women's rights movement and the publicity it received. He reports that it was among the educated public—those most exposed to the women's movement by the media—that the greatest changes in attitudes occurred. For example, among women college graduates, support for a female president rose from 51 percent

Belva Ann Lockwood stamp.
(Reproduced with permission of
Hamilton Projects, Inc.)

in 1967 to 88 percent in 1975; the figures for college men were actually higher—58 and 91 percent.[3] A 1996 Gallup poll found that 92 percent of women and 88 percent of men indicated they would vote for a qualified woman for president if she was nominated by their party.[4]

Willingness to elect women to other political offices, such as mayor or governor, also increased. As early as 1975, more than 80 percent of the public reported that they would support a qualified woman for those positions.[5] Similarly, in sharp contrast to the public's attitudes toward women judges in the 1930s (when three-quarters of those polled objected to a woman Supreme Court justice), Sandra Day O'Connor's appointment to the Supreme Court in 1981 was approved by 87 percent of all women and 84 percent of all men.[6]

By the 1990s, in the wake of government scandals such as the savings and loan crisis, the House check-bouncing fiasco, and the U.S. Senate Judiciary Committee's treatment of Anita Hill, voters began to turn to women candidates at the same time more women sought elective office. According to Patricia Ireland, president of NOW, "certainly voters perceive women candidates as more honest . . . and as advocating issues that make our world a better place to live."[7] In fact, a poll taken in 1992 showed that 74 percent of American women believed that the country would be "better off," and 27 percent believed it would be "much better off" if women held half of the elected offices. Over half of the men polled did too![8]

Continuing Cultural Barriers

Even with changes in cultural beliefs, stereotypes continue to impede women's political participation. In 1991, 19 percent of the public polled agreed that "women should run their homes and children and leave running the country to men."[9] Moreover, in a 1996 poll, only 73 percent of men and 76 percent of women disagreed with the statement, "Most men are better suited emotionally for politics."[10] When asked to list reasons why there were not more women in public office, the respondents to a 1989 poll said one of the most important factors was "Many Americans aren't ready to elect a woman to higher office."[11]

Some people continue to question the effectiveness of women elected officials. For instance, as shown in Table 2–1, a 1989 survey revealed that when asked whether a woman in public office would do a better job, a worse job, or just as good a job as a man in a variety of public policy topics, the respondents indicated there were areas where they believed a woman would do a worse job.[12]

Women public officials, however, were expected to do a better job than their male counterparts in assisting the poor, improving the educational system, providing support for working parents, and dealing with health problems, children and family problems, homelessness, and the concerns of senior citizens. In general, women receive higher marks on "domestic" issues, whereas men are seen as better at dealing with international affairs. The

TABLE 2–1 Percentage of the Public Who Believe Women in Public Office Would Do a Better Job Than Men[a]

Area	Believing Women Would Do a Better Job Than Men		Believing Women Would Do a Worse Job Than Men	
	Women	*(Men)*	*Women*	*(Men)*
Foreign Affairs				
Directing the military	6	(3)	42	(58)
Conducting diplomatic relations with other countries	14	(10)	17	(23)
Making war decisions	18	(12)	24	(37)
Working for world peace	38	(32)	5	(8)
Honesty				
Maintaining honesty and integrity in government	38	(31)	5	(7)
Domestic Affairs				
Assisting the poor	49	(46)	4	(5)
Improving education	48	(46)	3	(4)
Dealing with family problems	65	(60)	3	(4)
Dealing with health problems	44	(38)	3	(4)
Providing support for working parents	61	(57)	3	(3)
Dealing with homelessness	44	(38)	4	(4)
Assisting senior citizens	45	(38)	4	(5)
Protecting the environment	30	(31)	7	(8)

[a]Survey question: "When it comes to ———, do you feel that women in public office would do a better job than men, a worse job than men, or just as good a job as men in public office?" Figures represent the percentage of women (men) who indicate women would do a better or worse job than men.

Source: Data from the 1990 Virginia Slims American Women's Opinion Poll conducted by the Roper Organization. Data provided by the Roper Center for Public Opinion Research, Storrs, Connecticut.

percentages reported in Table 2–1, however, reflect improvement in the public's perception of women's abilities in traditional "male" areas. In 1972, for example, 69 percent of women and 75 percent of men felt women would do a worse job than men in directing the military.[13] A similar study in 1992 by the polling firm Greenburg-Lake reported similar, if somewhat smaller, differences. They also found that the public had questions about women's ability to be tough and effective, although women were given higher marks than men for empathy and honesty.[14] One researcher found these stereotypes may help to explain why women do less well than men when they run for some offices.[15]

Given these views, it is easy to see how some women are disadvantaged when they run for office, especially for higher office. Women candidates start out with a certain percentage of the electorate predisposed *not* to vote for them depending on the office. Moreover, questions still linger about women's abilities to perform well in certain positions. Relatedly, societal views may encourage many women to reject a role in politics, deeming it an activity more appropriate for the other sex.

POLITICAL SOCIALIZATION

One byproduct of negative cultural attitudes toward political involvement by women is that girls traditionally have not been socialized to take an active role in politics. Studies of young children show that boys and girls differ in significant ways in their orientation to politics. Most research finds young girls to be less attentive to, less informed about, and less interested in politics than boys.[16] In a similar vein, the 1990 Virginia Slims American Women's Opinion Poll found that more than 70 percent of the respondents believed that one of the main reasons there are so few women in politics is that young girls are not inclined to aspire to careers in politics.[17]

Research conducted in the mid-1980s, however, suggests it is not young women but young men who are particularly likely to think that women are not as qualified as men to run the country. Although 89 percent of adolescent girls in one study agreed that women were qualified, only 44 percent of young men rated women's political abilities favorably.[18] Boys were also much more likely to say they would *not* vote for a woman for president.

Surveys of more than a thousand college students in 1989 reported similar disparities.[19] Some have speculated that young men may be rejecting claims of gender equality as a way of maintaining male, and hence their own, power.[20] Young women, however, appear to be more supportive of women running for political office. There is also some limited evidence that they are becoming more willing to envision a political role for themselves.[21] Although other research suggests that while very young girls are likely to expect to be politically active, by adolescence, perhaps in reaction to the attitudes of boys, young women expect to be less politically involved than males of the same age.[22] Thus, women apparently are socialized to be less well prepared psychologically for political activity than men, although this may be less true of the generation coming of age today. Gallup surveys now find while there is reluctance among the public to have a child go into politics as his or her life's work, people are as willing to have a daughter as a son take up this career.[23]

Socialization does not end at age 18. Some political scientists think that the birth of a woman's first child is a critical point at which gender stereotypes come into play.[24] Other scholars have found that over the course of their adult lifetimes, many women, at least those living through the 1970s, became more politically active and aware, in part as a correlate to their increasingly gender-egalitarian beliefs.[25]

POLITICAL RESOURCES

The socialization of women into the dominant cultural beliefs about the appropriateness of politics for them has echoes in the relative levels of psychological involvement or preparedness of women to participate in politics. Relatedly, stereotypes about women's roles as breadwinners mean women are less likely to have the money or professional involvement necessary for some forms of political activity. Research on political participation of average men and women has found that the absence of both types of political resources—money and professional involvement—is part of the explanation for women's lower involvement in our country's affairs.[26]

Citizen Duty

The belief that a citizen has an obligation to vote is perhaps the most elementary civic attitude. It constitutes the single best predictor of whether a person casts a ballot in an election. In 1923, interviews with women nonvoters in Chicago indicated that more than 10 percent believed it was wrong for women to vote.[27] In fact, one female nonvoter's response was: "Women should not 'stick their noses in politics.' . . . Only men and widows should vote. Women do not understand politics and so should not 'butt in men's work.' "[28] As voting became a more acceptable activity for women, there was a corresponding increase in women's feelings of civic obligation. By 1980, women recorded slightly higher levels of citizen duty than men.[29]

Psychological Involvement in Politics

For participation other than voting, political scientists have emphasized the critical importance of political interest and attention to public affairs in determining who participates. These orientations have been labeled by Sidney Verba and Norman Nie as "psychological involvement" in politics.[30] When women and men are compared on these dimensions, we begin to see the legacy of the societal views examined earlier.

In one early survey, for instance, nearly 33 percent of all women nonvoters interviewed in Chicago in 1923 reported "no interest in politics" as their reason for not voting, as compared to only 15 percent of nonvoting men.[31] Even in the 1960s, the interest of women at all educational levels in politics and national affairs was lower than that of similarly educated men.[32]

The dawning of the women's movement and changes that began in the 1970s have not completely eliminated this disparity between the sexes. In 1989, 61 percent of men but only 45 percent of women said they followed what was going on in politics or public affairs most or some of the time.[33] In at least one area of politics—presidential campaigns—women are almost as involved as men. Whereas studies in the 1940s and 1950s found that women were less interested than men in presidential campaigns, in the 1964 election no such difference was found. Additionally, there is some indication that even in those elections since 1952 when women as a group indicated less campaign interest than men, the interest gap was much smaller or even nonexistent among citizens with at least some college education.[34]

Women's lower psychological involvement in politics appears to be closely associated with levels of political information. Analysis of data from the 1994 National Election Study (NES) found that 80 percent of all men knew that the Democratic Party controlled the House of Representatives, but only 68 percent of all women did. Women were also less likely to know a series of basic facts about the political system including who Al Gore, Boris Yeltsin, William Rehnquist, and Thomas Foley were, as well as who nominates federal judges and who is the final judge of the Constitution. Relatedly, women scored lower than men on all seventeen political information items in a 1988 national survey.[35] Examination of only college-educated men and women or young men and women did not decrease the knowledge gap. If anything, the gap is greater among younger people. Comparisons with information gaps in decades past, moreover, show no signs that things are improving. The only area where women appear to be as informed as men is local politics—the policy arena where their participation has been seen as acceptable for many decades.[36] This disparity in political information is likely to continue. A national survey of first-year college students conducted in the fall of 1996 reported that young women are less likely than young men (27 versus 33 percent) to identify keeping up with political affairs as essential or very important.[37]

Interestingly, in one other area of psychological involvement in politics, party identification, women reported higher scores than men in the 1980s and into the 1990s. In 1996, 70 percent of all women, but only 62 percent of all men, identified with a political party.[38]

Political Efficacy

Political efficacy is an individual's belief that he or she can influence governmental decision making. Confidence in one's ability to affect governmental actions is closely related to a willingness to undertake political activity. Early interviews with women revealed their lack of self-confidence about political matters. Although nearly equal numbers of nonvoting men and women doubted the effectiveness of their vote, women were more likely to report "timidity" when it came to casting their ballots. One female nonvoter explained why she had never voted: "I ain't got the nerve."[39]

Since the 1950s, women have routinely reported lower levels of efficacy in several areas. One involves awareness of and confidence in the use of political participation other than voting. In every presidential election between 1956 and 1972, women were more likely than men to believe that "voting is the only way to influence government."[40] By 1980, there was no significant difference between male and female respondents across educational categories.

In one respect, however, the political efficacy of women continues to lag behind men. Perhaps tied to their lower levels of attention to and information about politics, women still report much lower confidence in their understanding of politics. Our analysis of the 1994 NES found, for example, that 72 percent of women but only 58 percent of men indicated that politics was too complicated for them to understand. This difference continues even among the more educated citizenry. In contrast, the more nearly equal levels of local political interest and local political information between men and women result in more similar overall confidence in understanding of local issues and politics by the two sexes. One study, for example, found the difference between college-educated men and women in understanding local politics was less than half that found with respect to understanding politics "in general." Furthermore, participation by women in community action groups tends to break down this vicious cycle even for working-class women. Women reported higher confidence levels as a result of their interest in and subsequent action with respect to local problems.[41]

Perhaps as a result of their lower levels of psychological involvement in national politics, women in the 1994 NES were less likely than men to agree with the statement that they are qualified to participate in politics (48 percent of men and 29 percent of women think they are qualified). Correspondingly, 55 percent of women, but only 41 percent of men did not think they could do as well as others in a government position.

Other Resources

Although such attitudes go a long way toward explaining women's lower involvement in politics, recent research also finds that women may not be as active as men in some forms of political activity because they earn less than men or contribute a smaller share than their husbands to the family income. Relatedly, women's jobs are generally not as likely as men's to prepare them for political life. Women seem only to be advantaged by their involvement in nonpolitical organizations such as church groups, which boosts women's political activity more than men's.[42]

SEX DISCRIMINATION: THE HIDDEN BARRIER

Historically, sex discrimination has been a powerful deterrent to political activity. Unfortunately, discrimination is difficult to study or document. Few men are willing to admit that they discriminate. Additionally, what many women see as discrimination against them may be viewed otherwise by men who feel they are simply complying with traditional cultural mores or widely accepted patterns of political behavior.

Two factors seem to motivate most sex discrimination: (1) cultural stereotypes about the abilities and appropriate position of women in politics and (2) self-interest on the part of male voters and politicians who are reluctant to share their power with women or any other "out group." It is difficult, however, to determine where cultural attitudes end and self-interest begins. Politicians in the 1920s and 1930s, for example, could be openly hostile to the active participation of women in politics. For instance, a 1924 gubernatorial candidate proclaimed, "women's place in politics is about four feet from the kitchen sink."[43] Although today few would be so blunt, some have questioned the emotional stability of women to hold public office. In 1990, for example, when Ann Richards successfully ran for the governorship of Texas, her opponent, Clayton Williams, made much of her gender and her support from women's groups. Nevertheless, she was able to capitalize on her opponent's insensitivity to women, especially rape victims. At one campaign stop, upon encountering bad weather, Williams told those assembled, "Weather's like rape—as long as it's inevitable, sit back and enjoy it."[44]

Women of color often face discrimination from men of color who believe that after years of race discrimination, women should let men go first. Shirley Chisholm, who faced opposition from male political leaders in her first race for Congress, noted that "Black males feel that the political seats are owed to them because of historical circumstances; therefore, opportunities should redound to them first of all."[45]

POLITICAL INVOLVEMENT

Given the legacy of public attitudes about the appropriateness of political activity for women and the evidence of women's lower psychological involvement, we would expect women to be less involved as citizens than men. It is possible, however, that women overcome these factors and are equal to men in their participation in politics. An examination of various types of activities supports both of these predictions.

Voting

The first major study of women's electoral turnout in the 1923 Chicago mayoral election found nearly two-thirds of all men but only one-third of all eligible women voted. Other research on this era finds similar, if somewhat smaller, disparities.[46]

Many women chose not to vote in the early decades after ratification of the Nineteenth Amendment. Reluctance to vote was especially pronounced among classes of women—immigrant and uneducated women—where there were strong cultural stereotypes concerning appropriate male and female roles. In the South, where attitudes toward women's roles were more conservative, and where the poll tax and racial discrimination eliminated the possibility of voting for poor white women and African American men and women, only a few women went to the polls. In contrast, in the West, where support for women's suffrage had a long heritage, women were apparently voting in the early 1920s at rates nearly equal to those of men.[47]

Suffrage movement leaders saw women's lack of information and training as the main barriers to the full and equal participation of women in politics. To correct this problem, they established the National League of Women Voters (LWV) to help educate women about politics and political activity. Just how many women benefited from the League's efforts is difficult to measure, although only a small minority of the original suffrage movement members joined the new organization. Moreover, the League's policy of remaining aloof from partisan politics may have diminished the chances that those who became involved would become active in partisan politics, although many women elected officials claimed membership in it.[48] Although the League may have played a role in mobilizing middle-class women, Kristi Andersen's research indicates political parties probably were more important for women generally. Examination of the data on registration rates of women and men in the 1920s (where available) finds that in those areas where it was advantageous to political parties to register women, registration rates for women were higher.[49]

The Great Depression of the 1930s also played a key role in the mobilization of women, especially those with fewer resources, both political and economic. This crisis politicized large numbers of immigrants, lower-class women, and young people who had previously remained outside the political arena.[50] Work by Courtney Brown on the 1920 presidential election indicates that while women voters in that election overwhelmingly favored the Republican Party, voters who were drawn to the polls for the first time in their adult life by the economic crisis surrounding the 1932 election adopted strong ties to the Democratic Party—ties that served to bind them strongly to that party and to the electoral process.[51]

As revealed in Table 2–2, from 1964 to 1978, women continued to vote at rates slightly lower than men. Since the 1980 presidential election, however, women have usually voted at rates higher than men.

The gender gap in voter turnout is particularly large for some groups of men and women of color. In 1992, for instance, 56.7 percent of African American women voted in the presidential election. Only 50.8 percent of African American men voted. Similarly, among Hispanic voters, 30.9 percent of women but only 26.8 percent of men voted. In 1996, however, African American males reported a 53 percent increase in turnout from 1992, while African American and white women's turnout decreased. In general, African American women still outvote African American men at the polls.[52]

Sandra Baxter and Marjorie Lansing trace the higher participation rates of African American women to their greater feminist beliefs, products of being doubly oppressed by both sex and race discrimination.[53] It is also possible

TABLE 2–2 Sex Differences in Voter Turnout Rates, 1964–1994 (percentage of eligible adults who voted)

Year	Women	Men	Difference (% Women – % Men)
1994	44.9	44.4	+.5
1992[a]	62.3	60.2	+2.1
1990	45.4	44.6	+0.8
1988[a]	58.3	56.4	+1.9
1986	46.1	45.8	+0.3
1984[a]	60.8	59.0	+1.8
1982	48.4	48.7	-0.3
1980[a]	59.4	59.1	+0.3
1978	45.3	46.6	-1.3
1976[a]	58.8	59.6	-0.8
1974	43.4	46.2	-2.8
1972[a]	62.0	64.1	-2.1
1970	52.7	56.8	-4.1
1968[a]	66.0	69.8	-3.8
1966	53.0	58.2	-5.2
1964[a]	67.0	71.9	-4.9

[a]Presidential election years.

Source: "Sex Differences in Voter Turnout," *CAWP Fact Sheet,* December 1996. Data from the U.S. Bureau of the Census.

that the higher levels of voting by African American and Hispanic women is traceable to their greater ties to the community, especially to the church. Susan A. MacManus, Charles S. Bullock III, and Barbara P. Grothe speculated that the Mexican American women in their study might also participate more than the men in their community as a function of the role of women as agents of change and upward mobility for their families.[54]

In 1994, there was considerable speculation that women's failure to vote contributed to the Republican victory. Still, the 1994 gender gap in turnout at the polls caused EMILY's List and the League of Women Voters to try to mobilize more women to go to the polls. Analysis finds it was mostly poor and minority women (generally Democrats) who failed to vote in 1994.[55]

Although the barriers to women's voting have diminished significantly since 1920, the one factor that may still negatively affect the voting participation of some women is the presence of small children, who make it difficult for some women to get to the polls. This seems to be particularly true for single mothers.[56]

When the disparity in voter turnout is combined with the greater number of women in the electorate (52 percent of all voters were women in 1996), we can see what a powerful voting bloc women could form if they wanted to do so.[57] But do women cast their ballots differently from men? The leaders of the suffrage movement (and even suffrage opponents) clearly expected women would be distinct in their attitudes and political behavior. Until recently, however, these differences were not evident. A prerequisite to establishing the voting bloc envisioned by the suffrage leaders would be for women and men to take different stands on questions of public policy.

Issue Positions. Survey data reveal few significant gender differences across views about most issues, with a few notable exceptions. Since the 1930s, women have led men in their opposition to war and the use of force more generally. Tom Smith's extensive research on the use of military force from the 1930s through the 1980s found gender differences on 87 percent of the questions, with an average 9 percent gap.[58] In 1952, for example, 45 percent of the women compared to only 37 percent of the men interviewed believed the United States should have stayed out of the Korean War. Similar differences of opinion surfaced during the Vietnam War. Most recently, during Operation Desert Storm, women were on the average 14.3 percent more likely than men to think the United States had made a mistake in sending troops to the area. At one point, only 37 percent of women but 61 percent of men supported that war.[59]

According to one 1990 study, gender differences were still apparent on international issues.[60] More generally, the Center for the American Woman and Politics (CAWP) found, when compared to men, women are

- less militaristic on issues of war and peace
- more often opposed to the use of force in nonmilitary situations
- more likely to favor measures to protect the environment and to check the growth of nuclear power
- more often supportive of programs to help the economically disadvantaged
- more often supportive of efforts to achieve racial equality
- more likely to favor laws to regulate and control various social vices (e.g., drugs, gambling, pornography)
- less likely to be optimistic about the country's future[61]

Although some research suggests these gender differences in attitudes may be limited to only feminists or conditioned by the careers women and men choose,[62] a national survey of first-year college students in 1996 found large differences of opinion between men and women on prohibition of homosexuality, control of handguns, national health care, affirmative action, racial discrimination, and treatment of immigrants. On all but health care issues, the gap was over 10 percent, with women always more likely to choose the more liberal position.[63]

Party Identification. Party identity—whether or not an individual views himself or herself as a Republican, Democrat, or something else—generally is believed to be an exceptionally important determinant of the vote. Prior to 1968, however, men and women showed little difference in their tendency to affiliate with either party, when age and region of the respondents were controlled. In that year, however, significant differences began to occur in male-female patterns of party identification, with women significantly more likely than men to identify with the Democratic Party. Table 2–3 gives the difference since 1980.

Since 1982, the difference between men and women does not disappear when age, race, and education controls are introduced. Indeed, some of the greatest disparities are found among the youngest voters and the well-educated. In 1996, for instance, 38 percent of all women age eighteen to twenty-four were Democrats, as opposed to only 23 percent of men of this age.[64] Women tend to view the Democratic Party as more concerned about women's issues and closer to them on a wide range of domestic policy questions. This gap in party identification has parallels in the voting choices of women and men.

Voting Patterns

In recent years, gender-based differences in issue positions and party identification have tended to manifest themselves in what some term the *gender*

TABLE 2–3 Gender Differences in Party Identification

Year	Democrats		Republicans	
	Women (%)	*Men (%)*	*Women (%)*	*Men (%)*
1996	44	33	26	29
1995	31	25	29	36
1994	38	34	25	29
1993	38	30	28	30
1992	36	29	32	34
1991	38	26	28	31
1990	38	28	30	32
1989	36	32	31	31
1988	41	32	29	31
1987	44	35	30	31
1986	40	35	29	28
1985	38	30	31	28
1984	40	37	28	31
1983	43	32	21	25
1982	49	38	22	25
1980	44	37	23	22

Source: For 1983–1994, "The Gender Gap," *CAWP Fact Sheet,* July 1996. Data from CBS/New York Times polls, for 1980 and 1982, Henry C. Kenski, "The Gender Factor in a Changing Electorate," *The Politics of the Gender Gap,* ed. Carol M. Mueller (Beverly Hills, Calif.: Sage, 1988, 44).

gap—the difference in male-female support for political candidates. In 1980, for example, Ronald Reagan scored a nearly twenty-point advantage among men, while women split their vote more evenly between Reagan and Carter, producing a seven-point gender gap. In 1984, Reagan got 62 percent of the men's vote but only 58 percent of the women's. Likewise, in 1988, George Bush received 51 percent of the women's vote while securing 58 percent of the men's support.[65] The 1992 presidential race found women four percentage points more likely than men to vote for the Democratic candidate Clinton and five percentage points less likely to vote for the Independent Ross Perot.[66]

The 1996 election evidenced the greatest differences in men's and women's voting preferences to date. While men split their vote fairly evenly between Clinton (43 percent) and Dole (44 percent), a majority of women (54 percent) voted for the Clinton-Gore ticket. Only a third of all women voted for Dole-Kemp (38 percent). The eleven-point gender gap between men and women voting for Clinton persisted among most subgroups and even increased among young voters (under age thirty), where 17 percent more women than men voted for the president.[67] Dubbed the Year of the Soccer Mom because of Clinton's large lead among women in the polls, the gender gap was no accident. The Clinton campaign team deliberately focused on issues that women favored (v-chips, gun control, and family and medical leave) to strengthen the Democrats' natural advantage among women.[68] Dole seemingly cooperated with this strategy, arguing in vain that his tax cut would benefit women.

Polls suggest women were generally distrustful of the Republican Party's platform, especially its perceived threat to social programs. Even the showcasing of women like Susan Molinari (R-N.Y.), the keynote speaker at the Republican National Convention, apparently did not convince a majority of women that voting for the Republican Party's candidate was in their best interest.[69] As Debbie Walsh from the Center for the American Woman and Politics noted, "Women felt Bob Dole didn't understand the lives they were leading. . . . He didn't understand what it meant to juggle work and family in two-income families or women supporting families on their own."[70] Interestingly, in the final vote totals it was not the soccer moms that gave Clinton the big boost, but "waitress moms," women without husbands and in low-wage jobs. They split 55 to 28 percent for Clinton while suburban mothers (soccer moms) divided 49 to 42 percent for Clinton.[71]

Women Voters and the 1996 Elections

The 1992 elections were heralded as the Year of the Woman because an unprecedented number of women sought, and won, election at all levels of government. The 1994 elections were dubbed the revenge of angry white males, who voted overwhelmingly Republican and directly contributed to the GOP's takeover of the U.S. House and Senate.

In 1996, yet another force was recognized by pollsters: Voters whom many pundits termed soccer moms came to the fore. In early 1996, a *Washington Post* poll noted that women were more likely than men to be nervous about the economy and distrustful of the government. Fully three-quarters of the women polled believed that the economy was getting worse.[a] As a group, women, moreover, were concerned about the growing gap between the rich and the middle class. They also believed that government was making it worse by lowering taxes on the rich and doing too little for the needy.[b]

Many of those women, who ultimately voted Democratic in the 1996 elections, were called soccer moms. Why? They were the middle-class mothers who spent their afternoons shuttling their children from one after-school activity to another. Pollsters more narrowly defined these voters as married, in their mid-40s, college-educated, suburban white women with school-age children. They were said to be financially stressed and trying hard to balance the demands of career and motherhood. Although only about 5 percent of the voting public fits this description, these voters were considered swing voters by Republicans and Democrats. Both sides, therefore, fought hard to win these voters. Most of them, however, voted for Bill Clinton. The term went on to cause a considerable amount of controversy as being "somewhat dismissive and wimpy."[c]

Reproduced by permission of DePixion Studios.

[a]Steven Pearlstein, "Angry Female Voters a Growing Force," *Washington Post*, January 30, 1996, Al.

[b]Ibid.

[c]Clarence Page, "How About Paying Some Attention to Us Soccer Dads?" *Dallas Morning News*, December 8, 1996, 7J.

The gender gap in 1996 was not restricted to the presidential election. In House races, women gave the Democrats an eight percentage point advantage over men. In Senate races, women broke for the Democratic candidate by four or more percentage points in twenty-nine of the thirty-four races.[72]

Since 1980, in state and congressional races, women generally have differed from men in their preferences for candidates, supporting Democratic candidates but occasionally switching to the Republican candidate if the Republican is a woman supportive of women's issues.[73] In the 1990 governor's race in Texas, Ann Richards won because of the votes of women (59 percent of women but only 41 percent of men supported her). Overall, in 1994, in 81 percent of the races with exit polls, women voted differently from men and supported the Democrats in forty-nine of the fifty-one races with gender gaps.[74]

The 1992 election was particularly notable for the support women gave to women running for the U.S. Senate. In Dianne Feinstein's 1992 Senate race, she split the male vote evenly with her opponent, but racked up an impressive 64 percent of the women's vote, which provided her with the margin of victory. The other woman running for a Senate seat in California (there were two Senate races in California in 1992), Barbara Boxer, received 57 percent of the female vote and 43 percent of the men's. Feinstein, again, was the beneficiary of an eleven-point gender gap in her 1994 Senate race—52 percent of women but only 41 percent of men voted for her.[75]

Women's support of women candidates, especially Democratic women candidates in other races, has been documented by Jody Newman. She analyzed forty-one contests for senator and governor between a man and a woman in 1990, 1992, and 1994. She found that, on average, in races with a woman Democratic candidate, there was an eight-point gender gap. If the woman was a Republican, the gap narrowed to less than two points. In races with two men, the gender gap in the Democrats' favor averaged five points.[76]

As was clear in the presidential race of 1996, the power of the women's vote is beginning to influence the behavior of politicians. As NOW President Patricia Ireland notes, "Because of the gender gap, women's votes put us in the driver's seat."[77]

POLITICAL ACTIVITY

Political activity is another area where gender differences exist. Here, we divide our discussion into three sections: (1) lobbying and community involvement, (2) campaign and party work, and (3) office holding.

Lobbying and Community Involvement

Since the latter half of the nineteenth century, women have played a vital role in their communities, organizing charitable and civic projects and dominating the activities of groups like the PTA and local library boards. Women have also taken the lead in pressing local officials to include family, children's, and women's issues on the agendas of local legislative bodies. This practice of lobbying, petitioning, and protesting for social needs originated with women's groups because they were unable to pressure politicians with their votes. Kristi Andersen argues that as a result of women's domination of this activity at the turn of the century, it was not even seen as politics. Politics was connected with activities on behalf of political parties and elections and was the exclusive sphere of men.[78]

Recent research by scholars reveals the continued pervasive lobbying activity of women at the local level. Janet Boles and others have documented how women in feminist groups have altered the policies of local libraries to include more material of interest to women, worked to expand child-care services, broadened support for abused women and their children, and provided centers for victims of rape.[79] Similarly, conservative women's groups often lobby for the removal of certain books from libraries or for a return to traditional school curricula. Many of these issues have traditionally been seen as "outside" of politics, but women activists and elected officials are transforming the policy agenda to make personal matters political in nearly every community in the United States.

Some of the most underrecognized work has been done by African American women and other women from ethnic and racial minorities. African American women, for instance, played a vital role in antilynching campaigns and, more recently, the civil rights movement, organizing the bus boycott in Montgomery, managing the poor people's cooperatives in Mississippi, running freedom schools, and directing voter registration drives.[80] More recently, Nydia M. Veláquez, for example, organized a Hispanic voter registration drive in New York City. Unlike countless other women who have worked to expand opportunities for women in their communities, Veláquez's work resulted in her eventual election to the House of Representatives, where she became the first Puerto Rican woman to hold that office.[81]

Although women's contributions at the local level have been notable, a national survey of citizens in 1989 found men were slightly more likely than women to report that they had worked informally to deal with a community problem and to have contacted a public official with a problem. For women and men who engaged in some form of political activity other than voting, there was only a slightly greater tendency for women over men to restrict such activity to local affairs. Only with respect to religious institutions were women more active than men.[82] Interestingly, when women become active, they often focus on different issues than men. Compared with men, women generally are more concerned with education, and African American and Hispanic women more with basic human needs like drug and crime prevention.[83]

Campaign and Party Work

There are several reasons to expect that women will not participate as extensively as men in partisan activities. First, such involvement has often run counter to cultural expectations about a woman's role in public life. Whereas community involvement has been seen as a natural extension of women's homekeeping role, partisan politics was viewed as exclusively male. Party politics and campaigning in the nineteenth and early twentieth centuries in many ways took on the appearance of a "males only" sporting event with two groups of players: the candidates and their respective groups of partisan "fans." There were marching groups, parades, and smoke-filled rooms. Polling places often were located in pool halls and bars. While Progressive movement reforms, including the secret ballot, weakened political party machines, the Nineteenth Amendment and the addition of women to the electorate also altered the game of politics.[84] Even today, however, many citizens still see politics as "dirty" or corrupt and reject the idea of an active political role for women in party affairs and campaigns.

Second, while levels of interest in local affairs, especially among better-educated women, prepare them for community activities, the generally lower levels of political interest, involvement, information, and efficacy of women concerning politics or national affairs might be a serious obstacle to their participation in extralocal political campaigns and party work. Last, the relative absence of women in certain "power" positions, including those of union leaders and corporate executives, may result in women not being asked to become involved in campaigns.

In the years immediately following passage of the Nineteenth Amendment, women received a mixed message concerning party work. While some women leaders, including Carrie Chapman Catt, urged women to take an active role in the parties, the League of Women Voters itself adopted a nonpartisan posture.[85] Although a few followed Catt's advice, most women tended to avoid all partisan work including campaign activity. The decline of political machines eventually forced party leaders to rely on volunteers, including women, to run campaigns. Even so, the first national survey of citizen-level campaign activity in 1952 found that women were considerably less involved in campaigns than men.[86]

Since 1952, there has been a gradual decline in the overall disparity in campaign activity between the sexes. In 1980, only slightly fewer women than men reported engaging in at least one of the following campaign acts: contributing money, attending a political meeting, influencing another's vote, or displaying a button or poster. In 1992, our analysis of the National Election Survey data found that women continued to lag slightly behind men on these measures. For instance, in the most common form of campaign activity, trying to influence another person's vote, more men than women (44 versus 33 percent) reported engaging in this activity. Women also were less likely to wear a campaign button, attend a political rally, or contribute money to a candidate or political party. In 1994, when there was no presidential race, gender differences showed up only in the category of influencing another's vote. Studies suggest the small differences that do exist can be traced largely to women's lower level of political and economic resources. For instance, because women earn less than men, they generally are less frequent campaign contributors. The more developed civic skills of men also help to explain their slightly higher campaign participation.[87]

In spite of these continued differences, there is considerable evidence that women are essential to the maintenance of both parties. Informal reports and research on party activists indicate it is women who do the daily work of keeping the parties functioning.[88] One recent study, moreover, found few gender differences in the amount of time devoted to local party politics.[89] Indeed, because of the aggressive affirmative action efforts of the Democratic Party, about 50 to 60 percent of its state party officials are African Americans or women.[90]

At the national level, since 1972, both parties have included more women in their presidential nominating conventions than ever before. From 1980 to 1996, half of the delegates to the Democratic conventions, and more than one-third of those at the Republican conventions, have been women.[91]

There is some evidence that the women who take the most active roles in national campaigns, as participants in the party caucuses, are ideologically distinct from the men activists in their parties, with women more liberal on social and foreign policy questions and more supportive of women's issues in both parties.[92] A study of local party activists also found women in both parties to be more liberal on these issues.[93]

Office Holding

Women have long been severely underrepresented in elective office. During any single year between 1917 and 1970, women never constituted more than 5 percent (and generally far less) of the members of the U.S. Congress or of the state legislatures. In 1971, slightly more than 2 percent of the members of Congress and less than 5 percent of state legislators were women. By 1991, these numbers had climbed marginally, as women made up less than 6 percent of the Congress and 18.3 percent of the state houses.[94] (See Figures 2–1 and 2–2.)

Heralded as the Year of the Woman, 1992 was a breakthrough year for women candidates as they vied for all levels of political office in unprecedented numbers. In all, 108 women won their parties' nomination for seats in the House and eleven for positions in the U.S. Senate. Moreover, 2,375 women ran for state legislative posts, up from 2,063 in 1988. Even more importantly, more women than ever before were elected to the House and Senate. The elections of 1994 and 1996 saw much smaller gains, but the 105th Congress had a record number of women (fifty-one in the House and nine in the Senate), and women now hold 11.2 percent of the total seats in Congress.[95]

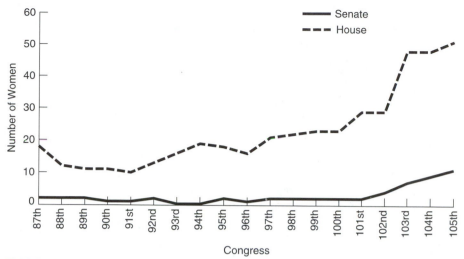

FIGURE 2–1 Number of women in the U.S. Congress, 87th to 105th Congresses.

Source: "Women in Elective Office 1997," *CAWP Fact Sheet,* March 1997.

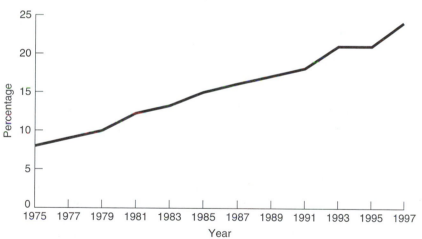

FIGURE 2–2 Percentage of women in U.S. state houses, 1975–1997.

Source: "Percentages of Women in Elective Offices," *CAWP Fact Sheet,* March 1997.

The gains in 1992 were particularly dramatic for women of color. The first African American woman ever to take a seat in the Senate, Carol Moseley-Braun, was elected from the state of Illinois. In the House of Representatives, five new African American women were elected, raising the total to nine. This number remained unchanged in 1997.[96]

At the state level, gains have come more gradually. By 1997, 21.5 percent of all legislators were women. More than 14 percent of all women state legislators were African American, 2.5 percent were of Hispanic heritage, 0.7 percent were Asian/Pacific American, and nine Native American women were state legislators.[97] In statewide elected offices, women now hold 25.3 percent of the executive positions.

At the local level in 1995, women were mayors in seventeen of the largest one hundred cities, 18.2 percent of the mayors in cities with populations over 30,000, and 22 percent of the city council members in cities with populations of 10,000 or more.[98] The ability of women to get elected to office below the national level is a good indicator of their future ability to achieve higher political office, as state and local offices often are a "jumping-off" point for political positions at the national level. From this perspective the local figures are both encouraging and a sign of how far women have yet to go before they achieve parity with men.

BARRIERS TO WOMEN IN ELECTED AND APPOINTED POSITIONS

Historically, the barriers that have kept women out of political office seem to fall into five general categories: (1) stereotypes, (2) career choice and preparation, (3) family demands, (4) sex discrimination, and (5) the political system itself. Although most of these barriers have been eliminated or weakened in the other areas of political activity, they continue to be much more powerful vis-à-vis political office. Moreover, other system-specific problems limit the likelihood that every election year will afford record gains like those made by women in 1992.

These barriers act in two ways to keep the numbers of women in public office low: First, they deter many women from running for office, and second, they keep those who run from succeeding. Studies of women who actually seek elective office indicate that this first set of hurdles, such as the initial decision to seek public office, can be the most formidable.[99] When women actually do run against nonincumbent men, the rate of electoral success of men and women is nearly equal. Since 1970, researchers have found very little or no difference in the percentage of the vote received by men and women candidates for Congress when party and incumbency of opponent and candidate were controlled.[100] Similar results were obtained in a comparison of men and women running for other political offices.[101] Thus, it is the failure of women to toss their hats in the ring that contributes most to the absence of women in the political arena.

Stereotypes

When public opposition to women running for political office was at its peak, the most likely explanation for women not running for office was that most women and men thought such activity was inappropriate. Evidence of the continued influence of these stereotypes can also be seen in places where women are still underrepresented in state legislatures, notably the South—a region where traditional views about women continue to hold sway. Seven of the ten state legislatures with the lowest percentages of women in 1997 were from this region.[102]

The legacy of cultural stereotypes is also apparent in the ambition levels of women participants in party politics. Research focusing on party activists in California from 1964 to 1986 finds women less likely at every time interval to be as interested as men in seeking elective and appointive office.[103] But paralleling the decline in the stereotypes, women are fast closing the disparity with men in ambition. This is particularly true of younger women and those who work outside the home who are active in feminist and community organizations—the very women most likely to have enlightened views on the appropriateness of office holding by women.[104] Not surprisingly, given their high levels of feminism, African American women are as politically ambitious as white women.[105] Younger African American women, like their white counterparts, also have the advantage of having more elected women role models and mentors than women of earlier generations. U.S. Representative Corrine Brown (D-Fla.), for instance, attributes her decision to get into politics to the encouragement of Gwendolyn Sawyer Cherry, Florida's first black state representative and a sorority sister at Florida A&M University.[106]

For women who actually decide to run for office, stereotypes about their abilities continue to present problems. Kim Fridken Kahn finds evidence of this in the press coverage of women and men candidates in Senate and gubernatorial races. She reports that women senatorial candidates are routinely portrayed as less viable than male candidates. Women also receive less issue coverage. No such bias was evident in the articles about women candidates for governor.[107] Using an experimental design, Kahn finds this difference contributes to voters rating men candidates as more competent to deal with military issues, and women candidates as less viable, more honest, and better able to deal with health issues. Kahn argues that this combination of stereotyping articles and reader reaction might help to explain women's lower success rates in races for the Senate, a legislative body that traditionally has focused more on defense than health issues. She reasons that because the press does not diminish the viability of women gubernatorial candidates, the same stereotypes about women's issue expertise help to explain their greater success in gubernatorial races, where key issues are those for which women are seen as better prepared.[108]

Women candidates who run for office also have to be mindful of public perceptions when they produce their campaign commercials. An analysis of the ads of men and women senatorial candidates in 1992 found that women dressed more formally and used male announcers, perhaps in a subtle effort to overcome stereotypes about competence and strength. Correspondingly, they stressed their compassionate side and their empathy for voters' needs more than men.[109] The emphasis on domestic issues as the Cold War ended also helped women candidates.

Career Choice and Preparation

The socialization of women to pursue occupations that are either incompatible with political careers or are perceived as such by officials who supervise candidate selection processes (or by voters) also constitutes a barrier to and limit on the potential number of female office seekers. Many traditionally female occupations such as teaching or nursing are less compatible with politics than are more male-dominated professions. Historically, women were barred from, or had difficulty entering, the legal profession, a common springboard to public office. R. Darcy, Susan Welch, and Janet Clark present convincing evidence that the relative paucity of women from the "eligible pool" of potential political candidates until recently is an important reason, although not the only one, for their relative absence from state legislatures, especially in the "upper" or more prestigious houses.[110] Christine B. Williams's research on the relationship between the number of women lawyers in a state and the number of women in the state legislature indicates that the lack of "eligible" women continues to help to explain the disparity between the number of men and women in state legislatures.[111]

Research suggests the careers of women and men running for Congress are increasingly converging. Although women are still less likely to be lawyers, the gap with men is declining. Of the newly elected women in the House of Representatives in 1992, one-quarter had law degrees, whereas one-half of the males were lawyers.[112] In the 105th Congress, 44 percent of the males were lawyers; only 18 percent of the female representatives were attorneys.

An examination of the careers of women officeholders, moreover, finds that many successful women candidates have pursued "women's careers."[113] In 1988, for example, forty nurses ran for various state offices and only seven lost. Barbara Burrell finds the most common career of women elected to the House before 1992 was educator, although Kathleen Dolan and Lynne E. Ford find women in state legislatures are increasingly in business.[114] It may be that as the public assesses the issues facing the nation in the twenty-first century, women's careers and experiences in education, health, and social services will make them more and more attractive candidates. As State Senator Nita Rinehart of Washington notes, the benefit from having more women in office may come from their difference from men in educational and career backgrounds: "There's a wider array of perspective now when you have more women."[115]

Family Demands

Another major barrier that has affected women candidates is a public perception that women with children (especially young children) are less suited for public office. According to one woman state legislator serving in the 1970s who had postponed running until her children were older: "To be very frank,

I couldn't have done it. I really couldn't have been an effective legislator if my children were little. . . . I would have carried too much of a load of guilt."[116] Half of the women in Jeane Kirkpatrick's 1974 study of female state legislators ran for office only after their children were grown. Only one had attempted it when she had a child under age six.[117] Interviews with a broader group of women political officials a decade later by CAWP also found that women officeholders were less likely than men officeholders to have young children. Moreover, these women officeholders were more likely to agree that "my children being old enough for me to feel comfortable not being home as much" was very important to their decision to run.[118] Men, however, did not appear to hold reservations about running for or serving in public office while they had children.[119]

Until recently, the conflict between parenthood and politics channeled many women away from not only elected office but also partisan or campaign activity, at least while their children were young. This gave women a late start in partisan politics, which had important ramifications on the eventual success of women in getting into office. Although research by Dolan and Ford found women state legislators in 1992 were younger and more likely to be married than their predecessors, Burrell finds some evidence of the continued effect of delayed entrance to politics in 1992 with newly elected women members of the House averaging six years older than newly elected males.[120] In 1997, 26 percent of the men in the House were under age forty-five; only 14 percent of the women were that young.

Even if a woman could reject or overcome the alleged incompatibility of the two roles of mother and politician, she might not run for office for fear of the public's or her own family's negative reaction. Mothers of young children who have run for office tell many stories about the hostile and snide questions asked by some voters and reporters about who was taking care of their children. This has often been a particular problem for women who run for national office, which necessitates a move to Washington, D.C. A study of 1992 candidates for the U.S. House, however, found that these attitudes may no longer be affecting women as negatively. Joanne Bay Brzynski and Bernadette Nye found that women candidates were, in fact, more likely than men candidates to have small children.[121] An update of this research found young children may produce another kind of problem or barrier for some women seeking elective or appointive office. Two women President Clinton considered nominating for attorney general in his first term withdrew from consideration after it was revealed that they had employed undocumented aliens to care for their children. On the heels of what many pundits dubbed Nannygate, Clinton then nominated Janet Reno, an unmarried, childless, Dade County, Florida, prosecutor, to the nation's top law enforcement position.

Historically, another closely related aspect of role conflict that has kept many married women out of politics was spousal preference. Surveys of political officeholders of both sexes in the 1970s found evidence that acceptance and encouragement of political activity by one's spouse and family were more critical for a woman than for a man.[122] Again, this may be especially true for offices that require relocation or spending considerable amounts of time away from home. It may be that one of the reasons why so few women ran for office before the 1970s was that husbands willing to provide the necessary support for a wife who wanted to be active in politics were rare. One of the benefits of the women's rights movement and a factor in the rise in the number of women in office may well be the growth of the idea of shared marriages where both partners have careers. Recent research, moreover, suggests women candidates today may be less concerned with spousal support than male candidates. Although more women than men officeholders claim their spouses are supportive, fewer women than men said that spousal support was important to their decision to run. The main reason for the difference seems to be that many more women than men elected officials are not married.[123] For instance, among those elected to the House before 1992, 58 percent of the women and 87 percent of the men were married at the time of their election. Analysis of the women serving in Congress in 1997 finds even greater disparity in marriage rates: 36 percent of the women but only 15 percent of the men were unmarried.[124]

Thus, women are apparently confronted with a conflict between their roles as mothers and wives and their political roles. When faced with this role conflict, following the pattern of women in other high-powered careers, women politicians appear to solve the problem either by remaining childless, having fewer children, delaying their political career until their children are older, remaining single, or marrying a supportive spouse.

Sex Discrimination

In the past, there was considerable reason to believe that the male gatekeepers of public office, the party leaders, were not very supportive of women candidates. Susan Carroll's survey of women who ran for state or national office in 1976 found women reported they often had to contact party leaders to seek their support. Leaders did not come to them to ask them to run. Moreover, women who sought party support were often discouraged from running, particularly for statewide or national office. When women were recruited to run, they were often meant to serve as "sacrificial lambs" in races they could not be expected to win.[125] Representative Patricia Schroeder (D-Colo.), however, presents a realistic view of the process: "A lot of women think they're going to be asked to run. But this is not a dance. There are a lot of sharp elbows trying to get to the front of the line."[126]

More recent research finds little continued discrimination by party leaders. Women and men were equally as likely to be recruited by party leaders, although there is evidence that women are still disproportionately encouraged to run in unwinnable races or where the seat is a "woman's seat," that is, one previously held by a woman.[127]

African American women and other women of color often face a special or double burden in running for political office because both their race and their gender limit their chances for success. R. Darcy, Charles D. Hadley, and Jason F. Kirksey point out that based on state legislative seats, African American women are more severely underrepresented than African American men.[128] They argue that African American men hold nearly 90 percent of the seats they could expect to hold at the state level based on population; African American women hold only 30 percent of the seats they "deserve." Irene Natividad of the National Women's Political Caucus argues that minority women are especially hampered by their perceived lack of credibility as serious candidates.[129] Other research by R. Darcy and Charles D. Hadley, however, suggests African American women have been able to do better than white women in securing elected office. For instance in 1985, when Darcy and Hadley did their research, African American women held 18.8 percent of all state legislative seats occupied by African Americans, while the percentage of white seats held by white women was 14.5.[130] Part of the problem facing women of both races is an electoral system that magnifies the disadvantages faced by women running for office.

The Political System

Several key components of the political system—money, campaign finance laws, party organization, winner-take-all electoral systems, and incumbency—all affect the ability of women to run and wage successful campaigns for public office.

Money. Adequate funding is the lodestone of a successful campaign. Most women candidates believe that it is more difficult for women than men to obtain the funds needed to run.[131] Burrell's research on women candidates for the House, however, finds the campaign fund deficit of women in the 1970s (except for 1972) declined in the 1980s. In 1988 and 1992, women actually outraised men once the status of the candidate (incumbency) and party were controlled.[132]

The large number of women who ran in 1992 made the ability of women to raise comparable amounts of money all the more impressive. Perhaps spurred on by the Clarence Thomas hearings and the picture they presented of a nearly all-male Senate, women donated millions of dollars to women candidates in unprecedented numbers. The founder of EMILY's List, Ellen Malcolm, commented on the change in women's behavior. "Women have learned that if they want to see themselves represented, they have to get behind women candidates with their contributions as well as their volunteer hours and their votes."[133] Two women, Barbara Boxer (D-Calif.) and Dianne Feinstein (D-Calif.), were among the top five fund-raisers for Senate races.[134] Indeed, four of the five women elected to the Senate in 1992 raised more money than their opponents. The exception was Patty Murray (D-Wash.).

The picture is not all rosy. Research by *Congressional Quarterly* and the National Library on Money and Politics, a nonpartisan research organization, found that the women candidates in 1992 had difficulty securing large contributions or donations from men and PACs.[135] Relatedly, women were not as well funded as their opponents in 1992.[136] This may be a function of the fact that women are generally challengers who have a more difficult time raising money than incumbents. Indeed, if women want to achieve political equality they will have to raise more money than the male incumbents they need to unseat. This is a difficult and daunting although not impossible task. In 1996, women challengers did especially well winning six of their sixty-five races against incumbents. This was possible because in five of these victories the woman challenger raised more money than the male incumbent.[137]

Although women overall may be facing an improved ability to raise funds, African American and other women of color may still have a particularly difficult time because of fewer contacts with monied individuals and the low economic status of the people living in their districts.[138] Cynthia McKinney's (D-Ga.) 1996 House race drew considerable national attention. Her 1992 newly created district was 63 percent black; her redrawn district in 1996 was only 33 percent black. Still, with considerable help from EMILY's List and NOW PAC, she raised five times as much as her opponent, who she defeated by a twenty-point margin.[139]

Campaign Finance Laws. Former Representative Geraldine Ferraro (D-N.Y.) had to sell property and take out personal loans to raise money for her campaign. She lamented, "Unfortunately, that's the way women have to do it. Women have got to learn to write checks for other women."[140]

Since 1984, many women have heeded Ferraro's words, and the growth of political action committees (PACs) made legal by the 1974 campaign finance reforms has helped. Recent efforts by women's PACs including EMILY's List, NOW PAC, the Women's Campaign Fund, Women in the Senate and House (WISH), and Republican Network to Elect Women (RENEW) have been critical in alleviating the financial obstacles faced by women candidates. However, problems may arise from this source if some of the proposed campaign finance reforms are adopted. Bundling, a tactic used successfully by EMILY's List, which bundles the donations of many small contributors, is being targeted for elimination by the Republican Congress. Relatedly, limits are being sought on donations from PACs and from people outside of the candidate's state. If these changes are enacted, women, especially those in small or poor states, may find that their primary sources of campaign funds will dry up.[141]

Party Organization. Historically, women candidates also faced another problem—limited organizational help in the form of campaign workers, in part because of marginal party support.[142] This, however, appears to have changed. Both parties now support the notion of electing more women. According to

Burrell's analysis, they have backed their statements with money and other forms of support.[143] An analysis of party contributions to candidates finds women may actually get more money than men from the party. Republican women appear to have a more difficult time, however, in securing their party's nomination than do Democratic women. In 1996, seventy-seven Democratic women were their party's nominee for a House seat as compared to forty-two Republican women. At both the state and national levels, the majority of elected women (55 percent of the state legislators and 69 percent of the congresswomen) were Democrats. Although Republican women made major gains in 1994, their troubles in the Republican Party may have been the result of the party's strength in the South, a region less hospitable to women candidates. The concentration of women in the Democratic Party may also be a function of women's greater dominance in the Democratic Party structure or the party's support of issues benefiting women.[144]

Interviews with elected officials indicate that groups other than parties, especially women's groups, now play a key role not only in funding women's races but in encouraging and championing them more generally. Support from feminist groups, especially the NWPC, was reported by sizable proportions of women serving in state legislatures.[145] Political consultant Cathy Allen noted in referring to the victories of women in 1992, "I call it the triple play of women in politics—more women deciding to run, more women contributing money, more women working in campaigns."[146]

Electoral Systems. The traditional barriers facing women running for office may be diminishing. Yet there are some problems unique to the U.S. political system that make it very hard for women to be elected in as large numbers as in other democracies. A 1986 study of women legislators in western democracies revealed only three countries (Greece, Japan, and Australia) had a smaller percentage of women than the United States in their national legislatures.[147] Work by Rebecca Davis, moreover, documents the advantages women have in obtaining political appointments in multiparty, multiple-member districts.[148]

One problem hindering women in the U.S. electoral system is its single-member "winner-take-all" structure, which means only one candidate wins in every district. Studies show that when a system has multiple winners (multimember districts) who are selected from lists of candidates prepared by the party, women are more likely to be included on these lists.

More women candidates generally means more women win a seat in the legislature.[149] This is true not only in other countries, but also in the United States. In the few states and localities where multimember districts exist, women have a much better chance of election. Indeed, a number of states with higher than average representation of women in their legislatures elect their officials this way.[150] In recent decades, however, the number of states using multimember districts has declined.[151] African American women seem particularly disadvantaged by this trend.

Incumbency. The political system favors incumbents. This incumbency factor makes it hard for newcomers, which most women are, to break into politics. During the 1980s, for instance, it was common for 90 percent or more of all members of Congress to seek reelection. More than 90 percent of the incumbent candidates won. Between 1976 and 1996, only 2 percent of the women who challenged incumbent senators and 4 percent of the women who challenged members of the House were successful.[152] Relatedly, one-third of the women elected to the House between 1979 and 1992 obtained their seats in special elections, races where the incumbent has left office between elections.[153]

Kim Fridkin Kahn and Edie Goldenberg's analysis of U.S. Senate races suggests that when women run in races where there is an incumbent, they get less media coverage than men in similar races. This hurts women's electoral chances in races already difficult.[154] Some commentators even argue that a "woman's nature" makes it more difficult for a woman to run against an incumbent. Jane Danowitz, former director of the Women's Campaign Fund, notes, "To get anyone out of office, you have to explain to voters why [that person] shouldn't be in office, and that means negative campaigning."[155] She says this is harder for women to do because it goes against their image of what women should do. This may be changing. In 1992, women candidates for the Senate were as likely as men to employ negative ads.[156]

Indeed, 1992 was the Year of the Woman in large part because there were an unprecedented number of open seats. A record number of House incumbents (fifty-four) did not seek reelection or were defeated in primaries (nineteen). This allowed more women candidates than ever—one-third of all candidates—to run in races where there were no incumbents, which greatly increased their chances of winning. The media's coverage of the Year of the Woman also may have made women look like more viable candidates. Given the special circumstances of 1992, it is not surprising the gains of that year were not repeated in 1994 and 1996 when there were far fewer open seats. One political innovation that may weaken the incumbency advantage is term limits. If incumbents, mostly men, were forced to retire after a few terms, women would be able to run for those open seats.

PROBLEMS FACED BY WOMEN IN ELECTED POSITIONS

Election to public office often does not end a woman's problems. Interviews with women public officials indicate that many of the barriers to election also may act to keep women in secondary positions once in office.[157]

Positions of power in legislatures are gained generally according to length of time served. Women often come to politics later in life due to child-rearing demands. This places them at a disadvantage in terms of seniority.

Women who break into leadership positions, moreover, usually have to fight male resistance to get there. A 1991 CAWP report, for example, found almost half of the women in state legislatures believe men try to keep women out of leadership positions.[158] This problem is not restricted to the state level. In fall 1996, Representative Louise Slaughter (D-N.Y.) was defeated in her effort to become the ranking member of the Budget Committee (the person who would become chair if Democrats controlled the House), even though she had the most seniority on the committee. Democratic women were especially angered by Slaughter's defeat because of the key role women had played in electing Clinton and House Democrats. As Slaughter rightly noted, "Half of our governing body of the United States doesn't have any representation."[159]

By some measures, however, women appear to be moving up in the power structure. Figures from 1991 indicate that 17.7 percent of all leadership positions in the state legislatures were held by women, a figure only marginally lower than their total seats (18.3 percent) in those bodies in that year. In state lower houses, women actually held proportionately *more* leadership posts than their numbers in the lower houses. Only a handful of women (fewer than five), however, were in the top positions of speaker of the state house or president of the state senate.[160] In the 105th Congress, women hold two of the seven Republican leadership positions and one of the four Democratic leadership slots.[161] Only Senator Barbara Mikulski has a leadership post among women in the Senate. All the positions held by women, however, have little real political clout.

Another indicator of the difficulties women face can be seen in their committee assignments. Most of the work of legislatures is done in committees. The appointment of women to committees that control important legislation is critical to their ability to influence legislation. Interviews at the state level in the late 1980s, however, found women more likely than men *not* to be appointed to at least two prestige committees—finance and revenue. Instead, they were appointed disproportionately to committees concerned with traditional women's issues such as health or education. Women also were more unhappy with their committee appointments than were men. Their discontent stemmed largely from being placed disproportionately on unpopular committees or as tokens on committees with few or no women.[162] Because they lack seniority, women are also considerably less likely to hold the all-powerful positions of committee chairs. This may be changing, however, as women now serve longer tenure than in previous decades.[163]

Although more women are getting prestigious committee assignments in Congress, their prospects for these slots are often worse than those for men in their same class. Most prestigious committees have but token positions for women.[164] Tokenism or not, in 1993 Senate leaders made certain that two women were appointed to the Senate Judiciary Committee, Dianne Feinstein (D-Calif.) and Carol Moseley-Braun (D-Ill.), to avoid further embarrassment for the members of that body who had been responsible for the Clarence Thomas–Anita Hill fiasco. The real power on a committee, moreover, goes to its chair, and no women hold such a position in either the House or the Senate in the 105th Congress. Nor are any women ranking members on any committee in either body.

IMPACT OF WOMEN IN ELECTED POSITIONS

Attitudes of men appear to be changing, especially toward the new breed of women legislators who are often drawn from the same mold as the typical male legislators. Attitudinal studies of men in state legislatures find they are not likely to downgrade the electability of their women colleagues, although they are more likely than women legislators to portray women as concerned with women's issues and to negate the need for more women legislators.[165] Interviews with women at the state and national levels also indicate that women are having some influence in breaking down the "old-boy" network of back-room and late-night deals that kept women and the public on the outside of the legislative process. Majorities of women state officials, for instance, believe that women are more likely to get legislative business conducted in public and less likely to socialize with lobbyists. Both men and women report having more women in the lawmaking body increases the access of the economically disadvantaged to the legislature.[166]

Indeed, there is agreement among women studied by CAWP that they are better public officials than are their male colleagues in some ways. On the plus side, majorities of women at all levels of public office agree that "women in office generally devote more time to the job than do men," and that "women in office are better at the 'human relations' aspect of the job."[167] Former U.S. Representative and now Senator Barbara Boxer notes, "You have to prove yourself constantly in ways a male colleague does not."[168] These beliefs, moreover, are supported by the actual reports of male and female officials regarding the number of hours a week they spend on their legislative work and the reported emphasis they give to constituents' problems.[169]

Research on the interaction of men and women in state legislatures and Congress, however, indicates that men persist in treating women unfairly in personal interactions. Analysis of committee hearings at the state level finds, even on committees with many women or a woman chair, that men control the floor.[170] Similar analysis of Senate hearings find that men interrupt women, challenge their expertise, and in many other ways make it more problematic for women to testify before committees.[171]

In spite of this discriminatory treatment, elected women influence public policy, especially as it affects women and children. Whereas in the early 1970s, there was little support for the women's movement or its policy goals among female state legislators (although almost all favored the equal rights amendment),[172] by 1988, interviews with women and men state legislators found women were more likely to call themselves feminists, favor the ERA, oppose parental consent for abortion, and oppose prohibiting abortion. In addition, women legislators were more likely to have an issue of concern to women as their top priority and to work on women's rights legislation.[173] African American women legislators were especially united on the policy priorities benefiting women, children, and the poor.[174] Both men and women agreed, moreover, that women in the lawmaking body increased the extent to which legislators consider how a bill will affect women, the number of bills dealing with women, and the spending priorities of the state.[175]

Not surprisingly, the success of bills affecting women is heavily dependent on the proportion of women in a state's legislature and their visibility.[176] In Washington State, for instance (where women comprise more than a third of the lawmakers), when a bill mandating coverage of mammograms by insurance companies was in trouble, women legislators donned "Ladies Sewing Circle and Terrorist Society" buttons. The message was heard. The legislature passed the bill, and the governor signed it.[177]

In Congress, lacking large numbers, women legislators gained visibility in the 1970s with the Congresswomen's Caucus (now called the Congressional Caucus for Women's Issues).[178] Paralleling the findings at the state level, most major pieces of national legislation affecting women have been introduced or sponsored by women legislators. For instance, 62 percent of congress*women* were sponsors of the Freedom of Choice Act in 1992, as compared to only 27 percent of congress*men*. A recent review of the voting behavior of women in Congress finds evidence, moreover, that they are more liberal and more supportive of legislation benefiting women. For instance, whereas 97 percent of all Democratic women and 75 percent of all Republican women voted for the Freedom of Access to (Abortion) Clinic Entrances Act, the figures for their Democratic and Republican male colleagues were 80 percent and 19 percent, respectively. This produced a gender gap of 17 percent for the Democrats and 56 percent for the Republicans. Even after controlling for a number of factors, Republican women are generally more liberal and supportive of women's issues than are their male party colleagues. The differences among Democrats are much smaller.[179] Women have also been able to use their positions on committees to bring about changes benefiting women. Representatives Nancy Pelosi (D-Calif.), Nita Lowey (D-N.Y.), and Rosa DeLauro (D-Conn.), for instance, were able to get the Appropriations Committee to add funds for research on breast, ovarian, and cervical cancer. As Pelosi pointed out, this was possible because "for the first time . . . there were four women on that committee, when there were none before."[180]

There is evidence that the most effective legislators for women's issues are those who are members of women's groups and are supported by those groups when they run for office.[181] If this trend continues to hold, the increased political activity and financial contributions of such groups as NWPC, NOW, EMILY's List, WISH List, and RENEW to women's campaigns, and the resultant election of women backed by these organizations, should mean even more success for legislation benefiting women in the future.

Clearly, women in public office still face many hurdles in being effective legislators. Nevertheless, considerable evidence exists that they have an impact. As U.S. Senator Patty Murray (D-Wash.) proclaimed with regard to the 1992 class of women in Congress, "You are going to see a coalition of women that will get to work from day one to get this country back on track."[182]

PROBLEMS FACED BY WOMEN IN APPOINTED POSITIONS

Many of the problems faced by women in elective office also apply to women in appointed governmental positions. Until recently, women have made few inroads in this area.

The Executive Branch

Franklin D. Roosevelt was the first president to select a woman to a cabinet-level position—Frances Perkins as Secretary of Labor in 1933. FDR also appointed an African American woman, Mary McLeod Bethune, to the board of the National Youth Administration. She and three other African American males constituted the "black cabinet" in the Roosevelt administration, advising the president on issues affecting their race.[183] Since Jimmy Carter's presidency, every president has appointed one or two women to his cabinet, as illustrated in Table 2–4. Clinton's desire to appoint a first-term cabinet that looked "like America," along with pressure from the Coalition for Women's Appointments, which decided it was time to go after one of the "big four" power positions—Defense, State, Justice, and Treasury—resulted in his selection of four women to that cabinet, including the first woman to serve as attorney general, heading the Justice Department.

In his second term, Clinton again nominated four women to cabinet posts, including the first woman, Madeleine Albright, to the second "big four" slot: State Department. "She's a strong lady. She is a courageous lady," said Senator Jesse Helms (R-S.C.), not one known for bestowing accolades on Democratic nominees.[184] A protégé of former National Security Advisor Zbigniew Brzezinski during the Carter years, Albright was serving as chief delegate to the United Nations when Clinton tapped her to lead his foreign policy team. Because, historically, women have often been considered ill-suited for foreign policy positions, her selection may be especially critical in reshaping the public's views about women's expertise in foreign policy.

Women are also making inroads at the subcabinet level. George Bush,

TABLE 2–4 Cabinet Positions Held by Women

Year Appointed	Department	Person	President
1933	Labor	Frances Perkins	Roosevelt (continued under Truman)
1953	Health, Education, and Welfare	Oveta Culp Hobby	Eisenhower
1975–77	Housing and Urban Development	Carla Anderson Hills	Ford
1977	Commerce	Juanita M. Kreps	Carter
1979	Housing and Urban Development	Patricia Roberts Harris	Carter
1979	Health and Human Services	Patricia Roberts Harris	Carter
1979	Education	Shirley Mount Hufstedler	Carter
1981	United Nations Ambassador[a]	Jeane Kirkpatrick	Reagan
1983	Health and Human Services	Margaret M. Heckler	Reagan
1983	Transportation	Elizabeth H. Dole	Reagan
1987	Labor	Ann Dore McLaughlin	Reagan
1989	Special Trade Representative[a]	Carla Anderson Hills	Bush
1989	Labor	Elizabeth H. Dole	Bush
1991	Labor	Lynn Martin	Bush
1992	Commerce	Barbara H. Franklin	Bush
1993	Energy	Hazel O'Leary	Clinton
1993/1997	Health and Human Services	Donna Shalala	Clinton
1993/1997	Attorney General	Janet Reno	Clinton
1993	United Nations Ambassador[a]	Madeleine K. Albright	Clinton
1997	State	Madeleine K. Albright	Clinton
1997	Labor	Alexis Herman	Clinton

[a]Presidents Reagan and Clinton included this as a cabinet position.

for example, responding to the NWPC Coalition for Women's Appointments, chose women for a then record 19.7 percent of his Senate-confirmed positions. Bill Clinton, in his first term, selected women for a record-breaking 27 percent of his top appointments and 41 percent of all noncareer executive branch jobs.[185] He also appointed the first open lesbian, Roberta Achtenberg, to be the assistant secretary for fair housing.

The Federal Judiciary

President Clinton also appointed record-breaking numbers of women to the federal bench. By the end of his first term, Clinton had nominated forty-five women (for 24 percent of his appointments) to the district courts and six women (for 19 percent of his appointments) to the appeals courts.[186] This record was an improvement over that of his predecessors. In 1981, Ronald Reagan had appointed Sandra Day O'Connor the first woman to the Supreme Court, but he nominated only 28 women to fill the 368 judicial vacancies that arose in his eight years in office. Most observers believe Reagan had a hard time finding women who could meet his strict test of ideological conservatism. George Bush appointed fewer women, but they comprised a larger percentage of his overall appointments than Reagan's.[187] Bush is likely to be remembered, however, for his nomination of Clarence Thomas to the Supreme Court, an act that mobilized many women to run against senators who voted to confirm the man accused of sexually harassing Anita Hill.

In sharp contrast, Bill Clinton's first appointment to the U.S. Supreme Court, Ruth Bader Ginsburg, was not only a coauthor of the first important text on sex discrimination,[188] she was also the architect of the legal strategy to convince the Supreme Court to apply the equal protection clause of the Fourteenth Amendment to invalidate gender-based laws.[189]

IMPACT OF WOMEN IN APPOINTED POSITIONS

With more women selected to serve in the executive and judicial branches, an interesting question is whether they, like their sisters in the legislative branches, act in ways distinct from men. Research on this question generally finds they do. Carter's executive branch appointees were found to be more feminist than the men in his administration; so, too, were women appointed to high state government positions.[190] Women appointees in the Clinton administration, moreover, appear to select more women to serve under them than do men, thus bringing more women into the opportunity structure.

The impact of women judges is beginning to be evaluated. There is evidence that women judges generally are more supportive of women in court.[191] Their very presence on the bench, particularly at the appellate level, seems to make other jurists more sensitive to problems of sex discrimination. And it appears that during her first term on the Supreme Court, Sandra Day O'Connor, although generally voting with the conservative bloc of the Court, adopted positions advocated by women's rights activists in gender-based discrimination cases 66 percent of the time. Just as important was the fact that all *eight* other justices became *more* supportive of women's rights claims after she joined the Court.[192] Clearly her vote in *Planned Parenthood of Southeastern Pennsylvania v. Casey* (1992)[193] was crucial in convincing two other justices not to overrule *Roe v. Wade* (1973).[194]

The fact that large numbers of women have been appointed to the federal bench has prompted more women to run for state court judgeships and has led to wider public acceptance of women in these positions. Ultimately, however, the number of women in appointed positions (both judicial and executive) will depend on the chief executive.

CONCLUSION

Five interrelated barriers exist that continue to prevent women from fully exercising their political rights: (1) stereotypes, (2) career choice and preparation, (3) family demands, (4) sex discrimination, and (5) the political system. As the discussion of various political activities has shown, these obstacles have gradually diminished. Indeed, with respect to certain citizen-level activities, women today face few difficulties in participating on an equal footing with men. Barriers to political activity, while diminished since 1920, can still be formidable. System-level barriers, especially those that favor incumbents, make it difficult for women to reach parity even if the public and male party officials are increasingly enlightened as to the need to elect and appoint more women to public office.

The women's rights movement has had an impact on all aspects of women's involvement in politics. Women's groups support women who run for office and pressure governors and presidents to appoint more women. And there is evidence that once they are in office, women, especially feminist women, are more likely to return the favor by supporting legislation and policies benefiting women.

Yet the nation is far from achieving the goal of political equality voiced by the women at Seneca Falls and supposedly achieved by the leaders of the suffrage movement. As former U.S. Representative Patricia Schroeder observes, "We've passed laws, but we haven't changed attitudes; we must now engage in some serious culture-cracking." She urged, "Young women, take government back. . . . Don't wring your hands about government—roll up your sleeves and do something about it!"[195]

NOTES

1. This figure and those that follow are reported in Hazel Erskine, "The Polls: Women's Role," *Public Opinion Quarterly* 35 (1971): 275–90.
2. Kristi Andersen, *After Suffrage: Women in Partisan and Electoral Politics Before the New Deal* (Chicago: University of Chicago, 1996), 13–14.
3. E. M. Schreiber, "Education and Change in Opinions on a Woman for President," *Public Opinion Quarterly* 42 (1978): 171–82. See also Myra Marx Ferree, "A Woman for President? Changing Responses: 1958–1972," *Public Opinion Quarterly* 38 (1974): 390–99.
4. "Men and Women Don't Disagree on 'Women in Politics,' but They Divide When Maternal Responsibility Is Invoked," *The Public Perspective* 8 (1997): 25.

5. Sandra Baxter and Marjorie Lansing, *Women and Politics: The Invisible Majority* (Ann Arbor: University of Michigan Press, 1980), 140.
6. *The Gallup Report*, no. 191, August 1981, 4.
7. "Election 1992," *Chicago Tribune*, June 28, 1992, 4C.
8. *Polling Report: Women's Voices*, September 1992, 28–29. James Allan Davis and Tom W. Smith, *General Social Surveys, 1972–1996*. Principal Investigator, James A. Davis; Director and Co-Principal Investigator, Tom W. Smith. NORC ed. Chicago: National Opinion Research Center, producer, 1996; Storrs, Conn.: The Roper Center for Public Opinion Research, University of Connecticut, distributor. This is the source for all the General Social Survey data reported in this book. See generally, Jody Newman, *Sex as a Political Variable: Women as Candidates and Voters in U.S. Elections* (Boulder, Colo.: Lynne Rienner, 1997.)
9. *General Social Surveys, 1972–1996*.
10. "Men and Women Don't Disagree," 25.
11. "The 1990 Virginia Slims Poll." Data made available through the Roper Center for Public Opinion Research, Storrs, Conn.
12. Ibid.
13. "The 1972 Virginia Slims American Women's Opinion Poll." (Louis Harris and Associates, 1971), 32.
14. Barbara C. Burrell, *A Woman's Place Is in the House: Campaigning for Congress in the Feminist Era* (Ann Arbor: University of Michigan Press, 1994), 27.
15. Leonie Huddy and Nayda Terkildsen, "Gender Stereotypes and the Perception of Male and Female Candidates," *American Journal of Political Science* 37 (1993): 127–44.
16. Dianne Owen and Jack Dennis, "Gender Differences in the Politicization of American Children," *Women & Politics* 8 (1988): 30–33.
17. "1990 Virginia Slims Poll."
18. Diane Gillespie and Cassia Spohn, "Adolescents' Attitudes toward Women in Politics: A Follow-up Study," *Women & Politics* 10 (1990): 5–7; Sue Tolleson Rinehart, "Gender Differences and Political Orientations of Southern College Students," *Women & Politics* 8 (1988): 69–86.
19. Kathleen Dolan, "Support for Women Political Candidates: An Examination of the Role of Family," *Women & Politics* 16 (1996): 54–55.
20. Gillespie and Spohn, "Adolescents' Attitudes," 14–15.
21. Rinehart, "Gender Differences," 77–79.
22. Owen and Dennis, "Gender Differences in the Politicization," 35–36.
23. Karlyn Bowman, "Do You Want to Be President?" *Public Perspective* 8 (1997): 39. In 1995, 34 percent of those polled would like to see their daughter (32 percent, their son) go into politics as a life's work.
24. Virginia Sapiro, *The Political Integration of Women* (Urbana: University of Illinois Press, 1983).
25. Sue Tolleson Rinehart, "The Life Course and Intergenerational Change: A Brief Note on the Transmission of Political Roles from Mother to Daughter" (paper delivered at the annual meeting of the American Political Science Association, Washington, D.C., 1988), 23.
26. Kay Lehman Schlozman, Nancy Burns, and Sidney Verba, "Gender and the Pathways to Participation: The Role of Resources," *Journal of Politics* 56 (1994): 984.
27. Charles Merriam and Harold Gosnell, *Non-Voting: Causes and Methods of Control* (Chicago: University of Chicago Press, 1924), 37.
28. Ibid., 113.
29. Nancy E. McGlen and Karen O'Connor, *Women's Rights: The Struggle for Equality in the 19th and 20th Centuries* (New York: Praeger, 1983), 89.
30. Sidney Verba and Norman H. Nie, *Participation in America: Political Democracy and Social Equality* (New York: Harper & Row, 1972), 83.
31. Merriam and Gosnell, *Non-Voting*, 161.
32. Judy Bertelsen, "Political Interest, Influence, and Efficacy: Differences between the Sexes and among Marital Status Groups," *American Politics Quarterly* 2 (1974): 415.
33. Unless otherwise indicated, the data analyzed in this chapter were made available by the Inter-University Consortium for Political and Social Research.
34. In 1940, only 23 percent of all women but 33 percent of all men in Erie County, Ohio, expressed an interest in that year's presidential campaign. Paul Lazarsfeld, Bernard Berelson, and Hazel Gaudet, *The People's Choice*, 3d ed. (New York: Columbia University Press, 1968), 45. See also Angus Campbell et al., *The American Voter* (New York: Wiley,

1960), 489; Susan Welch, "Women as Political Animals? A Test of Some Explanations for Male-Female Differences in Political Participation Differences," *American Journal of Political Science* 21 (1977): 723; McGlen and O'Connor, *Women's Rights,* 90.

35. Michael X. Delli Carpini and Scott Keeter, "The Gender Gap in Political Knowledge," *Public Perspective* 3 (1992): 23–26.
36. Laura van Assendelft and Karen O'Connor, "Backgrounds, Motivations and Interests: A Comparison of Male and Female Local Party Activists," *Women & Politics* 14 (1994): 77–92.
37. Mary Geraghty, "Finances Are Becoming More Crucial in Students' College Choice, Survey Finds," *Chronicle of Higher Education,* January 17, 1997, A43.
38. "The Gender Gap," *CAWP Fact Sheet,* July 1996.
39. Merriam and Gosnell, *Non-Voting,* 37.
40. John W. Soule and Wilma E. McGrath, "A Comparative Study of Male-Female Political Attitudes at Citizen and Elite Levels," in *A Portrait of Marginality,* Marianne Githens and Jewel L. Prestage, eds. (New York: McKay, 1977), 183.
41. Kathleen McCourt, *Working-Class Women and Grass-Roots Politics* (Bloomington: Indiana University Press, 1977), 174–84, 226; Laura Woliver, *From Outrage to Action: The Politics of Grass-Root Dissent* (Urbana: University of Illinois Press, 1993).
42. Schlozman, Burns, and Verba, "Gender and the Pathways," 972–85.
43. Quoted in Andersen, *After Suffrage,* 101.
44. John Leo, "Wit Is Opiate of Politics," *U.S. News & World Report,* November 26, 1990, 24.
45. Quoted in Irene Natividad, "Women of Color and the Campaign Trail," in *The American Woman: 1992–1993,* Paula Ries and Anne J. Stone, eds. (New York: Norton, 1992), 136.
46. Andersen, *After Suffrage,* chap. 3.
47. Ibid., 56.
48. Susan J. Carroll and Wendy S. Strimling, *Women's Routes to Elective Office: A Comparison with Men's* (New Brunswick, N.J.: Center for the American Woman and Politics, 1983), 88.
49. Andersen, *After Suffrage,* 66.
50. Kristi Andersen, "Generation, Partisan Shift, and Realignment," in *The Changing American Voter,* Norman H. Nie, Sidney Verba, and John R. Petrocick (Cambridge: Harvard University Press, 1976), 74–95. Other research suggests that the 1928 presidential campaign, with a Catholic presidential candidate, mobilized many immigrant women.
51. Courtney Brown, *Ballots of Tumult* (Ann Arbor: University of Michigan Press, 1992); Andersen, "Generation, Partisan Shift, and Realignment," 90.
52. "Increased Turnout by Black Male Voters; Politicians Note," *The Virginia Pilot,* February 15, 1997, A12.
53. Baxter and Lansing, *Women and Politics,* 101–2, 107–10.
54. Susan A. MacManus, Charles S. Bullock III, and Barbara P. Grothe, "A Longitudinal Examination of Political Participation Rates of Mexican American Females," *Social Science Quarterly* 67 (1986): 605, 610.
55. Susan Carroll, "The Gender Gap in 1996: Setting the Context," *CAWP News & Notes,* 11, no. 1 (1996): 2.
56. C. Richard Hofstetter and William A. Schultze, "Some Observations about Participation and Attitudes among Single Parent Women: Inferences Concerning Political Translation," *Women & Politics* 9 (1989): 93.
57. Marjorie Connelly, "Portrait of the Electorate," *New York Times,* November 10, 1996, 28.
58. Tom W. Smith, "The Polls: Gender and Attitudes toward Violence," *Public Opinion Quarterly* 48 (1984), 384–96.
59. "Women and the Use of Force," *Public Perspective* 2, no. 3 (1991): 85–86.
60. Pamela Johnston Conover and Virginia Sapiro, "Gender, Feminist Consciousness, and War," *American Journal of Political Science* 37 (1993): 1088–91.
61. Center for the American Woman and Politics, *CAWP Fact Sheet,* September 1992.
62. Pamela Johnston Conover, "Feminists and the Gender Gap," *Journal of Politics* 50 (1988): 985–1010. Others disagree with Conover's results; see Elizabeth Adell Cook and Clyde Wilcox, "Feminists and the Gender Gap—A Second Look," *Journal of Politics* 53 (1991): 1111–22. Research on women's foreign policy views finds occupation can make a difference. See Nancy E. McGlen and Meredith Reid Sarkees, *Women and Foreign Policy: The Insiders* (New York: Routledge, 1993).
63. Geraghty, "Finances Are Becoming More Crucial," A43.
64. "The Gender Gap," *CAWP Fact Sheet,* July 1996; "Gender and Party ID," *Public Perspective* 3, no. 5 (1992): 27–28.

65. "The Exit Poll Results," *Public Opinion,* January/February 1989, 24–25.
66. Susan Carroll, "The Gender Gap in the Presidential Race," *CAWP News & Notes* 9, no. 1 (1993): 5–6; "Portrait of the Electorate," *New York Times,* November 5, 1992, B9.
67. Connelly, "Portrait," p.28.
68. Thomas B. Edsall and Richard Morin, "Winning Over the Women," *Washington Post National Weekly Edition,* November 11–17, 1996, 12.
69. Blaine Harden, "Bob Dole's Garbled Message," *Washington Post Weekly Edition,* November 11–17, 1996, 8–9.
70. Quoted in Carolyn Barta, "Engendering Power, Women's Voting Pattern Has Implications Beyond Re-election of President Clinton," *Dallas Morning News,* November 30, 1996, 1C.
71. Ibid.
72. "Gender Gap Biggest in the DE and GA Contests, Small to Nonexistent in RI, NJ, WY, NM and AK," *Public Perspective* 8, no. 1 (1997): 28.
73. "Do Women Vote for Women?" *Public Perspective* 3, no. 5 (1992): 98–99; Tom W. Smith and Lance A. Selfa, "When Do Women Vote for Women?" *Public Perspective* 3, no. 6 (1992): 30–31.
74. "The Gender Gap," *CAWP Fact Sheet,* http://www.-rci.rutgers.edu:80/~cawp/ggap.html
75. Ibid.
76. Jody Newman, "Do Women Vote for Women?" *Public Perspective* 7, no. 2 (1996): 10–12.
77. Quoted in Diane Minor, "New Year, New Congress," *National NOW Times,* January 1997, 1.
78. Andersen, *After Suffrage,* 13–14.
79. Janet K. Boles, "Local Based Social Welfare Policies: The Impact of Local Feminist Networks" (paper delivered at the annual meeting of the Midwest Political Science Association, Chicago, 1988); Woliver, *From Outrage to Action;* Irene Diamond, ed., *Families, Politics, and Public Policy* (New York: Longman, 1983).
80. Vicki L. Crawford, Jacqueline Anne Rouse, and Barbara Woods, eds., *Women in the Civil Rights Movement: Trailblazers and Torchbearers, 1941–1965* (Brooklyn, N.Y.: Carlson Publishing, 1990); Jo Anne Gibson, *The Montgomery Bus Boycott and the Women Who Started It* (Knoxville: University of Tennessee Press, 1987).
81. Profile of Nydia M. Veláquez, "The New Congress," *Congressional Quarterly Report* 51, supplement to no. 3 (1993), 113.
82. Kay Lehman Schlozman, Nancy Burns, Sidney Verba, and Jesse Donahue, "Gender and Citizen Participation: Is There a Different Voice?" *American Journal of Political Science* 39 (1995): 274.
83. Ibid, 281–83.
84. Andersen, *After Suffrage,* chap. 6.
85. Ibid., 40–45.
86. Kristi Andersen, "Working Women and Political Participation, 1952–1972," *American Journal of Political Science* 19 (1975): 442.
87. Schlozman, Burns, and Verba, "Gender and Pathways," 980–85.
88. Edmond Costantini, "Political Women and Political Ambition," *American Journal of Politics* 34 (1990): 763–65.
89. van Assendelft and O'Connor, "Backgrounds, Motivations and Interests."
90. Natividad, "Women of Color," 129.
91. Burrell, *A Woman's Place,* 90.
92. Ronald B. Rapoport, Walter J. Stone, and Alan I. Abramowitz, "Sex and the Caucus Participant: The Gender Gap and Presidential Nominating Conventions," *American Journal of Political Science* 34 (1990): 725–40.
93. van Assendelft and O'Connor, "Backgrounds, Motivations and Interests."
94. "Women in the U.S. Congress 1993," *CAWP Fact Sheet,* January 1993, 2; "Women in State Legislatures 1993," *CAWP Fact Sheet,* January 1993, 1.
95. "Election Results," *Congressional Quarterly Weekly Report* 55, no. 7 (1997): 447–55.
96. "Women of Color in Elective Office 1996," *CAWP Fact Sheet,* August 1996. The 1997 figures were calculated by the authors.
97. "Solid Gains for Women in State Legislatures," *CAWP News & Notes* 9, no. 1 (1993): 3–4; "Woman of Color in Elected Office 1996," *CAWP Fact Sheet,* August 1996.
98. "Women in Elective Office 1997," *CAWP Fact Sheet,* March 1997.
99. Burrell, *A Woman's Place,* 42, 55.

100. R. Darcy and Sarah Slavin Schramm, "When Women Run Against Men," *Public Opinion Quarterly* 41 (1977): 1–12. Burrell found that sex was a negligible factor in explaining success rates of women running for Congress, *A Woman's Place,* 141.
101. A. Karnig and B. O. Walter, "Election of Women to City Councils," *Social Science Quarterly* 56 (1976): 605–13; Barbara Burrell, "The Political Opportunity of Women Candidates for the U.S. House of Representatives in 1984," *Women & Politics* 8 (1988): 51–68; Barbara Burrell, "The Presence of Women Candidates and the Role of Gender in Campaigns for the State Legislature in an Urban Setting: The Case of Massachusetts," *Women & Politics* 10 (1990): 85–102.
102. The states with the lowest percentages were Alabama (4.3), Kentucky (9.4), Oklahoma (10.2), Louisiana (11.1), Mississippi (11.5), Pennsylvania (12.3), South Carolina (12.9), Alaska (13.3), Tennessee (13.6), and West Virginia (14.9). The states with the highest percentage of women state legislators were Washington (38.1), Arizona (37.8), Colorado (35), Nevada (33.3), Vermont (31.7), New Hampshire (31.1), Minnesota (30.3), Maryland (29.8), Kansas (29.7), and Connecticut (28.9). CAWP, "Women in State Legislatures 1997," *CAWP Fact Sheet,* March 1997.
103. Costantini, "Political Women and Political Ambition," 749–51. See also van Assendelft and O'Connor, "Backgrounds, Motivations and Interests." Susan Carroll also finds some evidence of low career ambitions among women elected officials. Susan J. Carroll, *Women as Candidates in American Politics* (Bloomington: Indiana University Press, 1985), chap. 7.
104. Carroll, *Women as Candidates,* 755–59.
105. Jerry Perkins, "Political Ambition among Black and White Women: An Intragender Test of the Socialization Model," *Women & Politics* 6 (1986): 33.
106. Profile of Corrine Brown, "The New Congress," *Congressional Quarterly Report* 51, supplement to no. 3 (1993), 64.
107. Kim Fridken Kahn, "Does Gender Make a Difference? An Experimental Examination of Sex Stereotypes and Press Patterns in Statewide Campaigns," *American Journal of Political Science* 38 (1994): 168–70.
108. Ibid., 185–91.
109. Leonard Williams, "Political Advertising in the Year of the Woman," in *The Year of the Woman: Myths & Realities,* ed. Elizabeth Adell Cook, Sue Thomas, and Clyde Wilcox (Boulder, Colo.: Westview Press, 1994), 202.
110. R. Darcy, Susan Welch, and Janet Clark, *Women, Elections, and Representation* (New York: Longman, 1987), 93–108.
111. Christine B. Williams, "Women, Law and Politics: Recruitment Patterns in the Fifty States," *Women & Politics* 10 (1990): 103–23.
112. Congressional Quarterly, *The New Congress* (Washington, D.C.: Congressional Quarterly Press, 1993). Analysis by the authors.
113. Carroll and Strimling, *Women's Routes to Elective Office,* 17–23.
114. Burrell, *A Woman's Place,* 67; Kathleen Dolan and Lynne E. Ford, "Change and Continuity Among Women State Legislators: Evidence from 3 Decades," *Political Research Quarterly* 50 (1997): 137–51.
115. Andrea Stone and Dee Ann Glasmer, "Lawmakers and Laws Change," *USA Today,* February 12, 1993, 6.
116. Quoted in Jeane J. Kirkpatrick, *Political Woman* (New York: Basic Books, 1974), 235.
117. Ibid., 234–35.
118. Carroll and Strimling, *Women's Routes to Elective Office,* 28–29.
119. Virginia Sapiro, "Private Costs of Public Commitments or Public Costs of Private Commitments? Family Roles versus Political Ambition," *American Journal of Political Science* 26 (1982): 265–79.
120. Marcia Manning Lee, "Why Few Women Hold Public Office: Democracy and Sexual Roles," *Political Science Quarterly* 31 (1976); Dolan and Ford, "Change and Continuity Among Women State Legislators"; Burrell, *A Woman's Place,* 74.
121. Joanne Bay Brzynski and Bernadette Nye, "Recruitment of Women Candidates in the 1992 Congressional Election" (paper delivered at the annual meeting of the American Political Science Association, Washington, D.C., 1993), 6.
122. Johnson et al., *Profile of Women Holding Office,* 19A; and Carroll, *Women as Candidates,* 30.
123. Carroll and Strimling, *Women's Routes to Elective Office,* 24–26.
124. Thomas reports similar findings for women state legislators, *How Women Legislate,* 47.

125. Carroll, *Women as Candidates*, 30–56.
126. Elizabeth A. Brown, "Why Most Public Officials Are Still Men," *Christian Science Monitor*, February 15, 1991, 11.
127. Carroll and Strimling, *Women's Routes to Elective Office*, 61–82; Darcy, Welch, and Clark, *Women, Elections, and Representation*, 35–36.
128. R. Darcy, Charles D. Hadley, and Jason F. Kirksey, "Electoral Systems and the Representation of Black Women in American State Legislatures," *Women & Politics* 13 (1993): 73–76.
129. Natividad, "Women of Color," 134–38.
130. R. Darcy and Charles D. Hadley, "Black Women in Politics: The Puzzle of Success," *Social Science Quarterly* 69 (1988): 633.
131. Both the Carroll study of women candidates in 1976 and the Carroll and Strimling research on women elected officials in the 1980s found women complaining about a lack of funds. Carroll, *Women as Candidates*, 49–55; Carroll and Strimling, *Women's Routes to Elective Office*, 111–13.
132. Burrell, *A Woman's Place*, 105.
133. Quoted in Beth Donovan, "Women's Campaigns Fueled Mostly by Women's Checks," *Congressional Quarterly Weekly Report* 50, no. 41 (1992): 3270.
134. "Spending on Congressional Campaigns Hits New High," *New York Times*, October 29, 1992, A1, B11.
135. Donovan, "Women's Campaigns Fueled Mostly by Women's Checks," 3271–73.
136. Rebekah Herrick, "A Reappraisal of the Quality of Women Candidates," *Women & Politics* 15 (1995): 30–35.
137. Jonathan D. Salant, "Million-Dollar Campaigns Proliferate in the 105th," *Congressional Quarterly Weekly Report* 54, no. 50 (1996): 3450.
138. Natividad, "Women of Color," 133–34.
139. Salim Muwakkil, "Holding Pattern," *In These Times*, December 9, 1996, 18.
140. Quoted in Anita Shreve and John Clemans, "The New Wave of Women Politicians," *New York Times Magazine*, October 19, 1980, 31.
141. Salant, "Million-Dollar Campaigns," 3450–51.
142. Carroll, *Women as Candidates*, 51–56.
143. Burrell, *A Woman's Place*, 94–98.
144. "Women in State Legislatures 1996"; figures for the 1997 House calculated by the authors.
145. Carroll and Strimling, *Women's Routes to Elective Office*, 93–99.
146. Quoted in Stone and Glasmer, "Lawmakers and Laws Change," 6.
147. Wilma Rule, "Electoral Systems, Contextual Factors and Women's Opportunity for Election to Parliament in Twenty-three Democracies," *Western Political Quarterly* 40 (1987): 477–98.
148. Rebecca Howard Davis, *Women and Power in Parliamentary Democracies: Cabinet Appointments in Western Europe, 1968–1992* (Lincoln: University of Nebraska Press, 1997).
149. Rule, "Electoral," 481. The same problem affects women running for local office. In localities with multicandidate races women are more likely to get nominated and elected. Carroll, *Women as Candidates*, 40–41, 107–8.
150. Darcy, Hadley, and Kirksey, "Electoral Systems," 74, 85; Wilma Rule, "Why More Women Are State Legislators: A Research Note," *Western Political Quarterly* 43 (1990): 437–48.
151. Sue Thomas, "Women in State Legislatures: One Step at a Time," in *The Year of the Woman*, ed. Cook, Thomas, and Wilcox, 146.
152. "Women Candidates for Congress 1974–1996" *CAWP Fact Sheet*, November 1996.
153. David L. Nixon and R. Darcy, "Special Elections and the Growth of Women's Representation in the House of Representatives," *Women & Politics*, 16 (1996): 102.
154. Kim Fridin Kahn and Edie N. Goldenberg, "Evaluations of Male and Female U.S. Senate Candidates: An Investigation of Media Influence" (paper delivered at the annual meeting of the Midwest Political Science Association, Chicago, 1988). See also Pippa Norris, ed., *Women, Media and Politics* (New York: Oxford University Press, 1996); and Kim Fridkin Kahn, *The Politics of Being a Woman: How Stereotypes Influence the Conduct and Consequences of Political Campaigns* (New York: Columbia University Press, 1996).
155. Quoted in Brown, "Why Most Public Officials Are Men."
156. Williams, "Political Advertising," 206.
157. See generally, Karen Foerstel and Herbert N. Foerstel, *Climbing the Hill: Gender Conflict in Congress* (New York: Praeger, 1996); Clara Bingham, *Women on the Hill: Challenging the Culture of Congress* (New York: Times Books, 1997).

158. Debra L. Dodson and Susan J. Carroll, *Reshaping the Agenda: Women in the State Legislatures* (New Brunswick, N.J.: Center for the American Woman and Politics, 1991), 87.

159. Donna Cassata, "Leadership Lineup Stays Intact, but Centrists Gain Influence," *Congressional Quarterly Weekly Report* 54, no. 47 (1996): 3304.

160. "Women State Legislators: Leadership Positions and Committee Chairs 1991," *CAWP Fact Sheet*, February 1991.

161. Jackie Koszczuk, "Revolutionary Rhetoric Fades as GOP Softens Its Edges," *Congressional Quarterly Weekly Report* 54, no. 47 (1996): 3301; Cassata, "Leadership Lineup," 3304.

162. Susan J. Carroll and Ella Taylor, "Gender Differences in the Committee Assignments of State Legislators: Preferences or Discrimination?" (paper delivered at the annual meeting of the Midwest Political Science Association, Chicago, 1989).

163. "Women State Legislators," *CAWP Fact Sheet*, November 1991; Dolan and Ford, "Change and Continuity Among Women State Legislators."

164. Sally Friedman, "Committee Assignments of Women and Blacks in Congress: 1964–1990" (paper delivered at the annual meeting of the Midwest Political Science Association, Chicago, 1990).

165. Patricia K. Freeman and William Lyons, "Legislators' Perceptions of Women in State Legislatures," *Women & Politics* 10 (1990): 128; Thomas, *How Women Legislate*, 48.

166. Dodson and Carroll, *Reshaping the Agenda*, 79.

167. Johnson et al., *Profile*. See also Thomas, *How Women Legislate*, 48–49.

168. In Lois Ramano, "Capitol Hill: Is This Any Place for a Woman?" *Cosmopolitan Magazine*, March 1991.

169. Johnson et al, *Profile*.

170. Lyn Kathlene, "Power and Influence in State Legislative Policymaking: The Interaction of Gender and Position in Committee Hearing Debates," *American Political Science Review* 88 (1994): 565–69.

171. Laura R. Winsky Mattei, "Language, Power and the Participation of Women in the American Legislative Process" (paper delivered at the annual meeting of the American Political Science Association, San Francisco, 1996), 7–15.

172. Kirkpatrick, *Political Woman*, 164–76.

173. Thomas, *How Women Legislate*, 55–84; see also Sue Thomas, "Voting Patterns in the California Assembly: The Role of Gender," *Women & Politics* 9 (1989): 47–50; Susan J. Carroll, Debra L. Dodson, and Ruth B. Mandel, *The Impact of Women in Public Office* (New Brunswick, N.J.: Center for the American Woman and Politics, 1991), 25–31.

174. Edith J. Barrett, "The Policy Priorities of Mexican-American Women in State Legislatures: Is There a Black Women's Agenda?" (paper delivered at the annual meeting of the American Political Science Association, Washington, D.C., 1993), 14–16.

175. Carroll et al., *Impact of Women in Public Office*, 11–13.

176. Thomas, *How Women Legislate*, 100.

177. Stone and Glasmer, "Lawmakers and Laws Change," 6.

178. Joan Hulse Thompson, "The Congressional Caucus for Women's Issues: A Study in Organizational Change" (paper delivered at the annual meeting of the American Political Science Association, Washington, D.C., 1993).

179. Michele Swers, "Are Congresswomen More Likely to Vote for Women's Issues Bills Than Their Male Colleagues?" (paper delivered at the annual meeting of the Northeastern Political Science Association, Boston, 1996), 6. See also Burrell, *A Woman's Place*, chap. 8; Carroll, *Voices, Views, Votes*; Susan Welch, "Are Women More Liberal Than Men in the U.S. Congress?" *Legislative Studies Quarterly* 10 (1985): 125–34; Frieda L. Gehlen, "Women Members of Congress: A Distinctive Role," in *A Portrait of Marginality*, ed. Githens and Prestage, 304–19; "Women in Congress Support Women's Issues," *National NOW Times* 25, no. 1 (1993): 4.

180. Quoted in Carroll, *Voices, Views, Votes*, 10.

181. Carroll et al., *Impact of Women in Public Office*, 62–63. Note that men who received contributions from feminist groups were less likely than similarly supported women to have a women's concern bill as their legislative priority.

182. Dale Nelson, "Women Vow to Make Impact in Senate, House," *Buffalo News*, November 4, 1992, A7.

183. B. Joyce Ross, "Mary McLeod Bethune and the National Youth Administration: A Case Study of Power Relationships in the Black Cabinet of Franklin D. Roosevelt," in *Black*

Women in American History: The Twentieth Century, ed. Darlene Clark Hine (Brooklyn, N.Y.: Carlson Publishing, 1990), 1021–49.

184. Carroll J. Doherty, "Senate Confirms Albright," *Congressional Quarterly Weekly Report* 55, no. 4 (1997): 248.

185. Tom Raum, "Clinton Comes under Pressure to Name Women, Minorities to Key Posts," *Buffalo News,* November 30, 1996, A5; Nancy E. McGlen and Meredith Reid Sarkees, "Style Does Matter: The Impact of Presidential Management on Women in Foreign Policy," in *The Other Elites: Women, Politics, and Power in the Executive Branch,* ed. Janet Martin and Maryanne Borrelli (Boulder, Colo.: Lynne Rienner, 1997); Janet M. Martin, "Women Who Govern: The President's Appointments," in *The Other Elites: Women, Politics, and Power in the Executive Branch,* ed. MaryAnne Borrelli and Janet Martin.

186. Holly Idelson, "Clinton's Unexpected Bequest: Judgeships Bush Did Not Fill," *Congressional Quarterly* 51, no. 7 (February 13, 1993): 317–20. Richard L. Pacelle Jr., "A President's Legacy: Gender and Appointment to the Federal Courts," in Borrelli and Martin, eds., *The Other Elites,* 147–66.

187. Pacelle, "A President's Legacy."

188. Kenneth M. Davidson, Ruth Bader Ginsburg, and Herma Hill Kay, *Sex-Based Discrimination* (St. Paul, Minn.: West, 1974).

189. Karen O'Connor, "The Next Thurgood Marshall?" *Atlanta Journal and Constitution,* June 15, 1993, A23.

190. "Women Appointed to the Carter Administration" (New Brunswick, N.J.: Center for the American Woman and Politics, n.d.); Susan J. Carroll and Barbara Geiger-Parker, *Women Appointed to State Government* (New Brunswick, N.J.: Center for the American Woman and Politics, 1983). See, however, McGlen and Sarkees, *Women in Foreign Policy,* chap. 4, for some contrary data about Reagan appointees.

191. Elaine Martin, "The Representative Role of Women Judges," *Judicature* 77 (November/December 1993): 166–73; Sue Davis, Susan Haire, and Donald R. Songer, "Voting Behavior and Gender on the U.S. Court of Appeals," *Judicature* 77 (November/December 1993): 129–33.

192. Karen O'Connor and Jeffrey A. Segal, "The Supreme Court's Reaction to Its First Female Member," *Women & Politics* 10 (1990): 95–104.

193. 112 S. Ct. 2791 (1992).

194. 410 U.S. 113 (1973).

195. Quoted in Rep. Patricia Schroeder, "Viewpoint: Why I'm Leaving Congress," *Glamour,* February 1996, 106.

EMPLOYMENT AND EDUCATIONAL RIGHTS AND REALITIES

PART II

Women's struggle for equal educational and employment opportunities has been a long one. Even before the first woman's movement, feminist writers such as Mary Wollstonecraft argued:

> Mankind should all be educated after the same model, or the intercourse of the sexes will never deserve the name of fellowship, nor will women ever fulfill the peculiar duties of their sex, till they become enlightened citizens, till they become free by being enabled to earn their own subsistence, independent of men.*

Resolutions calling for equal educational, professional, and employment opportunities were regularly passed at women's conventions in the nineteenth century. But women still constitute less than one-third of all students receiving professional degrees, and a woman who works outside of the home can expect to earn only about 70 cents for every dollar earned by a man.

The efforts to rectify these inequalities and the barriers to success are the topics of the next two chapters. Chapter 3 covers the efforts of various women's movements to expand women's employment and educational rights and opportunities, and Chapter 4 examines the progress made and the barriers that remain.

Employment and educational rights—including equal pay for equal work and the removal of legal roadblocks to women's practice of some professions—are "rights" that affect only a limited number of women. Many laws that equalize employment and educational opportunities are nonthreatening because their effect is not always universal. Women can choose whether or not they wish to work outside the home or get a college degree, and whether or not they wish to take full advantage of antidiscrimination legislation. In the educational area, when barriers to admission are eliminated,

---

*Quoted in Alice S. Rossi, ed., *The Feminist Papers: From Adams to de Beauvoir* (New York: Columbia University Press, 1973), 76.

only some women will opt for certain kinds of training. Owing to the non-universal and therefore "non-lifestyle-endangering" nature of rights in these areas, strong opposition groups have not emerged to lobby against or challenge in court any of the recent employment and educational rights laws.

For the most part, conservative women's groups have not challenged specific laws designed to improve women's employment or educational status. In fact, these groups have viewed some pieces of antidiscrimination legislation, most notably the Pregnancy Discrimination Act, as fostering motherhood roles.

Most objections to expanded rights for women have come from men. Men's hostility toward equal educational and professional opportunities for women has been and continues to be a significant barrier to full equality.

3

The Struggle for Employment and Educational Rights

Distinct eras of women's gains in employment and educational rights and opportunities closely parallel (but are not identical to) the periods of women's movement activity noted in the Introduction. From 1820 to 1900, young, white, primarily unmarried women left their homes in increasing numbers to seek employment in the growing textile industry. Other more privileged women, often closely allied with the woman's rights activists, sought entrance into higher-prestige occupations, particularly medicine and law. Many of them were forced to break legal and social barriers to gain admission to professional schools and again later to earn even minimal acceptance in their chosen fields. During this period, and even earlier, a large number of women's colleges were founded, and some formerly "male-only" universities opened their doors to female students.

A second period of change—from 1900 to 1930—can be delineated. In those years, the composition of the female labor force was altered dramatically both by the influx of immigrant women into the labor force and by the growth of white-collar jobs for unmarried, middle-class women. These changes were accompanied by an alteration in the ideology of white middle-class women active in the drive for suffrage. Generally, they were less concerned with eliminating all legal, social, and economic barriers for women. Instead they worked to protect working women and children from unsavory working conditions. Employment legislation promoted by those active in the suffrage and progressive movements tended to be based on the same logic as their arguments for the vote-—namely, the view that a woman's proper role in life was that of devoted wife and mother. The dominant ideology of the time also was evident in the substandard preparation given to women in American colleges and in the lifestyles of female professionals.

World War II and the period of the 1950s and 1960s saw yet another radical alteration in the kinds and number of women working outside the home. Substantial legal changes designed to improve women's economic status, however, did not occur until passage of the Equal Pay Act in 1963. The period since then has been marked by the activity of women's groups and by the enactment of sweeping antidiscrimination legislation designed to improve women's employment status and educational opportunities. Many of these new laws, however, suffer from uneven enforcement. Thus, efforts to force compliance and to eliminate other barriers to economic and educational opportunity still occupy a good deal of the energies of members of the current women's rights movement. New issues also continue to emerge. In the 1980s, women's rights activists took up the fight for comparable worth. As women traditionally have been channeled into low-prestige, low-paying positions, activists argued that women's jobs should be reevaluated. In 1993, after long opposition from the Bush administration, women's rights groups were able to secure passage of the Family and Medical Leave Act.

This chapter also illustrates the tension between women's employment status and motherhood. Historically, a variety of laws and practices designed to "protect" women (and usually their childbearing functions) at work (or from too much education) have been enacted and then challenged as denying women equal rights. In this chapter we trace the evolution of those laws and practices.

THE WOMAN'S MOVEMENT

In colonial times, few individuals—male or female—sought employment outside of the home. Wives toiled beside their husbands in the fields, kept house, tended gardens, and raised poultry. Marriage was viewed as an economic necessity, and the contributions of both spouses were valued because the work of each was geared toward the survival of the household as an economic unit. The coming of the Industrial Revolution, however, altered this delicate balance. In the United States, as citizens and immigrants flocked to cities, men entered nonagricultural occupations; most women stayed at home and provided essential but nonremunerative services: cooking, cleaning, and child rearing. For middle-class whites, the business world was perceived as a "dog-eat-dog" existence from which a dutiful husband was expected to protect his wife. Thus, from the colonial period to the time of the first woman's movement, a woman's proper role did not include obtaining an education or accepting any type of employment unless it was essential for her survival. White women who worked outside the home were often looked upon as inferior and put in a class with prostitutes or indentured servants.[1]

Some women, including widows, unmarried women, and women whose husbands could not earn enough to support the family, found it necessary to work outside the home. Many used their "womanly" skills and became domestics. In the South, slavery held women in bondage to their masters whether they worked in the house or in the fields. Many women, particularly in the Northeast, found work in the fledgling textile industry, which relied heavily on cheap (i.e., female) labor. By 1831, women held 80 percent of the jobs in New England's textile mills. By 1850, over 225,000 American women were employed in that industry.[2]

The Seneca Falls Convention and the Woman's Movement

As opportunities for men expanded, societal restrictions on women's opportunities increased. These limits caused the women at Seneca Falls to demand equal educational and employment opportunities on the principle "that the equality of human rights results necessarily from the fact of the identity of the race in capabilities and responsibilities."[3]

Women and Higher Education

The first schools of higher education for women were called female seminaries, best exemplified by Troy Seminary, founded in 1821 by Emma Hart Willard, and Mount Holyoke, chartered in 1836 by Mary Lyon.[a] These seminaries offered subjects ranging from the ancient languages to the sciences, mathematics, and history. Indeed, most seminaries offered courses roughly similar to those taught in men's colleges. After the 1850s, many seminaries were replaced by teacher training (normal) schools and public high schools, whereas others came to call themselves colleges.

The first real women's colleges were private: Vassar, founded in 1865, Wellesley and Smith, both chartered in 1875, and Bryn Mawr, begun in 1884. Their goal was to prepare women for their domestic responsibilities and for teaching. Gradually, some public coeducational colleges were developed or created as a result of pressure from women and their tax-paying parents.

Women did so well in college and their numbers grew so rapidly that some universities, most notably Stanford and the University of Chicago, began to limit, restrict, or segregate women students. One problem confronting women seeking education was the prevailing view that women would not be able to absorb an education without encountering physical harm: Until the late nineteenth century, many people believed women's brains were much smaller than men's and would burst if filled with too much learning. Another concern was the "desexing" of educated women. Women who graduated from college, it was argued, either would not marry or, if they did, would disobey their husbands and refuse to have children.

The late 1940s and early 1950s witnessed continued educational setbacks for women, as returning veterans crowded women out of some college slots. But the number of women in college continued to grow, and by the early 1980s women outnumbered men in institutions of higher learning.

[a]See Barbara Miller Solomon, *In the Company of Educated Women* (New Haven, Conn.: Yale University Press, 1985).

Although deeply concerned about the economic and educational plight of women, those active in the first woman's movement did little to solve those problems. They were increasingly more concerned with suffrage. Most improvements in this sphere, therefore, came as the result of the efforts of individual women with only limited help from others in the movement.

Efforts on Behalf of Working Women. Most jobs open to women in factories and in the textile industry required long hours of work at low pay in substandard conditions. Eleven- or twelve-hour workdays were not uncommon. Hours aside, females were paid less than their male counterparts universally. These depressed wages were the result of a variety of factors. Many men believed that women were inherently inferior and, consequently, their labor was worth less. Moreover, rigid societal values limited the number of jobs open to women, which made competition for even low-paid jobs keen. Even many women employed in the textile industry were not troubled by these inequities. They viewed their jobs as only short term and saw factory employment as an escape route from the farm until a suitable mate was found.

While most women who worked during this period were employed in factories, a limited number held "prestige" occupations. It was from this limited pool of educated women that the woman's movement most frequently drew support. Leaders in the woman's movement often were tutored at home. A few, like Susan B. Anthony, attended female seminaries where women were trained to teach. From the time of the Seneca Falls Convention, in fact, the movement was largely dependent upon these white, educated, middle-class women not only to serve as leaders but also to form the core of its strongest supporters. Few African American women or poor women had the time or energy or, in the case of slave women, the basic freedom to become involved in the movement.

Professionalization and Education. During the 1800s, several roadblocks were erected that affected even educated women's abilities to enter most professions. One noteworthy barrier came in the form of "professionalization"; that is, a college education or advanced training was required before one could attempt to practice certain professions. Since women were routinely denied admission to most colleges and medical and law schools, they had no opportunity to pursue certain careers. Additionally, state licensing of "prestige" professions, most notably law and medicine, was another barrier to women's employment opportunities.

As the number of public elementary and secondary schools increased in this period, the teaching profession opened up to women. Many people believed that women were naturally suited to teaching given "the greater intensity of the parental instinct in the female sex, their natural love of children, and the superior gentleness and forbearance of their dispositions."[4] Some argued that the more moral and religious nature of women made them better teachers of young minds than men.[5]

Financial considerations, however, constituted the most important factor for allowing women to teach. As the nation committed itself to universal public education (at least for whites), thousands of new teachers were needed. Men could not be counted on to fill these positions because of the numerous, more profitable opportunities open to them. Indeed, because women were expected to teach only until they married, their salaries were often only one-third to one-half of those paid to males. Pay differentials were even worse for African American teachers. When economics was combined with the rising number of young women who wanted to work, the result was the massive influx of women into the teaching profession. By 1880, women constituted 57.2 percent of all elementary school teachers.[6]

THE SUFFRAGE MOVEMENT

During the suffrage movement, demands for women's educational and employment rights failed to attract even the limited support offered by the woman's movement. Because of the movement's narrow focus and conservative ideology, only a few of the groups affiliated with the suffrage cause, most notably the National Woman's Party (NWP), continued to work for equal rights for women in every facet of life. Real progress in these areas during this period—indeed, until the 1960s and the rise of the women's rights movement—was accomplished either by individual women or those acting in small groups. As in the earlier movement, this tended to result in severe limits on educational and employment opportunities for all women. Additionally, at least some of the "progress" made during the suffrage era was regressive. Conservative views about women's roles resulted in legislation and court cases that often limited the occupational opportunities available to women.

The narrow focus of the suffrage movement and its more traditional views about women explain much of the difference between it and the woman's movement. Another important difference between the two movements was their respective attitudes toward blue-collar workers. Most suffragists wanted little to do with immigrants, the poor, or African American women who worked in factories (or fields) at the turn of the century. Some suffragists, associating the plight of working women with the rights of foreign-born or uneducated individuals, appeared ready to abandon a whole class of women workers in their new emphasis on educated suffrage (discussed in Chapter 1).

As the twentieth century approached, however, some women, particularly those allied with the growing progressive movement and not necessarily the National American Woman Suffrage Association (NAWSA), saw the need to address the problems of working women. Increasingly during the last decade of the nineteenth century, some middle-class women began to recognize that most employed women were not working for fun but rather to help support themselves and their families. In fact, 43 percent of African American women, 25 percent of immigrant women, and 15 percent of American-born white women were employed outside the home by 1900.[7] Reformers realized that if these women were going to be able to fulfill their paramount roles as mothers and homemakers, the terrible conditions under which they toiled outside the home would have to change.

The Women's Trade Union League (WTUL) was formed in 1903 to organize women laborers into units to bargain for shorter hours and better wages. Its membership was varied and included individuals from the working-class trade union movement and upper-middle-class women from the settlement house movement.[8]

From the very beginning, the WTUL was dedicated to the cause of woman suffrage along with its other goals. It had some early successes in organizing women workers, but after 1909 it increasingly devoted its efforts to securing protective legislation for women workers.[9] The WTUL did not play an active role in the suffrage cause until after 1912, however, when working-class women's potential usefulness was finally recognized by NAWSA leaders.[10]

The Drive for Protective Legislation

The second strategy to improve the status of working women—passage of protective legislation—was also the main goal of another middle-class reform group, the National Consumers' League (NCL). It was dedicated to the improvement of working conditions in retail shops and factories.[11] Most NCL members believed that a woman's proper role in life was to be a good wife and mother. They believed that working long hours was detrimental to women's health and their ability to care for their families. Through education, legislation, and litigation, the NCL sought to educate the consuming public about substandard conditions in many shops and factories. These concerns were vividly brought home to most Americans in 1911 by the Triangle Shirtwaist Company fire in downtown New York City. As flames trapped workers—mostly young, poor, immigrant women—forty-seven leaped from the upper floors of a tall sweatshop to their deaths. Ninety-nine others died inside behind locked doors that barred their escape.

The NCL's efforts resulted in the passage of several state laws for women. These laws limited the number of hours a day a woman could work in any one establishment. This legislation, however, soon was attacked by employers.[12]

Maximum Hour and Minimum Wage Laws. In 1907, an Oregon employer was convicted for violating an NCL-backed state law that prohibited women from working more than eight hours a day. The U.S. Supreme Court had recently ruled that a similar New York law regarding the hours of bakers was unconstitutional. Thus, the NCL's lawyer, Louis Brandeis (who later became the first Jewish U.S. Supreme Court justice), submitted a lengthy brief to the Court, containing statistics indicating the negative impact of long hours of work on a woman's health and her reproductive capabilities. In essence, Brandeis's arguments echoed the ideology of the suffrage movement. He argued that women had unique characteristics and therefore were in need of special protective labor legislation.

The Supreme Court was receptive to his arguments. In upholding the constitutionality of the Oregon statute, in *Muller v. Oregon* (1908), the Court noted:

> That woman's physical structure and the performance of maternal functions place her at a disadvantage in the struggle for subsistence is obvious. This is especially true when the burdens of motherhood are upon her. Even when they are not, by abundant testimony of the medical fraternity, continuance for a long time on her feet at work, repeating this from day to day, tends to injurious effects upon the body, and, as healthy mothers are essential to vigorous off-spring, the physical well-being of woman becomes an object of public interest and care in order to preserve the strength and vigor of the race. . . .
>
> . . . Even though all restrictions on political, personal, and contractual rights were taken away, and she stood, so far as statutes are concerned, upon an absolutely equal plane with him [man], it would still be true that she is so con-stituted that she will rest upon and look to him for protection; that her physical structure and a proper discharge of her maternal functions—having in view not merely her own health, but the well-being of the race—justify legislation to pro-tect her from the greed as well as the passion of men.[13]

Muller v. Oregon established the principle that women workers could be treated differently from their male counterparts under the law. NCL leaders saw this decision as helping women by remedying at least one evil—long hours. In actuality, however, many employers used this decision to justify not hiring women or treating women workers differently from men. In New York City, for example, hundreds of women typesetters lost their jobs at sev-eral local newspapers. Their employers claimed that they would be in viola-tion of the law if they forced the women to work long hours on the night shift. The irony of this action was that these were high-paying positions that most of the women desperately wanted to keep. Other available "female" jobs paid far less.

Wages were another concern of the NCL and other progressive organi-zations. Fearing that low wages forced some women into prostitution, these organizations believed that it was absolutely necessary to secure state mini-mum wage laws to protect a woman's virtue. Again, little thought was given to the possibility that employers would or could hire men at wages lower than the statutory minimum for women, thereby making it a matter of busi-ness sense for employers to replace their female workers with cheaper males.

The NCL successfully lobbied several state legislatures for the adoption of minimum wage laws. These laws, like the maximum hour provisions before them, soon encountered challenges in the courts.

The first major case was *Adkins v. Children's Hospital* (1923), which challenged the District of Columbia's "living wage" standard for women.[14] The NCL again defended the constitutionality of minimum wage protections in court. In sharp contrast, however, the National Woman's Party, which viewed protective legislation as inconsistent with its support of an equal rights amendment, filed a brief in opposition to the NCL's arguments. The Supreme Court appeared mindful of this division. It declared minimum wage laws for women unconstitutional, noting:

> But the ancient inequality of the sexes, otherwise than physical, as suggested in the *Muller* Case, has continued "with diminishing intensity." In view of the great—not to say revolutionary—changes which have taken place since that utterance, in the contractual, political, and civil status of women, culminating in the Nineteenth Amendment, it is not unreasonable to say that these differences have now come almost, if not quite, to the vanishing point.[15]

Adkins probably accelerated the disintegration of the fragile suffrage movement coalition by presenting a major issue upon which component women's groups could not agree.

Women and Work After Suffrage

After *Adkins*, women's working conditions in the United States largely remained the same, but the kinds of work women obtained changed considerably. By 1930, 30 percent of the employed women in the United States were engaged in nonmanual occupations—often as clerical workers. In fact, a particularly significant phenomenon occurred during this period—the colonization by women of the new white-collar clerical and sales jobs. From 1890 to 1920, the percentage of all working women who were employed in these fields rose from 5.3 to 25.6.[16] This change in the composition of the female work force had an impact on the NCL's fight for improved labor conditions. As the proportion of women working in factories and other occupations notorious for their hazardous conditions declined, it became much more difficult to get people to rally for improved conditions. Immigrant women who were employed as factory workers, domestics, and office clerks often feared losing their jobs and resisted attempts at organization.

Lack of organization, occupational segregation of women, and employer intimidation resulted in low wages for women when compared to men both overall and within occupational categories. Like poor immigrant women, African American women often suffered from low wages and substandard conditions and very limited job opportunities.

The Great Depression intensified women's problems. Most people believed that men, rather than married women, should get the few available jobs. Some employers adopted policies prohibiting the hiring of married women or calling for a woman's immediate discharge upon marriage. In fact, during the Great Depression, over half of the states had laws specifically barring the employment of married women in some occupations. For example, most public school systems had policies against hiring married women, and a majority fired women upon their marriage. Similar laws were adopted in many states and municipalities. Even the national government passed legislation that prohibited the employment of more than one family member from one household—a practice that had a far greater adverse impact on women than men.[17]

Education and the Professions

The percentage of women with college educations and advanced degrees rose dramatically, as revealed in Table 3–1. But this apparent progress was in many ways deceptive. The expansion of coeducation to most state colleges and many private schools was met with resistance by many college

TABLE 3–1 Women's College Attendance Rates (women as a percentage of total)

| Year | Degrees | | |
	Bachelor's	First-Professional	Doctorate
1869–1870	15	a	0
1879–1880	19	a	6
1889–1890	17	a	13
1899–1900	19	a	6
1909–1910	23	a	10
1919–1920	34	a	15
1929–1930	40	a	15
1939–1940	41	a	13
1949–1950	24	a	10
1959–1960	35	a	10
1969–1970	43	5	13
1979–1980	49	25	30
1989–1990	52	36	38
1994–1995	58	41	39

[a]For this year first-professional degree figures are included with bachelor's degrees.

Source: Figures derived from National Center for Education Statistics, *Digest of Education Statistics* (Washington, D.C.: U.S. Department of Education, 1992), 125, and *Degrees and Other Awards Conferred by Institutions of Higher Education: 1994–1995* (Washington, D.C.: U.S. Department of Education). http://www.ed.gov/NCES

administrators and faculty. Admission of women was often motivated by the economic need of schools needing students' tuition payments to survive and not by acceptance of the idea that women could and should receive a college education.

In keeping with prevailing stereotypes about women's mental abilities and "natural" propensities, women students, or coeds as they were called, were channeled into liberal arts and other "female" majors. Entire curricula were developed for near-exclusive study by women. Most notable of these were social work, education, library studies, and home economics. Because many people believed that a young woman's ultimate "career" was wife and mother, they also believed she should take college courses concerned with the proper running of a home (sewing, cooking, and child care). This philosophy was, of course, entirely in keeping with the dominant suffrage view that a woman should devote her full energies and abilities to being the best possible mother and wife.

As more women sought college entrance, coeducational institutions began to limit the number of female students. In 1925 American medical schools even adopted a 5 percent quota for female students (a standard that was to remain in effect until 1945). Moreover, few—40 out of 482—hospitals in the United States accepted women as interns.[18] Not surprisingly, the number of women doctors declined from a high point of 6 percent in 1910. Similarly, the position of women in law remained abysmal. Although by 1916 all states in the Union allowed women to practice law, many law schools denied admission to women, as did many professional legal associations.[19] Moreover, the few women who were physicians and lawyers were relegated to doing what their colleagues viewed as low-status "women's work." Female attorneys generally practiced in the areas of matrimonial law or wills and estates, while female doctors became obstetricians or pediatricians, not surgeons.

While the situation of women in "male" professions improved only marginally, the crowding of women into their "natural" professions continued unabated. Indeed, virtually all of the "progress" women made in the professions during the suffrage era (the percentage of women working as professionals in 1920 was close to 12 percent) can be attributed to the opening of several new "learned" occupations for women.[20] Nurses and teachers, in fact, made up 75 percent of all female professionals.[21] Other women became librarians, home economists, and social workers. Many of these women became leaders in the suffrage movement.

Thus, even though large numbers of white women went to college, their training gave them a perspective largely incompatible with the principle of equal rights. Accordingly, the major legal advances won during this period concerned the legalization of protective legislation—judicial recognition of the fact that women workers needed protection—and were not grounded in notions of equality sought by women in the first woman's movement.

WORLD WAR II

The onset of World War II and the activation of men into the military reversed the economic climate of the 1930s. With men off to war, the U.S. government undertook a massive campaign to recruit women into the paid labor force. This campaign brought about the abolition of many of the employment restrictions affecting women in the 1930s, and women moved into the labor force in large numbers. Between 1940 and 1945, the percentage of employed women rose from 26 to 36 percent. Perhaps the most important aspect of this increase was the rise in the number of married women who joined the labor force. Between 1940 and 1945, the percentage of married women who worked rose from 15 to 24 percent.[22] During the war years, 75 percent of the new women workers were married.

As most prewar discriminatory hiring policies were abandoned, women gained employment in a variety of situations formerly closed to them. They became welders, airplane pilots, and Wall Street analysts, for example.

Liberalization of federal government employment practices resulted in the hiring of thousands of women in jobs vacated by men. The number of female doctors grew as the shortage of male physicians and male students forced the national government, medical schools, and hospitals to relax their previous restrictive practices. One million women were hired as clerical workers by the U.S. government to handle the new bureaucracy brought about by the war.[23]

During World War II, the War Production Coordinating Committee commissioned this poster of "Rosie the Riveter" to encourage women to leave their homes, work in factories, and help the war effort.

The national government furthered this progress by endorsing in principle the idea of equal pay for equal work. Unions, too, began to treat women workers more fairly. After congressional passage of the National Industrial Recovery Act in 1933, which recognized labor's right to organize, some unions began to concentrate their energies on mass production industries. In the late 1930s, the Congress of Industrial Organizations began to organize unskilled workers and often had to appeal to women in the factories where unionization attempts were being made. According to Barbara Deckard, the number of union women grew from 800,000 in 1939 to more than three million by the end of the war in 1945.[24] Unionization and employer need for women workers resulted in a tremendous improvement in women's earnings.

World War II and the employment conditions it created brought about an expansion of economic opportunity that women, acting alone or in small groups, had previously been unable to produce. These new rights, however, were limited by the fact that the conditions that necessitated them were temporary. The kinds of permanent legal changes required to produce real equal opportunity were not undertaken. For example, the U.S. government failed to adopt a law requiring equal pay for equal work; it simply endorsed the idea. Many employers also ignored the equal pay provision or circumvented it by reclassifying jobs performed by women workers. Similarly, it continued to be legal for employers to refuse to hire older or married women. And there were no national legal prohibitions against flat refusals to employ women at all. Thus, many job classifications remained male or were only temporarily staffed by women until a more "appropriate" person—a man—could be hired. Union protection of female members also often lagged behind that afforded to men. Separate seniority lists for each sex, for example, were not illegal or uncommon.

After the war it surprised many employers as well as the U.S. government that the women wanted to stay on the job. Many women, however, lost their positions to returning veterans, who, by law, were given preference. Within two months after the end of World War II, almost 800,000 women lost their jobs in the aircraft industry alone.[25]

Many corporations quickly moved to reestablish prewar prohibitions against the employment of married women, fearing a postwar recession. Much of the protective legislation concerning the hours, conditions, and kinds of work women could do was reinstituted. These actions clearly reflected a concerted effort to encourage women to return to their homes, husbands, and children. Within a few short years after the veterans' return, however, large numbers of women reentered the work force but did so by taking traditional jobs at far lower pay than they had enjoyed during the war.[26] African American women generally stayed in the work force regardless of changing attitudes. Facing pervasive discrimination, their total family income was generally much lower than that of white families, virtually necessitating a two-income household.

The reentry of white women into the work force was a particularly interesting phenomenon given the "return to the home" ethos that characterized the postwar period. Although popular magazines proclaimed the benefits and rewards of suburban living and the homemaker role as a rewarding full-time occupation, many married women abandoned this "ideal" for the working world. According to Betty Friedan, while the editors of the *Ladies' Home Journal, McCall's,* and *Redbook* magazines created a "feminine mystique" by depicting women as "young, frivolous, almost childlike; fluffy and feminine; passive, gaily content in a world of bedroom and kitchen, sex, babies, and home,"[27] millions of "contented" housewives sought employment outside of the home—most out of financial necessity. In 1950, for example, for the first time in American history, married women constituted more than 50 percent of all women workers. Nearly 25 percent of them had school-age children—a dramatic change from the prewar period. These trends continued unabated into the early 1960s.[28]

Changes in the number and kind of working women, however, were not accompanied by an improvement in the economic conditions or rights of women. For the most part, women still were clustered into female jobs. Few held prestigious occupations, while the "professions" open to women— nursing and teaching—continued to be almost totally dominated by females. Additionally, as larger numbers of women sought work outside of the home, the concentration of women in certain fields tended to drive wages downward—at least in relation to those of men. From 1940 to 1960, the wage gap increased steadily largely due to the ghettoization of female employees in low-paying fields and the nonexistence of national equal pay legislation.

Education after World War II

Just as returning veterans reclaimed jobs from women, they also had an effect on the proportion of women in colleges and universities. From 1940 to 1950, the percentage of baccalaureate degrees awarded to women declined precipitously, as revealed previously in Table 3–1. Part of this dramatic change was a direct consequence of government policy. Even though women helped in the war effort, they did not receive G.I. benefits. Thus, large numbers of returning veterans—most of them male—were able to attend college financed by the federal government. Before 1940, most men and women who enrolled in postsecondary education were from middle-class or well-to-do families. After the war, because of the tuition and living assistance grants available to returning veterans, many men who formerly would have been unable to afford a college education could do so. Without similar benefits for women, even though they had supported the war effort in the only way they were allowed to (by statute women could not be drafted), a large number of women were priced out of a college education.[29] Women who could afford to attend a college or university often met a "veterans first" policy or the stringent kinds of quotas that had been utilized to exclude women before the war.

The women who attended college after the war continued to face discrimination. They were encouraged to major in "women's" fields, especially teaching, where the demand for workers was high. Few tried to obtain professional or higher academic degrees; those who did were often denied admission because of their sex. Additionally, continued curricular emphasis on the rewards of motherhood and marriage led large numbers of women to drop out of school to marry. Even those who graduated almost invariably married soon after and never sought employment.

By the early 1960s, even when women had equipped themselves with the tools necessary for a career, ghettoization and the continuing myths about why most women worked resulted in low wages compared to those of men—even when they did the same work. As late as 1960, it was estimated that a woman with a college degree could only expect to earn the same wages as a man who had completed the eighth grade![30]

THE WOMEN'S RIGHTS MOVEMENT

As the 1960s approached, some women recognized that gender-based discrimination existed in all spheres. Many of them campaigned for John F. Kennedy, who they believed would support legislation to expand women's rights. When his first major appointees were announced and only 2 out of 240 were women, his female supporters were outraged. To appease them and, some believe, to avoid the equal rights amendment question, Kennedy signed Executive Order 10980 on December 14, 1961, creating the President's Commission on the Status of Women. (Mary Anne Baker et al. suggest that Kennedy hoped the commission would find facts to be used against passage of an ERA.[31]) The mandate of the executive order was to analyze and recommend changes to end the "prejudices and outmoded customs that act as a barrier to full realization of women's basic rights." When the commission's report was made public in 1963, perhaps its most concrete recommendations concerned employment and labor standards.

In terms of employment rights and the creation of a women's rights movement, the commission's importance cannot be overstated. It was chaired by former First Lady Eleanor Roosevelt, who had extremely close ties to women active in the progressive movement. The commission brought women together for the first time since the 1930s. Its members were drawn largely from the ranks of business and professional women's clubs with limited representation from organized labor. These women soon formed the leadership nucleus of the women's rights movement.

In addition to providing the leadership of the fledgling movement, the commission gave women an agenda and publicized that agenda, which helped produce some governmental action. Examples of responses to commission recommendations include several executive orders and passage of the Equal Pay Act (EPA). Only one year after the commission issued its recommendations, the Civil Rights Act of 1964 also was enacted.

The Equal Pay Act

Prior to congressional passage of the Equal Pay Act of 1963, several efforts were made to secure such a law. During World War II, the Women's Bureau, a division within the Department of Labor devoted to the improvement of the state of working women, called for women to be paid equal pay for comparable work. In 1945, legislation calling for equal pay was actually introduced in the House of Representatives but never came to a vote. Although similar legislation was introduced during every subsequent session of Congress until 1963, without presidential backing, equal pay supporters were unsuccessful. Once Kennedy threw his support behind the proposed equal pay amendment to the Fair Labor Standards Act of 1938, it passed quickly.

The Equal Pay Act, however, did not pass in the form advocated by its staunchest supporters. It exempted several classes of workers, and instead of guaranteeing *equal* pay for *comparable* work, it required only that *equal* pay be had for *equal* work. It forbade an employer to "discriminate on the basis of sex by paying wages . . . to employees at a rate less than that which he pays . . . employees of the opposite sex . . . for equal work on jobs the performance of which requires equal skill, effort, and responsibilities, and which are performed under similar working conditions." The act also allowed for four exceptions: (1) if sex differences were part of a seniority system or training program, (2) if earnings were dependent on a merit system, (3) if earnings were dependent on the quantity or quality of production, or (4) if salaries were based on any factor other than sex.

Department of Labor Enforcement. Initially, the Equal Pay Act's greatest impact was on working-class women. In fact, it was not amended to cover administrative, executive, or professional employees until 1972. The Wage Standards Division of the Department of Labor (DOL) was empowered to bring suits on behalf of women who alleged violations of the law. In general, DOL was very successful in terms of attempting to bring about compliance with the act's provisions. Since the act allows a woman to file a complaint anonymously and, therefore, not fear employer retaliation, many complaints were filed and then thoroughly investigated by DOL. By 1973, more than $200 million in back pay awards were secured by the agency for aggrieved employees, most of them women.[32] In fact, from 1963 to 1979, when DOL was divested of its enforcement powers, although the Equal Pay Act's language is written in terms of equal pay for equal work, DOL was able to convince the courts to interpret this provision to require that work done must be only "substantially equal."[33]

On July 1, 1979, however, over the protest of many women's groups, Equal Pay Act enforcement was transferred to the Equal Employment Opportunity Commission (EEOC). (The EEOC initially was created by Congress to enforce the provisions of the Civil Rights Act of 1964.) This was done as part of President Jimmy Carter's reorganization plan to streamline government. The EEOC has never been a particularly effective enforcement agency, and compliance efforts have lagged.

From 1980 to 1992, during the Reagan and Bush administrations (and with Clarence Thomas heading the EEOC), awards dropped to less than $2 million a year in contrast to the $20 million a year won by the DOL. During the Clinton administration, the EEOC has done only slightly better. In 1995, for example, the EEOC won $2.8 million in awards for plaintiffs but resolved only 16.1 percent of the charges filed with it.[34]

Over the years, however, fewer and fewer employers have continued to pay male and female employees blatantly different wages for the same or similar work. Still, as discussed in Chapter 4, women's wages continue to lag behind those of men.

The Civil Rights Act of 1964

Members of the Commission on the Status of Women recognized that employment discrimination was rampant, yet their final report made no specific call for new antidiscrimination laws. Nevertheless, in 1964, Title VII of the Civil Rights Act, which prohibits discrimination based on race, color, religion, national origin, or *sex* in all terms, conditions, or privileges of employment, was enacted. Like the Equal Pay Act, it also includes an exception: Discrimination based on *sex*, religion, or national origin (*but* not race) is permissible if it is "a bona fide occupational qualification reasonably necessary to the normal operation of that particular business enterprise." The Equal Employment Opportunity Commission was created to enforce its provisions.

The inclusion of the "sex" prohibition in the Civil Rights Act originally was tacked onto the bill by a southerner to make a joke of the bill, divide supporters, and thereby lead to its defeat. Martha Griffiths (D-Mich.) initially intended to sponsor the addition. Upon hearing of a southerner's plan to include sex in the bill, however, she deferred to him. She believed that his sponsorship, no matter what his intentions, could swing some conservative votes needed to pass the entire bill.[35] Griffiths calculated correctly.

Enactment of this major tool to fight sex discrimination is interesting. Unlike the large number of women's groups that testified in favor of the Equal Pay Act, no organized women's groups spoke on its behalf, although Griffiths and other female representatives lined up solidly behind its passage.

EEOC Enforcement. Ironically, it was not the actions of existing women's rights groups, but instead the EEOC's nonenforcement of the Civil

Rights Act that provided the catalyst for the formation of the rights branch of the current women's movement. From the beginning, EEOC officials refused to take its sex discrimination provision seriously, noting the absence of legislative history on its sex clause and the mirth that it inspired when it reached the floor.[36] Repeatedly, the agency failed to investigate complaints of sex discrimination, which prompted Griffiths to attack the agency's inaction from the floor of the House of Representatives. Griffiths was not the only person concerned with EEOC negligence. Many women, frustrated by the EEOC's incompetence and the inability of the Commission on the Status of Women to force the EEOC to act, formed the National Organization for Women (NOW) in 1966. One of NOW's first goals was the eradication of sex discrimination in employment, but without EEOC support, it could do little.

Unlike DOL's vigorous enforcement of the Equal Pay Act, the EEOC's enforcement of the Civil Rights Act's sex discrimination clause was totally inadequate. NOW and several other women's rights groups took a number of actions to remedy this problem. First, throughout 1966 they put pressure on the EEOC to initiate the steps necessary to draft regulations to implement the act's ban on sex discrimination in employment.

Second, women put pressure on employers and the EEOC to follow the letter and spirit of the law. New York City NOW members, for example, picketed the *New York Times*'s offices to protest its maintenance of sex-segregated employment advertisements. Later, in December 1967, NOW held what Jo Freeman calls "perhaps the first contemporary feminist demonstration."[37] NOW members and others picketed EEOC offices around the country to draw attention to the agency's inaction. NOW also filed suit against the EEOC for failing to enforce Title VII. In Pittsburgh, in response to a complaint filed by NOW, the city's Commission on Human Relations brought suit against a local newspaper, the *Pittsburgh Press*. It claimed that the paper's publication of sex-segregated advertisements violated Title VII of the Civil Rights Act.[38]

Third, NOW and other women's groups also began to lobby Congress for passage of the Equal Employment Opportunity Act (EEOA). They believed that the EEOC needed powers to bring suit if discrimination was found after an investigation. Without additional legislation, all the EEOC could do was seek voluntary compliance. EEOA, as ultimately passed in 1972, also widened the coverage of the Civil Rights Act to include employers and unions with eight or more workers, employees of both the state and the federal government, and employees of educational institutions.

Finally, women's rights groups recognized that they would need to litigate to obtain employment rights. Civil Rights Act or Title VII litigation, as it is often called, involves complex issues of fact and the introduction of statistical information, particularly where a pattern and practice of discrimination is alleged. Most aggrieved women do not have the resources necessary to retain attorneys to handle their claims. Thus, many women's rights groups have been extensively involved in both counseling and representing women who claim employment discrimination. In fact, NOW's recognition that political pressure alone might not be sufficient to change the EEOC's inaction concerning sex discrimination complaints led it to form a legal arm to litigate alleged violations of both the Civil Rights and Equal Pay Acts. Shortly after NOW's creation, those unhappy with some of NOW's policies on more controversial issues formed other women's rights organizations concerned with employment and educational discrimination. All, however, agreed that it was imperative to force the EEOC to treat sex discrimination complaints seriously. Thus, other groups such as the Women's Equity Action League also took steps to form legal funds to finance sex discrimination employment litigation.

This strategy was entirely in keeping with the ideology of the emerging rights branch of the movement. Women sought changes in discriminatory practices, some of which would allow them to better pursue motherhood and a career. In keeping with this philosophy, women began to use conventional political and legal pressure to expand employment rights under Title VII by attacking several types of discriminatory practices.

BFOQs and Protective Legislation. One of the first actions taken by NOW was an effort to limit the scope of the bona fide occupational qualification (BFOQ) exception of Title VII of the Civil Rights Act of 1964, which allows employers to take sex into account when it is a BFOQ for a particular position. Examples of legal BFOQs include hiring only females as wet nurses or hiring only male actors to play Batman. Interpretation of this vague provision, however, led to controversy. Some argued that an expansive interpretation of the BFOQ provision would allow most protective legislation to remain on the law books, whereas a narrow one would have invalidated most of these laws.

As soon as the potential ramifications of a narrow interpretation of the BFOQ were realized, several groups, including the NCL, the Young Women's Christian Association (YWCA), and the American Association of University Women (AAUW), wrote to the director of the EEOC urging him to construe Title VII to allow "differential legislation" for females, noting that it had beneficial effects on their health and well-being.[39]

In contrast, representatives from the National Woman's Party and from the National Federation of Business and Professional Women's Clubs (BPW) and Representative Griffiths spoke in favor of a narrow construction of the BFOQ, which would necessitate an end to protective legislation for women. Additionally, NOW testified in opposition to state maximum hour laws and laws setting weight-lifting maximums or limiting night work. A NOW representative stressed the fact that many state laws operated to deprive women of jobs they desperately needed to support their families. These sentiments were in sharp contrast to those of the NCL and other more conservative groups. An NCL representative testified, "While men may also require protection from over-time hours, as a group their need is less than that of women, who usually spend more time on family and home responsibilities."[40]

Although there was conflicting testimony from women's rights groups concerning the desirability of protective legislation, the EEOC took two actions signaling its support for women's rights groups. First, in 1968, it submitted a friend of the court brief in a case originally sponsored by NOW, arguing that Title VII invalidated California's laws that prohibited women from lifting certain weights or working overtime. The federal district court adopted the EEOC's position. In 1971 it ruled that a California law (limiting women's work hours and the weights they were permitted to lift, which was cited by the railway as its reason for not hiring women as agent-telegraphers) was a violation of Title VII of the Civil Rights Act.[41]

Customer Preference or Business Necessity? After that decision, some employers tried to justify discriminatory employment practices by equating business necessity allowed under the BFOQ with "customer preference." For example, in spite of contrary urgings from women's groups, airline companies had long refused to hire men as flight attendants, citing customer preference. They argued that traditionally women were viewed as the more nurturing and comforting of the sexes, and should an emergency arise in the cabin, male passengers would reject handholding-type overtures from male attendants. Ultimately, the airlines' refusal to hire male attendants was found to be illegal.[42]

Second, the EEOC enacted guidelines that interpreted the BFOQ very narrowly, and women's rights groups continued to challenge any kind of "protective" legislation in the courts, which had been very receptive to their activities. In fact, on only one occasion has the U.S. Supreme Court relied on the BFOQ to justify an employer's refusal to hire women. In *Dothard v. Rawlinson* (1977), the Supreme Court upheld Alabama's refusal to hire women as prison guards in the state's correctional facilities.[43] There, the Court, however, narrowly construed BFOQ. In essence, the Court took notice that conditions in Alabama's dormitory-style prisons were so bad that really no one should work in them, but since someone had to, it was reasonable for the state to hire only males.

Comparable Worth. Another issue that has arisen under Title VII is that of comparable worth. While the Equal Pay Act has been construed as encouraging equal pay for similar work, authors of the act deny that they meant anything other than that. Nevertheless, many women's rights groups have advocated that women be given "equal" or "comparable" wages for "equivalent" or "comparable" work. Such demands involve reassessment of the way that jobs are evaluated and worth assigned in this country. Thus, level of skill, effort, and responsibility are key, *not* the job itself. For example, using a point system based on four factors—know-how, problem solving, accountability, and working conditions—one employee-benefits firm has compared nurses and "sanitation engineers," also known as garbage collectors.

	Nurse	Sanitation Engineer
Know-how	150	60
Problem solving	75	40
Accountability	175	165
Working conditions	50	185
Total	450	450

Thus, according to this plan, these employees should earn equal wages.[44]

Comparable worth gained attention in 1981 when the U.S. Supreme Court ruled that female workers could sue for discrimination under Title VII even if they were not performing the same jobs as men. In *County of Washington v. Gunther* (1981), a group of female prison guards, called matrons, earned lower wages and benefits than their male counterparts, known as deputy sheriffs.[45] Their jobs differed in that women were required to guard fewer prisoners and to perform clerical tasks. The Court ruled that they could sue even though the jobs were different.

Although the idea of comparable worth received a lot of attention in the 1970s and 1980s, it has received little attention of late. Given poor EEOC enforcement, some argue that new, national legislation to alleviate wage gaps is imperative.[46] To reduce continued pay inequities, the Fair Pay Act was introduced in Congress in 1994. It would prohibit discrimination in equivalent jobs but is unlikely to get far in a Republican-controlled Congress.

This approach is not likely to bring about a quick resolution to the problems of equity faced by women in employment. On April 11, 1996, President Clinton proclaimed National Pay Inequality Awareness Day, because that was the day "on which American women's wages for 1996, when added to their entire 1995 earnings, finally equal[ed] what men earned in 1995 alone."[47] While this shows some support for bringing parity to the workplace, as discussed in Chapter 4, equal pay and equal opportunities are far from realization.

Some progress, however, has been made at the state level. Some states have relatively weak pay equity laws for state employees. Still, those laws encourage employers to rethink their pay scales, and as a result, there has been some equalization of pay between women and men doing different jobs of comparable worth.[48]

Affirmative Action

Affirmative action programs attempt to remedy past discrimination against women, minorities, and others by increasing recruitment, promotion, retention, and on-the-job training opportunities and removing barriers to admission to educational institutions. Because there has been a long history of discrimination against women and African Americans in particular, most affirmative action programs are geared toward helping those two groups.

Title VII of the Civil Rights Act of 1964 and presidential Executive Order 11246, as amended by Executive Order 11375 in 1967, provided the initial basis for affirmative action toward women in employment in the United States. Title VII, as already noted, outlaws discrimination by employers or unions. Executive Order 11246, issued by President Lyndon Johnson in 1965, bars discrimination on the basis of race, color, religion, or national origin in federal employment and in employment by federal contractors and subcontractors. This order specifically required all executive agencies to "maintain a positive program of equal opportunities." The order also requires contractors to "take affirmative action to ensure that applicants are employed, and . . . treated during employment without regard to their race, creed, color, or national origin." In 1967, with the issuance of Executive Order 11375, this provision was expanded to include women. Somewhat reminiscent of the EEOC's failure to enforce Title VII, women's groups were unable to secure enforcement of this order until 1973. Title IX, discussed later, also provides the basis for affirmative action in education. It requires educational institutions receiving federal dollars to take "specific steps designed to encourage individuals of the previously excluded sex to apply."

In a series of cases decided in 1978–1980, the U.S. Supreme Court upheld the constitutionality of affirmative action plans, and in one case ruled that Title VII permitted a steelworkers' union and an employer to reserve one-half of all job openings in a training program for black workers. In 1987, in *Johnson v. Transportation Agency,* the Supreme Court relied on these earlier rulings to uphold an affirmative action plan that resulted in the promotion of a woman worker.[49]

In 1978, Santa Clara, California, adopted an affirmative action plan to remedy the effects of past practices and to attain a more equitable representation of women. Sex was to be considered as one factor in choosing among qualified job applicants in fields where women were traditionally underrepresented.

Diane Joyce and Paul Johnson were two of nine applicants who applied for a road dispatcher job, which was classified as a skilled craft position, a position no woman had ever held. Both had worked for the agency for several years and, in fact, had worked as dispatchers without the title or extra salary. After a personal interview in front of two superiors, Joyce and Johnson were rated 73 and 75, respectively. After a second round of interviews, Johnson was recommended for the job, but Joyce was hired after the agency's affirmative action coordinator intervened.

Johnson then filed a complaint with the EEOC, which refused to make a decision. The district court ruled for Johnson but was later reversed by the

U.S. Supreme Court; the Reagan Justice Department filed a brief urging the justices to side with Johnson and against affirmative action programs. Women's rights groups lined up on the side of Joyce. In March 1987, the Supreme Court upheld the plan, concluding that Title VII permitted discrimination to end discrimination—even in situations where no showing of past discrimination was made. According to the Court, it was appropriate for the agency to take note of the *total* absence of women from the skilled craft jobs and to use sex as a factor in the appointment process.

The six-person majority was not a strong one. Justice Sandra Day O'Connor, then the lone female on the bench, concurred only because she believed prior intentional discrimination had occurred. In subsequent affirmative action decisions, however, Justice O'Connor has not found intentional discrimination. In fact, a series of seven conservative decisions involving race and sex discrimination decided in 1988 and 1989 led to congressional passage of the Civil Rights Act of 1991 after extensive lobbying by a coalition of women's and civil rights organizations. It eased substantive and procedural requirements on employees seeking to prove discrimination. It also provided new remedies for victims of intentional employment discrimination, including sexual harassment.

In spite of this congressional action, affirmative action as we know it is on its last legs. In 1995, the Supreme Court issued a ruling calling more affirmative action programs into serious constitutional question.[50] The 1996 Republican platform specifically called for an end to all federal affirmative action programs, and the Republican-controlled Congress has vowed to roll back these programs.

Affirmative action is a particularly thorny legal issue for African American women and other women of color. Not only do they often experience discrimination based on their gender, they often suffer on account of race too. Proving discrimination then can become much more complex.

Challenges to Affirmative Action: California and Clinton

In November 1996, California voters overwhelmingly approved the controversial California Civil Rights Initiative (CCRI), popularly called Proposition 209, which seeks to bar state and local governments from using race- and gender-based preferences in education, contracting, and hiring. If enforced, it would end most, if not all, of the state's affirmative action programs, from university admissions to contracting set-asides to recruitment. It would also end programs such as girls-only math classes.

A day after the measure passed, a group of civil rights organizations sued in federal court to prevent its enforcement. A federal district court judge stayed enforcement of the CCRI, finding that it prevented women and minorities from redressing government for discrimination, whereas other groups complaining of discrimination based on age, disability, or veteran status, continued to have access to the political process at all levels.[a] This decision will, in all likelihood, eventually end up before the U.S. Supreme Court.

Considerable controversy exists concerning how the CCRI will affect women. Clause C is particularly controversial. It specifies that "Nothing in this clause shall be interpreted as prohibiting bona fide qualifications based on sex which are reasonably necessary." Critics say that this provision not only lowers the standard of review from the current one, which says that the state cannot discriminate against women unless there is a "compelling need," but also that it will allow employers to ask female job applicants if they are married or have children, questions now illegal under federal law.[b] Others charge that CCRI would make it legal for employers to "reject women for firefighting positions or to shut down girls' sports teams at schools."[c]

The Clinton administration actively opposed Proposition 209 to little avail. And in 1997, a federal court of appeals ruled that the CCRI was constitutional, lifting a lower federal judge's stay of its enforcement.[d]

[a]Quoted in Reynolds Holding, "Judge Blocks Proposition 209," *San Francisco Chronicle,* November 28, 1996, A1.

[b]Marilyn Kalfus, "Focus on Politics: Proposition 209," *Orange County Register,* October 19, 1996, A18.

[c]Edward W. Lempinen, "Debate Over CCRI Effect on Women," *San Francisco Chronicle,* September 10, 1996, A1.

[d]"Prop. 209—Still Questions," *Christian Science Monitor,* April 14, 1997.

Sexual Harassment. Discrimination clearly continues to exist in the work force. Of late, however, the issue of sexual harassment in the workplace has garnered more attention than other forms of discrimination.

In some instances, sexual requirements have been placed on women workers as conditions for job retention, advancement, or salary raises. Other less flagrant forms of sexual harassment include verbal abuse, sexist remarks or "jokes," and offensive touching, patting, and leering. This kind of treatment makes working conditions difficult for women, causing them a tremendous amount of stress. Harassment often leads victims to seek other positions, thereby causing them to lose seniority and other accrued benefits. Problems of sexual harassment have not been confined to the working world either. In fact, the Legal Defense and Education Fund of the National Organization for Women established a special Sexual Harassment in Education Project to provide legal assistance for students and faculty members who find themselves victims of harassment.

Women, Sexual Harassment, and the Military

Today, women are an integral part of the military in the United States. As the size of the military decreases, the percentage of women in the military continues to rise. One-fifth of all recruits are now women, as is 13 percent of the armed forces; and the pressure is now on the military to treat women on an equal footing. Still, as the navy's 1991 Tailhook incident (when several navy and civilian women were accosted in a convention hotel hallway by male pilots) and the 1996 sexual harassment scandal at the Aberdeen Proving Ground in Maryland indicate, women are far from receiving equal treatment in the military. A survey released by the Pentagon in 1996, for example, revealed that 55 percent of the 50,000 women who responded believed that they had experienced sexual harassment in 1995.[a] The Marine Corps had the highest rate—64 percent. Ironically, the navy had the best rate, with 53 percent of the women there reporting some kind of sexual harassment.[b]

All branches of the services are trying to end sexual harassment, not just because it's wrong, but because the new army, for example, needs all of the women it can get. "If a secret blast went off right now, killing all the women, the army would cease to function," says a spokesperson for its personnel branch.[c] In 1994, the Pentagon opened up all positions to women except those in "direct combat."[d] Some argue that this has added to the confusion over women's role in the military, as women "can now participate in roles that seem to be in combat in everything but name."[e] Conservatives on the House National Security Committee argue that the army "has been naive in training women and men in the same boot camps, and in widening jobs open to women including flying combat jets and serving on warships."[f] In spite of these criticisms, the army continues to recruit women; at the same time it is instituting new procedures to handle sexual harassment complaints. The navy, too, has taken a more positive role in heading off sexual harassment. Training teams were sent to every base to teach personnel about sexual harassment and how to report allegations of abuse. It is likely that change will be a long time in coming, however. Only ten years ago, Marine Corps instructors led training exercises with chants such as "Five, six, seven, eight, rape, kill, mutilate."[g]

[a]Elizabeth Gleick, "Scandal in the Military," *Time,* November 25, 1996, 28.

[b]Genevieve Anton and Kelly Pearce, "Military Opening Its Eyes to Sexual Harassment," *Times-Picayune,* December 1, 1996, A15.

[c]Steven Komarow, "Army Wants More Than a Few Good Women," *USA Today,* March 11, 1997, 5A.

[d]Nolan Walters, "Women's Role in the Military Confuses Both Sexes," *Atlanta Journal,* December 8, 1996, A10.

[e]Ibid.

[f]Ibid.

[g]Linda Borg, "Tailhook Launched a Tidal Wave of Change for Women in Navy," *Houston Chronicle,* December 1, 1996, A23.

Public awareness of sexual harassment has evolved slowly. In the late 1970s, radical feminist scholar Catharine A. MacKinnon began to advance the idea that sexual harassment was employment discrimination actionable under Title VII.[51] In November 1980, at the urging of several women's rights groups, the EEOC adopted regulations making sexual harassment an impermissible form of sex discrimination prohibited by Title VII.

When more hearings were held on these guidelines in spring 1981, Phyllis Schlafly, head of the Eagle Forum, testified in opposition. She argued that harassment "is not a problem" and that only those who "ask for it" actually find themselves victims. And she asked commission members to rescind the regulations as inconsistent with Title VII.

Schlafly's comments surprised and angered many. Clearly, stringent regulations could be threatening to some men who harass women, but women had little to lose from the regulations. In fact, for conservative women, the regulations guarantee that women have recourse against inappropriate conduct; for women's rights supporters, they provide legal recourse for discriminatory conduct that has a pervasive impact on the employment status of many women.

In 1985, Congress finally codified sexual harassment as a form of discrimination prohibited under Title VII. Basically, two versions of harassment were made illegal: (1) the "quid pro quo" version in which employment terms and benefits are based on or are conditional on sexual favors, and (2) the offensive or hostile work environment that results from harassment, which does not necessarily involve salary or other job benefits.

Meritor Savings Bank v. Vinson (1986) was the first sexual harassment case to reach the U.S. Supreme Court.[52] A unanimous Court found that a bank manager's repeated demands for sexual favors created a "hostile environment" actionable under Title VII. Moreover, such sexual harassment is illegal not only when it results in the loss of a job or a promotion, but also when it creates a hostile work environment.

In spite of *Meritor*, the EEOC was not deluged with complaints. In 1987, the first year the EEOC kept records of complaints, only 5,499 complaints of sexual harassment were filed. In fact, a 1989 *Forbes* magazine article suggested that management consultants were blowing the problem out of proportion. Based on EEOC complaints, *Forbes* estimated that victims of harassment constituted only 0.0091 percent of the female work force,[53] but the magazine did not mention that many women victims are reluctant to complain.

Still, it wasn't until 1991, when the nation sat riveted before television sets during the Clarence Thomas confirmation hearings, that sexual harassment as an issue began to get a significant amount of media attention. The issue was debated not only all over Washington, D.C., but also in businesses, lunchrooms, and living rooms all over America. More women began to report harassment, and employers began to appear more sensitive to the problem. The EEOC, for example, reported that sexual harassment complaints went up 70 percent the year after the Thomas hearings, and 150 percent by the end of 1995.

The number of sexual harassment complaints filed annually continues to rise in the wake of the U.S. Supreme Court's 1993 decision, *Harris v. Forklift Systems*.[54] In *Harris*, the company supervisor admitted asking female employees to fish for coins in his front pants pockets, commenting on the size of a female employee's breasts and buttocks, and suggesting to one woman that they go to a hotel to negotiate her raise. The lower court did not think that this kind of behavior, which forced Teresa Harris to quit her job, was enough to be called sexual harassment actionable under law. A unanimous U.S. Supreme Court disagreed, concluding that for harassment to be actionable, the conduct in question need not "seriously affect [an employee's] psychological well-being" or lead the plaintiff to suffer an injury.[55]

EEOC Enforcement of the Equal Pay Act and Title VII of the Civil Rights Act

During the Reagan and Bush administrations, enforcement personnel and funding for the EEOC were slashed. Says Eleanor Holmes Norton, head of the EEOC during the Carter administration, "The EEOC was destroyed both operationally and legally."[56] But even with a sympathetic Democratic president, EEOC enforcement of the Equal Pay Act as well as the Civil Rights Act of 1964 has been lax. The chair of the EEOC notes several reasons for his agency's failures, including (1) the anti-affirmative environment of the courts, (2) a hostile Republican Congress that keeps slashing the EEOC's budget, and (3) a skyrocketing caseload caused by the agency's expanding statutory responsibilities as well as increased awareness of discrimination.[57] Public attitudes toward government, government regulation, and affirmative action don't make the EEOC's job any easier either. Still, in an effort to reduce its backlog of over 100,000 cases, the EEOC adopted a National Enforcement Plan in 1996 to help it better manage its responsibilities. To eliminate discrimination in the workplace, the agency now tries (1) prevention through education; (2) voluntary resolution of complaints; and (3) only when voluntary resolution fails, strong enforcement.[58]

Testing the Limits: The EEOC Backs Down

On November 15, 1995, Hooters of America, Inc., operators of 172 restaurants in thirty-seven states, launched an unprecedented media blitz to try to dissuade the federal Equal Employment Opportunity Commission (EEOC) from forcing it to hire "Hooters guys" to work with its "Hooters girls" in its restaurant chain. To publicize its case, the restaurant chain took out full-page ads in newspapers across the nation attempting to capitalize on the country's anti-Washington, anti-big-government, anti-unnecessary-governmental-intervention attitude by making fun of Washington and the EEOC, charging that the EEOC's investigation of its hiring practices was a waste of taxpayer monies. It also held a rally a few blocks from the U.S. Capitol complete with two dozen of its trademark scantily clad waitresses.

What caused Hooters to protest the EEOC's actions? After several men around the country applied for and then were denied jobs at Hooters, they filed complaints with the EEOC, which investigated Hooters for four years. (Persons who believe that they have been discriminated against can file a complaint with an EEOC field office, which then investigates their complaint. If the investigation establishes that there is reasonable cause to believe that the complaint is true, the agency first tries to mediate between the employee and employer. If that fails, the EEOC has the authority to file a lawsuit in federal court seeking to remedy the discriminatory treatment.)

In September 1994, the EEOC ruled that Hooters violated the Civil Rights Act of 1964 by failing to hire any men to act as servers in its restaurants. Hooters rejected the EEOC's settlement offer, which called for the chain to hire men and to put $22 million into a fund to pay male victims of its females-only hiring policy. The EEOC also wanted Hooters to conduct sensitivity training to combat sex discrimination in its restaurants.

Hooters contended, much like the airlines industry did when it tried to keep its all-female flight attendant policies, that federal law allows some gender-based hiring and that its customers want young attractive female servers. Hooters, which spent more than $2 million in legal fees and for its media blitz, countered that it was prepared to spend up to $10 million to keep its all-female staff. "There's a time when governmental intervention goes too far, and this is a perfect illustration of good intentions that have gone haywire," said Hooters vice president of marketing, Mike McNeil.[a] In response, Marcia Greenberger, copresident of the National Women's Law Center, characterized the Hooters publicity campaign as a "serious mischaracterization" of the facts and a "trivialization" of equal employment laws. "From our perspective," Greenberger said, "it's illegal for a restaurant to say it's only going to hire young, slim women that fit a particular stereotype."[b] Hooters's unprecedented media blitz triumphed in the end. In May 1996, the EEOC quietly dropped the case and said that it won't intervene in the class action sex discrimination lawsuit filed by several men. Nevertheless, in late 1997, Hooters agreed to begin to hire men in order to settle the men's suit.

[a]This paragraph draws heavily on William Claiborne, "Suit to Test Police Interrogations," *Washington Post*, December 30, 1995, A3.
[b]Ibid.

Employment Discrimination and the Consequences of Childbearing

Although the Equal Pay Act and Title VII of the Civil Rights Act are designed to remedy discrimination, from the beginning, the fact that only women bear children has had major consequences on their status in the work force.

Employers have tried to use a variety of tactics to penalize women who opt to have children.

Pregnancy Discrimination. Beginning in the 1970s and continuing today, many forms of pregnancy discrimination—including forced leave, loss of seniority, lack of medical coverage, and outright dismissal—have been challenged by women's rights groups. In a list of demands made at its first conference, NOW listed paid maternity leaves, laws to allow women to return to their jobs with no loss of seniority, and child-care centers. When NOW first decided to target pregnancy discrimination in employment, however, some women, including many in the Women's Equity Action League (WEAL), voiced their concern that the new group should focus its energies on less controversial issues.

The first real schism over how to deal with pregnancy discrimination occurred when the Women's Law Fund (WLF) was founded by some WEAL leaders who disagreed over WEAL's involvement in *Cleveland Board of Education v. LaFleur* (1974), a case challenging the automatic dismissal of school-teachers in their fourth month of pregnancy.[59] WEAL thought that pregnancy discrimination was too controversial to tackle. Nevertheless, both NOW and the ACLU's Women's Rights Project (WRP) filed friend of the court briefs to support the arguments made by WLF, which ultimately sponsored the case. In *LaFleur*, the Supreme Court ruled that it was unconstitutional for the school board to require pregnant women to take unpaid leaves five months before their due dates and prohibit them from returning to the classroom until the semester after their children were three months old.

LaFleur constituted an important victory for women's rights groups, but the Court failed to address whether employers should treat pregnancy like other medical conditions and not as one unique to women. In 1972, based on recommendations of the Citizens Advisory Council on the Status of Women (the new name of the President's Commission on the Status of Women) and women's rights groups, the EEOC adopted regulations that specifically rejected the "pregnancy is unique" argument. But in *Geduldig v. Aiello* (1974), a case challenging California's refusal to pay pregnancy disability benefits to women workers, the justices upheld the constitutionality of a plan that established a medical benefits fund for all workers but excluded any coverage for pregnancy, including normal hospital stays.[60] The justices found that the plan was a reasonable way for the state to limit expenses and that there was "no evidence in the record that the selection of the risks insured by the program worked to discriminate against any identifiable group or class in terms of the aggregate risk protection." Although *Geduldig* was a major loss for the women's rights groups involved, most commentators believed that this decision was grounded not in constitutional theory, but in economic realities—the California plan simply had not been set up to handle these additional claims. Prior to *Geduldig*, in two major cases, *Reed v. Reed* (1971) and *Frontiero v. Richardson* (1973) (see Chapter 1), the Supreme

Court struck down laws that treated women differently from men, holding that certain kinds of sex discrimination were prohibited by the Fourteenth Amendment. Because only women get pregnant, the justices found no sex discrimination in *Geduldig.*

Successes of women's rights organizations in litigating *Reed, Frontiero,* and *LaFleur* lulled attorneys into believing that the Court was willing to expand the protections of the Fourteenth Amendment to prohibit a wide variety of gender-based discriminatory practices. As *Geduldig* proved, however, this was not to be the case. Thus, given the Court's opinion in *Geduldig,* feminist lawyers turned to Title VII for possible relief against on-the-job pregnancy discrimination by private employers.

The first test of this strategy came in *General Electric Co. v. Gilbert* (1976).[61] Unlike the situation in *Geduldig,* in which a judicial finding of discrimination might have bankrupted the state's disability system, *Gilbert* involved a private employer's plan that contained a maternity exclusion clause similar to California's. Because *Gilbert* was styled as a Title VII class action lawsuit and involved only one, albeit large, company, many court observers believed that the justices would find in favor of the pregnancy discrimination claim. However, in rejecting the arguments put forth by Gilbert's lawyers that a penalty on the birth process was inherently discriminatory, the Court disregarded EEOC guidelines that interpreted such programs as discriminatory. It also found no Title VII violation, because there was *no* showing of employer discrimination. Writing for the Court, Justice William Rehnquist adopted the reasoning of the lower court, which had concluded that pregnancy "is not a disease at all and is often a voluntarily undertaken and desired condition."

Women's rights activists were outraged by the *Gilbert* decision and the justices' cavalier attitude toward pregnancy. In droves they descended on Congress to urge passage of an amendment to Title VII to ban discrimination based on pregnancy.[62] Their efforts resulted in passage of the Pregnancy Discrimination Act (PDA) of 1978 as an amendment to the Civil Rights Act of 1964. It requires employers to treat pregnancy like any other physical condition.

Not surprisingly, the legislation drew strong opposition from employer groups. In contrast, it was an issue that united women's groups on *both* sides of the ERA controversy. Most women agreed that pregnant women should be entitled to the same benefits as their male counterparts. Women's rights activists believed that the PDA would allow women with children greater career and childbirth options. The Eagle Forum and many conservative women, moreover, believed that the absence of such legislation encouraged abortion. Although the PDA provided a public good, it was not particularly threatening to women. Thus, the absence of opposition from conservative women is not surprising; there is nothing in the law that requires women to work. It simply allows those who wish to work not to be penalized for motherhood—a right strongly advocated by both pro- and anti-ERA camps.

The Difference Debate. As political scientist Judith A. Baer has noted, "amending the civil rights law has not settled all the difficulties involved, because pregnancy and childbirth are more than physical conditions."[63] Pregnancy makes some women ill, especially in the first trimester when nausea and fatigue are common. Most women also require some time to recuperate from childbirth. Indeed, a 1993 study concluded that some women take up to a year to recuperate fully from pregnancy.[64] Moreover, pregnancy is a condition unique to women.

Although the PDA requires employers to treat women and men *equally*, some states have opted to require employers to provide "extra" protection or benefits to pregnant workers. A California law passed in 1978, for example, *requires* employers to give employees up to four months of "pregnancy disability leave." But when Lillian Garland attempted to return to her receptionist's position at a California bank, she was told she had no job. She filed a complaint against the bank with the State Department of Fair Employment and Housing. Her employer argued that the California law was in conflict with and was preempted by the PDA because the California law discriminated *in favor of* pregnant workers. The department found in favor of Garland, and her employer filed suit in federal court. The director of the Department of Fair Employment and Housing, Mark Guerra, acted on her behalf in court.

By the time *California Federal Savings and Loan Association v. Guerra* (1987)[65] reached the U.S. Supreme Court, women's rights advocates were weighing in on both sides of the issue, which resulted in a situation that closely paralleled the early split among suffragists over the NWP's support of an ERA and the division that occurred in *Adkins v. Children's Hospital* (1923), described earlier in this chapter. NOW and the ACLU's WRP filed an amicus curiae (friend of the court) brief on behalf of the bank. They argued that application of a policy to women alone (Cal Federal did not guarantee jobs to men who returned from medical leave) would "reinforce stereotypes about women's inclinations and abilities" and "deter employers from hiring women of childbearing age."[66] Other feminists including Equal Rights Advocates, a California-based public interest law group, argued that this position denied the reality that women alone bear children; that difference, they argued, must be acknowledged.[67]

The Supreme Court never really addressed the debate over equality versus protection. Instead it concluded that the Pregnancy Discrimination Act was only a floor below which states could not go in treating pregnant workers. Writing for the Court, Justice Thurgood Marshall noted that the purpose of the 1978 act was "to guarantee women the right to participate fully and equally in the work force, without denying them the fundamental right to full participation in family life." Thus, although Garland had already been rehired by the bank, the decision put employers on notice that pregnancy discrimination would not be tolerated.

The Family and Medical Leave Act. The difference debate was also evident in early attempts to guarantee family and medical leaves for women workers. Representative Howard Berman (D-Calif.), who wrote the California pregnancy disability legislation at issue in the *Cal Federal* case, introduced similar legislation in Congress after Lillian Garland lost in the lower court. Women active in NOW, the Women's Legal Defense Fund (WLDF), the National Women's Political Caucus (NWPC), and the AAUW refused to support Berman's legislation (as they had in *Cal Federal*) because they were uncomfortable with his description of pregnancy as a disability.[68] They then persuaded Berman that parental leave for mothers *and* fathers would be more likely to garner wide support.

Representative Patricia Schroeder (D-Colo.), the cochair of the Congressional Caucus on Women's Issues, soon took up a leadership role on the parental leave bill. She liked the legislation because "it challenged the commitment of conservative family proponents head on while not doing harm to women's rights."[69] Schroeder reasoned that anyone interested in helping families would favor allowing a parent time off to care for a sick child.

The AAUW, ACLU, BPW, NOW, NWPC, WEAL, WLDF, and several labor unions supported the proposed legislation when it was first introduced in the House in 1985. Opposed were the Chamber of Commerce of the United States and the Reagan White House. The legislation soon got caught up in controversial welfare and child-care reform legislation as it was changed and amended. Finally, a watered-down version of the Family and Medical Leave bill passed in May 1990 but was vetoed by President Bush. Even though polls showed Americans were ready to accept maternity leave, the notion of paternity leave was harder to sell. Gender roles, as discussed in Chapter 4, die hard; and with a president in the White House who was hostile to the idea, supporters held little hope.

Child Care: An Obstacle to Equal Employment Opportunity?

In 1992, when asked what was the greatest problem facing them at work, women ranked "combining work and family" at the top.[a] Not only do a majority of all mothers work, over two-thirds of the employed mothers with children under age six work full time. Lack of adequate child care can be a particularly large obstacle to work for poor women, especially those who head their households.

In 1990, the National Child Care Study found that two-thirds of employed mothers used some form of nonparent child-care arrangement other than school. Day-care options most commonly included child-care centers, family day-care homes, and nonparental relatives. In-home care by unrelated providers was not an economically feasible option for most.

Over time, child-care arrangements have changed dramatically. In 1965, for example, only 6 percent of parents used day-care centers for young children; by 1990 that proportion had risen to 28 percent.

The high cost and lack of availability of quality child care often impede a woman's performance and advancement on the job. Even when women think they have made adequate arrangements, if a child or caregiver gets sick, these arrangements can fall apart quickly. Because women in traditional families often are the ones who then stay home when emergencies arise, employers often view them as less committed than their male counterparts.

On the national level, women's rights organizations have recognized this and lobbied hard for federal legislation to create new programs to make quality care accessible for more women. On most fronts, however, they have fierce opposition from the Eagle Forum and Concerned Women for America, which oppose the federal government's involvement in regulation of child care as unnecessary governmental intrusion into the family. In 1990, however, after a two-decade-long effort, Congress created the Child Care and Development Block Grant Program, which provides money to states for child-care programs. Most of this is to be used for the neediest families. Low-income parents, for whom the cost of day care probably hits the hardest, still need further relief. They do get a Dependent Care Tax Credit, but it covers only 30 percent of the cost of child-care expenses.

[a]Much of the information contained here is derived from the Children's Defense Fund, Child Care Section, "Child Care: Key Facts," updated September 1992. Washington, D.C.

The 1992 election of Bill Clinton, who had attacked Bush's veto of the Family and Medical Leave Act, changed the scenario. Congress quickly passed the act in 1993, and Clinton signed it into law with considerable fanfare, noting that it was "a matter of pure common sense and a matter of common decency."[70]

The act gives workers at companies of more than fifty persons the right to take up to twelve weeks of unpaid leave to care for a new baby or to help a family member with a serious health problem. On returning from leave, workers must be given their old job or its equivalent. The highest-paid 10 percent of employees at each company are not fully protected. These "key" employees can lose their jobs if employers can prove their reinstatement would cause "substantial and grievous" harm.

Since the act was passed, twelve million workers (through June 1996) took advantage of its leave provision. Moreover, more than 85 percent of the businesses covered by the act "found that it neither adds to the cost nor takes away from their profits." Forty percent of all workers polled believe that they will take leave under the act in the next five years.

In 1997, President Clinton proposed expanding the act to cover family obligations. Specifically, he requested Congress (and employers) to allow workers to take up to twenty-four hours of annual leave to attend parent-teacher conferences and to accompany a child, spouse, or elderly parent for routine medical and dental care.[71]

Department of Labor Enforcement of the Family and Medical Leave Act.
Congress charged the Department of Labor with enforcing the Family and Medical Leave Act. In 1994, 1,422 complaints were filed under the act; in 1995, DOL reported complaints increased by 53 percent to 2,179.[72] Donna Lenhoff of the Women's Legal Defense Fund, who also is the vice chair of the Commission on Family and Medical Leave, attributes this increase to the "ever increasing" number of employers and employees aware of the law.[73] Just as important, DOL enjoys a very high success rate (as it did when it was responsible for enforcing the Equal Pay Act), and "the vast majority of the complaints in which violations were found were resolved successfully."[74]

Reproductive Hazards and Fetal Protection Policies.
The fact that women have children has also been the basis for employer "fetal protection" policies that bar only women of childbearing age from certain jobs. Upon reaching her fiftieth birthday, Virginia Green considered herself done with childbearing, but her employer, Johnson Controls Inc. of Bennington, Vermont, apparently disagreed. The maker of automotive batteries demoted Green from her job as a lead plate stacker to a lower-paying one in the laundry for fear that lead in her blood (absorbed from the batteries) would pose a risk to any fetus she might conceive.

Eight years later the U.S. Supreme Court finally addressed her demotion and that of three of her female coworkers when it decided its first fetal protection case. Green's lawyers argued that the company's policy resulted in discrimination barred by Title VII. While Johnson Controls argued that its mandatory fetal protection policy was a bona fide occupational qualification permissible under Title VII, the Supreme Court disagreed. In a landmark sex discrimination employment case, the justices ruled that women could not be forced to choose between having a job and having children and that the roles of mother and employee are not mutually exclusive.

Initially, women's rights activists, although unanimous in their agreement that fetal protection policies were illegal, feared that the Court might opt to uphold these policies by construing the BFOQ exception liberally. But in *Automobile Workers v. Johnson Controls* (1991), a unanimous Court protected the rights of millions of workers for whom compulsory sterilization could have been made a legal term and condition of employment by ruling that fetal protection policies affecting women workers violate Title VII.[75] Groups on both sides of the pregnancy litigation in *Cal Federal* supported the decision, as did conservative women's groups who viewed the company's fetal protection policy as encouraging abortion.

Education

Women have suffered from unequal treatment in education as far back as records have been kept. In the 1960s, women, particularly those in the older branch of the women's rights movement, immediately recognized inequalities in the educational system, their impact on employment opportunities, and the need for concerted action to improve conditions. While many younger-branch women were instrumental in founding women's studies programs, older-branch women pushed for laws to end discrimination. And, even before the rise of the older, rights-oriented branch, the National Federation of Business and Professional Women's Clubs long urged abolition of quotas for women in schools (which were used to limit women's access) and actively encouraged women to go back to school. President Kennedy's Commission on the Status of Women even urged government support of continuing education for homemakers. But although commission members recommended "imaginative counseling, which [could] lift aspirations beyond stubbornly persistent assumptions about women's roles and women's interest,"[76] their comments clearly reflected the view that a woman's primary role was motherhood. Instead of criticizing the emphasis many colleges placed on home economics, for example, the commission bemoaned the fact that "even women's colleges have given remarkably little serious thought to the better preparation of their students for the homemaking most of them will do."[77]

NOW and later WEAL, however, soon began to call for educational equality for women, as did the few women in the U.S. Congress. Noting, in 1967, that the near absence of women in high-paying, prestige professions and in leadership positions was often a function of limited educational opportunities for women, NOW called for passage of federal and state legislation to ensure that women "be educated to their full potential."[78]

Title IX and the Constitution. Concern for a woman's right to achieve her full educational potential was a key element in the support that women's rights organizations gave to educational equity legislation. In 1970, with the full support of a wide variety of women's groups, Representative Edith Green (D-Oreg.) held hearings that revealed extensive discrimination against women in the nation's schools. Two years later, when Green and Representative Patsy Mink (D-Hawaii), the first Japanese American woman elected to Congress, consequently introduced Title IX as part of the Educational Amendments Act of 1972, they asked women's groups not to testify for the bill, believing chances of passage would be greatly enhanced if less attention were given to its provisions. No women's groups testified, and Title IX was voted into law. As enacted, Title IX prohibits sex discrimination in any elementary, secondary, or postsecondary school if the institution is the recipient of any federal monies. It also extended coverage of Title VII and the Equal

Pay Act to educational workers and authorized the U.S. attorney general to instigate lawsuits against educational institutions that fail to comply. The law itself is fairly simple; most of the controversy over it has occurred in the drafting of regulations and enforcement stages.[79]

Drafting regulations to implement Title IX became a battleground for conservative versus liberal women's groups' agendas. When regulations were finally adopted they prohibited gender bias in three major areas: (1) admissions, (2) student treatment, and (3) hiring and personnel practices.

Admissions. Title IX and its implementing regulations do not outlaw single-sex schools. They simply prevent public institutions that already receive federal money from becoming single-sex institutions. Historically, single-sex education has produced division even among women who advocate full educational equality. According to a 1973 Carnegie Commission report, "various studies have shown that women who attend women's colleges have academic records superior to those of their coeducational sisters, on the basis of such measures as persistence, proportion going on to graduate education, and the proportion receiving Ph.D.'s."[80] Findings of this sort have led many women to support sex-segregated colleges, and many men cling dearly to the concept of male-only institutions. The controversy surrounding Shannon Faulkner's efforts to enter the Citadel and then the treatment of Faulkner and the four women cadets who enrolled there in 1996 dramatically highlight these attitudes.

Some women argue that state maintenance of sex-segregated schools, particularly where *states* maintain superior "male-only" schools, denies them equal educational opportunities and equal protection of the laws as guaranteed by the U.S. Constitution. In June 1982, the U.S. Supreme Court ruled that a state's maintenance of a nursing school that admitted only women was unconstitutional. Writing for the Court in *Mississippi v. Hogan* (1982), Justice Sandra Day O'Connor noted:

> Although the test for determining the validity of a gender-based classification is straightforward, it must be applied free of fixed notions concerning the roles and abilities of males and females. Care must be taken in ascertaining whether the statutory objective itself reflects archaic and stereotypic notions. Thus, if the statutory objective is to exclude or protect members of one gender because they are presumed to suffer from an inherent handicap or to be innately inferior, the objective itself is illegitimate.[81]

Thus, although the Court relied on the Fourteenth Amendment and not Title IX, it was clear that some types of single-sex schools could no longer be maintained.

In the late 1980s and into the 1990s, the issue of single-sex schools again heated up. Some private women's colleges, such as Mills College in California, contemplated admitting men to bolster faltering revenues, while lawsuits were filed to open the doors of all-male state-supported colleges to women. In 1990, the U.S. Justice Department sued the all-male Virginia Military Institute (VMI) and accused it of violating the Fourteenth Amendment for its policy of excluding women. Governor L. Douglas Wilder of Virginia refused to defend the policy, so the school's board of visitors and alumni took up its defense. They argued VMI's rigid military-style training was especially beneficial to men, an argument ultimately rejected by a U.S. court of appeals. In taking note of the fact that the U.S. service academies opened their doors to women many years before, the appeals court said VMI must admit women or create a separate "parallel program" for women or forfeit state aid. The state then proceeded to create an alternative program for women, the Women's Institute of Leadership, at Mary Baldwin College, a private women's college close by.

In 1996, the U.S. Supreme Court, in a seven to one vote (Justice Clarence Thomas did not participate in the decision), found that VMI's all-male admissions policy discriminated against women and violated the Equal Protection Clause of the Fourteenth Amendment to the U.S. Constitution. Writing for the majority in *United States v. Virginia,* Justice Ruth Bader Ginsburg dismissed VMI's contention that admitting women would hurt the school. Ginsburg further noted her belief that the program set up at Mary Baldwin was a "pale shadow" of VMI because it lacked the military training, prestige, and tradition of the all-male school. "In myriad respects," said Ginsburg, the Mary Baldwin program "does not qualify as VMI's equal."[82]

The Court's decision did not mean an end to all single-sex public institutions. The Court was clear to point out that single-sex schools could pass constitutional muster so long as states provide opportunities "evenhandedly" to both sexes.[83]

Student Treatment. Although debate continues over the appropriateness of non-state-supported, sex-segregated schools, most women agree that female students should be treated equally in coed schools. Passage of Title IX was to have accomplished this, but women's groups are still pressing for its full enforcement.

After passage of Title IX, the Department of Health, Education, and Welfare (HEW) (the precursor to the Department of Education and the Department of Health and Human Services) was slow to draft regulations to implement its provisions. Once HEW acted, women's rights groups have been forced, over the years, to try to ward off efforts to undermine the law through amendment, weaker regulations, or judicial decisions. In *Grove City College v. Bell* (1984), for example, the Supreme Court limited Title IX by finding (as urged by the Reagan administration) that it only applied to specific programs within universities that actually received federal aid.[84]

Athletic programs, where Title IX has had tremendous impact, are often funded by ticket sales, alumni contributions, or the sale of television rights, and not by federal dollars. In essence, *Grove City* initially gave schools a new license to discriminate. Within six months, numerous Title IX actions were dropped, and charges of discrimination in women's sports programs were no longer being investigated.[85]

Women's rights groups began to lobby Congress to pass legislation that would overrule the Supreme Court decision immediately, but they were not successful until 1988. And although the Department of Education is charged with enforcing Title IX, many women's organizations routinely monitor Title IX compliance, and most universities have their own compliance officers.

Monitoring groups were especially necessary during the Reagan and Bush administrations. The Women's Legal Defense Fund and Women's Law Center filed several suits to force equal treatment of women students. Their cause was helped by a 1992 Supreme Court case that allowed monetary damages to be awarded in cases of deliberate discrimination.[86] Numerous Title IX lawsuits were filed involving reinstatement of women's sports programs, upgrading women's club teams to varsity status, and retaliatory firings related to Title IX complaints in reaction to the Court's ruling.[87]

In 1992, the powerful National Collegiate Athletic Association (NCAA) announced that it would pressure its member schools to offer *equal* opportunities to female athletes. In 1972, when Title IX was passed, only 294,000 girls played high-school sports. By 1996, that number had grown—in large part in response to Title IX—to more than 2 million.

Young women, however, continue to face tremendous inequalities in college-level sports. The Women's Sports Foundation estimates that in 1996 only 5 percent of all colleges actually complied with Title IX.[88] In 1996, Division I schools, for example, awarded $1,291,118 in scholarships to men and only $505,246 to women. Recruiting expenses for women athletes were less than 20 percent of those of men,[89] and for every "$1 a man's basketball coach is paid, the woman's coach is paid 55 cents."[90] This disparity continues in spite of the fact that women constitute the majority of undergraduates in the United States and on most campuses.

Until recently, a major problem with Title IX enforcement has been not knowing how much money a college spends on men's and women's sports programs. In 1994, an amendment to the Elementary and Secondary Education Act was proposed by Senators Carol Moseley Braun (D-Ill.) and Edward Kennedy (D-Mass.). As passed by Congress and signed by President Clinton, the Improving America's Schools Act of 1994 requires universities to disclose to students a variety of information related to gender equity, including funding and participation rates. The Office of Civil Rights in the Department of Education is charged with enforcing the act, as well as Title IX, and is now drafting regulations to implement it.

Increased emphasis on Title IX enforcement has led many women to file lawsuits to force compliance. In 1991, in an effort to trim expenses, Brown University cut two men's and two women's teams from its varsity rosters. Several women on the downgraded gymnastics team filed a Title IX complaint against the school, arguing that it violated the act by not providing women varsity sport opportunities in relation to their population in the university. The women also argued that cutting two women's programs saved $62,000, whereas the men's cuts saved the school only $16,000. Thus, the women's varsity programs took a bigger hit in violation of federal law.

A U.S. district court refused to allow Brown to cut the women's programs. A U.S. court of appeals upheld that action, concluding that Brown failed to provide adequate opportunities for its female students to participate in athletics.[91] In 1997, in *Brown University v. Cohen,* the U.S. Supreme Court declined to review the appeals court decision. This put all colleges and universities on notice that discrimination against women would not be tolerated, even when, as in the case of Brown University, the university had, since passage of Title IX, tremendously expanded sports opportunities for women.[92]

Test fairness is another area in which unequal treatment continues to harm women students. In 1985, an article by Phyllis Rosser in *Ms.* magazine looked at gender bias in educational testing.[93] The National Center for Fair and Open Testing (FairTest) then commissioned a study of the Scholastic Aptitude Test (SAT), and the House Judicial Subcommittee on Civil and Constitutional Rights held hearings. Those hearings and subsequent reports led the ACLU's Women's Rights Project to file suit on behalf of NOW and Girl's Clubs of America to challenge New York State's use of SAT scores to award $8.4 million in college scholarship money. Sole use of SAT scores resulted in girls receiving only 28 percent of Empire State Scholarships for Excellence

TABLE 3–2 Women and SAT Score Bias[a]

Year	Average Verbal Score			Average Mathematical Score		
	Total	Male	Female	Total	Male	Female
1966–1967	466	463	468	492	514	467
1971–1972	453	454	452	484	505	461
1976–1977	429	431	427	470	497	445
1981–1982	426	431	421	467	493	443
1986–1987	430	435	425	476	500	453

[a]Printed in National Center for Education Statistics, *Digest of Education Statistics* (Washington, D.C.: U.S. Department of Education, 1992), 125.

even though they were 53 percent of the test takers. As revealed in Table 3–2, women score much lower on SATs even though they earn higher grades in high school.[94] Commenting that "SAT scores capture a student's academic achievement no more than a student's yearbook captures the full range of her experiences in high school," a federal judge found that New York's awarding of state scholarships solely on the basis of SAT scores was "in violation of Title IX and the equal protection clause of the U.S. Constitution."[95]

Colleges, however, still make use of these tests for admissions and scholarship decisions. Although test preparers have been aware of the gender differences in scores, some continue to dismiss them. In 1996, for example, boys made up 61 percent of all National Merit Scholarship semifinalists (girls were 54 percent of the test takers), a designation based on preliminary SAT (PSAT) scores.[96] In response to charges from FairTest about continued bias, a public information officer from the National Merit Corporation said, "We are not convinced that the test is biased. . . . It could be showing a disparity in academic preparation. If girls are getting better grades in home economics or things like that, they're not better prepared."[97] If, indeed, girls are less well prepared for these tests than boys, one could argue that schools are violating Title IX by offering differing opportunities to female students.

Hiring and Personnel Practices. Title IX also prohibits employment discrimination in all educational institutions receiving federal assistance. Although the number of women Ph.D.'s continues to grow, as revealed earlier in Table 3–1, this growth has not been reflected in the faculties of most universities, particularly research-oriented institutions. Although women make up nearly 30 percent of all college faculty members, these women are often clustered at women's, small Catholic, or community colleges. Despite a 58 percent increase from 1982 in the number of women who were full professors, they filled only 14.4 percent of all full professor positions in 1996.[98]

Once employed, women often face a variety of forms of discrimination ranging from blatant to the most subtle. Although both Title VII and Title IX prohibit discrimination, the kinds practiced in academia are difficult to prove, owing in large part to the deference most judges give to the judgment of a woman's senior peers (often all white men) as to the quality of her teaching and research.

Women's groups and women's studies programs (many of them originally founded by members of the younger branch of the movement) have been instrumental in monitoring university practices. They often serve as a clearinghouse for information and/or as a support system for women on campus. Volumes of information about women's studies and about Title IX and how to monitor compliance, file complaints, and keep abreast of the latest developments now exist on the World Wide Web to provide a communications network and enhanced monitoring of continued discrimination.[99]

Opposition to Employment and Educational Equity

Phyllis Schlafly spoke out quickly and vigorously against defining sexual harassment as illegal employment discrimination. She also opposed comparable worth legislation. In 1985, appealing to class resentments, she argued that comparable worth "would empower 'bureaucrats' to freeze blue-collar wages, because the so-called 'scientific criteria' used to evaluate job worth mask biases against manual labor."[100] Representatives from Schlafly's Eagle Forum and Concerned Women for America (CWA) also testified against the Family and Medical Leave Act. They argued it was biased against the working poor, who could not afford to take unpaid leaves, and that it would encourage employers to discriminate against women of childbearing age.

Conservative women have also parted ways with other women over issues of educational equity. In 1975, shortly after the first set of Title IX guidelines was announced, a tremendous outcry was raised when HEW officials ruled that father/son breakfasts were prohibited by Title IX. ERA opponents charged that this was a first step toward destruction of the family and unwarranted governmental action.[101] Although this interpretation of Title IX resulted in extensive media coverage and angry letters to HEW from conservative women, conservative women's groups were even more upset about moves being made in the schools and by publishers to remove sex-role stereotyping from textbooks.

In 1979, Phyllis Schlafly, Concerned Women for America, and many Republicans urged passage of the Family Protection Act (FPA), which would have denied "federal funds for purchase of textbooks that 'belittle' women's traditional role in society."[102] Although the FPA died, CWA continues to be influential on the state level, especially in California and Texas, where conservative texts written to glorify women's traditional roles have been adopted in many elementary and secondary schools.

Conservative women's groups enjoyed tremendous access to the White

House and the agencies charged with enforcing educational equity during the 1980s. The New Right, in fact, of which conservative women's groups are a part, was instrumental in bringing about the election of Ronald Reagan in 1980, and it was rewarded for those efforts. Since 1992, however, many conservative groups have turned their attentions to local elections. For example, CWA is particularly concerned with what it calls the secular-humanist curriculum taught in many public schools and has taken an active role in trying to ban discussions of feminism and homosexuality in public schools. Since 1992, CWA, along with fundamentalist Christian groups, has supported thousands of candidates for local school board elections to further these interests.

CONCLUSION

Women have made enormous strides since they first gathered in Seneca Falls to demand greater educational and employment opportunities. Although the franchise was won in 1920, it was more than four decades later before national legislation guaranteeing some semblance of equality in wages and equal opportunity in the workplace was enacted.

Prior to the 1960s, most of the progress made in employment and education came about as a result of individual efforts or employer demand. Neither the early woman's movement nor the woman suffrage movement attempted to attack head-on the problems in either sphere, although each movement supported notions of increased opportunity.

Once the Equal Pay and Civil Rights Acts of 1963 and 1964, respectively, were signed into law, parity did not occur. In fact, the failure of the EEOC to enforce the Civil Rights Act was an important reason for the creation of the National Organization for Women: Women were enraged when legitimate complaints of discrimination were not investigated.

Over the years, women's rights groups have pursued several different courses of action in their quest to gain greater educational and employment opportunities free from discrimination. Since passage of the Equal Pay and Civil Rights Acts, women's rights organizations routinely have filed lawsuits to seek compliance with existing law. They have also lobbied the executive branch for better enforcement of existing statutes but, particularly during the Reagan-Bush years, to little avail.

Women's groups have also lobbied for additional legislation and regulations to ban discrimination in the workplace and in schools. The Pregnancy Discrimination Act of 1978, sexual harassment guidelines, and Title IX are examples of these efforts. Most recently, after several years of work, women in Congress, with the aid of women's rights lobbying (as well as popular support), secured passage of the Family and Medical Leave Act.

Gains in this area have been fostered by two factors. First, even some conservative women supported antibias employment legislation. Not only did some of the proposed laws protect motherhood—the Pregnancy Discrimination Act is one example—but also, according to some, the protections found in many of those laws negated any need for the ERA.

Second, there was little organized business opposition to most of these proposals. However, when more threatening, costly changes including comparable worth, affirmative action, and pregnancy disability payments, for example, began to appear in regulations implementing laws or executive orders, a strong backlash arose that was exacerbated by the economic downturn.

Many employers and white males in particular, threatened by a loss of jobs or lessened chances of promotion, immediately began to lobby, litigate, and/or simply ignore equal opportunity as well as affirmative action guidelines. They viewed quotas or goals as true public bads that could only hurt their ability to pursue their education or careers.

All of these various statutes, regulations, and judicial rulings combine to make most forms of sex discrimination unquestionably illegal. Yet women continue to be underrepresented in high-prestige occupations, clustered in low-paying jobs and frequently subjected to on-the-job abuse.

NOTES

1. Judith Papachristou, *Women Together: A History in Documents of the Women's Movement in the United States* (New York: Knopf, 1976), 126.
2. Mary Frances Berry, *The Politics of Parenthood: Childcare, Women's Rights, and the Myth of the Good Mother* (New York: Viking, 1993), 46.
3. Reproduced in Elizabeth Cady Stanton, Susan B. Anthony, and Matilda Joslyn Gage, eds., *History of Woman Suffrage*, vol. 1, 1848–1861 (Rochester, N.Y.: Charles Mann, 1887), 72.
4. Horace Mann as quoted in Thomas Woody, *A History of Women's Education in the United States*, vol. 1 (New York: Science Press, 1929), 463.
5. Kathryn Kish Sklar, "The Founding of Mount Holyoke College," in *Women of America, A History*, ed. Carol Ruth Berkin and Mary Beth Norton (Boston: Houghton Mifflin, 1979), 185.
6. Woody, *History of Women's Education*, vol. 1, 499.
7. Lois W. Banner, *Women in Modern America: A Brief History*, 2d ed. (San Diego: Harcourt Brace Jovanovich, 1984), 65–69.
8. James J. Kenneally, *Women and American Trade Unions* (St. Albans, Vt.: Eden Press, 1978), chaps. 5, 6.
9. Ibid., 479.
10. Ibid., 481–86. The union between suffrage forces and the WTUL was an uneasy one born from expediency. The WTUL started working hard for suffrage after its poor treatment at the hands of male unionists and after its change of policy favoring protective legislation. WTUL leaders believed it was necessary for working women to have the vote to get laws passed.
11. See generally, Maude Nathan, *The Story of an Epoch-Making Movement* (Garden City, N.Y.: Doubleday, 1926); Karen O'Connor, *Women's Organizations' Use of the Courts* (Lexington, Mass.: Lexington Books, 1980), chap. 4; Vivien Hart, *Bound by Our Constitution: Women, Workers, and the Minimum Wage* (Princeton, N.J.: Princeton University Press, 1994).
12. Clement E. Vose, *Constitutional Change* (Lexington, Mass.: Lexington Books, 1972), chap. 7. For a discussion of the legal arguments made in these cases, see Judith A. Baer, *The Chains of Protection: The Judicial Response to Women's Labor Legislation* (Westport, Conn.: Greenwood Press, 1978); Nancy Woloch, *Muller v. Oregon: A Brief History with Documents* (Boston: Bedford Books, 1996).
13. 208 U.S. 421 (1908).
14. 261 U.S. 525 (1923).

15. Ibid.

16. Lois Scharf, *To Work and to Wed: Female Employment, Feminism, and the Great Depression* (Westport, Conn.: Greenwood Press, 1980), 10. Also reflecting the changing job opportunities for women was the growth of professional business and commercial schools. Business colleges like Katherine Gibbs Schools mushroomed in response to the demand of business for trained young women to staff the expanding number of clerical and secretarial openings.

17. Data in this paragraph comes from Carol Hymowitz and Michaele Weissman, *A History of Women in America* (New York: Bantam Books, 1978), 306.

18. Barbara Sinclair Deckard, *The Women's Movement*, 2d ed. (New York: Harper & Row, 1979), 317.

19. For example, the New York City Bar Association refused to accept female members until 1937. This kind of discrimination, plus social mores that acted against women seeking careers in the law, resulted in women making up 2 percent or less of all attorneys through 1940.

20. Barbara J. Harris, *Beyond Her Sphere: Women and the Professions in American History* (Westport, Conn.: Greenwood Press, 1978), 104–5.

21. William H. Chafe, "The Paradox of Progress," in *Our American Sisters,* 2d ed., ed. Jean E. Friedman and William G. Shade. (Boston: Allyn & Bacon, 1976), 386.

22. William H. Chafe, *The American Woman* (New York: Oxford University Press, 1972), 144–45.

23. Hymowitz and Weissman, *History of Women,* 312.

24. Deckard, *Women's Movement,* 319.

25. Hymowitz and Weissman, *History of Women,* 314.

26. Harris, *Beyond Her Sphere,* 155.

27. Betty Friedan, *The Feminine Mystique* (New York: Dell, 1963), 30.

28. Additionally, by 1965, 35 percent of all married women with husbands present worked. In fact, 42.7 percent of mothers with school-aged children worked, as did 23.3 percent of those with preschool-aged children. U.S. Department of Labor, Bureau of Labor Statistics, *Perspectives on Working Women: A Databook* (Bulletin #2080) (October 1980), 27.

29. Women's Bureau, 1969 Handbook (Washington, D.C., 1969).

30. Hymowitz and Weissman, *History of Women,* 316.

31. Mary Anne Baker et al., *Women Today: A Multidisciplinary Approach to Women's Studies* (Monterey, Calif.: Brooks/Cole, 1980), 24.

32. Norma K. Raffel, "Federal Laws and Regulations Prohibiting Sex Discrimination," in *The Study of Women: Enlarging Perspectives of Social Reality,* ed. Eloise C. Snyder (New York: Harper & Row, 1979), 106.

33. *Schultz v. Wheaton Glass Co.,* 421 F.2d 259 (3d Cir.), cert. denied, 398 U.S. 905 (1970).

34. Equal Employment Opportunity Commission, "Equal Pay Act Charge Statistics," January 9, 1997. (mimeo)

35. Jo Freeman, *The Politics of Women's Liberation* (New York: David McKay, 1975), 53. Some today downplay the joke angle of the "sex" addition. See Ann N. Costain, *Inviting Women's Rebellion* (Baltimore: Johns Hopkins University Press, 1992), chap. 2.

36. The first director of the EEOC even went so far as to say that the law was "conceived out of wedlock" and that "men were entitled to female secretaries." Quoted in Jo Freeman, "Women and Public Policy: An Overview," in Ellen Boneparth, ed., *Women, Power, and Public Policy* (New York: Pergamon Press, 1982), 53.

37. Freeman, *Women's Liberation,* 77.

38. *Pittsburgh Press Co. v. Pittsburgh Commission on Human Relations,* 413 U.S. 376 (1973). NOW became party to the suit at the Supreme Court level and was supported with amicus curiae briefs from several women's rights groups. Although the EEOC had succumbed to feminist pressures and announced regulations prohibiting male and female help-wanted ads, the Supreme Court upheld the agencies' construction of Title VII by only a one-vote majority.

39. Barbara Allen Babcock et al., *Sex Discrimination and the Law: Causes and Remedies* (St. Paul, Minn.: West, 1975), 262. This book contains an excellent summary of the protective legislation controversy that actually began in the 1920s. See 229–82.

40. Statement by Katherine P. Elickson of the National Consumers' League before the Equal Employment Opportunity Commission, May 2, 1967, 1, reported in Babcock et al., *Sex Discrimination,* 266, n. 60.

41. 444 F.2d 1219 (9th Cir. 1971).

42. See *Diaz v. Pan American Airlines,* 442 F.2d 385 (5th. Cir. 1971), cert. denied, 404 U.S. 950 (1971).
43. 433 U.S. 321 (1977).
44. Kenneth Janda, Jeffrey M. Berry, and Jerry Goldman, *The Challenge of Democracy,* 2d ed. (Dallas: Houghton Mifflin, 1990), 20.
45. 452 U.S. 161 (1981).
46. Harry Bernstein, "Closing the Wage Gap," *Los Angeles Times,* April 8, 1993, B7.
47. 82 Weekly Comp. Pres. Doc. 651.
48. Ibid.
49. 480 U.S. 616 (1987).
50. *Adarand Constructors, Inc. v. Pena,* No. 93-1841 (1995).
51. Catharine A. MacKinnon, *Sexual Harassment of Working Women* (New Haven, Conn: Yale University Press, 1979).
52. 477 U.S. 57 (1986).
53. Gretchen Morgenson, "Watch That Leer, Stifle That Joke," *Forbes,* May 15, 1989, 69.
54. *Harris v. Forklift Systems,* 510 U.S. 17 (1993).
55. David Hancock, "End Sexual Harassment, Companies Urged," *Miami Herald,* March 3, 1993, B2.
56. David E. Rovella, "EEOC Chairman Casellas: We Are Being Selective," *The National Law Journal,* November 20, 1995, B1.
57. 1993 U.S. LEXIS 7155.
58. Martha Burke and Josh Feltman, "How to Get Paid," *Executive Female,* January 1995, 46.
59. 414 U.S. 632 (1974).
60. 417 U.S. 484 (1972). *Geduldig* was sponsored by Equal Rights Advocates, a California-based feminist public interest law firm. The firm received substantial amicus curiae support from WRP, NOW, and even WEAL, whose leaders by 1974 realized the pervasive consequences of pregnancy-based discrimination.
61. 429 U.S. 125 (1976).
62. Karen O'Connor and Lee Epstein, "Beyond Legislative Lobbying: Women's Rights Groups and the Supreme Court," *Judicature* 67 (1983): 134–43.
63. Judith A. Baer, *Women in American Law* (New York: Holmes & Meier, 1991), 109–10.
64. "Report Says New Mothers Take Longer Than Thought to Recover," Reuters, March 16, 1993, NEXIS.
65. 479 U.S. 272 (1987).
66. Baer, *Women in American Law,* 103.
67. For more information on the difference debate, see Flora Davis, *Moving the Mountain: The Women's Movement in America since 1960* (New York: Simon & Schuster, 1991), 475–83.
68. Berry, *Politics of Parenthood,* 160.
69. Quoted in ibid., 161.
70. "President Clinton Announces New Family-Friendly Workplace Proposals," June 24, 1996 (http://www.whitehouse.gov/WH/dispatch/062496.html). The other statistics contained in this paragraph can also be found there.
71. Ibid.
72. "Briefing," *The Times Union,* January 29, 1997, D2.
73. Ibid.
74. Ibid.
75. 111 S.Ct. 2238 (1991). See Sally K. Kenney, *For Whose Protection? Reproductive Hazards and Exclusionary Policies in the United States and Great Britain* (Ann Arbor: University of Michigan Press, 1993).
76. Commission on the Status of Women, *American Women: Report on the President's Commission on the Status of Women* (Washington, D.C.: U.S. Government Printing Office, 1963), 13.
77. Ibid., 17.
78. "NOW Demands," quoted in Papachristou, *Women Together,* 222.
79. For an excellent account of the lobbying activities that led to passage of Title IX, see Marian Lief Palley and Joyce Gelb, *Women and Public Policies: Reassessing Gender Politics* (Charlottesville: University of Virginia Press, 1996).
80. Quoted in Babcock et al., *Sex Discrimination,* 1014–15.
81. 458 U.S. 718 (1982).
82. 116 S.Ct. 2264 (1996).
83. Douglas Lederman, "Supreme Court Rejects VMI's Exclusion of Women," *Chronicle of Higher Education,* July 5, 1996, A21.

84. 465 U.S. 555 (1984).
85. Baer, *Women in American Law*, 227.
86. *Franklin v. Gwinnett County School District*, 111 S.Ct. 1028 (1992).
87. Carol Herwig, "Colgate Prevails in Title IX Appeal," *USA Today*, April 28, 1993, 9C.
88. Mariah Burton Nelson, "In Search of a Level Playing Field," *USA Today*, March 19, 1992, 11A.
89. Candiss Collins, "Women in Sports: No More 'Wait till Next Year,'" *USA Today*, February 10, 1993, 11A.
90. Nelson, "Playing Field," 11A.
91. *Cohen v. Brown University*, 101 F.3d 155 (1996).
92. *Brown University v. Cohen*, 117 S.Ct. 1469 (1997).
93. Phyllis Rosser, "Do SATs Shortchange Women?" *Ms.*, December 1985, 20.
94. See Kathleen Kelly-Benjamin, *The Young Women's Guide to Better SAT Scores: Fighting the Gender Gap* (New York: Bantam Books, 1990).
95. Quoted in ibid., 10.
96. "Boys Predominate in a Contest: Fueling Complaint of Test Bias," *New York Times*, May 26, 1993, B7.
97. Data obtained from Website that has been discontinued.
98. Robert J. Vickkers, "College Survey—Gender Gap Lingers in Academia," *Atlanta Constitution*, April 10, 1993, B1.
99. For more on Title IX see http://www.mcs.net/~sluggers/titleixpage.html
100. Susan E. Marshall, "Who Speaks for American Women: The Future of Antifeminism," *Annals*, May 1991, 58.
101. Joseph A. Califano Jr., *Governing America* (New York: Simon & Schuster, 1981), 223–24.
102. Carol Felsehthal, *Phyllis Schlafly: The Sweetheart of the Silent Majority* (Garden City, N.Y.: Doubleday, 1981), 319. See also, Janet K. Boles, "Social Movements as Policy Entrepreneurs: The Family Protection Act and Family Impact Analysis" (paper delivered at the annual meeting of the American Political Science Association, Washington, D.C., 1982).

Women's Economic and Educational Status

4

As detailed in Chapter 3, the expansion of employment and educational rights for women that occurred during the early woman's and suffrage movements failed to produce full and equal participation. Slow progress was due partly to the absence of any laws guaranteeing equal employment and educational rights for women. In fact, the "protective" legislation that was enacted at the urging of many women's groups during the suffrage era actually *reduced* women's employment opportunities in many fields.

The 1960s and the 1970s saw passage of several laws to improve educational and employment opportunities for women. These laws, however, have yet to be fully enforced. The decade of the 1980s was a particularly difficult time. Both the Reagan and Bush administrations actively sought to undermine full enforcement of antidiscrimination legislation. Thus, it is not surprising that women's gains in the employment and educational spheres, while often impressive, have not produced anything approaching equality in the marketplace.

Paralleling our findings in the political arena, the data in the economic sector show that legal change is a necessary but insufficient condition for equality. Additional legal guarantees and the active enforcement of existing laws are just part of the reason for the continued inequality of women. These changes alone, however, will not bring full parity. Rather, as in politics, additional barriers continue to limit the progress of women. More specifically, the advancement of women in the educational and employment spheres has been hampered by barriers that parallel those that have limited women's progress in politics, namely (1) cultural attitudes about the roles and abilities of women, (2) conflict between women's family roles and marketplace activity, (3) women's lack of preparation and resources for all aspects of marketplace involvement, (4) sex discrimination by employers and associates on the job, and (5) the structure and demands of the economy.

In the sections that follow, we explore how these barriers, both in the past and the present, have limited women's progress. We also examine how these barriers have changed over time, especially during the current women's rights movement. Finally, we try to identify what additional changes must be made before women can take an equal place with men in the marketplace in the twenty-first century.

ATTITUDES TOWARD WORK AND WOMEN

Before the Women's Movement

Many people looked down on the few women who worked during the colonial period. Women workers, however, encountered little resistance, largely due to the shortage of men to perform many jobs—including but not limited to physicians, innkeepers, and shopkeepers. The public was hesitant to condemn women who provided these necessary services, especially since many businesses were family owned and it was not unusual for a wife to continue the business upon the death of her husband.[1] Some historians even argue that in the early years of industrialization, the employment of young, single women in factories was viewed positively by many.[2] Few even questioned the practice of having slave women, married and unmarried, work long hours as field hands, domestics, or nannies.

As industrialization proceeded, the division of sex roles became more pronounced. Increasingly work that had been done at home was moved to the factory. Men went "out" to work, while women stayed "in" the home. The symbol of the new middle class became the wife of leisure, although there was little real leisure associated with running a home in the mid-1800s. Most poor, African American, or immigrant families could ill afford the luxury of an unemployed wife, yet the common practice even in these groups was for the wife not to seek paid employment if it was economically feasible. While married women were discouraged from working, there is considerable evidence that women participated in family-run businesses located in the home.[3] Moreover, among single women of both native-born and immigrant parents, census data suggest that they worked unless the family could afford otherwise. However, negative attitudes toward women's employment seemed to heighten with the economic recession and massive industrial unemployment of the 1870s and the 1890s, as some women appeared to be "taking jobs from men."[4]

At the dawn of the twentieth century, many new white-collar jobs were developed. It became increasingly acceptable for young, middle-class women to work outside the home. The era of the 1920s and the "new woman" may have been a particularly favorable time for young, white, working women. Attitudes toward the employment of married women, however, were decidedly negative in the first public opinion polls taken in the 1930s. Perhaps in part because of the depression, in 1936 only 15 percent of the public gave an unqualified favorable response to a question concerning the advisability of married women working. The reasons given most frequently by those who objected were: (1) women take men's jobs (36 percent), (2) a woman's place is in the home (35 percent), and (3) one is guaranteed a happier home life or healthier children if women do not work (21 percent).[5] In 1937 and 1938 when the question was rephrased to include the possibility of a married woman working "if she had a husband capable of supporting her," less than a quarter of the public (25 percent of the women but only 19 percent of the men) approved. There also was widespread support for the practice of refusing to hire or actually firing women who could depend on their husbands for support. Over half of all respondents, for example, declared they would favor a law prohibiting employment of a married woman for state or local government if the woman's husband earned $1,000 a year.[6]

World War II radically altered these views. Workers were in tremendous demand to replace men at war. Public support for a married woman working rose dramatically. Sixty percent of the public said married women should take jobs in the war industries. When the qualifier "without children" was added, this number climbed to more than 70 percent.[7] Polls revealed that women were more supportive of women working.[8] More than three-quarters of those queried also supported the concept of equal pay for equal work.[9]

These views were short lived. By the war's end, fueled in part by the fears of public officials and male workers about a shortage of jobs, the nation embarked on an effort to return women to the home. Popular magazines proclaimed the benefits and rewards of suburban living and caring for the home as a full-time, fulfilling occupation. This change in public sentiment was quickly reflected in the public opinion polls. In the immediate postwar years, only 18 percent of the public in a national sample gave unqualified approval to a married woman working if her husband was capable of supporting her. When the question raised the specter of a "limited number of jobs," 86 percent, a proportion higher than reported during the depression, disapproved of a married woman working if she had a husband capable of supporting her. Even when no mention was made of a limited number of jobs, and the question focused only on women with no children under age sixteen, only 34 percent of all men surveyed in 1946 gave unqualified approval. In contrast, 42 percent of all women viewed these women workers in a positive light.[10]

Women who worked often justified their employment by claiming economic necessity, an acceptable reason for many people.[11] While economic motives may have made employment more socially acceptable, most women who went to work enjoyed it.[12] As more women went to work, support for women's employment climbed, especially in the high-prosperity years of the 1950s when jobs were abundant.

Employers also played a catalytic role in attitudinal change. Their expanding demand for women workers (a result of new openings in traditional women's fields) made possible the increased employment of women.

Moreover, because demand occurred when there were fewer single women to fill it, employers were willing to discard many of their own prejudices and biases against hiring married women. Thus, the changing practices of women and employers set the stage for the women's movement and its message that women's employment was not only acceptable but also desirable.

The Impact of the Women's Movement

As early as 1969, before the message of the women's rights movement reached many in America, popular support for married women working had already climbed from its postwar low of 18 percent to a record 55 percent.[13] Figure 4–1 reports the percentage of the public from 1972 to 1996 that approved a married woman earning money in business or industry if she had a husband capable of supporting her. The figures show a rather steady climb during the twenty-five-year time frame. In 1996, less than 17 percent (in a national survey) objected to married women's employment.

FIGURE 4–1 Proportion of population that supports the idea of a married woman working, 1972–1996.

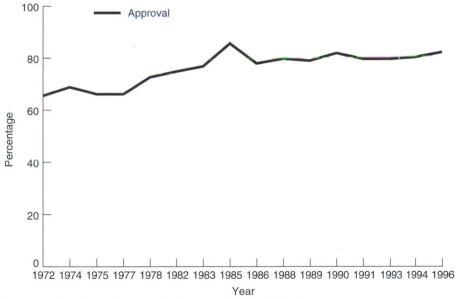

Survey question: Do you approve or disapprove of a married woman earning money in business or industry if she has a husband capable of supporting her?

Source: James Allan Davis and Tom W. Smith, *General Social Surveys, 1972–1996.* Principal Investigator, James A. Davis; Director and Co-Principal Investigator, Tom W. Smith. NORC ed. Chicago: National Opinion Research Center, producer, 1996; Storrs, Conn.: The Roper Center for Public Opinion Research, University of Connecticut, distributor.

There is some evidence, however, that some men still have reservations about a married woman working. For example, in the fall of 1996, 31 percent of first-year college men as compared to 19 percent of first-year women agreed "the activities of married women are best confined to the home and family."[14] The specter of women taking jobs away from men also seems to fuel resistances. In 1977, when asked if a married woman should work if there were a limited number of jobs and she had a husband capable of supporting her, 64 percent of the public disapproved of her working, a figure only 20 percent lower than the opposition to a similar question in 1946.[15] Although the question has not been repeated since 1977, the negative shifts in public sentiment toward women working in the late 1800s, the 1930s, and the postwar 1940s, which were tied to strong economic downturns or the prospect of such, raise the possibility that these attitudes are highly volatile. Indeed, a headline in 1993 proclaimed "Women Making Job Gains at Expense of Men,"[16] indicating that an artificial scenario about the battle for the scarce jobs of the 1990s may already be forming and may actually be behind much of the resistance to affirmative action (see Chapter 3).

Even though approval for a married woman working generally seems strong if the scenario does not include a job shortage, many people still believe a wife should place her career second to her husband's. Several questions tap this attitude. The first queries whether "it is more important for a wife to help her husband's career than to have one herself." In 1977, over half of the public (57 percent) agreed with this statement. Steady declines in the 1980s, however, still left one-fifth (21 percent) endorsing this view in 1996.[17] Relatedly, in the same year, a majority of the public (57 percent) agreed that it was better for society if the man is the achiever outside the home and the woman takes care of the home and the family.[18]

In response to the second more concrete set of questions about whether a woman or a man should give up her or his job if the spouse is offered a transfer, almost two-thirds of all women (62 percent) and more than half of all men (55 percent) surveyed in 1989 said the *wife* should give up her job if her husband is offered a very good job in another city. When the situation is reversed and the wife has the offer, only 29 percent of the women and 28 percent of the men believed the *husband* should quit and move with her.[19] A survey of college-educated men and women in the mid-1990s found that even among those who if forced to choose would prefer a career to marriage, more women (88 percent) than men (67 percent) were willing to move for the sake of their spouse's career. As the authors of this study note, "these women will be prone to experiencing an inner struggle as they weigh their conflicting commitments to their husbands and their own careers."[20] This conflict is even greater for women with children who want to work, as the public is even more adamant about a woman's need to sacrifice her career for her children.

ATTITUDES TOWARD MOTHERS WORKING

Early in the Industrial Revolution, in England and in some parts of the United States, whole families were often hired for factory work, apparently with public approval. By the mid-1800s, however, popular sentiment strongly opposed a mother working, although little thought was given to the hard work done by women in the home or on the family farm. Similarly, few objected to married African American women working. Indeed, in the South after emancipation it was expected that wives and children of sharecroppers would work alongside the man of the family in the fields.[21] Married African American women who were not sharecropping were expected to fill the housekeeping needs of white women, who generally gave little thought to the domestic concerns of their help. As the century progressed, the evils of factory life and the toll it took on working women (usually white) and their families were an important rationale for the enactment of protective legislation in the early 1900s.

The almost universal practice of white middle-class women leaving their jobs before the birth of their first child was in keeping with the popular notion that the roles of worker and mother were incompatible. Even in the 1920s, an era of relatively high support for women working, the majority of professional women saw their choice as *either* marriage and a family *or* work. During this period, only 19.3 percent of professional women were married, and most viewed a family and a profession as mutually exclusive.[22]

In the 1930s and 1940s, one of the most frequently cited objections to married women working was that the practice posed potential harm to children. Although the period from 1960 to the present has seen a massive increase in the number of mothers working, altering public sentiment toward their employment has been only partially accomplished. A 1994 national survey, for instance, found that although many interviewees thought it was acceptable for a woman to work full time after marrying and before she had children (84 percent), many fewer thought work was a good idea if there were children. For instance, if the youngest child was in school the percentage agreeing that full-time work was desirable dropped to 38 percent, although 54 percent thought part-time work was acceptable. If there was a child under school age, however, only 11 percent thought full-time work was acceptable and just 34 percent approved of part-time employment. Most of those interviewed (55 percent) thought that under these circumstances a woman should stay home.[23]

As revealed in Table 4–1, part of the objection to a mother working stems from a feeling that employment harms the mother-child relationship. Thus, in 1977, over half the public (52 percent) disagreed with the notion that a working mother could establish as warm and secure a relationship with her children as a mother who does not work. By 1996, opinion had shifted rather dramatically on this position, with two-thirds of the public (66 percent) agreeing with the statement.

**TABLE 4–1 The Mother-Child Relationship Is Not Hurt
by a Mother Working[a]**

Year	Strongly Agree (%)	Agree (%)	Disagree (%)	Strongly Disagree (%)
1977	16	33	34	18
1985	21	40	29	10
1986	22	40	30	8
1988	24	39	28	9
1989	22	42	30	7
1990	22	42	29	8
1991	20	45	28	6
1993	20	47	27	6
1994	23	46	26	5
1996	24	42	26	7

[a]Survey question: A working mother can establish just as warm and secure a relationship with her children as a mother who does not work.

Source: James Allan Davis and Tom W. Smith, *General Social Surveys, 1972–1996.* Principal Investigator, James A. Davis; Director and Co-Principal Investigator, Tom W. Smith. NORC ed. Chicago: National Opinion Research Center, producer, 1996; Storrs, Conn.: The Roper Center for Public Opinion Research, University of Connecticut, distributor.

A related question about the impact of a mother's job status on her preschool children produces a similar pattern of responses, but there is much greater agreement that a preschool child is likely to suffer if a mother works, as revealed in Table 4–2. More than two-thirds of all respondents (68 percent) felt this way in 1977. Although these feelings declined dramatically over the next decade, still nearly half of the people interviewed in 1996 (47 percent) thought this practice was harmful. Not surprisingly, working mothers, especially college-educated working mothers, are particularly likely to think that they are able to establish a warm relationship with their children and that working does not harm preschool children. Men, on the other hand, seem more likely to agree that both practices are harmful. In 1996, there was a gender gap of 17 and 14 percentage points, respectively, in these two questions.[24] Thus, even if a woman wants to work, she may find herself in conflict with a spouse who believes a mother should stay home. Moreover, as Lesley Lazin Novak and David R. Novak point out, many women "are likely to be caught in an internal bind between their personal aspirations and their culturally ingrained need to stay home after they become mothers."[25]

Attitudes toward the employment of women and the place of work in women's lives are not the only attitudinal barriers to the equality of women in the marketplace. One other set of very restrictive cultural views concerns the ability of women to perform certain jobs or to undertake appropriate training or education.

TABLE 4–2 Preschool Children Suffer if Their Mother Works[a]

Year	Strongly Agree (%)	Agree (%)	Disagree (%)	Strongly Disagree (%)
1977	21	47	28	5
1985	13	41	36	10
1986	11	40	40	9
1988	11	37	41	11
1989	9	39	42	10
1990	8	41	42	9
1991	9	39	42	10
1993	7	36	47	10
1994	8	35	47	11
1996	9	38	43	11

[a]Survey question: A preschool child is likely to suffer if his or her mother works.

Source: James Allan Davis and Tom W. Smith, *General Social Surveys, 1972–1996.* Principal Investigator, James A. Davis; Director and Co-Principal Investigator, Tom W. Smith. NORC ed. Chicago: National Opinion Research Center, producer, 1996; Storrs, Conn.: The Roper Center for Public Opinion Research, University of Connecticut, distributor.

Attitudes About the Abilities of Women

As we saw in Chapter 2, negative attitudes about the abilities of women have stymied their progress in securing high elective office. Many of these same stereotypes translate into similar doubts about the aptitudes of women in the economic realm.

In the nineteenth century, many commentators believed that women simply lacked the mental, physical, and emotional attributes necessary for work outside the home. Often such work, or the preparation for it in school, was seen as disastrous for the health of women. In the 1870s, a major medical text even claimed:

> During the epoch of development, that is the age from fourteen to eighteen or twenty . . . the system . . . is particularly susceptible, and disturbances of the delicate mechanism [the menstrual function] . . . , induced . . . by constrained positions, muscular effort, brain work, and all forms of mental and physical excitement, germinate a host of ills. Sometimes these causes, which pervade . . . our . . . schools produce an excessive performance of the . . . function, and this is equivalent to a periodic hemorrhage.[26]

This "knowledge" not only kept middle-class women out of the workplace, it was also used as a rationale to prevent them from acquiring an education or skills to prepare them for work outside the home.

With the growth of women's colleges and the entrance of a few women

into the professions, these stereotypes weakened but were far from eliminated. As late as 1891, some women in the suffrage movement believed:

> Women cannot maintain the same intellectual standards as men. The claim of
> the ability to learn, to apply knowledge . . . does not imply a claim to originate,
> or to maintain . . . the robust, massive intellectual enterprises which . . . are
> now carried on by masculine strength and energy.[27]

This line of reasoning was the cornerstone of the legal arguments for protective legislation.

Surveys taken in the 1940s show the intervening years did not completely dispel these views. Forty percent of the public continued to believe
that men were more intelligent than women. Additionally, a majority believed
that men were more creative than women. Pluralities of men and many
women also accepted the notion that men were more likely to possess a large
range of job-related emotional and mental traits, including the ability to
make decisions, handle people, accept new ideas, be even-tempered, and
maintain a level head. They also clung to the stereotype that men possessed
more common sense than women.[28]

Other clichés facilitated the view that women could not be as productive or as successful as men in many jobs. In the 1970s, for instance, most men
and women believed that women had less physical stamina and were more
emotional and less logical than men.[29] The women's movement and feminists have attacked these notions, but the rise of biological-based explanations for gender differences have made many of these stereotypes hard to
eradicate.[30]

Although evidence suggests that many of these ideas regarding women
are declining, many people still question women's ability to make it in the
business world. In 1994, 44 percent of women and 54 percent of men indicated that a reason (either major or minor) why few women were in high corporate positions was that "men are better suited emotionally for big business
than are women."[31] Large numbers of women and men (36 percent and 44
percent, respectively) also thought another factor was that "women aren't
tough enough for business."[32] Compared to a similar question in 1972 that
found 49 percent of all women and 56 percent of all men agreeing with the
statement that "men are better at economics and business than women,"
there seems to have been only minor changes in the negative view that
women are less qualified for business.

A related problem is that women are often viewed as less effective
bosses than men. Indeed, nearly half of all men and a third of all women in
the mid-1990s agreed that this is a reason why women are not in high corporate positions.[33] Table 4–3 gives the answers of men and women to a series of
questions asking them to indicate whether they associate each trait more
with a female or a male boss or manager. The responses point to several areas
where men are seen as better, namely toughness, level of awareness of business issues, effectiveness in dealing with competitors, decisiveness, effective-

TABLE 4–3 Public Perceptions of the Characteristics of Men and Women Bosses[a]

Characteristic associated with a

	Female Boss		Male Boss	
	% Women	(% Men)	% Women	(% Men)
Hard-working	22	(10)	18	(33)
Tough	10	(6)	47	(59)
Honest	35	(26)	7	(10)
Intelligent	18	(11)	7	(14)
Concerned about workers' rights	38	(31)	9	(14)
Well informed on business issues	9	(6)	30	(36)
Sensitive to employees' personal problems	49	(45)	7	(11)
Effective in dealing with competitors	10	(6)	31	(40)
Decisive	14	(7)	25	(38)
Loyal to employees	29	(22)	9	(17)
Effective in dealing with labor unions	8	(5)	41	(49)
Able to delegate responsibility	15	(7)	20	(32)
Respected by the people who report to them	12	(18)	26	(34)
Take a long-term view of things	19	(12)	18	(27)

[a]Survey question: "Now I'm going to read you a list of words and phrases. Thinking about the business world, for each one, would you tell me if you associate it more with a female boss or top manager, or more with a male boss or top manager?" Figures indicate the percentage of women (men) who responded that they associated the trait more with a female or male boss.

Source: Data from 1990 Virginia Slims American Women's Opinion Poll. Survey conducted by the Roper Organization. Data provided by the Roper Center for Public Opinion Research, Storrs, Conn.

ness in dealing with labor unions, ability to delegate responsibility, and level of respect by the people who report to them. Alternatively, women bosses are seen as better on honesty, concern about workers' rights, and sensitivity to employees' personal problems. Given these views, we can begin to understand why, if given a choice, men and women may prefer a man boss. In 1995, for instance, 46 percent of the public (54 percent of women and 37 percent of men) preferred a man boss.[34]

The liabilities that women bosses supposedly possess have parallels with the characterizations of women politicians reported in Chapter 2. Women are seen as less effective than men in standing up to competitors and unions in the same way they are expected to be less effective in dealing with the military, enemies, and trading partners.

Women's positive attributes are also similar in the political and economic spheres. They are identified as more concerned with "people issues" and more honest. In politics, women's attributes may be a plus in some races. Similarly, women may benefit if they are seen as having the abilities needed to manage the diverse work force of the twenty-first century. However, for the most important leadership positions of president of the United States or chief executive officer of a major corporation, women are characterized as "not tough enough" in the minds of many citizens. The stereotypes that persist in the political and corporate sectors may help to explain why there has never been a woman president and why very few women head Fortune 500 companies.

Stereotypes, moreover, are linked to deeply held views about the character traits of men and women. In 1995, for instance, a plurality of the public agreed that men are more aggressive, more courageous, more ambitious, and more easygoing, while women are seen as more emotional, more talkative, more patient, more creative, and more affectionate.[35] Other stereotypes about the abilities of women also persist. Perhaps one of the most damaging is the idea that women have lower mathematical and spatial abilities than men. This notion persists even though most research shows the differences to be minimal and probably the function of women taking fewer math courses, or the bias of tests or researchers, discussed in Chapter 3.[36] This stereotype, however, has devastating effects. High-school and college teachers and guidance counselors often track women students away from the natural sciences and engineering, the very courses necessary to enter some of today's most high-tech professions. There is suggestive evidence in a report by the American Association of University Women (AAUW) that teachers may even reinforce or produce the stereotype in the classroom, by allowing boys to do science experiments and diluting women's confidence in their mathematical abilities.[37] Public attitudes toward women's abilities also contribute to another barrier, women's preparedness for paid employment.

PREPARATION OF WOMEN FOR EMPLOYMENT OUTSIDE THE HOME

Early Training for Work

The review of the public's attitudes toward the relative importance and place of work outside the home helps us to understand the lower commitment of women, especially in the past, to salaried employment. Quite simply, prior to 1940, employment was looked upon by most women as something to do before they took up their real life's work—being wives and mothers. There is evidence, however, that many women desired to combine work and a family but were unable to do so.[38] Furthermore, married women who did work, notably African American women and women of limited economic means, faced a job market that took little cognizance of the difficulties they faced as they tried to combine both roles.

The absence of laws preventing discrimination in educational programs also contributed to the inability of all but a few women to acquire the educational preparation necessary for high-prestige fields such as law or medicine. In this climate young women were not encouraged and, as we have seen, were often discouraged from acquiring an education that would have prepared them for well-paying occupations and professions. The gradual expansion of academic opportunities for women, beginning in the late nineteenth century, did not always change the situation. Most women in high school and even some in college took home economics courses under the assumption that these programs were the best preparation for their future occupations as housewives and mothers. Even those who majored in other areas chose or were channeled into traditional fields such as teaching, nursing, clerical, or social work.

In the past, textbooks and schools also played key roles in narrowing the expectations of young women about lifetime work.[39] Recent examinations of children's literature and textbooks show a continued, though diminished, tendency to have more male characters and to portray women and girls in traditional roles with stereotyped characteristics of passivity, dependency, and a need to be rescued by males.[40] The AAUW study indicates that teachers still tend to encourage boys to do well more than girls, giving the former more classroom attention. African American girls and girls from economically impoverished backgrounds apparently get shortchanged the most.[41] This may help to explain the persistence of sex-role stereotyping of some fields and the finding that women are less confident than men about their own achievements.[42] It also may help us to understand why girls experience such a sharp drop in self-esteem in their teen years.[43] Not surprisingly, 56 percent of men and 63 percent of women believe an important reason why women have not risen in corporate ranks is because young girls are not encouraged to aspire to careers as managers.[44]

Take Our Daughters to Work

On April 28, 1993, the Ms. Foundation for Women sponsored an event entitled "Take Our Daughters to Work." This grass-roots public education campaign encouraged mothers, fathers, employers, teachers, and others to take nine- to fifteen-year-old girls to work with them to learn about the realities of work, employment opportunities, and the education and training jobs require.

The Ms. Foundation for Women received extensive response to the event. It is estimated that more than one million girls participated nationwide that first year. Employers such as the federal government, especially the Department of Health and Human Services, and the Lifetime Network played an active role in helping their employees bring their daughters to work.

This campaign evolved in response to research indicating that "girls emerge from adolescence with a poor self-image, relatively low expectations from life and much less confidence in themselves and their abilities than boys."[a] In a survey commissioned by the AAUW, adolescent girls were asked how often they felt "happy the way I am"; 60 percent responded "always." By high school that figure dropped to 29 percent. For boys, the figures dropped from 67 percent to 46 percent.[b] The Take Our Daughters to Work campaign is just a first step in combating these attitudes.

A program of the MS. FOUNDATION FOR WOMEN
Welcome to the OFFICIAL Home Page for

TAKE OUR DAUGHTERS TO WORK ®

FIVE YEARS OF WORK TOWARDS A LIFETIME OF CONFIDENCE

Thursday, April 24,1997

(ALWAYS THE 4TH THURSDAY IN APRIL)

Take Our Daughters to Work ® is designed to **CELEBRATE** Girls' Worth:

To value their opinions and ideas

To use their voice to speak their mind

To never stop asking questions

To live proudly in their bodies as they are

Website: Take Our Daughters To Work. (Take Our Daughters to Work® is a registered trademark of Ms. Foundation for Women.)

[a]Suzanne Daley, "Little Girls Lose Their Self-Esteem on Way to Adolescence, Study Finds," *New York Times,* January 9, 1991.
[b]Wellesley College Center for Research on Women, *The AAUW Report: How Schools Shortchange Women* (Washington, D.C.: American Association of University Women, 1992).

Although there is little evidence that women fear success, there may be some concern about doing gender-inappropriate activities that might, in turn, be tied to childhood socialization.[45] Indeed, research suggests people still continue to characterize jobs by gender. Certain careers, generally those with high pay, are identified as requiring "masculine" personality attributes, whereas others, often those that are less profitable, are seen as requiring "feminine" qualities.[46]

The Women's Rights Movement and Preparation for Work

Passage of Title IX and the message of the women's rights movement about the desirability of women having careers began to have a noticeable impact on the preparation of young women for the professions in the 1970s. In 1968, however, before the movement's message was popularized, surveys of white women born between 1944 and 1954, during the baby boom, found only 29 percent of them expected to be employed at age thirty-five. (In reality, more than 60 percent of the married women and 80 percent of the unmarried women were actually working when surveyed again at age thirty-five.) African American women were better at estimating their chances of working perhaps because their experiences were based on the employment record of their mothers, most of whom worked. Not surprisingly, the women who did not plan on being employed undertook much less job training and formal schooling.[47] These women were queried again about their work plans in 1973, after the message of the women's rights movement regarding women and work had gained prominence. These same young women had much more accurate estimates of their employment prospects then, although because they were older—nineteen to twenty-nine—many had passed the traditional time for acquiring the education that would prepare them for better jobs.[48]

More recently, interviews with first-year college students nationwide revealed that women are adopting many of the same work and status goals as men. In 1969, for instance, women were 22 percent less likely than men to list "being well-off" financially as a life goal; by 1996 they were only 4 percent less likely to have this goal than men. Relatedly, by 1996 men and women were equally likely to identify raising a family as an important goal. Women in their first year of college, however, were considerably less likely than first-year men, even in 1996, to want to become successful in a business of their own,[49] which is an interesting fact given that more than one-third of all small businesses are owned by women.

Education and Work Readiness. In 1969, when first-year college women and men were asked about their educational plans, only 42.8 percent of women expected to go beyond the associate or bachelor's degree. In contrast, 56.8 percent of men expected to continue their education. Twice as many men expected to get a Ph.D., five times as many men planned on law school, and three times as many men planned to become doctors or dentists.[50] By 1995, the educational plans of first-year women actually exceeded those of men. More women than men expected to obtain an advanced degree (67.2 percent versus 63.1 percent). Women were also more likely to plan on entering a Ph.D. program, law school, or medical school.[51]

Educational attainment of women and men is also increasingly similar. In the 1940s, men were slightly more likely to obtain a college degree (6.9 versus 4.9 percent in 1940), but men were much more likely to become medical doctors. Only 10 percent of all recipients of an M.D. in 1949 were women,[52] as revealed in Figure 4–2. On the eve of the popularization of the message of the women's movement and before Title IX, the gap between the educational attainment of men and women had grown. Of all women age twenty-five to twenty-nine in 1970, only 12.9 percent had completed college, in contrast to 20 percent of similarly aged men.[53] The percentage of medical degrees awarded to women had also declined to 8 percent. (They had actually slipped even lower to 6 percent in 1959–1960.) The percentage of women receiving law degrees was also dismally low at 5 percent, although this represented a doubling of the percentage from 1959 to 1960.[54]

Since the changes in cultural values and educational practices in the early 1970s, the number of college-educated women has increased dramatically, such that young women are now more likely than men to go to college. Moreover, in recent years more women than men obtained associate's, bach-

FIGURE 4–2   Percentage of professional degrees earned by women in medicine and law.[a]

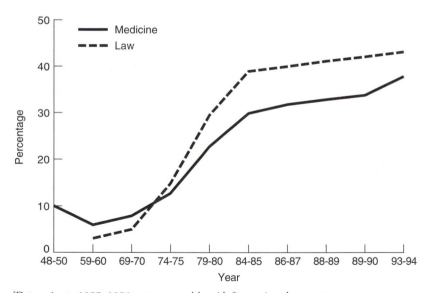

[a]Data prior to 1955–1956 not comparable with figures in subsequent years.

Source: U.S. Department of Education, National Center for Education Statistics, "Degrees and Other Formal Awards Conferred" and "Integrated Post-Secondary Education Data System (IPEDS), Completions Survey." Printed in National Center for Education Statistics, *Digest of Education Statistics 1989* (Washington, D.C.: U.S. Department of Education, 1989), 239; U.S. Department of Education. Reprinted in "Earned Degrees Conferred, 1993–94," *Chronicle of Higher Education Almanac* (Washington, D.C.: Chronicle of Higher Education, 1996), 22.

elor's, or master's degrees. In the mid-1990s, almost 40 percent of all Ph.D.s were given to women. Similarly, almost four out of ten medical degrees and more than four in ten law degrees are now earned by women, as revealed in Figure 4–2. African American women, moreover, are more likely to receive a college or professional degree at every level than their male counterparts. Similarly, Hispanic women now exceed Hispanic men in numbers of college and advanced degrees at all levels except the Ph.D.[55]

A closer examination of the fields in which women obtain their degrees, however, shows a persistence of some sex stereotyping. At least half of the doctoral degrees awarded in education and psychology go to women, whereas barely 11 percent of Ph.D.s in engineering, 21.7 percent of those in the physical sciences, and 28.2 percent of those in business go to women. Undergraduate degrees also show a concentration of women in the traditional fields of education (77.3 percent women), home economics (91.5 percent women), and health professions/nursing (82.5 percent women). The large number of undergraduate degrees to women in nontraditional fields such as business is indicative of the changed commitment of young women to the world of work, as noted in Table 4–4. The damaging stereotypes about the mathematical abilities of women are reflected in the small percentage of women getting their bachelor's degrees in engineering (16.4) and the physical sciences (33.6).[56]

Compared to women of an earlier generation, young women in college today are more likely to be preparing for a career at rates equal to their male contemporaries, yet their continued concentration in some traditional fields and their lack of parity in some degree programs have important implications for their ability to compete equally with men for the high-tech jobs of the twenty-first century.

TABLE 4–4 Earned Degrees Conferred by Gender, 1993–1994

Field	Degrees Earned by Women		
	% Bachelor's	*% Master's*	*% Doctoral*
Business and management	47.6	36.5	28.2
Communications	58.9	62.6	49.0
Computer, information sciences	28.4	25.8	15.4
Education	77.3	76.7	60.8
Engineering	16.4	15.4	11.1
Life sciences	51.2	52.1	40.7
Mathematics	46.3	38.1	21.9
Physical sciences	33.6	29.2	21.7
Psychology	73.1	72.1	62.2
Social sciences	46.1	44.0	36.1

Source: U.S. Department of Education. Reprinted in "Earned Degrees Conferred, 1993–94," *Chronicle of Higher Education Almanac* (Washington, D.C.: Chronicle of Higher Education, 1996), 22. Percentages calculated by authors.

The Chilly Climate for Women at Colleges and Universities

Women who attempt to earn an advanced degree face a number of special problems in universities and colleges. One of the most damaging is a classroom where their contributions are devalued and ignored.[a] Whereas white women often have to contend with professors who respond only to the questions of male students and refuse to call on the women in the classroom, women of color face the double burden of racism and sexism.[b] Not only are they ignored, but when they are called upon it is often to represent the views of members of their race, a situation that can be particularly embarrassing, demeaning, and racist.[c] Hispanic women, whose culture emphasizes politeness, may find their refusal to challenge a professor interpreted as a sign of a lack of independent thinking. Similarly, the competitiveness of academe may challenge Hispanic cultural values of cooperation and group cohesiveness.[d]

Professors are sometimes guilty of treating women students differently from male students in other ways as well. Women are less frequently encouraged to attempt difficult courses or curricula or to seek advanced degrees. Again, the abilities of women of color may be especially downgraded by both white male and white female faculty and male faculty from their own ethnic group.

The social setting of many universities may also make women feel undervalued and unwanted. In addition to the pervasive problem of sexual harassment by faculty and male students, women may find student activities are designed to benefit men more than women.[e] For instance, a 1991 study by the National Collegiate Athletic Association (NCAA) found that, contrary to the goals of Title IX, at most universities, male sports programs and male athletes receive a disproportionate share of the money in athletic programs.[f] The NCAA reported that although women number more than half of all students, male athletes outnumber women athletes by two to one, men receive twice as many athletic scholarships, men's teams get three-fourths of the operating funds, and recruiters for men's teams grab 80 percent of the funds for recruiting.[g] Follow-up studies by the *Chronicle of Higher Education* found small improvements in the 1990s.

Women of color face some special social problems. Because most directors of social activities are males, African American and Hispanic women often find their own interests are ignored by both the mainstream social activities and those designed for members of their race. Moreover, because of the greater number of African American women as compared to African American men on most campuses, the possibility of a heterosexual same-race social life is further limited. Many African American women complain about having to sit in their rooms because of the isolation they feel from campus activities.[h]

What is the climate for women in the classrooms and on the campus at your university? Do women of color face special problems? In addition to the problems already discussed, what special difficulties have you faced because of your sex, your race or ethnicity, or your sexual preference?

[a]Roberta M. Hall and Bernice R. Sandler, "The Classroom Climate: A Chilly One for Women?" (Washington, D.C.: Association of American Colleges, 1982); Bernice R. Sandler, Lisa A. Silverberg, and Roberta M. Hall, *The Chilly Classroom Climate: A Guide to Improve the Education of Women* (Washington, D.C.: National Association for Women in Education, 1996).

[b]Yolanda T. Moses, "Black Women in Academe: Issues and Strategies" (Washington, D.C.: Association of American Colleges, 1989); Sarah Nieves-Squire, "Hispanic Women: Making Their Presence on Campus Less Tenuous" (Washington, D.C.: Association of American Colleges and Universities, 1991).

[c]Moses, "Black Women in Academe," 4.

[d]Nieves-Squire, "Hispanic Women," 2–4.

[e]Roberta M. Hall and Bernice R. Sandler, "Out of the Classroom: A Chilly Climate for Women?" (Washington, D.C.: Association of American Colleges, 1984).

[f]Douglas Lederman, "Men Outnumber Women and Get Most of Money in Big-Time Sports Programs," *Chronicle of Higher Education* (April 8, 1992): Al, A37–A40; Douglas Lederman, "Men Get 70% of Money Available for Athletic Scholarships at Colleges That Play Big-Time Sports, New Study Finds," *Chronicle of Higher Education* (March 18, 1992): Al, A45, A46.

[g]Debra E. Blum, "Slow Progress on Equity," *Chronicle of Higher Education* (October 26, 1994): A45, A47–A51; Jim Naughton and Rachanee Srisavasdi, "Data on Funds for Men and Women's Sports Becomes Available as New Law Takes Effect," *Chronicle of Higher Education* (October 25, 1996): A45–46; Jim Naughton, "Women in Division 1 Sport Programs: The Glass Is Half Empty and Half Full," *Chronicle of Higher Education* (April 11, 1997): A39–A46.

[h]Moses, "Black Women in Academe," 2, 6–7.

Work-Force Commitment Attitudes. Surveys of women in the larger society show increasingly higher levels of commitment to the work force. Women are as likely as men to say they would continue to work if they did not need to financially, and that they get great or moderate personal satisfaction from working.[57] Today, more employed women say that they need to work to support themselves or their families. In 1970, 49 percent of working women gave "to earn extra money" as their reason for working. By 1994, only 23 percent listed this response; "to support self" (29 percent) and "to support family" (44 percent) were the most common reasons for working. Moreover, three-quarters of women indicated that their families would suffer financial hardships if they did not work.[58] A study in 1990 by the House Ways and Means Committee found women's earnings are increasingly important to a family's living standard.[59] This is especially true for African American women. According to a 1993 study, they contribute nearly 40 percent of their families' income. The percentage of family income contributed by Hispanic women is 32.2 percent, and by white women, 30.6 percent.[60] James Geschwender and Rita Carroll-Seguin argue that as white married women's employment rises, the relative income gains of African American families conditioned by the reliance on two incomes will be negated. Income inequalities between white families and other families, then, will rise.[61]

Public attitudes toward working mothers show considerable conflict between work roles and home roles. Perhaps as a consequence, working mothers report that they "frequently" or "sometimes" feel torn between the demands of their job and wanting to spend more time with their families.[62] When surveyed in 1994, four out of ten working mothers reported they would prefer to stay home rather than work if they were free to do either. Sixty-one percent of those not employed preferred staying home to working. Women were also more likely than men to prefer more opportunity to work at home.[63] Although many women with dual roles experience stress, most report that they are doing a fairly good job of balancing their jobs and their families.[64] Whether the dual roles limit their prospects at work is a topic we return to later.

Even if women are able to overcome traditional attitudes and prepare themselves to take an equal role with men, equality is not assured. Two important groups have acted, and probably will continue to act, to prevent women from achieving equality with men in the marketplace: employers and male workers.

SEX DISCRIMINATION

Discrimination by Employers

Sex discrimination by employers against women stems from two sources, cultural attitudes and economic self-interest. It is usually impossible to disentangle the two. Take, for example, the custom of employers hiring males for certain positions. Economists refer to this as "preference" or "taste." Preferences, in turn, are often cited as explanations for segregation of occupations and the lower wages paid to women.

A concrete example of this kind of discrimination in the first half of the twentieth century was the widespread practice of refusing to hire married women (referred to as a hire bar) or firing women who did marry (labeled a fire bar). Claudia Goldin's research on the practice of "marriage bars" has found that the practice began in public school systems sometime in the late nineteenth century. By 1928 (before the Great Depression), 61 percent of all school districts refused to hire married women and 52 percent fired women who married. As public sentiment against married women's employment grew during the depression, these figures rose to 87 percent of schools having hire bars and 70 percent having fire bars.[65]

The federal government and nine states also maintained a version of this policy during the depression.[66] Until 1970, the U.S. State Department continued to fire women in the Foreign Service who married.[67]

A 1931 survey of large firms in seven cities found the practice extended beyond government, as 12 percent of the firms had fire bars, and an additional 25 percent of firms had a discretionary policy that allowed firing of married women if the situation warranted. Additionally, 29 percent had hire bars, again with 50 percent of all surveyed firms having the discretionary ability to not hire married women. A follow-up survey in 1940 showed that the prevalence of the two types of bars increased during the depression. Collectively, the marriage hire and fire bars affected as many as 50 percent of the employed women in the sampled cities.[68]

The firms most likely to have either policy (the policies usually went together) were those that promoted from within, had fixed salary schedules, and had other benefits that accrued with years. The data, therefore, suggest that employers used societal distaste for married women working as an excuse for not hiring women or firing them so that women employees could be forced out before they qualified for maximum benefits.[69] The cumulative affect of the marriage bars, of course, was to reinforce cultural stereotypes against married women working and to discourage young women from preparing for a lifetime of work. Moreover, those married women who could find work were required to take jobs with considerably lower pay than they might have earned had they been able to seek employment with all businesses.[70]

Support for the economic self-interest explanation can also be seen in the hiring practices of firms in the 1950s. When the supply of single women declined, a result of the decline in the birth rate in the 1930s, most firms quickly dropped their hire and fire bars. A 1950 study of school districts found that only 18 percent still retained the hire bar and 10 percent the fire bar. In at least some firms and school districts the marriage bars were replaced with "pregnancy bars" that mandated the firing of women expecting a child or prohibited hiring of women with young children.[71] Most of these bars would themselves be eliminated as the supply of older married women declined and the practice was found illegal.

More pervasive than marriage or pregnancy hire and fire bars was the practice of most firms to not hire African American women or to limit the type of positions for which they could be employed. Surveys in the 1930s and 1940s, for instance, found that more than half of all firms queried had a practice of not hiring African American women as clerical or professional workers. Evidence suggests these official policies of discrimination persisted until at least the 1960s.[72]

Although most employers today readily employ married women and women with children, they are still influenced by racism and stereotypes about the work commitment and abilities of women. These kinds of attitudes form the basis for hiring practices that keep women out of management and decision-making positions. Francine D. Blau has documented that stereotypes about what women can do persist in some industries even when other industries are successfully using women workers in comparable job categories.[73] Economists trace such hiring practices to stereotypes about the productivity of women, women's supposed lack of certain qualities (strength, rationality, and mechanical ability), and fears that male employees will leave if women are hired.[74]

Whatever their source or rationale, stereotypes clearly affect women and influence the practices of employers. Perhaps as a result of the women's rights movement publicizing such activities, surveys of women show a growing awareness of this discrimination over the past twenty-five years, as revealed in Table 4–5.

In 1970, only 40 percent of those women surveyed believed women were discriminated against in obtaining top jobs in the professions. By 1994, this percentage was 53 percent, down slightly from its 1989 high of 58 percent. Similar results can be found regarding the problems faced by women in obtaining executive positions, skilled-labor jobs, and top jobs in the government. With respect to leadership responsibilities in groups of women and men, the perception of discrimination remains unchanged after increasing in the last two decades. Awareness of discrimination in the military is up perhaps because of the wider reporting of myriad sex scandals in the navy and army.

Whereas increased awareness of discrimination in the 1970s and 1980s may be a result of greater press attention, the decline in the 1990s may either signal actual decreases in discrimination or simply the perception that things are improving. When asked, most women report that salaries, job opportuni-

TABLE 4–5 Women's Perceptions of Discrimination[a]

Percentage of respondents answering affirmatively

	1970 (%)	1974 (%)	1979 (%)	1985 (%)	1989 (%)	1994 (%)
Obtaining loans, mortgages, charge accounts in their own names	NA	56	51	47	41	41
Obtaining top jobs in government	NA	55	55	58	64	56
Obtaining top jobs in the military	NA	NA	NA	42	55	61
Obtaining executive positions in business	50	54	58	57	61	59
Obtaining top jobs in the professions	40	50	52	56	58	53
Being given leadership responsibility in groups with both men and women	38	44	45	46	47	47
Getting skilled-labor jobs	40	47	48	51	52	49
Getting white-collar and clerical jobs	NA	13	13	14	15	17
Getting a college education	NA	9	7	10	10	12

[a]Survey question: "Do you feel women are discriminated against or not in——?"
NA = not applicable.

Source: The Virginia Slims Polls. Data provided by the Roper Center for Public Opinion Research, Storrs, Conn.

ties, and chances at top positions in government and in business have improved. Generally, however, that improvement is seen as a "little" and not a "lot." More than a third of women see the need for major change in all four areas to make women's lives better. Most other women see the need for some change. Interestingly, men are much less likely to think major changes are needed.[75]

Poor treatment by employers is not the only discrimination faced by women. The behavior of male employees also often serves as a barrier to some women's entry or success in a chosen job or career. Indeed, some researchers argue that hiring biases are not "economically rational" but reflect the desire of male employers in concert with male employees to retain male power and prestige in the larger society.[76]

Discrimination by Male Employees

The role of male workers in influencing women's job and wage opportunities cannot be ignored. In polls conducted in the 1930s, 1940s, and 1960s, fear that women would take their jobs was the second most commonly cited reason for men's opposition to women working.[77] Even in the 1990s, the specter of women taking jobs from men is raised by supporters of organized labor.[78]

Historically, male unionists, in particular, have viewed women workers as a threat. Women were barred from joining unions; when they could join, separate seniority lists were sometimes maintained, and some unions even negotiated differential wage scales for women and men. Judicial rulings eventually made these practices illegal. Even in predominantly female unions, women have faced discrimination in attaining leadership positions. As late as 1972, the International Ladies Garment Workers Union (ILGWU), whose membership is nearly 80 percent female, had only one woman official.[79] Similarly, a woman was not elected to the executive council of the American Federation of Labor–Congress of Industrial Organizations (AFL-CIO) until 1980.

The absence of union protection continues to help explain why the working conditions and pay scales of women lag behind those of men. Traditionally, union leaders, perhaps wishing to keep women out of certain job categories, have argued that women are difficult to organize. In 1996, only 12 percent of all working women were union members. New interest by union leaders in creating unions for those engaged in the clerical trades and other traditional women's jobs, however, has opened a whole new era in the relationship of women workers and the union movement. Thus, more union members are women today (39 percent) than twenty-five years ago (22 percent).[80]

Women breaking into the skilled trades still face a particularly difficult time in spite of recent court rulings. Unions and union apprentice systems seem especially reluctant to allow women entrance. Employers and unions have intentionally failed to notify women of openings, used questionable screening practices and age requirements, and mandated sponsors for entry in an effort to keep women out of the building and construction trades.[81] Even on job sites where employment goals to hire women exist, it is hard to monitor the number of women because jobs often last for only a few days. This makes it possible for companies to use their core (male) employees. In Buffalo, New York, for instance, construction jobs funded by government money supposedly are required to have women as 6.9 percent of the workers. However, analysis of the major construction sites found that women never were more than 4.5 percent of the workers, a percentage that also included women clerical workers in the field.[82]

Women who enter the skilled crafts where pay is high often face hostility, which makes success difficult. A comparison of women in the trades with those in clerical positions found that the former were considerably more likely to report sexual harassment and discrimination. Women in the trades were also exposed to more isolation, loneliness, and hostile supervisors and coworkers than women in traditionally women's fields. Not surprisingly, the tradeswomen were more dissatisfied with their jobs. African American tradeswomen appeared to face the most discrimination and ill treatment, reflecting the double influence of sex and race discrimination.[83] (Indeed, many employers whose policies prevented the hiring of African American women clericals claimed their policy followed from the preferences of their white employees, male and female.[84])

Women in other male-dominated professions also report problems with male colleagues. The most common difficulties revolve around being shut out of informal workers' networks. Closed out of the "old-boy" networks, women are denied the information and peer support necessary for success or promotion.[85] Women in the upper levels of management, the professions, and academia are particularly likely to encounter actions, whether conscious or unconscious, of male colleagues to thwart their upward mobility. In fact, in a 1992 study of top female executives, 25 percent reported that sexism was the greatest obstacle to success.[86]

The extent of male efforts to keep women coworkers from succeeding is difficult to measure, but women who work report widespread ill treatment. For instance, a 1994 survey found women agreed overwhelmingly (77 percent) that "women who try to rise to the top of major corporations get held back by the old-boy network."[87]

Sexual Harassment

Perhaps the most widely publicized form of "on-the-job" discrimination by male employers and employees is sexual harassment. In recent years a wide variety of reports of this behavior made headlines, with the most notorious case being Clarence Thomas's alleged harassment of Anita Hill.

As discussed in Chapter 3, sexual harassment, as defined by the Equal

Employment Opportunity Commission, is unwelcome sexual advances, requests for sexual favors, and other verbal or physical conduct of a sexual nature.

Studies of sexual harassment find that it takes a variety of forms from unwanted sexual remarks and suggestive looks to unwanted touching and pressures to have sex.[a] In the campus environment, peer harassment by male students of female students also runs the gamut from confrontation of women by men in groups, to sexual taunts or threats, to joking and put-downs of women in the classroom.[b]

There is debate over the extent of sexual harassment. A review by Rita Mae Kelly of major studies of harassment finds that, depending on the sample and the wording of the question, from 45 to 90 percent of all working women report having been sexually harassed.[c] At the college level, the few campuses where surveys have been conducted find over 70 percent of college women report peer sexual harassment.[d] Even young girls in elementary and high school report a rising tide of harassment by boy students.[e] Perhaps the most harassment occurs in the military where the recent scandals at the training bases show just how pervasive the problem is in this male-dominated institution.

In the aftermath of the Thomas hearings, surveys found that most of the public believed sexual harassment was a serious problem. Thus, a December 1992 poll found that 85 percent of women and men polled cited sexual harassment as a problem in the workplace, up from 74 percent a year earlier.[f] A 1994 poll, however, reported that only 25 percent of women believe there is a lot (51 percent think that there is some) sexual harassment in the workplace.[g] While more women than ever are filing complaints of sexual harassment, there is still a hesitancy to do so for fear of losing one's job.

Indeed, most researchers see sexual harassment as an attempt by men to exert their power over women. Psychologist John Gottman notes, "Sexual harassment is a subtle form of rape, and rape is more about fear than sex. Harassment is a way for a man to make a woman feel vulnerable."[h] Correspondingly, sexual harassment is most prevalent in professions and jobs where there are few women and where women are attempting to enter a previously male-only profession. Thus, men in blue-collar occupations use blatant sexual harassment to scare women out of occupations where men do not want them, and professional men make jokes at women's expense for the same effect.[i] For instance, in 1991, Professor Frances Cooley of the Stanford University Medical School announced she would resign, citing "pervasive and debilitating" sexual harassment. Although she stayed at the school, in 1995 she claimed, "The crotch grabbing and breast grabbing is out but there are still demeaning comments."[j]

[a]Deborah L. Siegel, "Sexual Harassment: Research and Resources" (New York: National Council for Research on Women, 1991), 5–6.

[b]Jean O'Gorman Hughes and Bernice R. Sandler, "Peer Harassment: Hassles for Women on Campus" (Washington, D.C.: Project on the Status and Education of Women, 1980), 3–5. See also, American Association of University Women, *Hostile Hallways: The AAUW Survey on Sexual Harassment in America's Schools* (Washington, D.C.: American Association of University Women Educational Foundation, 1993), 7–10.

[c]Rita Mae Kelly, *The Gendered Economy: Work, Careers, and Success* (Beverly Hills, Calif.: Sage, 1991), 89–91.

[d]Hughes and Sandler, "Peer Harassment," 2.

[e]Jerry Adler with Debra Rosenberg, "Must Boys Always Be Boys?" *Newsweek*, October 19, 1992, 77; American Association of University Women, *Hostile Hallways: The AAUW Survey on Sexual Harassment in America's Schools* (Washington, D.C.: Author, 1993).

[f]Richard Morin, "Sex-Harassment Issue Is Gaining Consensus," *Buffalo News*, December 19, 1992, A5.

[g]The 1995 Virginia Slims Poll. Data made available by the Roper Center for Public Opinion Research, Storrs, Conn.

[h]Quoted in Darrel Goleman, "Sexual Harassment. It's About Power, Not Sex," *New York Times*, October 22, 1991, C12.

[i]Ibid., C12.

[j]Quoted in Ben Gose, "Women's Place in Medicine," *Chronicle of Higher Education*, November 3, 1995, A49.

ECONOMIC AND MARKETPLACE FACTORS

Many economists who study the labor force participation rates of women focus on the influence of economic and marketplace factors on the propensity of women to work. Valerie Kincade Oppenheimer, for one, has traced the movement of women into the workplace after World War II to a change in the type of jobs available and the corresponding employer demand for women workers.[88] She argued that as the United States moved toward a service economy, women workers who had traditionally filled service jobs were more actively recruited into the labor force by higher wages and a corresponding elimination of the marriage, and later pregnancy, hire and fire bars.

Other economists focus on the role played by the income of other family members. They reason that women will be more likely to work if their spouse's income is low or if there is no other wage earner in the family.[89]

Claudia Goldin tested these propositions with data from 1890 to 1980. She found that the various economic factors did not have a consistent impact on the labor market activity of working women. In the early years of this century, her husband's income was an important determinant of whether a married woman worked; if his income was low, a woman was more likely to be employed. Later in the century, from 1940 through 1960, the most important variable became the wages paid to women. As wages rose, so too did women's employment levels. Interestingly, from 1960 through 1980, neither income of family nor women's wages were very good predictors of whether a married woman would work.[90] Research by Eileen Trzcinski suggests it may be the uncertainty of the husband's employment and/or the risk of divorce that explains women's greater work-force commitment,[91] although women's work-force commitments and developments in the workplace are also important.

IMPACT OF BARRIERS ON THE POSITION
OF WOMEN IN THE MARKETPLACE

Just as in the case of politics, the barriers to equality for women in the marketplace go beyond legal ones. Thus, we should not expect that simply
removing legal barriers will result in women assuming a comparable position with men in the educational and occupational arenas. The persistence of
attitudinal stereotypes about the abilities of women and the place of work in
women's lives, the lack of preparation on the part of some women for certain
types of economic activity, and discrimination all combine to restrict the
progress of women in the marketplace.

Attempts to identify how these barriers limit women in the educational
and economic arenas and how they might continue to do so in the future are
complicated by the interrelationships and interaction of the barriers. Moreover, not all women are equally affected by all of the barriers, or at least are
not affected in the same way. Young college-educated women who desire a
career may confront quite different problems from what older, high-school-
educated women who would prefer to be full-time homemakers would confront. With these caveats in mind, we turn to an examination of the historical
progress of women in obtaining job and pay equality with men.

Employment Levels of Women

Early census data about women are somewhat suspect because questions
about women's employment were not routinely included. Claudia Goldin's
examination of the limited data that exist suggests that as many as a third or
more of single women may have been employed in 1850.[92] By the turn of the
century, this number rose to over 35 percent for single women age fifteen
to twenty-four and 50 percent for women age twenty-five to thirty-four.
Foreign-born and African American women were much more likely to be
employed than single white women. In 1890, the participation rate of unmarried foreign-born women was 70.8 percent; for nonwhite women, it was 59.5
percent; and for white women, 38.4 percent.[93] Since 1890, official census figures reveal that the participation rate of single white women has continued
to climb so that two-thirds of all single women were employed in 1995. These
figures are just marginally lower than the figures for similarly aged single
men.[94]

Because of negative attitudes toward the employment of married
women, most people assume married women did not work in the past century. However, Goldin found that 44 percent or more of all female heads of
households may have worked before 1820. Her reanalysis of 1890 census
data, which includes both work at home and in family businesses such as
boarding houses and farms, indicates perhaps 12.5 percent of white married

women worked, a 10 percentage point increase from the official figures. The situation was dramatically different for African American women. According to 1890 official statistics, 24.5 percent of them worked.[95] The true figure is probably about twice that if women working on family farms and in family businesses are included.

Employment of married women increased only gradually in the next fifty years, probably because of the marriage hire and fire bars and negative public opinion. Thus, in 1940, about 15 to 17 percent of married women under age thirty-four were working. Older married women were even less likely to work outside the home. African American married women of all ages continued to be employed at higher rates than their white counterparts.[96]

World War II dramatically altered the pattern of married women's employment, as illustrated in Figure 4–3. Older married women with children who were grown or of school age entered the labor force in large numbers in reaction to the government's propaganda campaign and the availability of employment opportunities brought about by the war. In 1950, more than a quarter of all married women age thirty-five to forty-four were working.[97] The 1950s and 1960s saw the recruitment of even more older married women into the labor market. As the number and availability of single women declined, employers dropped their marriage bars, and occupations considered to be "women's" in the service and trade sectors grew.[98] Therefore, by 1970, nearly half of all women with school-age children and almost a

FIGURE 4–3 Labor-force participation rates of married women, husband present, by presence and age of children, 1950–1996.

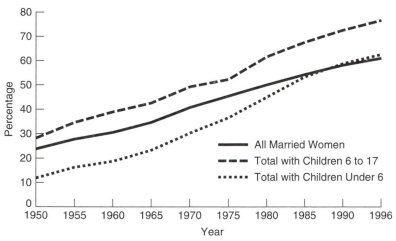

Source: U.S. Department of Labor, Bureau of Labor Statistics, *Perspectives on Working Women* (June 1980) and U.S. Department of Labor, Bureau of Labor Statistics, Marital and Family Characteristics of the Labor Force from the March 1996 Current Population Survey (December 1996).

third of women with preschool children were in the labor market. It should be noted that these employment figures come *before* most women had heard about the women's movement, at a time when support for a working mother was quite low.

The message of the women's rights movement, and its impact on public opinion, combined with the downturn in the economy (the 1970s witnessed stagflation [inflation plus low growth], and the 1980s saw declining wage rates, especially for young males), heightened the trend toward married women and women with children, especially young children, working. In 1996, therefore, nearly 63 percent of all married women with children under age six and 77 percent of married women with school-age children worked. The employment figures for divorced women with children were even higher. In 1996 over 76 percent of mothers with school-age children were working. Nearly 63 percent of those women with children under six were employed.

The combination of these trends has resulted in a dramatic increase in the overall employment rates of women, as illustrated in Table 4–6. When these rates are combined with the declining participation rates of men (because of earlier retirement and poor job prospects), we see that women in the 1990s are working at a rate only marginally lower than men. Indeed, while women constituted 43 percent of the labor force in 1983, by 1993 they made up 46 percent. Projections into the twenty-first century suggest that by 2005, women will be nearly 48 percent of those employed. There will be less than a 12-percentage-point gap in the employment rate of all men and women, and for African Americans an even narrower 7-point difference. The gap for whites will be 11 points. For Hispanics, it will be 23.[99]

TABLE 4–6 Labor-Force Participation Rates of Women and Men, by Race (in percentages)

Year	All Women	All Men	White Women	White Men	Black Women	Black Men	Hispanic Women	Hispanic Men
1958	37.1	NA	35.8	NA	48.0	NA	NA	NA
1970	43.3	79.7	42.6	80.0	49.5	76.5	NA	NA
1982	52.6	76.6	52.4	77.4	53.7	70.1	48.2	79.5
1991	57.3	75.5	57.4	76.4	57.0	69.5	52.3	80.1
1996	59.3	74.9	59.1	75.8	60.4	68.7	53.4	79.6
2005[a]	61.7	72.9	62.6	73.9	58.8	65.8	53.6	76.1

[a]projection
NA = not available.

Source: U.S. Bureau of Labor Statistics, "Employment in Perspective," Report 765, The Statistical Abstract of the United States, 1992, 381; and Howard N. Fullerton Jr., "The 2005 Labor Force: Growing but Slowly," *Monthly Labor Review* 118, no. 11, 39.

Work-Force Commitment of Women

In the past, white women who got married or had children dropped out of the labor market, generally permanently. In the 1950s many firms adopted a policy of offering part-time jobs to mothers and wives to facilitate the combining of multiple roles.[100] Many women took advantage of this practice. Other women opted for less than year-round work, or opted out of the marketplace for several years while they reared their children. These attempts to lessen the conflict between work and family roles were often used by employers as evidence of women's lower commitment to work. Recent evidence suggests these practices are declining. During the 1980s, the proportion of women working full time, year-round rose sharply. By the early 1990s, half of all working women worked full time.[101]

Many women continue to work part time. More than two-thirds of part-timers are women. Part-time employment is especially common if women have small children. About two out of five part-timers are mothers, although this practice also appears to be declining.[102] In 1970, only 16 percent of all mothers worked year-round full time; by 1993, 37 percent did so.[103] Part-time work is concentrated in several traditionally "women's fields," notably sales and service occupations, where 40 percent of the women work part time. Professional and managerial women are much less likely to work part time. Moreover, not all part-time work is by choice. About one out of seven women employed in part-time work would prefer full-time work.[104] Additionally, many of the part-time women workers hold more than one part-time job.

With lower wages and more uncertain work schedules, women generally are increasingly likely to be employed at more than one job. In 1970, only 2.2 percent of women held multiple jobs; by 1996, 6.2 percent of all women had multiple sources of income. Most of this increase has occurred since the mid-1980s. Women now constitute almost half (46.5 percent) of persons with two or more jobs.[105] Widowed, divorced, and separated women are actually more likely to hold two jobs than are similarly situated men. The need to meet household expenses is the most common reason given for their extensive job market activity.[106]

Another sign of women's increased commitment to the workplace is the short time many professional women now take off when a child is born. In 1990, 53 percent of women returned to work one year after having a baby. College-educated women and those in well-paying jobs are even more likely to rejoin the labor force shortly after the birth of a child.[107]

Interestingly, as women's commitment to the labor force has increased, men are decreasing their activity. In the ten-year time period from 1983 to 1993, the percentage of men working or seeking jobs declined 1.4 percent while women's rate of participation in the labor force rose 5.2 percent.[108] The decline for men occurred in all age groups, whereas only women under nineteen were less active in the 1990s, largely because they were spending more time in school preparing for work. Although increased school time may also help to explain some of men's lower participation rates, early retirement and being "unable to work" are the more important factors. What is implied by the latter is not clear, although it is a more common reason given by poorly educated men. Economists expect the decline in work-force involvement by men and the increase by women will continue into the next century, largely because the fields in which many men are concentrated are those experiencing the most rapid declines in employment (basically goods-producing jobs such as industrial manufacturing), while occupations in which there is a concentration of women (basically service-producing jobs such as teaching and health services) increase or remain stable.[109]

Even though more women than ever before work full time, year-round, and at multiple jobs, there is evidence that some women are having a difficult time managing their careers and their mother roles. Faced with this conflict, some women choose to delay marriage and/or children. Others attempt to do it all, often at the expense of their jobs, their families, or their leisure time. These problems are particularly acute for single mothers who lack the support of spouses.

To summarize, the movement of women into the marketplace is a function of five factors. Goldin's work on economic correlates of women's work-force activity over the last century shows quite clearly that attitudes, preparation, family roles, discrimination, and market demands all play a role. In the early years of this century when attitudes toward women working were highly negative and having a working wife was seen as an indication of the husband's failure to provide, married women worked only if the family's income necessitated it. This helps to explain the relatively high participation rates of African American and foreign-born women whose husbands faced severe discrimination and very low wages. Moreover, because most married women had not readied themselves for work, only the better-educated single women could be drawn into the work force by the higher wages of the new clerical positions. Later on, in the 1940s and 1950s, as more women obtained an education, they were able to be lured to work by the high wages offered by employers in the war and postwar decades as the economy needed more skilled women workers. Only more recently have women's decisions to seek employment been weakly shaped by market considerations. With societal and employer barriers to women working declining, high divorce rates lessening the tie between economic security and marriage, and more women preparing for full-time employment, women's decision to work, like that of men, is less influenced than in the past by economic factors. This is not to say these considerations are completely unimportant. As we shall see in the next section, the 1980s was a period of declining income for young men. This may well help to explain the high employment rates of mothers of young children. But most women today are as committed to work as men. Neither high wages nor inadequate family income are needed to draw them out of the home.

Wages of Women

The dramatic changes in women's employment have been accompanied by somewhat less impressive gains in the relative earnings of women. It is estimated that in terms of hourly wages, women in 1920 earned 43 percent as much as men; in 1950, 48 percent; in 1980, 53 percent; and in 1995, 75.5 percent.[110] The overall wage gap in annual income, however, is greater because women are more likely to work only part-time and/or part of the year. In 1995, women's annual earnings were 71.4 percent of men's.[111] (See Figure 4–4.) Part of the gain in women's relative income is a function of men's incomes actually declining. As a result of a weak economy and diminished numbers of well-paying jobs in traditionally male fields, during the 1980s the median annual salary of men declined 8 percent, while women's increased 10 percent.[112]

The decline in the salaries of young men with fewer educational skills was particularly striking. Using constant dollars, male high school dropouts in the 1980s saw their incomes decline nearly 30 percent relative to dropouts in the 1970s, whereas high school graduates saw a 27 percent decline. Even male college graduates experienced a 13 percent decline in their wages relative to the income of male college graduates in the 1970s. The salaries of female high school graduates also declined relative to similarly educated

FIGURE 4–4 Women's wages as a percentage of men's, 1979–1996.

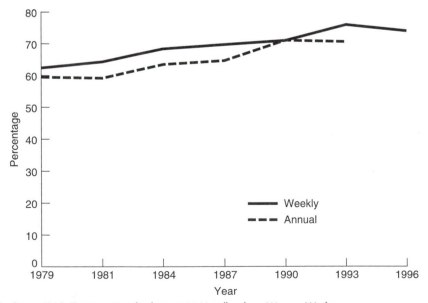

Source: U.S. Department of Labor, *1993 Handbook on Women Workers;* "Employment and Earnings," January 1997; "Employment in Perspective: Women in the Labor Force," Report 872; Department of the Census, oral communication.

young women in the 1970s, although much less sharply than for men. The result for all education groups of young adults was a fairly sizable narrowing of the wage-gender gap, almost entirely as a result of men's wages declining while women's increased slightly or declined less significantly.[113] For all workers in the 1980s, women's wages increased 5.7 percent, whereas men's were falling over 10 percent.[114] Most of this gain for women came in the increased number of middle-wage jobs, whereas men's middle-wage incomes declined.[115]

From 1989 to 1995, male wages continued to decrease at a constant rate (6.3 percent for the period). For the first time, women's wages also started to slide (1.7 percent). Thus, the wage gap continues to narrow, but at a slower rate. The impact of declining male wages (and now women's), moreover, helps to explain the greater work-force commitment of women. Most families can no longer survive on a single wage earner's salary. A bipartisan report to Congress found that the typical family in which the husband is a high school graduate is losing ground even as the wife doubles her work hours and provides a larger share of the family's income (up from 19 percent to 31 percent). The family in which the husband is a college graduate saw a slight increase in the family income due entirely to the greater work-force commitment and wages of the wife.[116] Of course, single heads of household, mostly women, are generally unable to prevent a downward slide. At the other end of the continuum, at the highest executive levels where salaries skyrocketed in the 1980s and 1990s, both men and women saw their salaries rise. In 1996, however, women still constituted a mere 2 percent of the top-paid executives in the Fortune 500 corporations.[117]

Although the overall wage gap in terms of weekly earnings has declined to 75 percent in 1996 from 62.5 percent in 1979, an examination of women and men in different age groupings shows the wage gap is narrowest for young men and women under age twenty-four. Those women earn 95 cents for every dollar made by men. Women age twenty-five to thirty-four earn 83 percent of men's salaries; women thirty-five to forty-four earn 73 percent; and women age forty-five to sixty-four earn about two-thirds of the weekly wages of men. African American and Hispanic women's wages come close to those of men of the same race (88 and 89 percent, respectively), whereas white women earn only 74 percent of what white men earn. The difference, of course, is a function of the fact that white men still dominate the high-paying jobs in our society.[118]

Economists have developed several explanations for the continuing lower earning power of women that parallel and overlap our five barriers to women's marketplace activity. The first focuses on the relative preparedness of women and men for work. Called the human capital theory by economists, the idea is that women earn less because they are less committed to the work force than men.[119] The reasoning is based on the notion that because women see their primary responsibility as taking care of their families, they will not be as willing to prepare for work as men. The largest single variable in the human capital theory is education; however, women earn less than men in every educational level.[120] Other human capital variables include on-the-job training, labor experience, and work effort. Some studies include an even wider variety of personal characteristics.[121]

Women's lack of work-force commitment is also thought to be exemplified by absences from the workplace for days, weeks, or years when family needs require it. Women who take time out from working to be with young children—which lowers their labor experience, on-the-job training, seniority, skills, and professional contacts—do pay a heavy price in terms of their future salaries. One study found that women who had a work gap of a year earned 30 percent less the first year back to work compared to women who did not leave. Even after 20 years back, they still earned 7 percent less than women who had not taken time off.[122] Attempts to control for all the human capital factor differences between men and women generally reduce the wage gap by, at most, 50 percent.[123]

Job segregation of women and men may be included as an explanatory factor in many human capital theory models. Proponents argue that women, because they do not expect to be as committed to the work force as men, choose occupations that allow them either to do less preparation or to combine working with homemaker duties more easily.[124]

Others argue that the occupational segregation of women's and men's work has as much or more to do with the discriminatory behavior or "preferences" of employers. They propose that such segregation should be treated as a separate explanation. This is often called the crowding hypothesis because women are crowded into a few low-paying jobs by employers' refusal to hire them for a wider variety of occupations. Barbara F. Reskin and Patricia A. Roos posit that employers prefer to hire men workers because they believe they are more productive or because of other prejudiced views about women workers, for instance that they will take time off to meet family commitments. Only if there are not enough men or they can hire women more cheaply for jobs that have often been "de-skilled" will employers hire women.[125] Of course, the socialization of boys and girls that channels each into gender-traditional fields is also at work.

The crowding hypothesis has historical roots in the early occupational profile of women who took jobs as domestics and textile workers for which they could readily transfer their homemaking skills. This crowding of women into a few blue-collar jobs was paralleled in the white-collar occupations and the professions, where women soon constituted the overwhelming majorities of the clerical, teaching, and nursing fields.

Regardless of the source, occupational segregation is a persistent reality. Table 4–7 gives the proportion of women in some of the more "crowded" and "uncrowded" fields and the average pay in each occupational category. The segregation of women even within broad classifications of workers is notable. Although more than half of all professionals are women, they are found in a few fields (nursing, teaching, social work). Men professionals are

TABLE 4–7 Occupational Segregation, 1996

Occupation	Women in Field (%)	Earnings Ratio, Women's/Men's
Executive, Administrative, Managerial	44	.69
Personnel and labor relations	52	
Administrators, protective services	31	
Managers, medicine and health	75	
Funeral directors	12	
Personnel training and labor relations specialists	66	
Managers, marketing, advertising, public relations	38	
Construction inspectors	7	
Professional Specialty	53	.76
Registered nurses	93	
Teachers, prekindergarten and kindergarten	98	
Teachers, secondary school	56	
Librarians	83	
Social workers	69	
Teachers, college and university	44	
Health-assessment and -treating occupations	86	
Computer systems analysts and scientists	28	
Physicians	26	
Lawyers	30	
Veterinarians	34	
Architects	17	
Dentists	14	
Clergy	12	
Engineers	9	
Pharmacists	43	
Service Occupations	59	.77
Child-care workers	97	
Private household workers	95	
Cleaners and servants	94	
Protective services	17	
Dental assistants	99	
Nurse's aides	88	
Food servers	78	
Janitors	35	
Cooks	42	
Pest controllers	3	
Firefighters	2	
Police and detectives	16	

TABLE 4–7 *(cont'd)*

Occupation	Women in Field (%)	Earnings Ratio, Women's/Men's
Precision, Production, Craft, and Repair	9	.67
Mechanics and repair persons	4	
Automobile mechanics	1	
Dressmakers	90	
Upholsterers	20	
Tool and die makers	2	
Operators, Assemblers, and Inspectors	38	.70
Textile sewing machine operators	84	
Metalworking and plastic-working machine operators	15	
Welders	5	
Assemblers	43	
Technical and Related Support	53	.70
Dental hygienists	98	
Legal assistants	81	
Engineering and related technologists	20	
Airplane pilots and navigators	1	
Sales	50	.60
Cashiers	75	
Salespersons, motor vehicles and boats	9	
Salespersons, apparel	81	
Salespersons, real estate	49	
Salespersons, securities and financial service	30	
Sales representatives, commodities, except retail	25	
Administrative Support	79	.80
Secretaries	98	
Typists	95	
Traffic, shipping and receiving clerks	30	

Source: U.S. Department of Labor, Bureau of Labor Statistics, Reprint of 1996 Annual Average Tables from the January 1997 Employment and Earnings.

similarly concentrated in "their" professions of engineering, dentistry, medicine, and architecture. Because the latter professions pay much better than the former, women professionals earn only 76 cents for every dollar a professional man earns, as the table shows. Similar instances of occupational segregation can be seen in the other job classifications. Notice how some fields are highly sex segregated.

Occupational segregation helps explain about a quarter to a third of the gap in men's and women's wages, depending on the study.[126] Of course, the gender segregation of jobs in the last two decades has meant that men, clustered in manufacturing jobs, have seen their job openings and wages fall, whereas women, working in the service sector, benefited from increased jobs and wages.

Research suggests that two-thirds of all working women or two-thirds of all working men would have to change jobs to achieve complete occupational integration.[127] Moreover, the most rapid declines in occupational segregation occurred in the 1970s, with more modest changes in the 1980s and 1990s, suggesting a persistent problem. Even in those fields that saw some occupational desegregation, women often made little or no wage gain because of the internal differentiation in men's and women's jobs in the profession or because the salaries of both sexes fell.[128]

A variation on the crowding hypothesis is an argument that women are further pushed into a few jobs by the failure of whole industries or firms to hire women for occupations they are performing elsewhere in the economy.[129] Thus, even if women have good jobs in the industries where they can find work, their incomes are lower than men's in similar positions in industries or firms that have higher pay scales and do not hire women. Economists estimate this industry or firm segregation also contributes to the disparity in women's and men's wages, perhaps as much as 12 to 17 percent.[130]

Three ideas closely related to industrial segregation are the glass ghetto, the glass ceiling, and the glass ladder. The glass ghetto refers to the hiring of women for the same occupations as men but in parts of the profession or field that do not pay as well or have the same prestige or status as the jobs for which men are hired. For instance, women medical doctors often become pediatricians, whereas men are trained as surgeons. Michael J. Carter and Susan Boslego Carter posit that the problem faced by many women who enter traditionally male fields is that they arrived "too late."[131] The Carters argue that many of these formerly prestigious professions have become two-tiered. One tier consists of prestige jobs with autonomy, opportunities for promotion, and good pay, whereas the other tier involves routinized, dead-end, lower-paying positions. According to the Carters, women are found overwhelmingly in the lower tier, primarily but not exclusively because they arrive late in these professions.

The Carters note, for instance, that although the number of women in academia is increasing, most have entered at a time when the position of university professor is becoming less well paid and offers reduced autonomy. Moreover, the women in academia tend to be concentrated in schools in which these conditions are most pronounced: junior colleges and undergraduate teaching positions. More recent research has also found women professors holding an inordinate number of the positions with the least status: part-time and nontenured slots.[132]

The Carters make a similar argument for the second-tiering of women in law and medicine. They note that the recent increase in the number of graduates from both types of schools has resulted in what is rapidly becoming an oversupply of lawyers and certain types of physicians. Thus, recent women graduates face stiff competition from men for the dwindling number of good jobs. The result is that women lawyers and doctors tend to be found in the most underpaid, routinized, nonautonomous sectors of those professions, namely, positions in the recently created legal clinics, health care centers, and hospital-based practices. In private law firms, moreover, lucrative partnerships are no longer always available even as tiers of partnerships have been created.

Research by Reskin and Roos, moreover, finds the problem extends beyond the academic, legal, and medical professions. Their study of traditionally male occupations where women made the largest gains in the 1970s found that these tended to be professions men were leaving because of a deterioration in the working conditions. For instance, the traditionally male occupation of pharmacist saw a dramatic increase in the number and percentage of women in the last three decades. This occurred at the very time, and probably because, many men were choosing not to become pharmacists. The male exodus was precipitated by the declining prestige of being a pharmacist. Large chains have eliminated the opportunity to own your own drug store, and computer technology reduced the autonomy of individual pharmacists.[133]

The story is little different in the other occupations that saw large numbers of women enter during the 1970s and 1980s. Indeed, there is considerable evidence that many of these occupations were internally resegregated as women who entered took the less prestigious, often new sectors in the field. A good example is women's admission into the occupation of baker. Most of the new women bakers were hired to bake prepared bread dough sold in grocery stores, whereas male bakers continued to work in the more profitable full-line bakeries.[134] Thus, the glass ghetto often finds women from a wide variety of jobs and professions isolated into the lower-paying sectors of even the most prestigious of occupations.

The glass ceiling operates in almost the same fashion. Women are hired into the lower ranks of a profession but find their path to the upper levels of the field are blocked. This practice seems most notable in the business sector, although it exists in all fields. If we look at the largest U.S. corporations, we find that only a handful of women have made it to the "top." In 1996, a study of Fortune 500 companies found that only 10 percent of the corporate officers were women. Moreover, only 57 women held the top slots of executive vice president or higher. There has been some improvement in this sector. In 1990, fewer than 3 percent of all corporate officers were women, and the percentage of companies with women in these slots rose from 69 percent in 1993 to 83 percent in 1996. Not surprisingly, the women executives are best represented in the soaps and cosmetics industry, where they are 19 percent of the directors.[135]

The situation is so bad that the U.S. Department of Labor instituted a Glass Ceiling Initiative in 1991 to break the ceiling in firms doing business with the federal government. When the Glass Ceiling Commission issued its report in 1995, it indicated that the barriers to women's and minorities' advancement were considerable. Among its twelve recommendations were calls for more CEO commitment to eliminating the barriers, the establishment of family-friendly programs, more diversity programs, and the implementation of affirmative action plans.[136]

The work of researchers connected with the Center for Creative Leadership finds several problems facing corporate women.[137] First, women in corporations are often placed in positions with no "path to the top," namely, staff and personnel slots. These specialties (that fit stereotypes about women's management strengths) do not allow the occupants to make "profit-determining" decisions that would show the corporate officers how they could make money for the firm. Second, women in business face many conflicting expectations about appropriate behavior. On one hand, they cannot be too feminine; on the other, they cannot be too masculine. Third, women do not receive the mentoring help of corporate males, nor are they given the same opportunities for on-the-job training. Fourth, women with family demands become exhausted by the burdens of the multiple roles they have to face. For many women the task is too daunting and they start their own business. Indeed, women in the 1990s were starting businesses at twice the rate of men. These firms, which are less prone to failure than new enterprises started by men, constitute one-third (36 percent) of small businesses, employ more than 18 million persons (one out of every four U.S. workers), and produce revenues of nearly $2.3 trillion.[138]

The glass ladder (or glass elevator) is the reverse of the glass ghetto. It is the tendency of employers to move men in women-dominated jobs to higher positions with better pay. Evidence of this phenomenon can be seen in the pay differentials of men and women in fields dominated by women. In 1995, for instance, male registered nurses earned $715 per week; women earned $693. The gap between what men and women elementary school teachers earned per week was $86; for cashiers, $20; for clerks, $29; and for health aides, $60.[139]

The last explanation for the wage gap is employer discrimination or, in the terms of economists, employer preference. This is difficult to measure and is often assumed to equal the percentage of the wage gap that is not explained after human capital and occupational and industry controls have been introduced. Of course, some of these latter factors, particularly occupational and firm differences in the employment of women and men, and the glass ghetto, glass ceiling, and glass ladder, also contain elements of employer-based discrimination if women are not being hired for certain jobs or by certain firms or are not being promoted because of stereotyped views about the work qualifications of all women. Generally, as much as 22 to 43 percent of the wage gap remains "unexplained" once human capital, occupational, and industry factors are accounted for. As we noted, this may actually underestimate the amount of the wage gap that is attributable to sex discrimination by employers.

African American Women Workers

Historically, African American women have worked at much higher rates than white or Hispanic women. This was especially true of married women. African American women were the backbone of the cotton industry, and many also worked as domestics. Indeed, on the eve of World War II, 60 percent of employed African American women were working as domestics.[a] Their concentration in these low-paying fields served to depress their wages considerably relative to African American and white men and white women. Domestics, for instance, earned just 16 percent of what the average working woman was being paid in 1945. Farm workers' salaries were just as dismal.

Since 1940, there has been a dramatic change in the occupations of African American women. Many fewer are domestics and farm workers. In 1940, 73 percent of African American women workers were employed in these two fields, but fifty years later fewer than 4 percent were working at these jobs. One result of the changing job distribution of African American women has been to narrow considerably their occupational dissimilarity with white women. This reduced gap in the employment distribution of women accounts for most of the reduction of racial segregation in the past several decades.[b]

African American women workers have not completely been able to overcome the legacy of occupational and racial discrimination. For one thing, fewer than 6 percent of all the women in the high-paying jobs of lawyers and other professionals are African American. Correspondingly, with the exception of elementary school teacher and registered nurse, the top ten fields employing African American women are generally low paying. Moreover, some of these fields (textile sewing machine operators, private household cleaners) are expected to need many fewer workers in the next century.[c] Perhaps in part because of this, the dramatic decline in the occupational segregation of African American and white women in the 1960s and 1970s slowed considerably in the 1980s and 1990s. The result was a growing wage gap. In 1990, African American women's weekly wage had climbed to 86 percent of white women's weekly wage, but by 1996, this had slipped to 84.6 percent. Because of the larger percentage of African American women in less than full-time year-round work, the overall gap is larger. Additionally, the employment rate of African American women has slipped below that of white women and is expected to continue to do so.

The future for African American women workers is clouded not only by continued gender and racial discrimination in the workplace but by the failure of public school systems to adequately prepare them (and African American men) for good jobs.[d] The increased college-entrance rate of African American women, however, is a very positive trend.

The lower wages of African American women, their higher unemployment, and higher divorce and premarital childbirth rates combine to place families headed by African American women at great risk of poverty. Indeed, over 50 percent of these families have incomes below the poverty level.

[a]Mary C. King, "Occupational Segregation by Race and Sex, 1940–1988," *Monthly Labor Review* 115, no. 4: 30.

[b]Ibid., 33.

[c]U.S. Department of Labor, Women's Bureau, *1993 Handbook on Women Workers: Trends & Issues* (Washington, D.C.: Author, 1994), 49–51.

[d]Phyllis Kemoff Mansfield, Patricia Barthalow Koch, Julie Henderson, Judith R. Vicaty, Margaret Cohn, and Elaine W. Young, "The Job Climate for Women in Traditionally Male Blue-Collar Occupations," *Sex Roles* 25, no. 112 (1991): 72, 75. See *The AAUW Report,* 33–36, for a discussion of the failure of elementary and secondary schools to adequately prepare some children, especially African American girls of low socioeconomic status.

Solutions to Pay Inequity

Examination of historical data by Claudia Goldin suggests that there have been two eras when women's earnings grew at a relatively rapid rate compared to those of men. From 1815 to 1850, women's wages rose from 28 to 50 percent of what men earned in the manufacturing sector. And from 1890 to 1930, women's earnings continued to grow as they entered the clerical fields and the traditional women's professions.[140] Goldin argues that both of these previous declines were tied to the better fit between women's skills and the new jobs that were opening to them, a modified version of the human capital theory. She argues further that the period starting from the 1980s may be a third epoch of declining wage disparity, especially as women who were socialized to, and prepared for, a lifetime of work enter the labor force.

Our review of the components of the wage gap suggests that although the increased supply of human capital by young women will lead and has led to a narrowing of the gap, the other factors producing the gap show only small signs of declining. Moreover, some of the factors contributing to wage disparity may actually be increasing as women find themselves hampered by occupational segregation, the glass ghetto, the glass ceiling, the glass ladder, and employer discrimination.

Most recent discussions of the wage gap have focused on the factor of occupational segregation. In part, this is because of the persistence and importance of the disparity between men and women. Indeed, there is even some evidence that the wage gap between men's and women's occupations is actually growing.[141] The solution that has been proposed to eliminate or reduce that part of the wage gap attributable to occupational segregation is known as comparable worth or pay equity, which Rita Mae Kelly and Jane Bayes define as "having comparable salaries for jobs requiring comparable effort, skill, responsibility, and working conditions."[142]

Implementation of comparable worth involves two steps. First, all jobs in a business or government are evaluated by a weighted set of compensatable factors including qualifications and responsibilities. All jobs are then assigned a total "job value" based on the evaluation. The second step is to recalculate wages so that positions with the same "job value" are accorded equal pay.

Studies using comparable worth evaluation systems (the first step) have found that women-dominated jobs pay about one-third less than men-dominated jobs of the same "job value." For instance, a 1982 study of state government jobs in Minnesota found that (mostly women) registered nurses' jobs rated 275 points, as did (mostly male) vocational education instructors' jobs. However, the registered nurses were being paid $1,732 a month, while the vocational education instructors were being paid $2,260 a month or $6,000 more a year.[143]

Comparable worth schemes have mostly been implemented (the second step) in state and local governments, in part because of the relative political ease of convincing governments as compared to businesses to adopt comparable worth studies and because wages and job descriptions are more readily accessible in government than in private industry. The Women's Bureau Fair Pay Clearinghouse reports that half the women in two-thirds of the states that have undertaken such a study have seen wage increases.[144] Public service unions also can and have put pressure on governments and some private industries.[145]

Most studies of the process of implementing these pay schemes, however, indicate they generally are far from completely successful in eliminating the wage gap due to unequal pay for jobs of comparable worth. Unions, professional organizations, administrators, state legislators, and women's groups all attempt to influence the final package, and the women workers often appear not to get their full pay adjustment. A study of the implementation process in Iowa found that the 8.8 percent potential gain to women employees determined by the job evaluators was reduced to a 1.4 percent gain by the time all the participants had their say and the plan was fully in place.[146] On university campuses, pay equity studies have become especially controversial, with male professors claiming such studies fail to adequately measure research productivity, which they claim explains men's higher salaries.[147]

Even if comparable worth plans did equally reward men's and women's jobs, they would not eliminate the problem of occupational segregation, mainly because the plans have been restricted to the public sector. More importantly, comparable worth schemes do not tackle the other problems that we have identified as contributing to the wage gap.

Affirmative Action

Few firms adopt affirmative action policies unless they are mandated to do so by the government or by a court. When such plans are implemented with the express purpose of increasing the number of women and minorities, however, the research suggests they can be quite effective in increasing both the number of women and their positions within the business.[148] Business and public resistance to affirmative action, especially among men, is growing stronger, however. A 1995 poll, for instance, found that whereas 53 percent of all men favored affirmative action to help women get better jobs and educations, 69 percent of women supported these plans. More importantly, among college-educated men who are most likely to be managers, only 43 percent supported affirmative action. College-educated men were also very opposed (66 percent) to giving preference to women where there is evidence of past discrimination.[149]

Family Leave, Day Care, and Flexible Jobs

Most other attempts to assist women workers have focused on helping women manage the multiple roles of wife, mother, and worker. In this way, these other reforms are indirectly designed to reduce the wage gap by increasing women's commitment to work, that is, by reducing human capital differences between women and men. The need for change is critical. A majority of all working mothers in one study reported that without these supports they could not take on additional job responsibilities.[150]

One solution that has engendered much political debate is allowing women and men time off to take care of a sick child or elderly parent. In 1996, the absence rate and the lost work time rate for women workers in all age groups was higher than for men. The disparity between women and men workers was greatest for those who are most likely to have young children, those age twenty to twenty-four. Among this group, women had an absence rate for reasons other than illness or injury that was three times higher than men of the same age.[151] A 1990 study by the Department of Labor found most of the reasons given for the absence rate of mothers of young children involved child-care problems.[152]

As discussed in Chapter 3, the Family and Medical Leave Act was passed in 1993. Before its passage, only a third of all employees had unpaid maternity leave.[153] Still, only 40 percent of workers are covered under the new act. The bipartisan commission to review the law's impact found that twelve million workers had taken leaves under the act by 1996. Although the figure sounds impressive, because the legislation requires only unpaid leave (a luxury few working women can afford), this law alone will not eliminate the difficulty of conflicting roles. The commission found that 64 percent of the employees could not afford to take the leave for which they were eligible.[154]

A more pressing need is affordable, quality child care for children of working mothers. A majority of the working women with young children who responded to a survey by the Women's Bureau in 1995 were concerned about their ability to find quality child care.[155] Other surveys find that women report that when their day-care arrangements fail it causes problems at work; relatedly, if they have to work late it creates conflict at home.[156] William T. Gormley Jr. argues that inadequate or poor quality day care also has negative repercussions for businesses in the form of lowered productivity and for our nation's children.[157]

The most common form of child care for children under five with a working mother is care provided in the child's own home by the father (15.9 percent) or a grandparent (16.5 percent). The second most common form is in a day-care center or nursery school. This practice, which is now used by 30 percent of all families, has climbed sharply during the past two decades. The third most common arrangement is care by a nonrelative in another home (16.6 percent). A very small percentage of women (6.2 percent) are able to care for their children at work or while they work at home.[158] The cost of these day-care services for a working mother can be sizable. For those living below the poverty level, a fifth of their income goes to child care. For other families, 7 percent of their family income goes for these expenses.[159]

Employers in the last two decades have become increasingly involved in helping their employees with child care. They have undertaken this assistance largely because of the increasing number of working mothers. Research shows that such assistance reduces turnover of employees and increases productivity. It is estimated that in the early 1990s fewer than 10 percent of businesses that employ one hundred or more workers provided some kind of child-care assistance.[160] This help includes work-site day-care centers, sponsorship or cosponsorship of day-care centers, referral services, and some financial help for child care. The latter ranges from outright money grants to help in locating care.

More recently, a few firms have developed some form of help for the increasing number of women who have to care for elderly relatives. Only a handful of employees currently have elder-care assistance, but it may become more common in the next decade as baby boomers begin to have to care for ill and aged parents.

Employers have also developed a number of other programs to assist women (and to a lesser extent men) who wish to combine work and family responsibilities. The most common is flextime, which allows employees to clock in early or work late in any configuration as long as they work forty hours per week. Thus, one parent can stay home until the children go to school and the other, by starting early, can be home when the children return. The practice helps to increase worker productivity and reduce turnover.

Other employer practices that may help working women combine their roles are the availability of part-time work and the related practice of job sharing. The former, as already discussed, has been used extensively by women since the 1950s to ease the burden of dual roles. It is a practice, however, with heavy costs for the employees, who may find themselves without health insurance or other employer benefits. It is also not very conducive to developing human capital, as few part-timers have access to on-the-job training or promotion. Job sharing is designed to overcome some of the problems of part-time work. With job sharing, two individuals agree to jointly undertake a single position.

Other employers have begun to modify other company practices that harm dual-career families such as limiting transfers or helping find jobs for spouses of transferred employees. With almost all of these employer assistance packages, the number of employees covered is small. In a 1994 survey, the percentages of working women reporting that their employer offered these family-friendly policies were as follows: unpaid leaves (27 percent), paid maternity leave (26 percent), job sharing (13 percent), flextime (32 percent), and part-time work (34 percent).[161] Moreover, with the exception of part-time work, the programs generally are most often accessible to the professional and administrative staff. Production and service employees, jobs where an inordinate number of women are employed, are much less likely to have the full range of options.[162] Responding to the need for these programs expressed by women workers, the Women's Bureau has begun to recognize firms that adopt policies that benefit women with its Honor Roll Report and the establishment of a network of Partners for Change, firms committed to making work better for women. Its first Honor Roll recognized almost fifty firms and governments for their efforts to support and reward women workers.[163]

Not all women or women's rights activists are convinced that these employer benefits are beneficial. Many worry that women who take advantage of them will jeopardize their chances to make it in the business world. Other feminists reason that without these programs women will have to make a choice between work and family. The controversy over the "Mommy track" exemplifies the debate. This idea, first proposed by Felice N. Schwartz, would allow firms to hire women who planned on having children for separate, less demanding career tracks than those that men and women who do not want a family would take. Many feel this would permanently ghettoize women workers and prevent them from ever reaching equality with men.

CONCLUSION

Although barriers facing women in the marketplace have diminished over the past few decades, women still face some serious hurdles in their effort to achieve equality. Although the public no longer objects to married women working, there are still vestiges of the traditional notions about the secondary place of work in the lives of mothers and wives that continue to hamper women's full integration into the marketplace. Even today, the influence of stereotypes about women's abilities results in women not being hired in leadership positions and the lack of readiness even of young women for the technical jobs of the twenty-first century. Discrimination by employers and male employees also continues to restrict the hiring and promotion opportunities of women.

The parallels with what we uncovered in the political realm are striking. In both, the barriers facing women are greatest for those positions with the most prestige and power. Additionally, in politics and the marketplace some of the most pressing problems involve conflict between the domestic roles of women and their efforts to assume equal positions with men. Thus, many of the changes that are needed before all the barriers are eliminated are tied to traditional notions of child care and women's place in the family.

NOTES

1. Sharlene J. Hesse, "Working Women: Historical Trends," in *Working Women and Families*, ed. Karen Wolk Feinstein (Beverly Hills, Calif.: Sage, 1979), 38–39; Claudia Goldin, *Understanding the Gender Gap: An Economic History of American Women* (New York: Oxford University Press, 1990), 48–49.
2. Gerda Lerner, "The Lady and the Mill Girl: Changes in the Status of Women in the Age of Jackson," in *A Heritage of Her Own*, ed. Nancy F. Cott and Elizabeth H. Pleck (New York: Simon & Schuster, 1979), 182–96; Goldin, *Understanding the Gender Gap*, 50–53.
3. Goldin, *Understanding the Gender Gap*, 43–46.
4. Ibid., 53.
5. Reported in Valerie Kincade Oppenheimer, *The Female Labor Force in the United States: Demographic and Economic Factors Governing Its Growth and Changing Composition* (Berkeley, Calif.: Institute of International Studies, 1970), 53.
6. Hazel Erskine, "The Polls: Women's Role," *Public Opinion Quarterly* 35 (Summer 1971): 282.
7. Ibid., 284.
8. Leila J. Rupp, "Women's Place Is in the War: Propaganda and Public Opinion in the United States and Germany," in *Women of America: A History*, ed. Carol Ruth Berkin and Mary Beth Norton (Boston: Houghton Mifflin, 1979), 351.
9. Erskine, "The Polls," 286–87.
10. Ibid., 283–85.
11. Ibid., 285.
12. Alfreda P. Ingelhart, *Married Women and Work* (Lexington, Mass.: Lexington Books, 1979); William H. Chafe, *The American Woman: Her Changing Social, Economic, and Political Role, 1920–1970* (New York: Oxford University Press, 1972), 178–79, reports that in New York 80 percent and in Detroit 75 percent of working women interviewed by the Women's Bureau wanted to continue work at the end of the war.
13. Erskine, "The Polls," 283.
14. Mary Geraghty, "Finances Are Becoming More Crucial in Students' College Choice, Survey Finds," *Chronicle of Higher Education*, January 17, 1997, A43.
15. James Allan Davis and Tom W. Smith, *General Social Surveys, 1972–1996*. Principal Investigator, James A. Davis; Director and Co-Principal Investigator, Tom W. Smith. NORC ed. Chicago: National Opinion Research Center, producer, 1996; Storrs, Conn.: The Roper Center for Public Opinion Research, University of Connecticut, distributor.
16. Joseph P. Ritz, "Women Making Job Gains at Expense of Men," *Buffalo News*, April 10, 1993, A6.

17. General Social Surveys. Made available by the Roper Center for Public Opinion Research, Storrs, Conn.

18. "Personal Values: A Fairly Traditionalistic Public," *Public Perspective* 8, no. 2 (February/March 1997): 18.

19. Data from the 1979 and 1990 Virginia Slims Polls. Made available by the Roper Center for Public Opinion Research, Storrs, Conn.

20. Lesley Lazin Novak and David R. Novak, "Being Female in the Eighties and Nineties: Conflict between New Opportunities and Traditional Expectations among White, Middle Class, Heterosexual Women," *Sex Roles* 35 (1996): 66–67.

21. Susan A. Mann, "Slavery, Sharecropping, and Sexual Inequality," *Signs* 14 (Summer 1989): 779–86.

22. This, however, was an increase from the 12.2 percent of all professional women who were married in 1910. Frank Stricker, "Cookbooks and Law Books: The Hidden History of Career Women in Twentieth-Century America," in *A Heritage of Her Own,* ed. Cott and Pleck, 486.

23. Percentages are based on only those who chose one of the three options: work full time, work part time, stay home. The 1994 General Social Survey, 1994 ISSP Module: Women and Work. Data made available by the Roper Center for Public Opinion Research, Storrs, Conn.

24. "Men and Women Don't Disagree on 'Women and Politics,' but They Divide When Maternal Responsibility Is Invoked," *Public Perspective* 8, no. 2 (February/March 1997): 25.

25. Novak and Novak, "Being Female in the Eighties and Nineties," 67.

26. Edward H. Clarke, *Sex in Education,* a book written during the 1870s and quoted in Robert W. Smuts, *Women and Work in America* (New York: Columbia University Press, 1959), 114.

27. Ibid., 112, quoting Mary Putnam Jacobi, a prominent woman physician, in 1891.

28. Erskine, "The Polls," 387–88.

29. The 1972 Virginia Slims Poll. Data made available by the Roper Center for Public Opinion Research, Storrs, Conn., and Connie De Boer, "The Polls: Women at Work," *Public Opinion Quarterly* 41 (Spring 1977): 275.

30. Cynthia Fuchs Epstein, *Deceptive Distinctions: Sex, Gender, and the Social Order* (New Haven, Conn.: Yale University Press, 1988), does a good job of showing how weak the data are on biological-based explanations of gender differences. The focus of much of the research now is on brain differences.

31. The 1995 Virginia Slims Poll. Data made available by the Roper Center for Public Opinion Research, Storrs, Conn.

32. Ibid.; The 1979 Virginia Slims Poll. Data made available by the Roper Center.

33. 1995 Virginia Slims Poll.

34. George Gallup Jr., *The Gallup Poll: Public Opinion 1995* (Wilmington, Del.: Scholarly Resources, 1996), 255.

35. Gallup, *The Gallup Poll,* 254–55.

36. Janet Shibley Hyde, "Meta-analysis and the Psychology of Gender Differences," *Signs* 16 (Autumn 1990): 55–73. See also Epstein, *Deceptive Distinctions,* generally on the question of biological differences between women and men and the absence of data to sustain the stereotypes.

37. Wellesley College Center for Research on Women, *The AAUW Report: How Schools Shortchange Girls.* (Washington, D.C.: American Association of University Women, 1992), 27–28, 70; Sheila Tobias, "The Mathematics Filter," *National Forum* (Fall 1981): 17–18.

38. Stricker reports that professional women were much more eager to combine roles than the percentage of them who were married suggests; "Cookbooks and Law Books," 486. Goldin's work, using old census data and surveys, finds evidence that for the generations of women born around 1900 to 1910 the desire to work and be married was particularly strong and may be reflected in the high percentage of this cohort who went to work as married women in the 1950s; *Understanding the Gender Gap,* 148–49.

39. Judith Stacey, Susan Bereard, and Joan Daniels, eds., *And Jill Came Tumbling After: Sexism in American Education* (New York: Dell Publishing, 1974).

40. Piper Purcell and Laura Stewart, "Dick and Jane," *Sex Roles* 22, nos. 3/4 (1990): 177–85; Carole M. Kortenhaus and Jack Demarest, "Gender Role Stereotyping in Children's Literature: An Update," *Sex Roles* 28, nos. 3/4 (1993): 219–42; Diane M. Turner-Bowker, "Gender Stereotyped Descriptors in Children's Picture Books: Does 'Curious Jane' Exist in the Literature?" *Sex Roles* 35, nos. 7/8 (1996): 461–88.

41. Center for Research on Women, *The AAUW Report,* 68–71.
42. Ibid., 28–30.
43. Ibid., 12; Emily Hancock, *The Girl Within* (Cambridge, Mass.: Harvard University Press, 1993).
44. 1995 Virginia Slims Poll.
45. Cecilia Ann Northcutt, *Successful Career Women: Their Professional and Personal Characteristics* (New York: Greenwood Press, 1991), 31–35; Hugh Lytton and David Romney, "Parent's Differential Socialization of Boys and Girls: A Meta-Analysis," *Psychology Bulletin* 109, no. 2 (1991): 267–96.
46. Peter Glick, "Trait-Based and Sex-Based Discrimination in Occupational Prestige, Occupational Salary, and Hiring," *Sex Roles* 25, nos. 5/6 (1991): 351–64.
47. Goldin, *Understanding the Gender Gap,* 155–56.
48. Ibid., 156.
49. Geraghty, "Finances Are Becoming More Crucial," A43.
50. Robert Fiorentine, "Increasing Similarity in the Values and Life Plans of Male and Female College Students? Evidence and Implication," *Sex Roles* 18, nos. 3/4 (1988): 151.
51. "Attitudes and Characteristics of Freshmen, Fall 1995," *Chronicle of Higher Education: Almanac Issue* (Washington, D.C.: Chronicle of Higher Education, 1996), 19. The percentage of women (men) expecting to complete each type of degree was as follows: master's 37.6 (36.3); Ph.D. or Ed.D. 14 (13.7); M.D., D.O., D.D.S., or D.V.M. 10 (7.7).
52. U.S. Bureau of the Census, Current Population Reports, Series P-23, no. 173, *Population Profile of the United States, 1991* (Washington, D.C.: U.S. Government Printing Office, 1991), 5; National Center for Education Statistics, *Digest of Education Statistics, 1989* (Washington, D.C.: U.S. Department of Education, 1989), 239.
53. Bureau of the Census, *Population Profile,* 5.
54. Center for Education Statistics, *Digest of Education Statistics,* 239.
55. "Earned Degrees Conferred, 1993–94," *Chronicle of Higher Education: Almanac Issue,* 22.
56. Ibid.
57. The 1985, 1990, and 1995 Virginia Slims Polls. Data made available by the Roper Center, Storrs, Conn.
58. The 1995 Virginia Slims Poll. In 1994, 32 percent of men said they worked to support themselves and 63 percent said to support their families.
59. John E. Yang, "Women's Earnings Important to Families," *Buffalo News,* June 19, 1990, A6.
60. Bureau of Labor Statistics, "Employment in Perspective: Women in the Labor Force," Report #832 (Washington, D.C.: Department of Labor, 1993).
61. James Geschwender and Rita Carroll-Seguin, "Exploding the Myth of African American Progress," *Signs* 15, no. 2 (Winter 1990): 290–93, 298.
62. 1989 *New York Times* Poll, "Women's Lives: A Scorecard of Change." Data made available by the *Times.*
63. Karlyn Bowman, "Opinion Pulse: Women and Work," *American Enterprise* (March/April 1996): 91.
64. Eleven percent of all working women agreed strongly and 27 percent agreed to a certain extent with the statement, "The conflicting demands of family and job put me under a lot of stress." To the statement, "All in all, I do feel that I do a good job of balancing my job and my family life," 40 percent of working women agreed strongly and 31 percent agreed to a certain extent. 1989 Virginia Slims Poll.
65. Goldin, *Understanding the Gender Gap,* 161–63.
66. Ibid., 165–66. Twenty-six states had proposed the legislation to bar married women from state government jobs.
67. Nancy E. McGlen and Meredith Reid Sarkees, *Women in Foreign Policy: The Insiders* (New York: Routledge, 1993), chap. 3.
68. Goldin, *Understanding the Gender Gap,* 171–78.
69. Ibid., 171–74.
70. Ibid., 163.
71. Ibid., 163, 176.
72. Ibid., 147.
73. Francine D. Blau, *Equal Pay in the Office* (Lexington, Mass.: Lexington Books, 1977), chap. 4.
74. Barbara F. Reskin and Patricia A. Roos, *Job Queues, Gender Queues: Explaining Women's Inroads into Male Occupations* (Philadelphia: Temple University Press, 1990), 35–37.
75. The 1995 Virginia Slims Poll.

76. Reskin and Roos, *Job Queues, Gender Queues,* 37–38, 309–10.
77. Smuts, *Women and Work,* 119–20; Oppenheimer, *Female Labor Force,* 51–55.
78. Ritz, "Women Making Job Gains," A6.
79. Sally Hilsman Baker, "Women in Blue-Collar and Service Occupations," in *Women Working: Theories and Facts in Perspective,* ed. Ann H. Stromberg and Shirley Harkess (Palo Alto, Calif.: Mayfield, 1978), 352.
80. U.S. Department of Labor, Bureau of Labor Statistics, "Reprint of the 1996 Annual Average Tables from the January 1997 Issue of Employment and Earnings" (Washington, D.C.: Author, 1996), 211.
81. Baker, "Women in Blue-Collar Occupations," 355–63; studies of women receiving vocational education in the trades find that they face greater unemployment problems. Center for Research on Women, *The AAUW Report,* 42.
82. Pat Swift, "Women Still on the Margins in Construction," *Buffalo News,* February 1, 1997, C7.
83. Phyllis Kernoff Mansfield, Patricia Barthalow Koch, Julie Henderson, Judith R. Vicary, Margaret Cohn, and Elaine W. Young, "The Job Climate for Women in Traditionally Male Blue-Collar Occupations," *Sex Roles* 25, no. 1/2 (1991): 71–73.
84. Goldin, *Understanding the Gender Gap,* 147.
85. Roberta T. Anderson and Pauline Ramey, "Women in Higher Education: Development through Administrative Mentoring," in *Women in Higher Education,* ed. Lynne Welch (New York: Praeger, 1990).
86. Erica Littlejohn and Hank Ezell, "Women Chip Away at 'Glass Ceiling,'" *Atlanta Constitution,* June 30, 1993, A1.
87. 1995 Virginia Slims Poll.
88. Oppenheimer, *The Female Labor Force.*
89. Eileen Trzcinski, "Effects of Uncertainty and Risk on the Allocation of Time of Married Women," *Journal of Family and Economic Issues* 17, nos. 3/4 (Winter 1996): 343–44; Goldin, *Understanding the Gender Gap,* 124–26.
90. Goldin, *Understanding the Gender Gap,* 136–38.
91. Trzcinski, "Effects of Uncertainty, pp. 343–45.
92. Goldin, *Understanding the Gender Gap,* 17.
93. Ibid.
94. U.S. Department of Labor, Women's Bureau, "Marital and Family Characteristics of the Labor Force" (Washington, D.C.: Author, 1996).
95. Goldin, *Understanding the Gender Gap,* 18, 44–49.
96. Ibid., 25, 38.
97. The figures were almost as high for the youngest group of married women, aged 15 to 24. Ibid., 18.
98. Oppenheimer, *The Female Labor Force,* 136–39.
99. All data in paragraph from Howard N. Fullerton Jr., "The 2005 Labor Force: Growing, but Slowly," *Monthly Labor Review* 118, no. 11 (1995): 39.
100. Goldin, *Understanding the Gender Gap,* 180–83.
101. Paul Ryscavage, "Gender-Related Shifts in the Distribution of Wages," *Monthly Labor Review,* 117, no. 7 (1994): 7.
102. Bureau of Labor Statistics, "Employment in Perspective: Women in the Labor Force," Report no. 824 (Washington, D.C.: U.S. Department of Labor, 1992).
103. Bureau of Labor Statistics, "Employment in Perspective: Women in the Labor Force," Report no. 879 (Washington, D.C.: U.S. Department of Labor, 1994).
104. Bureau of Labor Statistics, "Employment in Perspective: Women in the Labor Force," Report no. 770 (Washington, D.C.: U.S. Department of Labor, 1989).
105. U.S. Department of Labor, "Marital and Family Characteristics," 203.
106. John F. Stinson Jr., "Multiple Jobholding Up Sharply in the 1980s," *Monthly Labor Review* 113, no. 7 (1990): 3–5.
107. Meredith K. Wadman, "Mothers Who Take Time Off Find Their Careers Pay a Heavy Price," *Wall Street Journal,* July 16, 1992, B1.
108. Fullerton, "The 2005 Labor Force," 33–34.
109. William Goodman, "Women and Jobs in Recoveries: 1970–93," *Monthly Labor Review* 117, no. 7 (1994): 28–36.
110. U.S. Department of Labor, Women's Bureau, *1993 Handbook on Women Workers: Trends & Issues* (Washington, D.C.: Author, 1994), 30–33.

111. Ibid.

112. "Closing the Gender Gap," *Society* 30, no. 3 (1993): 3.

113. Bureau of Labor Statistics, "Work and Family: Changes in Wages and Benefits Among Young Adults," Report no. 849 (Washington, D.C.: Department of Labor, 1993).

114. "Working Men, Women See Their Pay Decline as Top Execs' Compensation Soars," *Buffalo News,* September 2, 1996, A10.

115. Ryscavage, "Gender-Related Shifts in the Distribution of Wages," 5.

116. Robert A. Rosenblatt, "Buying Power of Couples Is Declining, Study Reports," *Buffalo News,* September 13, 1996, A10.

117. Maggie Jackson, "Women Inch Their Way to the Top at U.S. Firms, Survey Says," *Buffalo News,* October 18, 1996, A13.

118. *Employment and Earnings,* January 1997, 204.

119. Margaret Mooney Marini, "Sex Differences in Earnings in the United States," *American Sociological Review* 26, no. 15 (1989): 352.

120. In 1994, college-educated women earned almost $12,000 less than college-educated men. U.S. Department of Labor, Women's Bureau, "Facts on Working Women."

121. Ibid.

122. Joyce P. Jacobsen and Laurence M. Levin, "Effects of Intermittent Labor Force Attachment on Women's Earnings," *Monthly Labor Review* 118, no. 9 (1995): 16–18.

123. Marini, "Sex Differences in Earnings," 352–56; Elaine Sorensen, "The Crowding Hypothesis and Comparable Worth," *Journal of Human Resources* 25, no. 1 (1990): 62–66. Most economists doubt the validity of studies that include hundreds of "human capital" variables that "explain" all of the gender gap.

124. Marini, "Sex Differences in Earnings," 351–52; Jacobsen and Levin, "Effects of Intermittent Labor Force Attachment," 14–16.

125. Reskin and Roos, *Job Queues, Gender Queues,* 35–38.

126. Sorensen, "The Crowding Hypothesis," 62–63.

127. Mary C. Icing, "Occupational Segregation by Race and Sex," *Monthly Labor Review* 115, no. 4 (1992): 30–36.

128. Reskin and Roos, *Job Queues, Gender Queues,* 81–84.

129. Ibid., 60–61.

130. Erica L. Groshen, "The Structure of the Female/Male Wage Differential: Is It Who You Are, What You Do, or Where You Work?" *The Journal of Human Resources* 26, no. 3 (1991): 457–72; Sorensen, "The Crowding Hypothesis," 73.

131. Michael J. Carter and Susan Boslego Carter, "Women's Recent Progress in the Professions or, Women Get a Ticket to Ride After the Gravy Train Has Left the Station," *Feminist Studies* 7, no. 3 (1981): 475–92.

132. Nancy E. McGlen and Meredith Reid Sarkees, "Political Science: A Hostile or Friendly Institution for Women" (paper delivered at the annual meeting of the American Political Science Association, Washington, D.C., 1997).

133. Reskin and Roos, *Job Queues, Gender Queues,* 111–27.

134. Ibid., 257–74.

135. *1996 Catalyst Census of Women Board Directors of the Fortune 500 Companies.*

136. U.S. Federal Glass Ceiling Commission, *A Solid Investment: Making Full Use of the Nation's Human Capital: Recommendations of the Glass Ceiling Commission* (Washington, D.C.: Government Printing Office, November 1995).

137. Ann Morrison, Randall P. White, Ellen Van Velsor, and The Center for Creative Leadership, *Breaking the Glass Ceiling* (Reading, Mass.: Addison-Wesley Publishing, 1992), 139–54.

138. Pat Swift, "Opportunity Abounds, and It's There for the Taking," *Buffalo News,* January 25, 1997, C7; The National Federation of Women Business Owners, "Women-Owned Businesses in the United States: 1996, A Fact Sheet" (Washington, D.C.: Author, 1996). Linda N. Edwards and Elizabeth Field-Hendrey, "Home-Based Workers: Data from the 1990 Census of the Population," *Monthly Labor Review* 119, no. 11 (1996): 26–34.

139. U.S. Department of Labor, Women's Bureau, "Facts on Working Women," No. 96–2, September 1996.

140. Goldin, *Understanding the Gender Gap,* 58–73.

141. Sorensen, "The Crowding Hypothesis," 72.

142. Rita Mae Kelly and Jane Bayes, *Comparable Worth, Pay Equity, and Public Policy* (Westport, Conn.: Greenwood Press, 1988), 4.

143. Sara M. Evans and Barbara Nelson, *Wage Justice: Comparable Worth and the Paradox of Technocratic Reform* (Chicago: University of Chicago Press, 1989).
144. U.S. Department of Labor, Women's Bureau, "Worth More Than We Earn: Fair Pay for Working Women," *Fair Pay Clearinghouse*, September 1996.
145. U.S. Department of Labor, Women's Bureau, "What Works: Fair Pay for Working Women," *Fair Pay Clearinghouse*, September 1996.
146. Peter F. Orazem and J. Peter Mattila. "The Implementation Process of Comparable Worth: Winners and Losers," *Journal of Political Economy* 98, no. 1 (1990): 149; Joan Acker, *Doing Comparable Worth: Gender, Class, and Pay Equity* (Philadelphia: Temple University Press, 1989).
147. Robin Wilson, "Equal Pay, Equal Worth?" *Chronicle of Higher Education*, November 24, 1995, A15–16.
148. Alison M. Konrad and Frank Linnehan, "Formalized HRM Structures: Coordinating Equal Employment Opportunity or Concealing Organizational Practices?" *Academy of Management Journal* 38, no. 3 (1995): 787–803.
149. "Affirmative Action, Welfare, and the Individual," *Public Perspective* 6, no. 4 (June/July 1995): 39.
150. U.S. Department of Labor, Women's Bureau, *The Working Women Count Honor Roll Report* (Washington, D.C.: Author), 19.
151. U.S. Department of Labor, "Reprint of 1996 Annual Average Tables," 215.
152. Bureau of Labor Statistics, "Employment in Perspective: Women in the Labor Force," Report no. 791 (Washington, D.C.: U.S. Department of Labor, 1990).
153. Stephanie L. Hyland, "Helping Employees with Family Care," *Monthly Labor Review* 115 (1990): 23.
154. U.S. Department of Labor, *Working Women Count*, 24.
155. U.S. Department of Labor, *Working Women Count*, 20.
156. 1995 Virginia Slims Poll.
157. William T. Gormley Jr., *Everybody's Children: Child Care as a Public Problem* (Washington, D.C.: The Brookings Institute, 1995).
158. U.S Department of Commerce, Bureau of the Census, "Percent of Children Under 5 in Selected Child Care Arrangements: 1977–1993," http://www.census.gov
159. U.S. Department of Commerce, Bureau of the Census, "Weekly Child Care Costs Paid by Families with Employed Mothers: 1985–1993," http://www.census.gov
160. Marcia Eldridge, "The State of Dependent Care," *National Business Women* (Spring 1993): 11–14.
161. 1995 Virginia Slims Poll.
162. Hyland, "Helping Employees," 23.
163. U.S. Department of Labor, *Working Women Count*, details the types of programs implemented by the honored firms in three areas: pay and benefits, balancing work and family policies, and respect and opportunity on the job.

PART III

FAMILIAL AND REPRODUCTIVE RIGHTS AND REALITIES

The changes sought in familial and reproductive rights are the most controversial of all the issues discussed thus far. More than political or employment rights, familial and reproductive rights are most likely to be universal in application and therefore perceived as threatening to the greatest number of people.

Efforts to change traditional practices in this arena had to be postponed until greater political and economic rights were obtained.* Without political rights, women had little chance of gaining or maintaining economic and social rights. Without economic opportunities to earn wages outside the home, few women had any options in life other than to marry and remain at home under the "protection" of their husbands. This was especially true when women had little or no control over reproduction. Without the ability to limit the number or timing of the arrival of children, women were made even more dependent on men for their livelihood.

Because of their inferior political and economic status, women were reluctant to challenge the institution of marriage or to make demands for significant changes in its structure. Without alternative lifestyle options, loss of this institution would have plunged most women into the depths of poverty and to the bottom of the political underclass. Early efforts in this arena were therefore limited to gaining control over reproduction—a prerequisite for any other changes in family structure.

The achievement of political and economic rights eventually made possible attempts to reform the traditionally male-dominated institution of

*The ideas of much of the following discussion draw heavily on Barbara Easton, "Feminism and the Contemporary Family," in *A Heritage of Our Own: Toward a New Social History of Women,* ed. Nancy F. Cott and Elizabeth H. Pleck (New York: Simon & Schuster/Touchstone Books, 1979), 555–77. See also Betty Friedan, *The Second Stage* (New York: Summit Books, 1981), 83–123.

marriage. Parallel to these efforts were ones centering on a woman's right to control reproduction.

As we have seen, women's economic opportunities and political power still are unequal to men's. Some women thus remain dependent on the institution of marriage. Real or even imagined threats to marriage can be very disturbing to women who believe they have little chance to support themselves or their families without it.

Sexuality is an additional complication. Sexual identity has been linked to gender, and gender roles have been linked to roles within the traditional family. In turn, family roles have defined gender role behaviors. Thus, for some, challenges to the traditional family pose a serious threat to sexual identity.

A vocal, well-organized, well-financed, and, in the early 1980s, politically powerful countermovement arose to prevent changes in familial and reproductive rights. This movement, threatened by changes in family and gender roles, appears to recognize the connection between economic and political power and change in the family. Thus, the "New Right" wants to roll back rights in all three areas, and especially abortion rights. The outcome of this struggle may hold the key to the future of the women's movement.

The Struggle for Familial and Reproductive Rights

5

According to noted historian Carl N. Degler, the period around 1830 signaled the development of what he terms the *modern family*.[1] Changes in the institution of marriage and thus the family were characterized by

1. Marriages based on mutual affection and not parental arrangement
2. "Separate spheres" for the sexes in which "a woman's life was physically spent in the home and with the family, while the man's life was largely outside the home, at work"
3. A focus on the importance of child rearing
4. Smaller families[2]

In this modern family, a woman's place was indisputably in the home. As the keeper of the family, a wife was regarded as the moral superior of her husband, although this "superiority" did not necessarily carry over into their interpersonal relations or into laws concerning a woman's place in the family. Relegation of women to the home also put married women in the position of near-complete economic dependence on their husbands, which was further exacerbated by laws that treated women, at best, as no better than children.

In this chapter, we examine the laws and social policies relating to marriage, the family, and reproduction that have affected women. Major societal changes have occurred: Most women work outside, as well as within, the home, and few individuals live in "traditional" families as defined by television's *Leave It to Beaver* or even *The Brady Bunch*. We focus on how each of the women's movements pursued changes in a woman's place in the family and the choices open to her. As family roles and values have changed, many of the struggles for women's rights have been closely tied to a woman's role—and expectations about that role—in the family, especially her motherhood role. Deep-rooted notions about women's "proper" role continue. Thus,

In 1996, President Clinton was assured the support of many women when he enthusiastically endorsed forcing health care plans to stop requiring new mothers to leave the hospital immediately after delivery. Women who had "drive-through deliveries" were shown to have higher rates of infection and their babies required more emergency room visits than mothers and babies who were allowed to stay in the hospital for longer periods of time. (Reproduced with the permission of the *Buffalo News*.)

opposition to a woman's equality in the family or concerning her reproductive rights continues to rage.

THE WOMAN'S MOVEMENT

During the 1848 Seneca Falls Convention, participants were very concerned about the laws and practices that made women inferior to men in family matters. The Declaration of Sentiments included accusations that men had

- made [a woman] if married, in the eye of the law, civilly dead.
- taken from her all right in property, even to the wages she earns.

- compelled [her] to promise obedience to her husband, he becoming, for all intents and purposes, her master—the law giving him power to deprive her of her liberty, and to administer chastisement.
- framed the laws of divorce, as to what shall be the proper cause.
- [assigned] guardianship of the children . . . upon a false supposition of the supremacy of man, and giving all power into his hand.
- created a different code of morals for men and women.

Effects of the Common Law

Historically, many of the problems described previously stemmed from women's legal inferiority, which was directly traceable to the English common law, adopted by the colonists. One common law doctrine, termed *coverture,* provided that women lost all legal capacity upon marriage. Married women ceased to be persons in the eyes of the law because their legal identities merged with those of their husbands. In essence, behind Mary Jones's new name, Mrs. John Smith, Mary Jones ceased to exist. Married women had no right to contract, to sue (or be sued) in their own names, or to own property. Perhaps the greatest effect of coverture was in the simple issue of control: As it evolved, coverture produced and legitimized almost total male domination over women. A married woman lost claim to her name, her assets, and even her children. As the sole *legal* guardian of his offspring, a man could, by will, transfer custody of his children to someone other than his wife. Slave women had even fewer rights. They were chattels to be bought and sold, and their marriages were not even legal.

To remedy these inequities (as they affected white women, at any rate), many women lobbied various state legislatures for reforms. In 1848, for example, New York passed a Married Woman's Property Act, which gave women the right to control property acquired by "inheritance, gift, bequest, or devise." Women continued to be denied control over their wages and earnings, and still were denied custody of their children and the right to divorce drunken or abusive husbands.

These successes led women to lobby for similar and more extensive changes in other states. For example, New York passed additional legislation in 1860 expanding women's control of their inheritances and wages and allowing them to make contracts and sue in their own names. Women were given joint custody of their children for the first time. A widow was also permitted to inherit at least a third of her husband's estate, regardless of whether he left a will to the contrary.

Divorce Reform

As early as 1852, Elizabeth Cady Stanton, as president of the New York Woman's Temperance Society, shocked many of its members when during its convention she urged:

> Let no woman remain in the relation of wife with a confirmed drunkard. Let no drunkard be the father of her child. . . . Let us petition our State government so to modify the laws affecting marriage and the custody of children that the drunkard shall have no claim on his wife or child.[3]

The radical nature of Stanton's demand—at the time only one state allowed a woman to divorce her husband for drunkenness—led supporters of temperance to distance themselves from Stanton's demands and the woman's movement. It appears that even temperance supporters did not want to complicate the drinking issue with a more controversial one—divorce—although it was clear that many unhappy marriages resulted from drinking problems. A drunken husband could spend all of his wages, sell his and/or his wife's property, or apprentice his children to work for others without consulting his wife. Even so, many temperance workers feared that their goals would be harder to achieve if they were allied with calls for other, more radical reforms.

Undaunted, Stanton continued to press for sweeping reform. In 1853, she wrote to Susan B. Anthony, "It is in vain to look for the elevation of woman so long as she is degraded in marriage."[4] At the 1860 National Woman's Rights Convention, Anthony noted, "By [marriage] man gains all; woman loses all; tyrant law and lust reign supreme with him. . . . "[5]

These comments horrified many women in attendance. In her autobiography Stanton wrote, "So alarming were the comments on what had been said that I began to feel that I had inadvertently taken out the underpinning from the social system."[6]

Divorce reform, like domestic violence reform today, was viewed by many as a basic threat to the stability of the family. In contrast, married women's property acts, especially those that gave women joint custody of their children, were generally viewed as strengthening women's proper role—motherhood. Also, on a more practical level, some legislators believed that their daughters needed protection from wandering or shiftless husbands. Under coverture, a man could dispose of all assets that a woman received from her family. Changes in divorce laws, however, were not without critics. In 1870, for example, Horace Greeley predicted that "easy divorce would destroy America blasted by the mildew of unchaste mothers and dissolute homes."[7]

Birth Control

While divorce reform was viewed by many as radical, at least some women spoke out in favor of reform. This was not the case with birth control. As early as 1856, Lucy Stone aptly captured women's consensus about the issue: "It is very little to me to have the right to vote, to own property, etc., if I may not keep my body and its use my absolute right. *But we are not ready for that question*"[8] (emphasis added).

Some reformers did, however, try to discuss controversial issues. *The Revolution*, for example, published by Anthony and Stanton, often included discussions of prostitution, free love (see Chapter 1), rape, and even spousal abuse. But views like these, declining birthrates (indicating that some form of family planning was being used by some), and a general concern with declining morals led to the passage of a series of laws banning abortion and obscenity. In 1873, for example, the U.S. Congress passed the Comstock Act. It prohibited the use of the U.S. mail for distribution of any "obscene" materials. It specifically labeled as obscene "the dissemination of any pornography, abortion devices, and any drug, medicine, article or thing designed, adapted, or intended for preventing *conception*"[9] (emphasis added). It also branded as "smut" and therefore "obscene" many essays that urged abstinence as a method of family planning.[10] Proponents of the act, including its sponsor Anthony Comstock, believed that this kind of information could lead only to moral decay and more abortions. Nevertheless, an 1871 American Medical Association report found that 20 percent of all pregnancies were deliberately terminated.[11]

Birth Control Advice in the 1800s

Ironically, much of the information concerning birth control that Anthony Comstock and others tried to stop was woefully inaccurate. As early as the 1830s, for example, a number of handbooks and guides written by physicians contained instructions on family planning. Many authors advocated periodic abstinence but often misjudged the safe period. One author advised, "if intercourse is abstained from until ten or twelve days after cessation of the menstrual flow, pregnancy will not occur." (We now know that information is totally incorrect.) Others advocated douches, condoms, or more unusual methods including "intercourse on an inclined plane so as to avoid dislodging the egg from the ovary" or dancing or horseback riding over a rough road after intercourse.[a]

[a]Carl N. Degler, *At Odds: Women and the Family in America from the Revolution to the Present* (New York: Oxford University Press, 1980), 216. The quotation and information in the paragraph are also found in Degler, *At Odds*, 214.

Voluntary Motherhood. During this period, many moral reformers and most woman's rights advocates supported the idea of "voluntary motherhood," a woman's right to limit her family size by natural means.[12] They and even radical "free lovers," such as Victoria Woodhull, believed that contraceptive devices were "a standing reproach upon, and a permanent indictment against American women."[13] Distaste for artificial birth control, "the washes, teas, tonics, and various sorts of appliances known to the initiated,"[14] stemmed from two sources. First, in keeping with notions of romantic love that pervaded this era, women believed that the use of contraceptives somehow destroyed the love act. Second, many married women feared an increase in marital infidelity.[15]

In an era when a woman's identity, livelihood, and status depended on a stable marriage, threats to that institution were avoided at all cost. This is not to say, however, that these women wished to have children every year. Stanton, who herself had eight children, believed that before women could gain full equality, they had to have control over their bodies. A staunch supporter of voluntary motherhood, Stanton frequently addressed all-women audiences during the suffrage campaign. At those meetings she regularly talked about the need for women to limit the size of their families to improve their overall status as well as their health.[16]

Cries for divorce reform and voluntary motherhood brought condemnation from the press and the pulpit. It seemed that the controversial changes sought by Stanton and some of her followers were never likely to be adopted. Women did secure positive changes in property and divorce laws before and during the Civil War. But once morals and birth control became issues, the passage of restrictive laws virtually stopped any additional moves for change. It was not until the suffrage era that significant new advances were made in women's status in the family.

Clothing and a Woman's Rights

Birth control was not the only controversial issue addressed by women. As early as the 1850s, woman's rights proponents risked ridicule when they rejected restrictive forms of dress that they believed negatively affected women's lives and were simply another form of male control. From the early 1800s to around 1890, women wore corsets "made of silk or cotton and ribbed with several dozen whalebone or steel stays which were girded to the female body from the chest to the hips."[a] These corsets were laced very tightly to produce an "hourglass figure" and often made breathing difficult. A metal hoop skirt, measuring four or five feet in diameter, was worn over the corset, severely restricting movement.

Firmly believing that changing a woman's apparel was closely related to changing her way of life, Susan B. Anthony, Elizabeth Cady Stanton, the Grimké sisters, Lucy Stone, and Amelia Bloomer, among others, adopted what came to be called "bloomers." Actually, the outfit was a loose tunic-type knee-length dress worn over long, harem-type trousers.

After tremendous ridicule, most women abandoned these less-restrictive garments. Although this episode may seem silly, think of the attention and consequences of women's clothing today that often set them apart. Are women in very short skirts treated as seriously as men in suits? How do high heels, platform shoes, or pointed-toe shoes affect women?

© Collection of the New York Historical Society.

[a]Carol Hymowitz and Michael C. Weissman, *A History of Women in America* (New York: Bantam Books, 1978), 70.

THE SUFFRAGE MOVEMENT

Like women in the movement before them, most women in the suffrage movement eventually came to view divorce reform as possibly strengthening the family. Although divorce laws generally held men and women to the same moral standard, suffragists did not take a public stand on the reform issue. Advocates of divorce reform generally were associated with the several smaller, radical movements that developed during the suffrage era. From 1895 to World War I, for example, the philosophies of Charlotte Perkins Gilman, an early radical feminist, were the most widely reported. For example, in *Women and Economics* (1898), she urged radical changes in the family and child care.[17] She called for professional day care and communal living arrangements with central kitchens, which would allow women the freedom to advance in the economic arena. Critics took these calls as the logical consequences of woman suffrage. Even most suffragists rejected Gilman's radical views.

Educated Motherhood

While rejecting most of the reforms suggested by Gilman and others, women in the suffrage and progressive movements worked for some changes that would benefit the position of women in their role as mothers. After woman suffrage was won, the seriously high infant and female childbirth mortality rates in the United States were some of the first problems sought to be remedied. Concern for the high number of birth-associated deaths was a natural response for the women who had sought the vote based on their claims as mothers. Stressing the idea of "educated motherhood,"[18] they called for federal legislation to give money to the states to set up clinics where expectant women and young mothers could be taught preventive health care. In many ways, these proposals perpetuated the idea of a woman's "separate sphere" by aiding her efforts to be a better mother.

During 1920 and 1921, the Women's Joint Congressional Committee (WJCC) and each of its constituent organizations lobbied for passage of the Sheppard-Towner Maternity Act (STMA), a bill that embodied many of the proposals behind the ideas of educated motherhood. It called for money to be paid to states to promote welfare and hygiene in maternity and infancy.

Not all women who supported suffrage favored the STMA. Just as the National Woman's Party (NWP) clashed with the dominant suffrage groups over strategy for the vote, it also strongly opposed the ideology behind the STMA.[19] Though never challenging traditional marriage itself—in fact, the NWP was on record as "dedicated to finer homes and better marriages"[20]—it believed passage of this law would legally sanction the treatment of women as "mothers not persons." This, NWP leaders believed, would simply reinforce the entire notion of separate spheres, as women would be singled out for special treatment solely on account of their reproductive capacity. This kind of treatment was at odds with the party's support of an equal rights amendment.[21] However, neither equal rights for women nor the idea that women should be anything other than mothers first was particularly popular in the 1920s.

Although the STMA was passed and became the first dividend of universal suffrage for women,[22] it did so over vigorous opposition. Many of its strongest opponents had lobbied *against* the Nineteenth Amendment. Now, they viewed the STMA as an unwarranted invasion of the family by the federal government. Nevertheless, frightened legislators believed women would vote against those who opposed the act; eight years later when it became clear to members of Congress that women did not vote in a bloc, the law failed to win an extension.

Birth Control in the Suffrage Era

Birth control was an exceptionally controversial issue during the suffrage era. The Comstock Act barred dissemination of birth control information through the mail. Nevertheless, many educated, middle-class women clearly used artificial forms of contraception or somehow restricted their fertility. Poorer and immigrant women, however, continued to have very large families. Soon Margaret Sanger and a growing number of women active in the progressive movement began to believe that family planning was the only way out of poverty for many.

Sanger traveled to Europe to learn more about contraceptive devices since there was no ban on their dissemination there. On her return, she began publication of *The Woman Rebel,* in which she explained available contraceptive devices, called on women to limit the size of their families, and urged them to revolt against "patriarchal society."[23] Sanger was indicted for violating the Comstock Act, but charges were dropped. Sanger then sought legal changes to allow physicians to fit birth control devices. This move made her goals more acceptable to physicians, a powerful political group, and to many suffragists.

Sanger's arguments for birth control closely paralleled those made earlier by suffragists during their educated suffrage phase. She presented birth control as a social reform, not a woman's issue. Sanger faced an uphill battle, however; birth control was far more controversial than suffrage. Even after ratification of the Nineteenth Amendment, Sanger was unable to attract the support of many women's organizations to her largely separate movement.[24]

Hostility to Sanger and public discussion of birth control was evidenced by the refusal of the General Federation of Women's Clubs to even discuss a birth control resolution at its national meeting. A similar position was also taken by the League of Women Voters. In fact, the only women's organization to go on record publicly in support of the activities of Sanger's National Birth Control League (NBCL) was the National Women's Trade Union League. Even the liberal National Woman's Party refused to adopt a resolution favoring birth control, fearing it would confuse public perceptions of its lone goal—passage of an equal rights amendment—which had nothing to do with birth control. In fact, NWP leaders took great pains to disassociate their goals with any ideas that could be considered to be antifamily.

The failure of many of the major women's groups to support the birth control movement is not surprising. It was vehemently objected to by many ministers and priests and even suffragists. In declining to be a sponsor of the NBCL, Carrie Chapman Catt, president of the National American Woman Suffrage Association, wrote to Sanger, "Your reform is too narrow to appeal to me and too sordid."[25] Even many socialists believed that an association with birth control made their economic radicalism less acceptable. In fact, many rejected birth control, and some even adopted the argument put forth in the first woman's movement, namely, that artificial contraception only reinforced the moral double standard.[26] Thus, declining support from conservative feminists and isolation from many radicals and socialists largely account for the relative lack of progress by the birth control movement during this period.

The suffrage movement was well defined by its name. A wide variety of groups, often diverse in purpose, came together to secure passage of the Nineteenth Amendment. Few were interested in marriage reform or other reforms affecting families. Some, like Sanger, however, believed that women would be better off if they could limit their families. But she and many others preferred to cast birth control as a social issue and not as a woman's issue.

THE CURRENT WOMEN'S RIGHTS MOVEMENT

Women from both branches of the women's rights movement have been active in the areas of family rights and reproductive freedom. In fact, those in the younger branch probably did more to change the institution of marriage and the family than women in the older branch. They also urged a reexamination of women's sexuality and often were at the forefront of moves for lesbian rights. Younger-branch women enthusiastically embraced many of the reforms sought during the first woman's movement, as well as those pursued by radicals like Charlotte Perkins Gilman during the suffrage movement.

Another phenomenon that has occurred concerns the older branch's growing acceptance, and indeed advocacy, of changes first advanced by those in the younger branch, including marriage reform, better birth control, and legal abortion. Indeed, Flora Davis and others have speculated that by 1975 the two branches had actually merged.[27] This has led to a movement fairly united in purpose although not necessarily in tactics. However, because the combined forces of both branches of the movement lobbied and continue to lobby for change in the family and for reproductive freedom, a strong countermovement arose to fight for the status quo and against what its followers believe to be the pure public bads advocated by the women's rights movement. Phyllis Schlafly's Eagle Forum and Beverly LaHaye's Concerned Women for America (CWA) were the major groups formed in reaction to these efforts.

Marriage

With the call "the personal is political," women in the younger branch initially challenged all aspects of the sexual relationship between men and women. Groups including the Redstockings, a New York–based, militant activist group, tried to develop a female class awareness among all women. This was often done through consciousness-raising groups. In them, women were expected to see how their individual and common experiences were the product of the same patriarchal system.

The Redstockings and many other groups demanded the elimination of the institutions that perpetuated male and female roles—including marriage. Shulamith Firestone, for example, a leading New York City feminist and author of *The Dialectic of Sex*, painted a future of cybernetic socialism. In it, reproduction was to be done by artificial means, the nuclear family would be replaced by communelike "households," and both men and women would share parenting and other domestic roles, although most tasks would be performed by machines[28]—a future very similar to the one proposed earlier by Charlotte Perkins Gilman.

Most women in the older branch initially tried to disassociate themselves from the tactics and ideology of the younger branch. The women who founded the National Organization for Women (NOW) in 1966 strongly supported both marriage and the family but thought that some legal changes needed to be made so that women could more easily pursue careers while continuing to be good wives and mothers.

Demands for reasonable pregnancy leaves without loss of seniority, tax deductions for child-care expenses, and establishment of child-care centers all reflect concern with the family. Although women in the younger branch also advocated the creation of more child-care centers, they viewed them as but a first step toward eliminating sex-role stereotypes about parenting. In contrast, NOW members and other older-branch women saw them as simply facilitating women's entrance into the work force and allowing them to combine their worker and motherhood roles more easily.

Older branch women also were very concerned with the position of women more generally within the marriage institution. While unswerving in their belief in the family, they agreed that wives should be treated as equal partners within the institution of marriage. Like Elizabeth Cady Stanton, they viewed inequalities in marriage as the root of the problems faced by women. Thus, they called for reforms both in marriage and in the legal treatment of married women, both during and upon the dissolution of a marriage.

Marriage and the Loss of Identity

Under the common law notion of coverture discussed earlier, a woman technically ceased to exist legally upon marriage.[29] Today, this no longer happens, but a woman can lose some of her identity if she takes the last name of her husband.

Names. Since Lucy Stone's marriage to Henry Blackwell in 1855, a small number of women have followed her lead and not adopted their husband's surname. Like most practices involving marriage, laws and requirements for name changes have been left to the states and thus vary from state to state. Laws in Kentucky and Alabama that require a woman to obtain her driver's license in her husband's surname, regardless of the name she uses in other situations, were upheld by the U.S. Supreme Court in the 1970s.[30] Until the mid-1970s, the U.S. Passport Office refused to issue passports in a married woman's birth name—even if it was the only name by which she was known. Eventually, pressure from a variety of women's rights groups forced the office to end this practice.

This kind of lobbying was also exerted in most states to gain passage of laws that allow women (and men in some states) to choose the name they would like to be known by after marriage. Thus, a woman may choose to retain her birth name, she may hyphenate her last name with that of her husband, or she and her husband may choose to be known by a new name altogether.

Women's Names Continue to Trouble Many

In the wake of the women's rights movement, some women decide to retain their birth names upon marriage. Others combine their name with that of their husband. The *New York Times*'s society editor estimates that one out of three married women do one or the other. In one study of women living in the suburbs, three out of four women took their husbands' names. In New York City, in contrast, it was estimated that 75 to 80 percent of the women either kept their birth names or combined them with that of their husbands.[a]

During the 1992 presidential campaign, and then after Bill Clinton took office in 1993, his wife's name seemed to be as great a national fixation as her hairstyles. As a practicing attorney in Little Rock, Arkansas, the governor's wife was known as Hillary Rodham. When her husband failed to win reelection as governor in 1980, some questioned her failure to change her name. She then began to go by Hillary Rodham Clinton, and Bill Clinton was reelected the next time he ran for governor. Through much of 1992, press accounts of her activities referred to her as Mrs. Clinton or Hillary Clinton. After the 1993 inauguration, however, she quickly reestablished herself as Hillary Rodham Clinton. What was the public's reaction? Although a *Wall Street Journal*/NBC poll found that 74 percent of those polled believed that she was a "positive role model for women," only 6 percent favored her using Rodham in her name, with 62 percent opposing her use of her birth name.[b]

When people were asked more generally about their views of the trend for some women to keep their birth names, one 1993 study found that one-quarter of southerners and one-fifth of nonsoutherners believed that this "was a change for the worse." Clearly this is an issue that continues to divide. Apparently it also "marks" women.

Deborah Tannen, the author of *You Just Don't Understand: Women and Men in Conversation*, has noted how "[W]omen can't even fill out a form without telling stories about themselves." Women are given the options of checking "Mrs.," "Miss," or "Ms." And each carries with it certain "markers": married, unmarried, traditional, untraditional, etc. In contrast, men simply check "Mr.," which carries no markers with it.

Similarly, women's surnames are marked. If a woman takes her husband's name she is "traditional"; if she retains her birth name, she has accomplished something: "She has kept her own name." And if she uses her husband's name and her own—with or without a hyphen—she is also marked and often has a "tongue-tying string." She stands out. Just look at Hillary Rodham Clinton.[c]

[a]Arthur Higbee, "American Topics," *International Herald Tribune*, March 29, 1993, NEXIS.

[b]Jeanne Freeman, "What's in a Name? Lots, When It Is First Lady's," *San Diego Union Tribune*, February 12, 1993, E1; "62% Say First Lady Should Drop 'Rodham,'" *USA Today*, January 29, 1993, 4A.

[c]Deborah Tannen, "Wears Jump Suit. Sensible Shoes. Uses Husband's Last Name," *New York Times Magazine*, June 20, 1993, 18.

Marriage and Divorce Law

Laws governing marriage and its dissolution have long discriminated against women. Women's rights activists recognized that discriminatory state laws needed change, but women's groups were often weak organizationally at the state level. Some organizations with strong state affiliates such as NOW, the National Federation of Business and Professional Women's Clubs, and the League of Women Voters have made considerable inroads to reform, but progress in individual states has not been uniform.

In the 1970s and 1980s, the Eagle Forum and CWA mobilized at the state and local levels. These groups drew supporters from a conservative religious base that saw an easy accommodation between religion and politics. In 1972, Phyllis Schlafly founded STOP ERA to do just what its name implied. Schlafly labeled feminists supporting the equal rights amendment "the unkempt, the lesbians, the radicals, the socialists."[31] She claimed that ERA supporters had abandoned their God-given roles of wife and mother. Schlafly and her supporters created the Eagle Forum as an outgrowth of STOP ERA in 1975 to represent the interests of conservative women in a variety of issue areas. From the beginning, its state affiliates and strong ties to the religious right have allowed it to lobby effectively against family law changes on the state level.

To get around the "state problem," several national liberal women's organizations have concerned themselves with national solutions to issues including violence against women, divorce, alimony and child support enforcement, child custody, and homemaker rights. As early as 1963, the Commission on the Status of Women suggested the elimination of laws discriminating against women in the marriage relationship and in the dissolution of marriage.[32] Later, NOW drafted an Equal Rights Divorce Reform bill, which called for a greater recognition of a woman's economic contribution to marriage and a right to an equal division of the couple's property.

In 1977, the National Women's Conference, which was supported by the U.S. government as part of the United States International Year of the Woman observance, met in Houston, Texas. More than twenty thousand women came together (two thousand of them as state delegates) to adopt a twenty-six-plank National Plan of Action, which they submitted to President Carter in March 1978. Federal and state lawmakers were urged to enact the economic provisions contained in the Uniform Marriage and Divorce Act, a proposed law supported by the American Bar Association.[33] In documenting the need for such provisions, the conference report noted that in 1977, in Georgia, if a house was titled in a husband's name, it "belonged only to him, even if the wife was the wage earner and made all payments."[34] Further, "in Arkansas, a husband could dispose of all property, even jointly owned, without his wife's consent."[35]

To protest the use of government funds, Phyllis Schlafly held an alternative conference to create a new conservative coalition called the Pro-Family Movement.[36] This brought unwanted controversy to a meeting where women's rights groups failed to foresee one. Not only did the National Women's Conference reveal divisions among women as a group, it also fostered the creation of another conservative women's group, Concerned Women for America. Deriving its base more from the religious right than the political right (where Schlafly had originally found many supporters), CWA's founder, Beverly LaHaye, created the group after the Houston conference. Unlike the Eagle Forum, it has a legal staff that tries to file lawsuits in what it calls profamily cases.[37] It also has a political action committee.

It is not surprising, then, that liberal reform in family law has been slow, as reform has largely had to proceed on a state-by-state basis. The U.S. Supreme Court, however, which rarely involves itself in state domestic disputes, ruled that laws like Arkansas's that allow husbands to dispose of property without spousal consent are unconstitutional.[38]

Divorce and Custody Laws. Women still experience legal inequality within marriage under some state laws. They also often fare even more inequitably upon the dissolution of marriage. The 1970s and 1980s brought dramatic changes in state divorce laws. Not only did divorce become easier to get, but the process also became nearly impossible for one spouse to block, even if he or she didn't want a divorce. Guilt no longer became an issue, and "no-fault" divorces are now available in all fifty states.[39]

Many argue that divorce reform has been disastrous for women, although no-fault divorce accompanied by a state-level ERA actually may prove advantageous to women. In the absence of state ERAs, women's and children's standards of living often drop dramatically after divorce. The Uniform Marriage and Divorce Act of 1974—a model law suggested for states— is written in terms of women's needs. Nevertheless, women often get low financial awards from state judges. In the 1980s and 1990s, for example, numerous state commissions on gender bias in the judicial system concluded that women fail to receive adequate alimony, child support, and/or equitable distributions of marital property. All states have laws allowing for awards of alimony, but few women actually receive it.

For several years, NOW, other women's groups, and the Children's Legal Defense Fund (of which Hillary Rodham Clinton was once president of its Board of Directors) repeatedly asked Congress to pass a comprehensive Women's Economic Equity Act (WEEA). The act was initially composed of twenty-six separate bills when it was introduced in 1981; several dealt with alimony, child support, and property settlement enforcement. Many of those provisions have yet to win legislative approval; but Congress did pass tougher enforcement of child support laws, and U.S. Attorney General Janet Reno has made their enforcement a priority.

Child custody, too, has been another area of concern to women's rights activists. At the time of the Seneca Falls Convention, laws favored fathers in custody disputes. Over time, however, laws changed, reflecting consideration of the best interest of the child. As a result, by the 1930s, most state courts awarded custody of children to their mothers *unless* the mothers were deemed unfit.

By the 1980s, however, as more fathers began to seek custody, most state courts abandoned the presumption that children were best left in the care of their mothers. Fathers often present courts with promises of higher economic standards for their children. One study found that as many as 90 percent of fathers who sought custody actually won.[40]

Just as troubling of late are the actions of some state court judges who have actually *taken away* child custody from biological mothers who are lesbians. Although some states such as Massachusetts allow the nonbiological mother in a lesbian couple to adopt the child, in 1993 a Virginia judge terminated a lesbian mother's legal custody of her child because, as a lesbian, the court found her to be "unfit" and "immoral." Custody was awarded to the child's grandmother in spite of the fact that it is estimated that there are between 4 and 6 million gay and lesbian parents.[41]

One new area of concern to feminist legal scholars has been the trend to remove divorce and child custody proceedings from courtrooms to less formal alternative dispute resolution (ADR) processes. Several state commissions on gender bias document that women often fare unequally before male judges in terms of alimony, property distribution, and even child custody awards.[42] To remedy this, some advocate use of ADR. Some states require court-connected conciliatory services.[43] Mediation, however, assumes that both parties approach the bargaining table on equal footing. As our discussion in Chapter 6 reveals, women are rarely equal in any marriage. Thus, ADR has been criticized by some as simply perpetuating inequalities.[44]

Motherhood and New Issues of "Family"

Today, many women face several dilemmas regarding motherhood. Should they have children? Must they be married to have children? Will they be able to conceive or adopt? If they have children, how can they reconcile motherhood roles and jobs or careers?

The Decision to Have Children.   Few question the decision of a married woman to have a child. Many, however, often look unfavorably on those who choose to have children without the benefit of marriage. Nevertheless, teenage pregnancy rates are high, as are the pregnancy rates of older, unmarried women. Some career women opt to bear children or to adopt without the benefit of a traditional marriage, as illustrated by the case of fictional television character Murphy Brown or real-life people such as Rosie O'Donnell. No state laws prohibit an unmarried woman from bearing her own child. But some states prohibit adoption by unmarried women, and many women's groups have lobbied to repeal those laws. Even in the absence of restrictive state laws, some state social service adoption agencies rarely place children in the homes of unmarried women.

Domestic Partnerships or Gay Marriages?

The move to recognize lesbian and gay marriages legally gained momentum in the 1990s. Early in the decade, many city councils enacted what are called domestic partnership laws. These laws come in a variety of versions. Most generally allow adults who live together but who cannot legally wed to register at city hall as domestic partners. Registration then provides the couple with certain legal rights that they would not otherwise enjoy in relationship to each other. Domestic partners often gain access to family health, dental, and even life insurance plans, which generally cover only married persons. (Domestic partnership provisions are especially useful should one partner die or become ill.)

At this writing, no state law recognizes same-sex marriages. In 1993, however, a decision of the Hawaiian Supreme Court called that state's ban on homosexual marriages into constitutional question. After three homosexual couples were denied marriage licenses by the state Department of Health in

1990, they filed suit in 1991 alleging that the state violated their rights to equal protection under the Hawaiian Constitution, which prohibits discrimination based on sex. In 1993, the state Supreme Court ruled that the homosexual couples' rights appeared to have been violated and sent the case back to the lower court with instructions that the state must show a "compelling state interest" to continue to deny marriage licenses to same-sex couples. In June 1994, the governor signed a law stating that marriage licenses could only be for male-female couples and stipulating that state policy can be changed only by the legislature, not the courts. The bill also called for the creation of a Commission on Sexual Orientation and the Law. On December 9, 1995, the commission recommended that Hawaii legalize marriage between same-sex couples or set up comprehensive domestic partnership laws.

The Hawaii Supreme Court is expected to issue a final decision in 1997 upholding the constitutional right of homosexuals to marry. Citizens in Hawaii are now mired in other legal challenges, including one involving whether a constitutional convention can be held to amend the Constitution to ban homosexual marriages, which would negate any judicial action. Since this case was litigated under the Hawaiian Constitution, however, no appeal to the U.S. Supreme Court is possible.

The U.S. Constitution requires that all states give "full faith and credit" to the laws of and contracts made in the other states. Thus, if a couple gets married in Texas, they are still recognized as being married in California if they move or vacation there. The specter of Hawaii's legalization of same-sex marriages has therefore thrown many state legislatures into a tizzy. By mid-1997, conservative legislators in more than half of the states passed legislation to specifically ban same-sex marriages. Others have enacted legislation stating that no matter what Hawaii does, they will not recognize such marriages performed there. The federal government has even weighed in on the issue. In late 1996, Congress passed and the president signed into law the Defense of Marriage Act, which is a statutory attempt to allow states not to recognize same-sex marriages performed in other states. The constitutionality of this provision, however, is in question.

Childbearing and adoption have been especially crucial areas to lesbians who cannot legally marry. Many states prohibit the placement of children in lesbian homes. Moreover, lesbians who choose to bear their own children often encounter discrimination from physicians when they seek donor insemination services or in vitro fertilization. Women in the younger branch of the women's movement, particularly those associated with the Federation of Feminist Women's Health Centers, have tried to alleviate this problem by expanding their health services to include donor insemination programs. Usually, a majority of their clients are lesbians, who were refused artificial insemination elsewhere.

Artificial insemination, the process by which sperm from a donor is injected into a woman, has been in use since the 1890s.[45] In vitro fertilization, a process by which a woman's ova are removed from her body, fertilized (*in vitro* means "in a glass" in Latin), and frozen for later implantation, is a much newer process. It is much more expensive, less commonly used, and less successful than artificial insemination. The development of these technologies and their potential was not lost on lesbians. Many women from the younger branch viewed these technologies as a mechanism by which to further separate themselves from a patriarchal society.

Feminist health centers have taken the lead in donor insemination services as well as in dealing with other specialized health care concerns of lesbians. Conservative women and the New Right have attacked the idea of lesbian parenting, and many have even opposed in vitro fertilization of married women who have been unable to conceive.

There is much concern in the feminist and women's health communities about new reproductive technologies and pregnancy medicalization and their impact on women. Laura Woliver, for example, among others, argues that these new technologies actually decrease women's control and options over maternity.[46]

Surrogacy. Artificial insemination, egg donation, and in vitro fertilization resulted in the emergence of another issue—surrogate parenthood. There are four types of surrogacy: (1) gestational surrogacy, in which both partners can produce viable embryos, which are carried in another woman's uterus; (2) egg donation fertilized with a husband's sperm and implanted in his wife through in vitro fertilization; (3) egg donation with implantation in a third woman; and (4) traditional surrogacy in which the woman who donates her egg also carries the child to term.[47] Surrogacy often questions our traditional definitions of the terms *mother* and *motherhood.* In 1986, surrogate parenting became a media sensation when Mary Beth Whitehead was paid $10,000 to be artificially inseminated with William Stern's sperm. Whitehead signed a contract agreeing to bear the child and then give it to Stern and his wife, a pediatrician. Whitehead, however, changed her mind after the birth. A judge ordered her to give the baby to the Sterns. Both parties then went to court. After a well-publicized trial, the Sterns were awarded custody, and Whitehead, the natural mother, was deprived of *all* parental rights. The judge insisted that his ruling was based on the best interests of Baby M (as the child had come to be known).

In 1988, the New Jersey Supreme Court upheld the custody award to William Stern but reinstated Whitehead's parental rights, which then allowed her visitation rights. Most important, the court ruled that surrogate parenting was illegal in New Jersey because it violated state adoption laws that banned baby selling.[48]

Since 1980, nearly 10,000 babies have been born through surrogates.[49] Still, surrogacy brings up troubling questions for the courts and feminists. In 1989, the American Bar Association endorsed a model state law that had two options: (1) States could make surrogate contracts illegal (and, therefore, unenforceable) or (2) states could regulate surrogate contracts like adoptions. The model law also suggested that surrogate contracts be limited to married couples with one person having a genetic link to the child. The legal community appears to be leaning toward genetic bonds as a prerequisite for legal surrogacy. In cases where women have simply carried another woman's fertilized eggs, courts have been uniform in their decisions against the surrogates.

In spite of thorny legal, moral, and philosophical issues, some women's rights advocates argue that women should be allowed to do what they want with their bodies.[50] Others fear that surrogacy contracts simply reinforce the stereotype "woman as womb."[51] Surrogacy arrangements also have a deep class dimension; they disproportionately affect poor women, who are more likely to use their reproductive capacities out of simple economic need.[52]

REPRODUCTIVE FREEDOM

The current women's rights movement is also concerned with issues of reproductive rights. According to Gloria Steinem, "reproductive freedom signifies an individual's basic human right to decide whether or not to have children," whereas the phrase rejected by feminists, "population control," "legitimizes some external force or power over women's lives."[53] To remove this external force, women continue to press for improved methods of contraception to allow them greater control over their lives. They also lobby for improved sex education and access to contraceptives to remedy teenage pregnancy. Additionally, younger-branch women have not only started feminist-run health clinics to avoid reliance on male physicians, they have also written self-help books, including *Our Bodies, Ourselves,* with the goal of giving women information about, and therefore more control over, their bodies.[54]

Birth Control

By the dawn of the women's rights movement, groups such as Planned Parenthood, created during the second movement, were well established. Still, by the 1960s, two states (Connecticut and Massachusetts) had Comstock-like laws that banned the sale or use of birth control devices or information, although these laws were not well enforced. Elsewhere, women could get prescriptions for diaphragms. By 1960, birth control pills were available from private physicians. No public clinics were available, however, to provide poor women with these types of birth control. After efforts to change these state laws failed, Planned Parenthood opened a clinic in New Haven, Connecticut, specifically to challenge the law. After its director and doctor were tried, convicted, and fined for violating the state law prohibiting dissemination of birth control devices, its challenge to the Connecticut law was ultimately heard by the U.S. Supreme Court. In *Griswold v. Connecticut* (1965), the Court ruled that the Connecticut statute was unconstitutional.[55] In *Griswold,* the Court concluded that the Constitution contained a broad right to *privacy,* which was created by "penumbras emanating" from several specific guarantees in the Bill of Rights. These include the First Amendment, which protects association; the Third Amendment, which bars the quartering of soldiers in private homes in peacetime without consent; the Fourth Amendment, which protects Americans from unreasonable searches and seizures of their homes and property; the Fifth Amendment, which guarantees the freedom from self-incrimination; and the Ninth Amendment, which gives to citizens rights not specifically enumerated in the Constitution. Once this right to privacy was established, the Court went on to conclude that a married couple's right to privacy included the right to have access to and use of birth control.

Adolescent Access to Birth Control. Although *Griswold* upheld the right of a married woman to use birth control—and in 1972 the Supreme Court again used the privacy doctrine to invalidate a state law barring unmarried women from access to birth control[56]—during the 1980s, the Reagan administration tried to limit teenage women's access to birth control. In 1981, for example, the first federal legislation specifically designed to deal with teenage pregnancies was passed.[57] The Adolescent Family Life Act placed emphasis on encouraging self-discipline rather than contraceptive services as a method of birth control. It also banned the use of any federal funds for abortion counseling in spite of the fact that the United States has the highest teen pregnancy rate in the Western world. Although many of the providers of counseling were religious groups that counseled teens that "God wants us to be pure,"[58] in 1989 the U.S. Supreme Court upheld what many called the gag rule.[59]

Parental consent policies, heavily lobbied for by the Eagle Forum and CWA, have reflected similar conservative values. In 1981, for example, a Department of Health and Human Services regulation required parental notification for adolescents seeking birth control devices in all federally funded clinics.

Women's rights groups have objected to both types of programs. Representative Patricia Schroeder (D-Colo.), for example, spoke out loudly against the Reagan and Bush administrations' exclusion of funding for most programs except those that teach abstinence. Most women's rights activists believe that teenagers must be given access to birth control information and devices not only as an important step in stopping teen pregnancies but also in stopping the spread of AIDS. U.S. Surgeon General Joycelyn Elders, the first African American woman to hold that position, has long espoused this view, which she steadfastly defended during her Senate confirmation hearings in 1993. Eventually, however, after she suggested, during a speech on

AIDS prevention, that masturbation is "part of something that perhaps should be taught" in school, President Clinton demanded her resignation.[60]

AIDS continues to be a particularly threatening issue for women of color. In the United States, the incidence of AIDS in Hispanic women is nearly eleven times that of white women. More than half of all women with AIDS are African American and 80 percent of all pediatric cases are Latino or African American.[61] Thus, feminist women's health centers, the Coalition of Women of Color for Reproductive Health, and the National Black Women's Health Project have been at the forefront of education on this issue.

Abortion

Whereas birth control, especially as it concerns teenagers, has been controversial, abortion has been even more so. States first began to enact statutes outlawing abortion except when necessary to protect the life and health of mothers around 1820. During both early women's movements, women procured abortions. But even progressive women such as Elizabeth Cady Stanton and Margaret Sanger preferred not to get involved in any move to change existing abortion laws. Sanger even publicly denounced abortion.

Not until the 1960s did many individuals come to recognize the need for changes in restrictive state abortion laws. In 1959, the influential American Law Institute (ALI) suggested that state laws be revised to decriminalize abortion in three circumstances:

1. When continuation of the pregnancy would gravely impair the physical or mental health of the mother
2. When the child might be born with a grave physical or mental defect
3. When the pregnancy resulted from rape, incest, or other felonious intercourse, including illicit intercourse with a girl below the age of sixteen

Soon after the ALI-proposed change, a number of events occurring almost simultaneously led to an abortion movement in the United States. Physicians began to lobby for reform. In 1962, abortion became an issue of heated public debate when Sherri Finkbine, a children's television show host, sought an abortion after she realized that she had taken thalidomide, a drug proven to cause fetal abnormalities. For the first time in history, abortion received prominent national attention. Finkbine was forced to fly to Sweden to get an abortion because she was unable to secure a legal one in the United States. Her plight was broadcast in minute detail. Attention also turned to scientific advances that lessened the medical risks associated with abortion.

Soon after the Finkbine incident, a German measles epidemic swept the United States in 1963 and 1964. If a woman contracts measles during the first three months of her pregnancy, there is a high probability that the fetus will suffer from interrupted development. As more and more pregnant women found themselves exposed to measles and unsuccessfully sought legal abortions, public concern over abortion reform increased. Even though more than twenty thousand children were born with various developmental problems directly traceable to measles, concern and publicity were still inadequate to forge an abortion movement.

Taken together, however, these factors prompted several individuals to become increasingly concerned with abortion reform. By the mid–1960s, Lawrence Lader, the author of a book about Margaret Sanger, began to advocate abortion reform in public speeches and to refer women to physicians who would risk performing the illegal procedure.[62] Around the same time, Patricia Maginnis, a California woman who had undergone three illegal abortions, began publicly to advocate total repeal of all abortion laws—a radical proposal that went far beyond the ALI proposals.

These isolated actions of Lader and Maginnis, even when coupled with news accounts of the horrors of illegal, back-alley abortions and the birth of abnormal children, were not enough to start a movement. It took the infusion of potential supporters provided by both branches of the women's rights movement to forge a pro-choice submovement within the existing movement. In fact, the first *formal* call for the repeal of restrictive abortion laws can be traced to the Bill of Rights for Women adopted by NOW at its first annual convention in 1967. The last section demanded:

> The right of women to control their own reproductive lives by removing from the penal codes laws limiting access to contraceptive information and devices and by repealing penal laws governing abortion.[63]

The provision was passed over strong opposition. Some members believed that abortion was not a civil rights issue; others argued that NOW's association with abortion would bring unfavorable publicity that would make other more attainable goals increasingly difficult to achieve.[64]

NOW's public support of abortion attracted additional members and even some of the leaders necessary to start a real move for change. Soon after NOW's call for repeal, for example, other "rights"-oriented organizations followed suit. In 1968, the Citizens Advisory Council on the Status of Women called for the repeal of all restrictive abortion laws, as did the ACLU.

Women from both branches of the women's rights movement became increasingly active in campaigns to repeal restrictive state laws. In 1969, the National Association for the Repeal for Abortion Laws, which later was to become the National Abortion Rights Action League (NARAL) was formed. In 1994, it changed its name again. NARAL now stands for National Abortion and Reproductive Rights Action League. Lader helped establish NARAL, as did many NOW members, including Betty Friedan.

NARAL, Planned Parenthood, the YWCA, and other groups used conventional lobbying methods to pressure state legislatures for abortion reform. The more radical, younger-branch Redstockings held a "speak out" where prominent women spoke out about their own abortions. In spite of pressure from the Roman Catholic Church not to do so, in 1970, New York State passed the most liberal abortion law in the United States. This victory fueled the pro-choice movement; it also provided the catalyst for a fledgling anti-abortion movement. Thus, by 1972, pressure from right-to-life forces, heavily supported by the Catholic Church, led the New York legislature to repeal the 1970 law. This action was vetoed, however, by Governor Nelson A. Rockefeller.

Advocates of repeal of restrictive abortion laws also had other legislative setbacks because of the efforts of the growing right-to-life movement. In Michigan and North Dakota, for example, proposals for abortion law reform were put to the voters and were overwhelmingly rejected. Increasingly, those women in the older branch in particular, but not exclusively, began to believe that the courts were their best chance for change.

Consequently, between 1969 and 1973, scores of cases were brought by attorneys and/or abortion rights groups generally on behalf of physicians who performed abortions and later on behalf of women who sought abortions but were unable to secure them legally. Within this setting and amid growing support for change among women's rights groups, the U.S. Supreme Court agreed to hear two more cases involving abortion rights. *Roe v. Wade* (1973) involved a pregnant woman's challenge to a Texas law that prohibited abortions except to save a mother's life.[65] Because "Jane Roe's"* pregnancy was not life threatening (which would have made her eligible to get a legal abortion in Texas), she was advised to seek one out of state. She did not have the money to do so. After seeking legal counsel, she went to court to challenge the constitutionality of the Texas law. Her lawsuit alleged that the Texas law deprived "women and their physicians of rights protected by the 1st, 4th, 5th, 9th, and 14th Amendments" and that she was deprived of the "fundamental right . . . to choose when and where to have children." Her lawyers relied heavily on the right to privacy enunciated by the U.S. Supreme Court in *Griswold v. Connecticut.*

Unlike the Texas law, the Georgia statute challenged in *Doe v. Bolton* (1973), the companion case to *Roe*, was based on the ALI's Model Penal Code. Doe's lawyers (acting on behalf of Planned Parenthood and several doctors, nurses, clergy, and social workers) alleged that the Georgia law was an undue restriction of personal and marital privacy and a denial of equal protection of the laws.[66]

These abortion cases marked the first major direct national confrontation of pro- and antiabortion forces. Amicus curiae (friend of the court) briefs in support of *Roe* and *Doe* were filed by several physicians' groups and organizations representing the older branch of the women's movement (including the YWCA, NOW, and Planned Parenthood) as well as the younger branch. While not as numerous, antiabortion groups including Americans United for Life, Women for the Unborn, and Women Concerned for the Unborn Child also filed friend of the court briefs in large numbers.

*Most abortion cases involving individuals use pseudonyms for the women.

On January 22, 1973, the Supreme Court handed down its momentous decision. While the justices did not adopt the view that abortion was totally a private matter not to be regulated, as urged by younger-branch women, seven justices concluded that a woman's *constitutional right to privacy* was more important than a state's right to regulate abortions.

Thus, going further than simply finding the two state laws unconstitutional, the justices effectively invalidated the abortion laws of nearly all the states. In *Roe*, the justices divided pregnancy into trimesters and found different rights in each. The Court held that during the first trimester a woman had an absolute right to obtain an abortion free from state interference. In the second trimester, the Court found that the "state, in promoting its interest in the health of the mother, may, if it chooses, regulate the abortion procedure in ways that are reasonably related to maternal health." In the last trimester of pregnancy, the justices concluded that the state, to promote its interest in "potential human life," could regulate or prohibit abortions, except when they were necessary to preserve the "life or health of the mother."

While this decision was met with enthusiasm by women in the abortion and women's rights movements, it provided the catalyst for major organizational efforts on the part of the antiabortion movement. In fact, in the aftermath of the abortion cases, several antiabortion organizations were formed or reformulated. For example, the National Right to Life Committee (NRTLC), which originally was only a small coordinating unit within the National Conference of Catholic Bishops, became an independent organization in 1973 directly "in response to" the Court's abortion decisions.[67] From its inception, NRTLC's ultimate goal has been a constitutional amendment that would give full legal rights of personhood to the fetus from the moment of conception.[68] It is closely allied with the Roman Catholic Church, which has provided it with an important source of members and considerable financial support.

The moral issues underlying the abortion debate and opponents' depiction of abortion as murder immediately made the controversy front-page news across the country, providing free publicity to the growing movement. In addition, just as the women's rights movement had provided an organizational base for pro-choice forces, antiabortion advocates benefited when Phyllis Schlafly, herself a Catholic, publicly attacked the Court's decision. For example, shortly after *Roe*, she effectively linked abortion rights to the ERA. Schlafly charged that *Roe* was an example of the havoc that would be wreaked on traditional values if the ERA was ratified. Antiabortion advocates blamed the Court's decision for the increasing decline of morals and the destruction of the family.

Within months after *Roe*, state legislatures were deluged with antiabortion bills. These proposed laws included provisions regulating clinics and requiring parental or spousal consent, waiting periods, and the description of the physical and psychological development of the particular fetus before a patient could give her consent for the procedures. Generally, these laws or regulations were enacted at the suggestion of or with the support of NRTLC members. The enactment of this kind of legislation immediately placed pro-choice advocates on the defensive. All around the country, they were forced to expend large sums of money and considerable energy to challenge the constitutionality of these laws.[69] While pro-choice advocates were defending the rights guaranteed by *Roe*, right-to-lifers continued to lobby Congress for a constitutional amendment to ban abortions.

Although early efforts to secure a constitutional amendment were unsuccessful, in 1976 Congress passed legislation (generally referred to as the Hyde amendment for its sponsor Henry Hyde [R-Mo.]) that prohibited the use of federal funds such as Medicaid for abortions for poor women in all but three circumstances:

1. When the mother's life was in danger
2. When two physicians certified that a woman would suffer "severe and long lasting damage"
3. When the pregnancy was the result of rape or incest as reported to the proper authorities

Although the ACLU had specifically created a Reproductive Freedom Project (RFP) in 1974 to ensure compliance with *Roe*, most pro-choice activists were caught off guard by Henry Hyde and well-organized state groups that lobbied to see restrictions and conditions placed on women's access to abortion. For example, although the RFP, supported by an amicus curiae brief from NOW, successfully challenged a Missouri law that required women to sign detailed consent forms prior to an abortion, the Supreme Court upheld various record-keeping requirements of the law.[70] (In 1972, many of the RFP's lawyers formed the independent Center for Reproductive Law and Policy.)

With the passage of the Hyde amendment, however, some women's rights groups turned their attentions to Medicaid funding and went to court to block the amendment's implementation. Initially, they charged that Medicaid's refusal to pay for abortions was unconstitutional because it discriminated against poor women.

A series of Supreme Court decisions, however, dealt this argument a stunning blow in 1977. In three separate challenges by women's rights groups and Planned Parenthood to state Medicaid programs that financed childbirths but not abortions, the Court concluded that these practices did not violate a woman's constitutional right to secure an abortion even though some women could not afford them.[71] As a result, the number of publicly funded abortions declined precipitously.

These losses in 1977 mobilized women's rights groups just as *Roe* and *Doe* had done for the right-to-life movement. While new groups were not created, the ACLU, RFP, and NARAL immediately launched a "Campaign for Choice," which was supported by most other women's rights groups. At the 1977 National Women's Conference in Houston, delegates passed a resolution opposing "the exclusion of abortion . . . from Federal, State, or local funding of medical services," over the strenuous objections of right-to-life delegates.[72]

To implement this resolution, NARAL began a grass-roots campaign and founded NARAL-PAC to raise money for pro-choice candidates. Again, however, this was a reactive move designed to counter the growing political forces of the antiabortion movement. But the political winds were blowing in another direction. In 1980, Ronald Reagan, bolstered by the New Right and the Moral Majority, ran a successful campaign for the presidency. He was avowedly against abortion and ran on a campaign platform that contained a plank calling for him to appoint to the federal courts only judges who supported strong family values and who opposed abortion. In fact, his first appointment to the Supreme Court, Sandra Day O'Connor, was criticized because pro-life forces feared that she would not be a vote to overrule *Roe*.

Right-to-life activists' fears were somewhat assuaged in *Akron v. Akron Center for Reproductive Health* (1983).[73] Although Akron became the first case in which the Justice Department advanced a pro-life position before the Court (claiming that "the time has come to call a halt" to judicial limitation on state regulation of abortion), the Court struck down a vast majority of the restrictions at issue, including those preventing second-trimester abortions in outpatient clinics and requiring a twenty-four-hour waiting period. Justice O'Connor, Reagan's lone appointment to that date, joined the dissenters, noting her belief that *Roe* "was on a collision course with itself" because the trimester approach was "unworkable" in light of changing medical technology.

Over and over again, well-organized right-to-life groups convinced state legislatures to pass restrictive state abortion laws, sensing that the Court—especially if Reagan could make more appointments to it—was close to overruling *Roe*. And eventually, through Reagan's appointment of new justices to the Supreme Court plus the elevation of Associate Justice William Rehnquist (one of the two dissenters in *Roe*) to the position of chief justice, the scope of *Roe* was slowly limited.

The move to overrule *Roe* judicially picked up during the Bush administration. During George Bush's 1988 campaign for the presidency, he urged "adoption not abortion" as a solution to unwanted pregnancies and resurrected the call for passage of a constitutional amendment to ban abortions. Also adding fuel to the fire was the formation of Operation Rescue, a national group that used more aggressive methods to stop abortions, including trying to bar access to clinics where they were performed. It first made its presence felt at the 1988 Democratic National Convention in Atlanta, Georgia, when it blockaded several local clinics and a feminist health center.

In response to these growing threats to abortion rights, Kate Michelman, the executive director of NARAL, decided to launch a major national campaign to let women know that *Roe* was in jeopardy. Working closely with other groups including Planned Parenthood, NOW, and the Coalition of Women of Color for Reproductive Health, NARAL designed a two-part strategy. The first was to let women know that *Webster v. Reproductive Health*

Services, a case that was pending before the Supreme Court, might be used by the Court to overturn *Roe.*[74] The second part of the strategy was to educate the public to understand that even if *Roe* was not overturned, *Webster* could be a major setback if the Supreme Court was no longer willing to preserve a woman's right to an abortion using the *Roe* framework. NARAL's scheme was to get Americans to ask, "Who decides?"

During the Bush years, abortion became an even more publicized issue. When *Webster* was finally announced in July 1989, four justices—Reagan appointees Antonin Scalia and Anthony Kennedy and Chief Justice William Rehnquist and Byron White (who was the second dissenter in *Roe*)—seemed willing to overrule *Roe.* They were unable to muster the support of a fifth justice, however. Thus, *Roe* was not overturned. But Missouri's restrictions on abortions in public hospitals and tests required for fetal viability were upheld. The opinion also read like an invitation to the states to pass additional restrictions. After *Webster,* Michelman warned, "The Court has left a woman's right to privacy hanging by a thread and passed the scissors to the state legislatures."[75]

Webster mobilized forces on both sides as marches were held around the country, and even sitting justices began to voice their fears about a post-*Roe* nation. In the wake of *Webster,* pro-choice groups including NARAL, NOW, the Fund for the Feminist Majority, and Planned Parenthood met to devise a strategy to use at the state and national levels. At the same time, the National Right to Life Committee moved to get more restrictive state laws passed throughout the country. One of the first states to act was Pennsylvania.

In 1989, Pennsylvania passed the Abortion Control Act. It included, among other things:

1. Lectures by doctors on fetal development (informed consent)
2. A mandated twenty-four-hour delay after the lecture
3. Reporting requirements that subjected providers to harassment
4. Spousal notification
5. More stringent parental consent rules requiring parents to come to a clinic with the minor or, if the parents wouldn't come, judicial approval[76]

As the challenge to the Pennsylvania law was working its way through the judicial system, George Bush appointed David Souter to the Court in 1990 to replace Lewis Powell. Pro-choice forces lobbied hard against his appointment but to no avail. In the first abortion-related case Souter participated in, he sided with the conservative majority. In *Rust v. Sullivan* (1991), the Court upheld regulations promulgated by the Reagan administration that barred family planning clinics receiving federal funds from discussing abortion. In spite of arguments that this gag rule violated physicians' rights to free speech, five justices voted to uphold the regulations.[77]

Pro-choice activists then tried again to raise public awareness of the direction in which the Court was going. Soon after *Rust* was announced, on

the last day of the 1990–1991 term of the Court, the pro-choice Justice Thur-
good Marshall resigned and George Bush nominated the conservative
African American federal judge Clarence Thomas to replace him. In spite of
concerted lobbying by women's rights groups and questions about Clarence
Thomas's alleged sexual harassment of Anita Hill, Thomas took the liberal
Marshall's place on the Court.

In keeping with their strategies announced earlier, pro-choice groups
opted to raise the stakes politically. At a joint press conference, the heads of
Planned Parenthood, NARAL, and the ACLU, and Kathryn Kolbert of the
RFP, who was set to argue against the constitutionality of Pennsylvania's
Abortion Control Statute before the Supreme Court, decided to intensify the
abortion debate *before* the 1992 elections. Thus, they asked the Court to come
right out and either reaffirm that abortion was a fundamental right or to
overrule *Roe* if that was what it was going to do. Said Faye Wattleton of
Planned Parenthood:

> Even if [the Court's ruling] does not come before the election, it will still be a
> major issue in this election. This is not whether it's better for us politically, but
> what is better for women. We will not permit the courts to have the last word
> ever again, and we will show our strength in the polls because we simply will
> not go back.[78]

In the Bush administration's amicus curiae brief in *Planned Parenthood of
Southeastern Pennsylvania v. Casey,* as the challenge to the Pennsylvania law
had come to be known, the Bush administration urged the Court to overrule
Roe. Joining the U.S. government in support of Casey (the governor) were
groups including Feminists for Life, the U.S. Catholic Conference, and the
National Right to Life Committee. Lining up in opposition to the regulations
were 178 organizations including the National Council of Negro Women,
the Women's Legal Defense Fund, NOW, NARAL, the YWCA, the National
Women's Health Network, the Federation of Feminist Women's Health Centers, and the National Women's Political Caucus.

Given the close nature of *Webster* and *Rust* and the addition of two Bush
appointees, many Court watchers expected that the Court would use *Casey*
to overturn *Roe.* In addition to filing briefs, women's groups sponsored the
March for Women's Lives on April 5, 1992, to attract more public and media
attention to the issue. Drawing between 500,000 and 700,000 marchers, it was
the largest pro-choice march ever.

Nearly four months after oral arguments, as tensions on both sides
mounted, Justices O'Connor, Kennedy, and Souter announced a joint opinion
that, while upholding a woman's right to an abortion, gave the states even
greater leeway than *Webster* to limit abortions. In redefining what *Roe* stood
for, the plurality opinion rejected *Roe*'s trimester approach to balancing the
interest of women and the state. The Court also overturned portions of sev-

eral other abortion rights cases that had struck down informed consent, parental consent, and abortion counseling requirements as unconstitutional infringements of *Roe*. But most critically, seven justices rejected the idea that a woman's right to an abortion was a fundamental right. Instead, the plurality opinion of O'Connor, Kennedy, and Souter redefined that "central principle" of *Roe* and replaced it with a lesser standard. According to them, states could enact abortion restrictions so long as they did not place an "undue burden" on a woman's right to an abortion. In *Casey*, none of the state's impediments to abortion noted earlier, except the one requiring spousal consent, was deemed an "undue burden."

Casey meant "full employment for reproductive rights lawyers," said Kathryn Kolbert, because it pushed the question back to the states. Said one National Right to Life Committee official, "We're back to where we were in the 1970s and 1980s, testing limits of what the Court will allow."[79]

Recognizing their historic weaknesses at the state level, pro-choice forces renewed efforts for a federal Freedom of Choice Act and focused on the outcome of the 1992 presidential campaign. In 1992, both major candidates made much of their respective views on abortion, which differed widely. The Democratic Party platform called for a strict adherence to the standards originally set out in *Roe v. Wade* and support for public funding of abortions. In contrast, the Republican Party platform supported a constitutional amendment to ban abortions except in cases where a mother's life is in danger. In that regard, it went even further than the views of George Bush, who argued that exceptions should be made for cases of rape and incest.

A Pro-Choice Administration

The election of Bill Clinton in 1992 and a large number of new female pro-choice national and state legislators sharply altered the abortion horizon. Just two days after his inauguration, Clinton issued an executive order repealing the Reagan-Bush gag rule on abortion counseling. He also lifted bans on fetal tissue research, abortions on military bases, and the testing of RU-486, an abortion pill. He also nominated Dr. Joycelyn Elders, a strong proponent of *Roe v. Wade*, to be the U.S. Surgeon General, further trumpeting a change in administrative policy. Perhaps the most important signal concerning his support for abortion rights, however, was his appointment of the women's rights, pro-choice pioneer Ruth Bader Ginsburg to the Supreme Court.

After *Casey*, even before Ginsburg's nomination, many in the right-to-life movement stepped up their efforts in the states to secure new abortion restrictions. Others began to direct more hostility, harassment, and violence at abortion clinics, providers, and those seeking abortions. One NARAL official speculated, "opponents haven't won in the political system, so they're apparently determined to shoot, stalk, and murder their way to their goal."[80]

Litigating to Stop Violence

Pro-choice groups initially were caught off guard by clinic violence. They realized, however, the tremendous toll that years of right-to-life activism were taking on the right to choose. By the end of the Reagan years, in spite of the fact that the vast majority of all obstetricians-gynecologists believed that "abortion should be legal and available," most did not perform any abortions. The few who did, didn't perform many.[81] At the same time, fewer medical schools were even training medical students to perform abortions. To stop this backslide, and energized by the Reagan administration's refusal to investigate clinic violence, NOW decided to take legal action to stop groups that were attempting to interfere with the daily routine of abortion clinics.

In 1986, long before Clinton's election, in the wake of an upsurge of clinic violence, NOW filed suit on behalf of two clinics' owners trying to stop Joseph Scheidler's Pro-Life Action League (PLAL) from picketing their clinics and disrupting their businesses. NOW argued that PLAL's activities were part of a massive conspiracy to shut down clinics. After a series of legal maneuverings, the Court finally slated *NOW v. Scheidler* for oral argument in 1993.

In *Scheidler,* NOW alleged that the Racketeer Influenced and Corrupt Organizations Act (RICO), which was initially enacted by Congress as a prosecutorial tool against mob activity and organized crime, could be applied to anti-choice violence even though the perpetrators were not trying to interfere with business practices for their own economic gain.[82]

By the time *Scheidler* got to the Court, President Clinton had replaced one of the original dissenters in *Roe* with the pro-choice Ginsburg. Just the year before, however, only days before Clinton took office, the Court had ruled that an old federal law designed to stop KKK activity could not be used to deter abortion protestors because their activities were not designed to discriminate against women as a class. *Bray v. Alexandria Women's Health Center* (1993) called into question the legality of at least twenty injunctions that were in place around the nation.

Congress Acts

The Court's decision appeared to embolden some in the right-to-life movement. Scheidler, in fact, called clinic bombers "good citizens," and the month of February saw a rash of clinic fire bombings nationwide at the same time that the homes of physicians who performed abortions were picketed and their children followed to school.[83] In response, the Fund for a Feminist Majority offered a $20,000 reward for the arrest of clinic harassers and urged pro-choice supporters in Congress to enact legislation to outlaw violent protest activity.

Just as pro-choice groups began to press for legislation to guarantee clinic safety, Dr. David Gunn was shot and killed outside a clinic in Florida where he worked. Two weeks later, in her first press conference, Attorney General Janet Reno called for federal legislation to protect women. The Freedom of Access to Clinic Entrances Act (FACE) was also introduced in both houses of Congress in March.

As FACE was debated in Congress, another physician was shot by an associate of Gunn's murderer. Reno then testified before Congress on behalf of the administration, urging congressional passage of FACE, saying that it was "essential legislation." FACE, as proposed, made it a federal crime to block access to reproductive health clinics and to harass or use violence against women seeking reproductive health care and those providing it. The proposed legislation also gave federal courts jurisdiction to order injunctive relief and damages while specifically allowing for First Amendment protections for peaceful demonstrations. While versions of the bill were passed in both houses, the House and Senate were unable to reconcile the differences in their bills prior to the Christmas recess.

Meanwhile, in response to *Bray*, while waiting for the U.S. Congress to act, several states enacted their own antiviolence clinic statutes. A Florida antistalking law, however, did not deter Paul Hill of Defensive Action from shooting and killing a physician and his escort as they were leaving a Pensacola clinic where the physician performed abortions. With national attention focused on this latest incidence of violence, it was the straw that broke the camel's back. FACE was passed by the House on May 5, 1994, on a vote of 241 to 174 and by the Senate on May 15 by a vote of 69 to 30.

NOW v. Scheidler *Decided.* While Congress was considering FACE, the Court heard oral arguments in *Scheidler.* The Clinton administration filed an amicus curiae brief on the side of pro-choice activists and became the first administration ever to weigh in on the side of abortion rights. In January 1994, the Court ruled *unanimously* that economic motive was not critical to RICO actions so long as a conspiracy that negatively affected a business was present.[84] This ruling gave the pro-choice movement a "powerful tool" in its arsenal to combat the escalation of violence, said Ellie Smeal of the Feminist Majority Foundation.[85] In 1997, the Supreme Court ruled that a fifteen-foot barrier around abortion clinics was also constitutional.

The Freedom of Choice Act. FACE was not the only pro-choice legislation debated by Congress, although, ultimately, it was the only pro-choice legislation passed. As early as 1990, sensing the direction the Supreme Court was going in terms of accepting restrictions on abortion rights, the ACLU and other pro-choice groups began to seek cosponsors for the Freedom of Choice Act (FOCA), which would prohibit state restrictions on abortion. It initially was drafted to codify *Roe* by protecting the right of a woman to an abortion before viability and prohibit restrictions such as parental notification and consent, as well as any requirements that all abortions be performed in hospitals, at a time when the Court appeared poised to overrule *Roe*. President Bush promised to veto the act, so House and Senate leaders did not push for a vote.

After Clinton's election and the election of more than twenty new pro-choice women to the Democratic-controlled Congress, pro-choice activists failed to seize upon the opportunity to pass pro-choice legislation without fear of a presidential veto. In August 1993, FOCA became bogged down over major issues including minors' access to abortion and public funding of abortions for indigent women. The ACLU and NOW withdrew their support, arguing the deletion of those provisions would discriminate against poor women and minors. In contrast, NARAL and Planned Parenthood believed that compromise on minors' access and funding was reasonable.

November 1994: The Death Knell for Further Protection of Abortion Rights?

In speaking about the new Republican majority in the new Congress, Kate Michelman of NARAL remarked, "The 104th Congress could well be the most anti-women, anti-choice Congress in our history."[86] How right she was. The 104th Congress reversed the pro-choice 103rd Congress's liberalization of the Hyde amendment, which for the first time had eased the restrictions on federal funding of abortions to include instances of rape and incest. The 104th Congress also enacted a ban on abortion coverage for federal employees and refused to remove a ban on abortions in overseas military hospitals. (In prior years, the ban was implemented through a 1988 agency memo interpreting a federal law; in January 1993, President Clinton reversed that interpretation.) It also passed an unprecedented law called the Partial Birth Abortion Act that was an attempt to criminalize the performance of certain infrequently used abortion techniques for late-term abortions. President Clinton vetoed this bill when it reached his desk. It was reintroduced in the 105th Congress where the House passed it again. At this writing, the Senate had not acted on it again because there was not a veto-proof majority there.

While the Republican Congress continues to find ways to restrict abortion rights, since *Webster* and *Casey* nearly all of the states have enacted one or more abortion-specific restrictions. Some states have no restrictions; others have a variety including bans on the performing of abortions in public hospitals or by physicians on the public payroll, parental consent requirements, twenty-four-hour waiting periods that often require women to travel long distances and spend the night before obtaining an abortion, and detailed informed consent procedures designed to deter a woman from exercising what is still a constitutional, albeit limited, right. In 1997, several states passed their own versions of the Partial Birth Abortion Act.

NEW FRONTIERS IN REPRODUCTIVE RIGHTS

Although many states continue to add restrictions concerning abortions to their law books, RU-486, a new drug, has become available following approval by the Food and Drug Administration (FDA). It induces abortions without surgery. Two additional drugs (methotrexate and misoprostol) also can be used to produce a "safe and effective alternative" to surgical abortions when used in combination.[87] Initially, RU-486 was available by prescription in only France and Germany. Initial tests also show that RU-486 is more reliable than currently used morning-after pills to terminate pregnancies. When taken within the first seven weeks of pregnancy, RU-486 causes shedding of the fertilized embryo after implantation in the uterine wall 95 percent of the time. There are also indications that it can be used to treat endometriosis, a leading cause of infertility. Thus, somewhat ironically, the same drug that can be used to terminate a pregnancy can potentially be used to facilitate pregnancies. This possibility, however, did not stop right-to-life activists and the Roman Catholic Church from denouncing the drug and pressuring the Reagan and Bush administrations to outlaw its testing or use in the United States, despite the fact that it had been used with such success in France that Sweden and Great Britain have also licensed the drug.

In 1989, after pressure from the Roman Catholic Church and pro-life groups, the FDA issued an "Import Alert" barring the import of RU-486 into the United States even for personal use because it had not been approved by the agency. The federal government also prohibited trials of the drug here.

Immediately after taking office in 1993, President Clinton ordered his administration to "promote the testing, licensing, and manufacturing" of RU-486. He also lifted the Import Alert, thus allowing importation of RU-486 for personal use.

RU-486 and combination medications move many first-term abortions out of clinics into myriad physicians' offices, allowing abortion to become a truly private decision, although still not an easy one for millions of women. The widespread availability of RU-486 and the use of methotrexate and misoprostol could truly transform the abortion debate, a possibility that is all too real for those who oppose abortion under any circumstances. "You can't stop a woman from visiting a doctor," said one drug industry analyst. "It becomes a private transaction. And that's the end of the abortion battle."[88] Thus, abortions would become much more difficult to regulate as they become simpler, safer, much cheaper, and able to be done *anywhere at any time.*

Right-to-life activists have vowed to make RU-486, or any other drugs used to induce abortion, a national issue. Joseph Scheidler has cautioned, "we will probably know which physicians were dispensing it. We'll sneak in women to ask for RU-486. . . . There will be doctors who will not deal with it. For those who do, we'll go to their homes, to their offices, to their hospitals."[89]

CONCLUSION

Women's family status and their reproductive choices have improved remarkably since women met in Seneca Falls in 1848. Women are no longer civilly dead upon marriage, and family law reform continues today.

Birth control has also improved, yet debate continues over issues of access and health. In recent years, much of the debate and controversy in women's rights has centered around abortion.

The abortion issue clearly mobilized members of a flagging movement to act. But unless abortion is in imminent danger of being dramatically limited, marginal changes in abortion law have failed to draw concerted, prolonged mobilization of women. Issues of child care, pay equity, and how to combine both *are* central concerns to most women, yet unlike threatened abortion rights, they are hard to sum up on a bumper sticker. Many laws are now in place to prevent discrimination against women in marriage. Yet the combined weight of her motherhood role and gender-based assumptions about her abilities that often stem from her childbearing capabilities still leave women as less than full citizens.

NOTES

1. Carl N. Degler, *At Odds: Women and the Family in America from the Revolution to the Present* (New York: Oxford University Press, 1980), chap. 1.
2. Ibid., 8–9.
3. Quoted in Ida Husted Harper, *The Life and Work of Susan B. Anthony*, vol. 1 (Indianapolis, Ind. and Kansas City, Mo.: Bowen Merrill, 1899), 67.
4. Quoted in Degler, *At Odds*, 175.
5. Quoted in Elizabeth Cady Stanton, *Eighty Years and More: Reminiscences 1857–1897* (1898; reprint, ed. T. Risher Urwin, New York: Schocken Books, 1971), 215–26.
6. Ibid., 225.
7. Quoted in Sara M. Evans, *Born for Liberty* (New York: Free Press, 1989), 143.
8. "Lucy Stone to Elizabeth Cady Stanton, October 22, 1856," Theodore Stanton and Harriet Stanton Blatch, eds., *Elizabeth Cady Stanton as Revealed in Her Letters, Diaries and Reminiscences*, vol. 2 (New York: Harper, 1922), 67–68.
9. Lois Banner, *Women in Modern America* (New York: Harcourt Brace Jovanovich, 1974), 17.
10. James Reed, *From Private Vice to Virtue: The Birth Control Movement in American Society since 1830* (New York: Basic Books, 1978), 37. The inadequacies of birth control and ignorance about fertile periods may have helped make birth control unpopular. For example, one popular pamphlet on birth control counseled women to refrain from sex at all times except in the middle of the menstrual cycle.
11. Kristin Luker, *Abortion and the Politics of Motherhood* (Berkeley: University of California Press, 1984).
12. Linda Gordon, *Woman's Body, Woman's Right: A Social History on Birth Control* (New York: Penguin Books, 1977), 95.
13. Ibid., 97.
14. Ibid.
15. Ibid., 97–98.
16. Degler, *At Odds*, 204.
17. Charlotte Perkins Gilman, *Women and Economics* (1898; reprint, New York: Source Book, 1970).

18. Sheila M. Rothman, *Woman's Proper Place* (New York: Basic Books, 1978), 221.
19. The National Woman's Party was not against the act itself, but it believed that the orientation of the proposed legislation should be changed so that pregnancy would not be treated as something that made woman unique. Rothman, *Woman's Proper Place*, 157–58.
20. William L. O'Neill, *Everyone Was Brave* (Chicago: Quadrangle, 1969), 303.
21. Rothman, *Woman's Proper Place*, 157.
22. Stanley J. Lemons, *The Woman Citizen: Social Feminism in the 1920s* (Urbana: University of Illinois Press, 1973).
23. Reed, *From Private Vice to Virtue*, 87.
24. Gordon, *Woman's Body, Woman's Right*, 221.
25. Quoted in ibid., 228.
26. Ibid., 242.
27. Flora Davis, *Moving the Mountain: The Women's Movement in America since 1960* (New York: Simon & Schuster, 1991), chap. 8.
28. Shulamith Firestone, *The Dialectic of Sex: The Case for Feminist Revolution* (New York: Bantam Books, 1970).
29. See Deborah L. Rhode, *Justice and Gender* (Cambridge, Mass.: Harvard University Press, 1989), 10, 24, 25.
30. In 1972 and late 1976, the Court upheld the right of Alabama and Kentucky to mandate a woman's use of her husband's surname when applying for a driver's license. The Kentucky suit was brought by a NOW member with NOW support. A woman's right to retain her maiden name is clearly a right largely determined by state law, and the Supreme Court is unwilling to get involved in the issue of sex discrimination as found in Kentucky/Alabama-type statutes.
31. Quoted in Evans, *Born for Liberty*, 304.
32. Report of the President's Commission on the Status of Women, 1963, 46–48.
33. *What Women Want, from the Official Report to the President* (New York: Simon & Schuster, 1979), 129.
34. Ibid.
35. Ibid.
36. Ibid.
37. Susan E. Marshall, "Who Speaks for American Women? The Future of Antifeminism," *Annals* (May 1991): 57.
38. See *Kirchberg v. Feenstra*, 450 U.S. 455 (1981), and *Farrey v. Sanderfoot*, 1991 U.S. LEXIS 2906.
39. For an excellent discussion of divorce reform see Martha Fineman, *Divorced from Reality, the Illusion of Equality: The Rhetoric and Reality of Divorce Reform* (Chicago: University of Chicago Press, 1991).
40. Georgia Commission on Gender Bias, Task Force Report, 1991.
41. David Bradvica, "Life with a Father . . . and a Father," *The Press Enterprise*, February 23, 1997, NEXIS. See also *Bottoms v. Bottoms*, 1997, Va. App. LEXIS 505.
42. See New York Task Force on Women in the Courts, "Report of the New York Task Force on Women in the Courts," *Fordham Law Review* 15 (1986): 211–35.
43. See Jana B. Singer, "The Privatization of Family Law," *Wisconsin Law Review* 5 (1992): 1497–1567 in particular.
44. Ibid.
45. Judith A. Baer, *American Women in Law* (New York: Holmes & Meier, 1991), 179.
46. Laura Woliver, "The Deflective Power of the New Reproductive Technologies: The Impact on Women," *Women & Politics* 9 (1989): 17–49.
47. Michael Lollar, "Alternate Path to Parenthood," *Commercial Appeal*, December 10, 1995, 1E.
48. See Gayle Binion, "Surrogate Parenting, Reproductive Freedom and Public Policy" (paper prepared for delivery at the Western Political Science Association, San Francisco, 1988).
49. Lollar, "Alternate Path."
50. Lori B. Andrews, "Surrogate Motherhood: Should the Adoption Model Apply?" *Children's Legal Rights Journal* 7 (Fall 1986): 13.
51. Janice G. Raymond, "International Traffic in Reproduction," *Ms.*, May/June 1991.
52. See, for example, Woliver, "New Reproductive Technologies."
53. *What Women Want*, 16.
54. Boston Women's Health Book Collective, *The New Our Bodies, Ourselves* (New York: Simon & Schuster, 1992).
55. 381 U.S. 479 (1965).

56. *Eisenstadt v. Baird,* 405 U.S. 438 (1972).
57. Rhode, *Justice and Gender,* 216–17.
58. Quoted in ibid., 216.
59. *Bowen v. Kendrick,* 487 U.S. 589 (1987).
60. Ruth Marcus, "President Clinton Fires Elders," *Washington Post,* December 10, 1994, A1.
61. Loretta Ross, Sherrilyn Ifill, and Sabrae Jenkins, "Emergency Memorandum to Women of Color," in Marlene Gerber Fried, ed., *From Abortion to Reproductive Freedom: Transforming a Movement* (Boston: South End Press, 1990), 148.
62. Lawrence H. Lader, *Margaret Sanger and the Fight for Birth Control* (Boston: Beacon Press, 1955).
63. National Organization for Women, *NOW Bill of Rights,* Washington, D.C., 1967.
64. See Karen O'Connor, *Women's Organizations' Use of the Courts* (Lexington, Mass: Lexington Books, 1980), chap. 5.
65. 410 U.S. 113 (1973).
66. 410 U.S. 179 (1973).
67. Constance Balides et al., "The Abortion Issue: Major Groups, Organizations and Funding Sources," in *The Abortion Experience,* ed. Howard Osofsky and Joy Osofsky (New York: Harper & Row, 1973), 513.
68. Deirdre English, "The War against Choice—Inside the Antiabortion Movement," *Mother Jones,* February/March, 1981, 17.
69. See Eva R. Rubin, *Abortion, Politics, and the Courts* (Westport, Conn.: Greenwood Press, 1982).
70. *Planned Parenthood v. Danforth,* 428 U.S. 52 (1976).
71. *Maher v. Roe,* 432 U.S. 464 (1977); *Beal v. Doe,* 432 U.S. 438 (1977); *Poelker v. Doe,* 432 U.S. 519 (1977).
72. *What Women Want,* 160.
73. 462 U.S. 416 (1983).
74. 492 U.S. 490 (1989).
75. Quoted in Lawrence H. Tribe, *Abortion: The Clash of Absolutes* (New York: Norton, 1992), 176.
76. See American Civil Liberties Union, *Reproductive Rights Update,* July 27, 1990.
77. 111 S.Ct. 1759 (1991).
78. Quoted in R. Berke, "Groups That Back Right to Abortion Ask Court to Act," *New York Times,* November 8, 1991, A1.
79. Quoted in R. Marcus, "Court's Ruling Assures More Abortion Litigation," *Washington Post,* July 1, 1992, A1.
80. Much of this section is derived from Karen O'Connor, *No Neutral Ground: Abortion Politics in an Age of Absolutes* (Boulder, Colo.: Westview Press, 1996), chap. 7.
81. Dallas A. Blanchard, *The Anti-Abortion Movement and the Rise of the Religious Right: From Polite to Fiery Protest* (New York: Twayne, 1994).
82. 506 U.S. 263 (1993).
83. Blanchard, *The Anti-Abortion Movement,* 100.
84. 510 U.S. 249 (1994).
85. Quoted in Steve McGonigle, "Abortion Rights Backers Win High Court Ruling," *The Dallas Morning News,* January 1, 1994, 1A.
86. "Election Heightens Pro-Choice Rhetoric," *Charlestown Gazette,* December 10, 1994.
87. Mathew Brelis, "Drug Induced Abortions Cleared for Trial in Boston, Other Cities," *Boston Globe,* September 12, 1996, A3.
88. David Van Bierra, "But Will It End the Abortion Debate?" *Time,* June 14, 1993, 52.
89. Ibid.

Women's Place
in the Family

The review presented in Chapter 5 of the struggle for women's rights as they relate to marriage, the family, and reproduction sets the stage for an examination of the current status of women in these areas. As we saw in our discussion of political and economic rights, laws alone are rarely sufficient to bring about full equality. The situation is little different with respect to the position of women in the family. Indeed, as we have seen, women's family roles and positions generally serve to undermine efforts to implement women's legal achievements in the political and economic sectors. More specifically, assigned the extra duties of wife, mother, and homemaker, women often find they are hindered in their attempts to achieve an equal footing with men in the wider public world. Hence, an examination of the problems and barriers preventing an improved status for women in this last area is critical to our understanding of why women's progress in other sectors has been delayed.

One of the problems limiting progress of women in the family has been the nature of many of the proposed new rights. Women's rights advocates often encounter staunch opposition in this sphere because the changes they seek often are seen by some as undermining the institution of the family. One result, as we saw in Chapter 5, is that the current women's movement has faced strong opposition from organizations opposed to change. Moreover, women who benefit, or believe they benefit, from the current structure of the family, have joined the opposition, often dividing many homemakers from women's rights advocates.

In addition to the organized opposition and conflict among women themselves, efforts to alter women's reproductive and family roles have confronted many of the same barriers that we identified as factors limiting women's equality in the political and economic realms, namely, cultural stereotypes, differential resources of men and women, and discrimination or at least a reluctance to change by men. In the sections that follow we discuss these barriers, how they have been modified over time, how they have prevented or delayed change, and what the prospects are for their elimination in the near future. We focus first on the most immediate and important barrier: cultural stereotypes concerning women's role in the family and a woman's right to control her reproductive capabilities.

ATTITUDINAL CHANGE TOWARD MARRIAGE AND THE FAMILY

As noted earlier, our ability to gauge public attitudes before the 1930s is hampered by the absence of public opinion polls. In the case of the family, we have even fewer data sources before the 1950s than we did for the political and economic realms, perhaps reflecting the perception that the institution of the family was immutable. We can get some idea of societal views during earlier periods, however, by examining actual marital practices or what popular writers and average citizens had to say about marriage.

Pre-Twentieth-Century America

In colonial times, marriage was perceived as a virtual economic necessity. Divorce was infrequent, and most marriages lasted until the death of one of the partners. The nature of the marital relationship and cultural attitudes about the appropriate placement of authority favored a male-dominated union. However, the scarcity of women relative to men, the need for workers to grow food and deliver rudimentary services, and the Protestant faith of the colonists all created a situation of somewhat greater equality in marriage in the colonies than in Europe.

Homemaking was often a shared task with both spouses responsible for providing food and basic needs for the family. Housekeeping was of less concern in the barren existence of most colonial homes. The mother's role was also diminished, in part because of high infant mortality that lessened the importance of individual children and made pregnancy an almost constant condition. Abortion, legal until "quickening" (movement in the womb, or "life" in the science of the day), may have been common.[1] Child rearing was a joint endeavor, although the primary parent was the father. This is reflected in parental guides which stressed the father's responsibilities and rarely mentioned the mother.[2]

The roles of men and women in the family, though more equitable than in the Old World, were far from equal. Only women could be found guilty of adultery.[3] More importantly, by law, men were the ultimate authority in all family decisions, and women were cautioned that the "proper attitude of a wife toward her husband was a reverend subjugation."[4]

On account of slavery, family life for African American men and women was different from that of whites. Robert Staples and Leanor Boulin Johnson note that the institution of marriage "was one of the most important survival mechanisms for African people held in bondage."[5] Although marriage between slaves lacked legal guarantees because slaves could not sign contracts, men and women in bondage still were intensely committed to their families. Masters knew this and often threatened to sell or punish members of a slave's family to keep him or her from rebelling or escaping.[6] On occasion, owners arranged marriages between slaves to encourage the birth of slave children, which added value to the owners' property. This practice increased after the importation of slaves was halted in 1808.

Slave family life was often very difficult. Men and women worked hours in the fields and had few resources with which to create a home. Nevertheless, sex roles existed, with men claiming the position of head of the family and women assuming more responsibility for child rearing. On at least some plantations, domestic tasks were undertaken communally to allow time for women slaves to work in the cotton fields or in the "Big House."[7]

One substantial difference between slaves and other women was the precarious status of slave women's control of their sexuality. Slave owners and other white men could rape African American women with no fear of retribution. Many slave women and their husbands put up a fierce resistance, but there was little either could do in a society that considered them the property of their masters.[8] After emancipation, African Americans made every effort to create family structures that solidified the bonds that were maintained with great difficulty under slavery. Thus, in the 1890 census, the first to collect information on family status, marital patterns of African Americans and whites differed little.

In the postcolonial era, the "modern family" emerged with its emphasis on love or mutual attraction rather than economic necessity as the basis of marriage. Remaining single and even divorce in rare circumstances became alternatives to an unhappy marriage. However, mutual emotional support was probably still more an ideal than a reality, and unlike earlier times, women's sexual needs were increasingly downplayed in a Victorian culture that expected only men to have such urges.[9]

Moreover, the "separate spheres"—women in the home and men in the business world—divided women's and men's roles in the family more clearly than they had been divided in the past. Men became the breadwinners, and women assumed responsibility for housekeeping and the children. Men's authority in important family decisions remained supreme, although their increasingly long absences from the home gave women an opportunity for daily decision making on many child-rearing and housekeeping matters.[10]

After slavery was abolished in 1865, African American women often tried to confine their activities to the home at least in part to limit the prospect of rape by white bosses or other men. The economic needs of their families often made this impossible. Sharecropping by whole families became the preferred solution. Many women, however, were forced to spend hours away from their families working as domestics.

With the division of roles in place, homemaking and motherhood achieved a new importance, and the status of women often depended on how well they performed these roles. Few persons, with Elizabeth Cady Stanton being one notable exception, questioned the primacy of motherhood for a woman. Corresponding to this increased emphasis on motherhood, abortion and the distribution of birth control information were outlawed.

The dawn of the twentieth century reinforced the trends begun in the nineteenth. The romantic ideal, and the increasing importance of sexual satisfaction for women as well as men, became the clear basis of marriage. Role divisions between men and women became more distinct. Housework became a science as home economics courses were developed at the high school and college levels to prepare women for their careers in the home. Motherhood took on a new meaning as well with the development of eugenics and Freudian psychology, which stressed the importance of the mother on the mental and physical development of the child. Even calls to limit the number of children a woman could have were tied to the need for women to devote more time to each child, lest she damage the child's psyche. Accordingly, the desire for birth control information increased. A 1937 poll, for instance, found 79 percent of all women believed in limiting the number of births.[11] As women's ties to the home were strengthened, men continued their retreat from the family. Fatherhood demands were increasingly limited to earning a wage to support the economic needs of wife and children. Automobile magnate Henry Ford's family wage plan sought to advance this notion by setting a man's wage at what was necessary to maintain a family.[12]

Throughout the nineteenth and early twentieth centuries, a period of family transition, many women continued to contribute to the household economy, both through their employment outside the home and their unpaid work in the house or family business. At least one social scientist estimates that women contributed 25 percent of family income, broadly interpreted, in the early part of the twentieth century.[13] Therefore, women's entry into the labor market during World War II was not as dramatic a break with "tradition" as it is so often portrayed.

The movement of women into the marketplace during and after World War II, however, did little initially to alter the public's perception of appropriate role divisions. Indeed, the 1950s saw the development of, in Betty Friedan's terminology, the *feminine mystique,* that is, the notion that a woman's fulfillment in life could only come through her total commitment to the roles of mother, wife, and homemaker.[14] Interviews with wives living in the Chicago area in the late 1950s and 1960s found considerable support for the triple roles of mother, wife, and homemaker. Almost all full-time homemakers identified their most important job as that of mother. The roles of wife and homemaker were close seconds. Even among women working outside the home, the same three roles dominated.[15]

Correspondingly, this era saw men's tasks as limited to breadwinner, with only a handful rating fatherhood as the most important role for a man.

Men assumed the breadwinner position, even if their wives went to work. Domestic and parental role sharing was rejected.[16] Authority in family decision making remained with husbands. To illustrate this point, only a third of all women in a Detroit area poll disagreed with the following statement: "Most of the important decisions in the life of the family should be made by the man of the house."[17] Thus, it appears that the initial entry of large numbers of women into the workplace did little to alter views about family life that had been in place since the Industrial Revolution.

The Women's Rights Movement and Attitudes Toward Marriage and Family

As recounted in previous chapters, one of the main goals of the current women's rights movement is the abolition of the stereotype that a woman's place is solely in the home. Paralleling this objective, and partially as a result of it, has been the massive flow of married women into the work force. Moreover, the working wife has increasingly become the working mother and, since the 1980s, the working mother of very young children. The combination of the movement's ideology and the changing demands on women has had a major effect on attitudes toward marriage and family roles.

Attitudes Toward Marriage. In the mid-1950s, nearly every woman believed that to find fulfillment in life she had to marry. This view may be less common today. Many women are overwhelmingly in agreement that a woman can have a complete and happy life if she remains single.[18] Relatedly, there is nearly universal disagreement with the statement that a bad marriage is better than no marriage at all.[19]

The desire to marry, however, continues to be very strong.[20] As Table 6–1 indicates, few people believe the most satisfying and interesting way of life for them excludes marriage. In 1974, only 2 percent of women opted for an unmarried lifestyle. Twenty years later, this figure was only 8 percent. What had changed is the type of family desired. In 1974, the "ideal" was a traditional marriage with a husband assuming responsibility for providing for the family and the wife running the house and taking care of the children. By 1994, a shared marriage with both spouses working, raising the children, and doing the housework was the preferred choice of a majority of women and men.[21] Indeed, 66 percent of a 1977 poll sample agreed with the idea that it is much better for everyone involved if the man is the achiever outside the home and the woman takes care of the family; by 1996 only 41 percent of a national sample held that opinion.[22]

Other evidence that Americans favor shared roles can be found when questions are raised about housework. Research by Arland Thornton and Deborah Freedman found that in one sample of married women taken between 1962 and 1977, the percentage believing a woman should expect help from her husband around the house increased from 46 to 62 percent.

TABLE 6–1 What Would Be the Most Satisfying and Interesting Way of Life?

	1974*	1979		1985		1989		1994	
	Women (%)	Women (%)	Men (%)	Women (%)	Men (%)	Women (%)	Men (%)	Women (%)	Men (%)
A traditional marriage with husband assuming the responsibility for providing for the family and the wife running the house and taking care of the children	50	42	43	37	43	38	39	37	36
A marriage where husband and wife share responsibilities more; both work, both share homemaking and child responsibilities	46	52	49	57	50	53	50	50	47
Living with someone of the opposite sex but not married	1	2	4	2	3	3	4	3	5
Remaining single and living alone	1	2	2	2	3	2	3	3	4
Remaining single and living with others of the same sex	**	**	**	**	1	0	1	1	1
Living in a big family of people with similar interests in which some people are married and some are not	1	1	1	1	0	1	1	1	1
None; don't know	2	1	2	1	1	2	1	5	5

*No men were polled in 1974.
**Less than 1 percent.

Source: Data from the 1974, 1979, 1985, 1990, and 1995 Virginia Slims Polls, made available by the Roper Center for Public Opinion Research, Storrs, Conn.

The more educated, younger, or working women were even more likely to favor this practice.[23] More recent research suggests women are increasingly willing to share domestic roles with men. For example, the 1995 Virginia Slims Poll found that 60 percent of the women polled believed that men should help out more with household and child-care responsibilities to allow working women to balance their jobs, marriages, and children. Among men, 53 percent agreed on the need for male help.[24] In a similar vein, both men and women are more willing to assign the breadwinning and parental roles equally to both mothers and fathers. Thus, whereas in the early 1970s most men and women said they would lose respect for a man who stayed home to take care of the children while the wife worked, two decades later only one-fifth of men and women said they would lose respect for a man who made such a decision.[25] A survey in 1994 found only 23 percent of the public agreed with the statement that it is not good if a man stays home and cares for the children and the woman goes out to work.[26]

Men and women are also in agreement on the need for emotional expression in a marriage. As indicated in Table 6–2, majorities of men and women believe the ingredients to a good marriage include "being in love," "keeping romance alive," "having a good sexual relationship," "being able to talk together about your feelings," and "your spouse having an understanding of what you do every day." However, with the exception of good sexual relations, women are more likely to think these dimensions of a marriage are important. For example, 67 percent of women but only 57 percent of men agree on the need for an understanding spouse. Women are also much more likely than men to think sexual fidelity is important to a good marriage.[27]

With marriage increasingly based on mutual emotional satisfaction, divorce has become the answer to an unhappy marriage. The proportion of women who find it an acceptable solution has risen from 52 percent in 1970 to 62 percent in 1979, declining to 57 percent in 1985.[28] In 1994, 48 percent agreed and 32 percent disagreed that divorce is usually the best solution when a couple can't work out their disagreements.[29] Divorce is seen as less acceptable if there are children under the age of five.[30] Moreover, older and less-educated women are less willing to see divorce as an acceptable solution. Interestingly, a plurality of the population would like to see divorce made more difficult to obtain.[31]

TABLE 6–2 Important Qualities in a Good Marriage

	Men (%)	Women (%)
Liking the same kinds of life, activities, and friends	62	64
Being in love	84	87
Keeping romance alive	76	78
Having children	41	48
Having similar ideas about how to raise children	63	72
Having a good sexual relationship	74	72
Sexual fidelity on the part of your spouse	78	85
Having similar ideas about how to handle money	66	71
Financial security	61	63
Having similar backgrounds	29	34
Being able to talk together about your feelings	76	84
Your spouse understanding what you do every day	57	67
Both being able to see the humorous side of things	69	76

Source: Data from the 1990 Virginia Slims Poll, made available by the Roper Center for Public Opinion Research, Storrs, Conn.

Perhaps because of these changing attitudes and the practices that accompany them, there is growing concern about the future of marriage. In 1989, three-fifths of men and women in a national survey thought the institution of marriage was weaker than ten years ago.[32] Women were nearly divided in 1994 over the question of whether the marriages of women have improved (42 percent) or gotten worse (37 percent) since the 1970s.[33] For the vast majority of Americans, having a good family life is extremely important, and threats to the institution are disconcerting.[34] Yet the public is deeply divided about whether it is the responsibility of the government to uphold traditional family values, with 40 percent rejecting and 53 percent endorsing this position.[35]

Attitudes Toward Motherhood. In the past, motherhood ranked second only to marriage as a woman's objective in life. Today, however, many women no longer identify motherhood as the route to happiness or the primary goal in life. As early as 1979, 82 percent of women disagreed that children are essential to a full and happy marriage.[36] By 1994, only 13 percent of the public believed the main purpose of marriage is to have children.[37]

Attitudes are also changing on the acceptability of having a child outside of marriage. A 1994 poll found that although a sizable majority of the public agreed, almost one out of five disagreed with the statement that people who want children ought to get married. Other polls have found young people are more accepting of out-of-wedlock births.[38]

Polls, moreover, continue to show that among those desiring a family, the ideal number of children has declined dramatically since the 1950s. In 1996, more than half of those surveyed chose two as the best number. Those wanting four children dropped to 11 percent from a high of 58 percent in 1959.[39] Interestingly, there seems to be a slight increase in those wanting only one child, up from 1 percent in 1952 to 4 percent in 1996.[40]

Along with a decreased emphasis on motherhood has come an increased focus on fatherhood. Half of the public (52 percent) agreed in a 1996 poll that if fathers would focus more on their families and less on other things it would help to improve this country a lot; 40 percent said it would help somewhat. Interestingly, far fewer felt that if women gave up their jobs and stayed home to care for their children it would help a lot (26 percent) or somewhat (32 percent).[41]

Sexuality and Birth Control

One of the most controversial issues of the women's rights movement has been the effort of women to control their reproductive capabilities. The major battles in this area have been over abortion. Closely tied to this effort has been the notion that women as well as men have sexual drives independent of the desire to have children.

TABLE 6–3 Should Abortion Be Legal?[a]

Year	Legal under Any Circumstances (%)	Legal Only under Certain Circumstances (%)	Illegal in All Circumstances (%)
1975	21	54	22
1977	22	55	19
1979	22	54	19
1980	25	53	18
1981	23	52	21
1983	23	58	16
1988	24	57	17
1989	29	51	17
1991	33	49	14
1996	25	58	15

[a]The question asks: Do you think abortions should be legal under any circumstances, legal only under certain circumstances, or illegal in all circumstances?

Source: George Gallup Jr., "Public Generally Supports a Woman's Right to Abortion," *Gallup Polls.* http://www.gallup.com/poll/news/960815.html

Attitudes on abortion (see Table 6–3) have been among the most frequently polled in the past two decades. Over time, the polls show that the proportion of the public favoring legality under all circumstances has grown only marginally, rising from 21 percent in 1975 to 25 percent in 1996.[42]

When pollsters ask general questions about the legality of abortion, majorities appear to support a woman's right to choose. But when more specific questions are asked about the legality of abortion in a variety of circumstances, support drops off considerably, as revealed in Table 6–4. When asked if abortion should be legal if the baby might have a serious defect, if the woman's health is endangered, or if the pregnancy is the result of rape, clear majorities support a woman's right to choose. On the other hand, if the decision is a function of economics, an out-of-wedlock pregnancy, or the desire to limit family size, support for abortion declines to below 50 percent.

During the past two decades, the proportion opposing abortion under all circumstances has declined from 22 percent in 1975 to 15 percent in 1996. Conversely, the majority of Americans surveyed in both 1975 and 1996 favor some restrictions on abortion.[43] While women and men overall are nearly equally likely to consider themselves pro-choice (52 percent of women are pro-choice as compared with 54 percent of men), women college graduates are much more likely to adopt the pro-choice label (75 percent of women, 54 percent of men).[44]

African Americans are less supportive of abortion than are whites.[45] While controls for demographic characteristics reduce the differences, they do not eliminate them. Moreover, attitudinal controls for sexuality and women's rights increase racial disparity. Factors associated with pro-choice

TABLE 6–4 Circumstances When Abortion Should Be Legal, 1996

Do you think it should be possible for a pregnant
woman to obtain a legal abortion if . . . ?

	Percentage Answering Yes
There is a strong chance of a serious defect in the baby	79
The woman's own health is seriously endangered by the pregnancy	89
The woman became pregnant as a result of rape	81
The family has a very low income and cannot afford any more children	45
The woman is not married and does not want to marry the man	43
The woman is married and does not want any more children	45
The woman wants an abortion for any reason	43

Source: James Allan Davis and Tom W. Smith, *General Social Surveys, 1972–1996.*
Principal Investigator, James A. Davis; Director and Co-Principal Investigator, Tom W.
Smith. NORC ed. Chicago: National Opinion Research Center, producer, 1996; Storrs,
Conn.: The Roper Center for Public Opinion Research, University of Connecticut,
distributor.

views are also different for the races. For whites, being Catholic, living in a
rural area, or having a low income or a low education is linked to a pro-life
position on abortion. For African Americans, the key correlates of pro-life
views are being male and growing up in the South.[46] It is, of course, the question
of what restrictions should be imposed that has engaged the public and
courts in heated battles during the past decade. A poll taken in July 1996
found that more than 70 percent of the public favored the following laws
restricting abortion: doctors required to inform patients of alternatives to
abortion, a 24-hour waiting period, parental consent for women under eighteen, a ban on "partial birth" abortions, and spousal notification. Only 38
percent, however, supported a constitutional ban on abortion.[47]

Since the Supreme Court's first major case upholding a wide variety of
abortion restrictions in *Webster v. Reproductive Health Services* in 1989, public
attitudes on abortion are increasingly finding their way into state and
national elections. Research by the Center for the American Woman and Politics during four gubernatorial campaigns held in 1989 and 1990 found that
attitudes on abortion influence the voting behavior of many citizens.[48]
Women and persons with consistent pro-choice or pro-life positions were the
most likely to cite the abortion issue as an important concern for them in the
election. Similarly, both pro-choice and pro-life voters who felt strongly
about the issue and were aware of the candidates' positions were most prone
to cast their ballots for the candidate who closely reflected their views. This
was especially true in the campaigns held a few months after *Webster,* and
where the abortion issue was politicized by the media and the candidates.[49]
At the presidential level, Alan Abramowitz's research on the 1992 election

found abortion was the most important issue for voters, and Mark J. Wattier, Byron W. Daynes, and Raymond Tatalovich report that pro-choice women were particularly mobilized by the election that year.[50]

Beliefs about a woman's right to abortion are often linked more generally to attitudes about a woman's right to control her sexuality. Earlier generations clearly thought men had this freedom, but only in the past few decades have public attitudes begun to allow women some of the same privileges. In 1953, for instance, 33 percent of the public agreed that no decent man can have respect for a woman who has had sexual relations before marriage.[51] Today, most young women do not believe premarital sex is always or almost always wrong.[52] Moreover, by the end of the 1980s, most men and women thought a single woman should enjoy the same kind of freedom as a single man;[53] although few people today believe that it is a good idea for a couple to live together before marriage.[54]

There are, however, large differences between women and men in this area. Though, overall, 42 percent of all first-year college students in 1996 agree with the view that "it is all right for two people who really like each other to have sex even if they've known each other for a very short time," men are much more likely to agree (54 percent) than women (32 percent).[55] Men also have very different views from women about when sexual behavior is appropriate. Among young men, one-fifth disagreed with the view that "just because a man thinks that a woman has 'led him on' does not entitle him to have sex with her." Virtually all young women (93 percent) agreed with this view.[56] Similarly, 88 percent of women but only 77 percent of men consider it rape when a man has sex with a woman who has passed out from drinking too much.[57] In a variety of other circumstances, men are more likely than women to think forced or pressured sex is not rape.[58] Attitude differences like these help to explain the inability of many men who rape their dates to recognize that they have committed a crime or the failure of (mostly male) district attorneys to believe victims or to prosecute cases of acquaintance rape.[59] Not surprisingly, given these mixed messages about women who are sexually active and men's continuing belief in their "right to sex," women and men in national samples agree that the double moral standard still exists.[60]

In polls, majorities of Americans are still strongly opposed to instances of homosexual relations.[61] This seems to be particularly true of men. For instance, even among men in their first year of college, 45 percent support laws prohibiting homosexual relations, while only 24 percent of first-year college women support such laws.[62] Similarly, women in a national sample are much less willing to think that homosexuality is always wrong and are much more willing than men to include in the definition of family a lesbian or gay couple living together or raising a child together.[63]

Differences Among Women. The dynamic attitudinal changes in the past two decades have been more warmly supported by some women than by others. Feminists have generally been the most willing to endorse new views, while conservative women have been strongly opposed to any change that threatens the traditional division of family roles.[64] Working women are also more likely to take more progressive positions. Homemakers, however, have increasingly diverged from the feminists and working women in their views on changing marital and sexual relationships.

Jennifer Glass's research on attitudinal change of working women and homemakers from 1972 to 1986 found a widening gap among women on a range of issues. Part of the difference was attributable to growing demographic differences. Housewives were older, less well educated, and had more children and lower incomes than working women. Even controlling for these variables, however, women working full time were more accepting of abortion for married women, less willing to think a husband's career should come first, less willing to think men should run the country and women run the homes, and less in agreement with the view that maternal employment was detrimental to young children.[65] Glass argued that the political implications of the class and ideological gap between working wives and housewives was "profound."[66] That the women's rights movement has played a role in this gap is reflected in a poll question that found most people (90 percent) believed the movement had benefited professional women and working class women (75 percent) but had actually been detrimental (20 percent) or had made little difference (33 percent) to housewives.[67]

Homemakers' more traditional views of women's roles are not the only problem limiting women's attainment of equal status in marital and sexual relationships. In addition to organized opposition, women's own lack of preparation (or socialization to traditional roles) also hampers them as they bargain for greater equality.

WOMEN'S AND MEN'S RESOURCES IN THE STRUGGLE FOR EQUAL ROLES

In attempting to explain the subordinate position of women in the family, many sociologists have focused on the wives' inferior resources with which to demand or to bargain for more equitable roles in marriage. The lack of resources is itself partly traceable to the cultural stereotypes discussed previously. With respect to economic worth, for example, one of the direct results of the traditional cultural view that the proper role for women is to marry was that, until recently, few women prepared for a full-time career. As a result, as we have seen in Chapter 4, few women had jobs. If they worked, few had jobs that paid as well as their husbands'. Related resource discrepancies still exist in age and educational attainment, with women generally marrying men who are older and who have more formal years of schooling.

Women also are often at a disadvantage when physical force becomes an issue in marital relationships. Studies of family violence make it clear that men are much more likely than women to use acts of violence in a dating or marital relationship. Indeed, in 1996 an estimated 2 million women were physically assaulted by spouses or partners.

Most women have also not been as well prepared as men to bargain or negotiate. Women have especially been less conditioned to engage in conflict or to be assertive, which may be necessary prerequisites for getting a spouse to do housework, for example.[68]

The inability to change men's behavior is also conditioned by sex role socialization that makes talking about certain topics taboo or potentially explosive. Researchers who have studied women partners of men who are intravenous drug users, for instance, find the women are often reluctant to raise the issue of condom use even though they recognize they are at risk to contract AIDS.[69] Among the women there was a general expectation that their partners would respond violently or simply refuse to consider the woman's request. Hispanic women, whose culture tends to frown on women talking about sex, were even more reluctant to ask their partner to practice safe sex. For women who did ask, the predicted reactions were indeed what they encountered.[70] With heterosexually transmitted AIDS among women the major factor in making women the fastest growing number of AIDS cases (accompanied by the very real threat of giving birth to infected babies), we can see that unequal sex roles in relationships can have deadly consequences.

Violence Against Women

The American Medical Association has labeled domestic violence against women a problem of "epidemic proportions."[a] The estimated percentage of women subject to abuse varies from study to study. Work by Murray A. Straus and Richard J. Gelles, using their measure of domestic violence based on surveys of men and women, find that one in eight men engage in domestic abuse.[b] While most of the violence measured in their study is not life threatening (pushing, slapping, throwing something), Straus and Gelles report that severe physical violence by men may occur in three out of one hundred marriages in a single year. Given the time focus of Straus and Gelles (one year), most observers argue it is probable that during the course of a marriage the amount of battering a woman could expect would be much higher. Correspondingly, some studies report as many as one in four women will be seriously abused in their lifetime, and as many as two-thirds of all women will be hit by a spouse while married.[c] The measure developed by Straus and Gelles also leaves out some of the more common acts of marital violence including verbal abuse and rape. The latter may occur in as many as 14 percent of all marriages.[d]

Women who are not married are not exempt from violence at the hands of their male partners. Estimates are that the chances of being raped or assaulted are actually higher in dating or cohabitation relationships than in marriages.[e] Interviews with women on college campuses find that date rape has become a major concern, as well it should with rape by someone a woman knows much more likely to happen than rape by a stranger.[f]

The results of violence against women can be life threatening. The American Medical Association estimates that as many as 35 percent of the women who come to the nation's emergency rooms are victims of marital violence. In the most severe cases, wife abuse can lead to death, with women twice as likely to be murdered by a husband or boyfriend as by a stranger.[g]

Most researchers believe marital violence is the result of a number of factors. Many see it as an attempt by men to control their wives' behavior; others argue it is a byproduct of a patriarchal culture than condones male violence or violence generally.[h] Support for the latter can be found in the data showing that women also use violence, against both their spouse and their children.[i]

In recent years, the women's movement and public officials have begun to take action to limit spousal abuse. At the community level, the most common strategy is to start a shelter for victims of domestic abuse. Since the early 1980s, most police agencies have also adopted a strategy of arresting offenders, although there is a debate today about whether this is an effective strategy for preventing future abuse. African American scholars suggest that both of these solutions have not addressed the special needs of women of their race who are less likely to find shelters in their communities and whose fears of police brutality might limit their willingness to call for help.[j]

In 1994, Congress passed the Violence Against Women Act. It contained a number of provisions aimed at curtailing domestic violence and other crimes against women, including financial aid for domestic abuse shelters, support for state programs to prosecute rape and other crimes against women, and a closer monitoring of sex offenders.[k] The otherwise conservative 104th Congress also responded to public pressures by making interstate stalking a federal crime and making rape a federal crime if committed during a carjacking.[l]

[a]Quoted in Sarah Glazer, "Violence Against Women: The Issues," *CQ Researcher* 3, no. 8 (1993): 171.

[b]Murray A. Straus and Richard J. Gelles, "How Violent Are American Families? Estimates from the National Family Violence Resurvey and Other Studies," in *Physical Violence in American Families,* ed. Murray A. Straus and Richard J. Gelles (New Brunswick, N.J.: Transaction Publishers, 1990), 96.

[c]Glazer, "Violence Against Women," 171, 180.

[d]Anna Scheyett, "Marriage Is the Best Defense: Policy on Marital Rape," *Affilia* 3, no. 4 (1988): 9–10.

[e]Jan E. Stets and Murray A. Straus, "The Marriage License as a Hitting License: A Comparison of Assaults in Dating, Cohabiting, and Married Couples," in *Physical Violence in American Families,* ed. Murray A. Straus and Richard J. Gelles (New Brunswick, N.J.: Transaction Publishers, 1990), 227–28, 231–35.

[f]Glazer, "Violence Against Women," 172.

[g]Ibid., 171.

[h]Richard J. Gelles and Claire Pedrick Cornell, *Intimate Violence in Families,* 2d ed. (Newbury Park, Calif.: Sage, 1990), 72–78; Kersti A. Yllo and Murray A. Straus, "Patriarchy and Violence Against Wives: Impact of Structural and Normative Factors," in *Physical Violence in American Families,* ed. Murray A. Straus and Richard J. Gelles (New Brunswick, N.J.: Transaction Publishers, 1990), 383–398.

[i]Straus and Gelles, "How Violent Are American Families?," 9.

ʲJo-Ellen Asbury, "African American Women in Violent Relationships: An Exploration of Cultural Differences," in *Violence in the Black Family,* ed. Robert L. Hampton (Lexington, Mass.: Lexington Books, 1987), 99–101.

ᵏHolly Idelson, "A Tougher Domestic Violence Law," *Congressional Quarterly Weekly Report* 52, no. 25 (1994): 1714.

ˡDavid Hosansky, "GOP Confounds Expectations, Expands Federal Authority," *Congressional Quarterly Weekly Report* 54, no. 44 (1996): 3119.

The lack of a strong sense of independence in women also limits women's ability to leave bad relationships. Socialization studies find that while young boys are encouraged to be independent, young girls often are not.[71] This may result in women's unwillingness to leave less-than-satisfying relationships or marriages. The added responsibility of children may also limit a woman's sense of independence.

In the twin areas of child care and housework, however, women may have been overtrained to take charge. Studies measuring differences in play activities encouraged or discouraged, toys purchased, and household chores assigned make it clear that parents, especially fathers, encourage sex-role-type activities in their children.[72] As a result, girls are trained to be homemakers and mothers, and boys are not. At adulthood, these roles are hard to change. Moreover, because of their early training, women's expertise in these tasks may make some unwilling to give up the jobs to not-as-well-trained males. Correspondingly, males may feel inadequate to undertake the task, having little experience in cleaning the house or taking care of babies.

Thus, until very recently, as a result of cultural stereotypes that narrowly defined their roles as wife and mother, women have not always had the same resources as men to assume, negotiate, or demand. Our review of cultural stereotypes suggests some of these barriers may be changing, especially among the young, educated, and working women. For some segments of women, however, traditional views persist. Even if all women were to demand an equitable, shared marriage, their success in achieving that goal would be limited unless they can overcome another important barrier—men's attitudes, prejudices, and simple unwillingness to change.

DISCRIMINATION BY MEN IN THE FAMILY

Men's reluctance to share in all facets of marriage is conditioned by a number of factors. Among the most important has been the unwillingness of men to give up the privileged position that they hold even in modern-day marriages. The system benefits men, and most proposed changes would require them to give something up, either time or power or both. The unequal benefits of traditional marriage help to explain the more conservative or traditional views of men on the gender roles. This seems to be especially noticeable among the young, where women's attitudes have changed more rapidly than men's. A 1980 survey of teenagers, for example, found 49 percent of the boys but only 35 percent of girls felt that the person whose salary was the most important to the family should make most of the decisions.[73] Even in 1996, first-year male college students were much more likely than women students (31 versus 19 percent) to agree that married women's activities are best confined to the home.[74] Often men's ideas on gender roles cover hidden qualifications of women.

Even among men who want to share, they may find their own socialization has ill prepared them for certain tasks, such as laundry or mending. Although parents may be more willing today then in the past to assign certain chores to both boys and girls, research suggests that in many homes boys and girls do not have the same responsibilities.[75]

Another barrier to equality may be the attitudes of employers. Some evidence suggests that employers do not think family issues are as important to men as they are to women.[76] This may make it hard for men to ask for time off for child-care or household responsibilities.

Although men may be beginning to want more equitable marital arrangements, alteration of old practices will not come quickly or easily. Even more so than political and economic changes, new proposals regarding family life require men to relinquish some of the power and leisure that they have enjoyed in the past. As we shall see, for many men, these changes are very difficult to make.

IMPACT OF CULTURAL ATTITUDES, LACK OF RESOURCES, AND DISCRIMINATION ON THE POSITION OF WOMEN IN THE FAMILY

Marriage Rates

During the colonial period, cultural standards and the economic needs of both women and men resulted in virtually all men and women marrying. Unlike their Western European counterparts, women settlers in the New World married at a relatively young age.[77] In the nineteenth century, the new emphasis on marrying "for love" and the initial drive for autonomy on the part of women resulted in a gradual increase in the number of women remaining single. Yet the absence of economic alternatives for most women kept this figure low.[78] In the first half of the twentieth century, this pattern was reversed. With the exception of the Great Depression years, the percentage of women who never married and the age at which women actually married fell steadily until 1960. This corresponds to our discussion of the popularity of marriage, especially in the profamily era of the "feminine mystique."

Starting in the mid-1960s, the age of women marrying and percentage of women and men not marrying rose (see Table 6–5). For instance, in 1995, the median age of first marriage for women was twenty-five and for men it was twenty-seven (see Table 6–6). Additionally, among persons age fifteen and over in 1995, 31 percent of men and 24 percent of women had never married. This compares to 22 percent of men and 14 percent of women who were unmarried in this age category in 1965.[79] The probability of marrying is very much related to race. Among whites, 29 percent of all persons age fifteen and over are never married; among African Americans the figure is 47 percent.[80]

TABLE 6–5 Percentage of People Never Married, by Age and Sex, 1960–1995

Year	Women	Men	Year	Women	Men
	Ages 20 to 24			*Ages 35 to 39*	
1960	28	53	1960	NA	NA
1970	36	55	1970	5	7
1980	50	69	1980	6	8
1990	63	79	1992	13	18
1992	66	80			
1995[a]	74	86		*Ages 40 to 44*	
			1960	NA	NA
	Ages 25 to 29		1970	5	6
1960	11	21	1980	5	7
1970	11	19	1992	8	9
1980	21	33	1995[a]	11	17
1990	31	45			
1992	33	49			
	Ages 30 to 34				
1960	7	12			
1970	6	9			
1980	10	16			
1990	16	27			
1992	19	29			
1995[a]	27	39			

NA = Not available.

[a]The 1995 figures are for age groups 18–24, 25–34, and 35–44.

Source: U.S. Bureau of the Census, Current Population Reports, P23–181, *Households, Families, and Children: A 30-Year Perspective* (Washington, D.C.: U.S. Bureau of the Census, 1992); U.S. Bureau of the Census, Current Population Reports, Series P20, no. 468, "Marital Status and Living Arrangements: March 1992" (Washington, D.C.: U.S. Government Printing Office); U.S. Bureau of the Census, Current Population Reports, Series P20, no. 484, "Marital Status and Living Arrangements: March 1995" (Washington, D.C.: http://www.census.gov)

TABLE 6–6 Median Age at First Marriage

Year	Men	Women
1890	26	22
1900	26	22
1910	25	22
1920	25	21
1930	24	21
1940	24	22
1950	23	20
1960	23	20
1970	23	21
1980	25	22
1990	26	24
1995	27	25

Source: U.S. Bureau of the Census, Current Population Reports, Series P20 no. 484, "Marital Status and Living Arrangements: March 1995" (Washington, D.C.: http://www.census.gov) and earlier reports.

Estimates are that only 75 percent of all African American women will marry, considerably lower than the 90 percent projected rate for white women.[81]

Explanations for the declining marriage rate are varied. One issue is the availability of "marriageable" mates, men who by traditional standards would be good providers. In the past, this meant a man who was older than the woman, better or as well educated as the woman, and gainfully employed. A reason for the lower marriage rates of African American women, then, is the lack of men with jobs and/or education equal to or greater than that of the women.[82] Women of both races born at the early stages of the baby boom (1946–1955), when birthrates were high, also face the difficulty of finding men who are both older and as well or better educated. Birthrates were lower in the 1930s and early 1940s, and men born during these years were less highly trained than baby-boom women.[83]

The declining importance of marriage in women's lives, noted in our earlier discussion of attitudes toward marriage, and the increased importance of obtaining an education and pursuing a career are also important factors in the avoidance or delay in marriage among young women. As Frances Goldscheidner, an editor of *Demography* magazine, notes, "Unmarried women do well if they have enough money. They can support themselves in reasonable style. They don't define themselves around men."[84] She calls women's growing lack of interest in marriage in the past twenty years "a real revolution."[85] Just as revolutionary is the dramatic jump in marriage age, which has risen five years for women since 1960. By delaying marriage until their mid-twenties, more women have experienced work outside the home before marriage.

Although demographers and sociologists expect most persons will eventually marry, it is estimated that as many as 15 percent of young adult women may not.[86] Some researchers believe that many women with successful careers may avoid marriage if they perceive the conflicts between marriage and career that may await them. Indeed, 60 percent of single women in a 1989 survey felt their status was a lot easier than being married, and 57 percent felt they were happier than their married friends.[87] One result is that many women "go it alone," living by themselves and often buying their own homes.[88] Other women prefer female partners.

Another indicator of the trend away from marriage is the phenomenal growth in the number of couples who live together without the benefit of marriage. At the beginning of the 1990s, there were almost three million households of unmarried couples, plus an unknown number of homosexual couples who were cohabitating. This figure represents a fourfold increase in such households from 1970.[89] Many of these arrangements involve children. Research suggests a large number of these unions (37 percent) will result in marriage in two years or less. However, 23 percent of such couples dissolve their relationship in the same time frame, and 40 percent merely maintain their unmarried couple status.[90]

Companionship Marriage

Our earlier discussion of changing public views toward marriage found that, whereas few reject the institution, most prefer a role-shared union where both spouses work and take care of children. This attitude, however, is relatively recent. In the 1950s and 1960s, most women expected to take care of the home and children while the husband financially supported the family. Given the relatively recent change in public attitudes, we might expect to find that behavior has not "caught up" with opinions. As we saw in Chapter 5, in at least two aspects of role sharing—working outside the home and contributing to the family income—wives are increasingly assuming an equal role with husbands. But what about the reverse of this? Are men sharing housekeeping and child-rearing roles?

Research conducted in the 1950s and 1960s reveals that few men did much role sharing in the first wave of women's move into the work force. An examination of the way women and men spent their days in 1965 and 1966, for instance, found that husbands with employed wives contributed no more time to housework than those with nonemployed spouses.[91] More recent studies still find little evidence that the desired equality in task sharing has been put into practice. Most men are doing more than their fathers, but the amount of time they contribute is still only a small proportion of that given by women.

Examining the period from 1965 to 1985, one researcher found that the proportion of traditionally female tasks (cooking, meal clean-up, housecleaning, laundry, and ironing) done by women had only decreased from 92 to 80 percent.[92] In 1965, employed women did 90 percent of these tasks, and in 1985, 79 percent. Other research finds even greater disparities. A 1987 survey looking at a mix of traditionally male tasks (paying bills, auto maintenance, yardwork, and driving) and traditionally female tasks (preparing meals, washing dishes, cleaning house, and shopping) found that in terms of average hours per week, working wives estimated they were putting in 32 hours on all household tasks, while men's own estimate of the hours they spent was under 19.[93] Although younger couples shared tasks more equally, even among married men and women under age 25, men reported fewer than 29 hours devoted each week to these chores, while wives indicated that for 41 hours of the week they were working on housework and home maintenance.[94] Surveys of married and cohabiting men and women in 1994 found that women still had the responsibility in most households for the laundry, ironing, grocery shopping, menu planning, and chauffeuring children to appointments. Men, on the other hand, had responsibility for yardwork, household repairs, servicing the car, and barbecuing. What distinguishes the two sets of tasks are the everyday demands of women's household roles.[95] Combining housework and work for pay, a 1990 study of 60,000 employees of fifteen major corporations found women were averaging forty-four hours at work and thirty-one hours of family responsibilities, in contrast to men, who were spending forty-seven hours at the office and fifteen hours on child care and household tasks, for a thirteen-hour "leisure gap."[96]

Although men may be contributing more time to housework today, research indicates that most of the similarity in hours spent by men and women in housework is a function of working women doing considerably less housework than their mothers. In the mid-1960s, the typical full-time housewife spent thirty-four hours per week doing household chores.[97] Today, housewives spend twenty-four hours on housework, and working women, fifteen hours. More telling, studies of couples find only marginal differences (less than two hours) in the housework contributed by men of working wives relative to that contributed by husbands whose wives stay home.[98] Thus, most of the role-sharing changes seem to be the result of women annexing men's role as breadwinner, not men taking on traditional women's roles.

Most recent research has attempted to explain this failure to share roles by focusing on four sets of variables: ideological acceptance of role sharing, relative resources of men and women, economic dependency, and time availability. These overlap with the three barriers to women's equality that we identified earlier (cultural stereotypes, differential resources, and discrimination or unwillingness on the part of men to change). With respect to ideology, most researchers find that in couples with more egalitarian attitudes, men generally do more around the house than when attitudes are more traditional. Only in households where *both* the man and the woman hold egalitarian views do men contribute much to household labor. Egalitarian wives married to men with traditional views can expect little assistance.[99] The more egalitarian views of African American men and women contribute to the greater role sharing found in such families.[100] However, even in families (including African American families) where men agree that women should be equal or that the man should not be the sole breadwinner, tasks are far from equally shared. Philip Blumstein and Pepper Schwartz report egalitarian men with working wives only did 8.4 hours of housework compared to 7.33 hours for all men with working wives.[101] Findings that African American men are more likely to share housework and Hispanic men are less likely to do so probably reflect the cultural differences between the two groups in their attitudes toward men's and women's roles.[102] In the same vein, the presence of young children increases family workload considerably and reinforces stereotyped roles. Even though men help out, studies indicate that young children may actually increase role divisions, as women take on even more responsibility under these circumstances.[103]

Feminists argue further that the failure of men and women to share housekeeping may stem from the meaning each assigns to housework. For many if not most people, housework "defines" a person's gender. People who do it are gendered women; people who avoid it are gendered men. To quote Sara Fenstermaker, "The doing of housework provides the occasion for the accomplishment of work and the affirmation of the essential natures of women and men."[104] Thus, both men and women may avoid role sharing because role sharing threatens not only their sense of self-identity as men or women but also the proper fulfillment of roles that identify men and women in the larger society.

Another critical factor is the resources of the spouses. In general, the more money a woman makes, the less housework she does. The same, however, is true of men. Because in most families men earn more (hence women are economically dependent), they are able to "buy their way" out of housework. This phenomenon persists even when both spouses work full time,[105] although the influence of money is lessened when couples reject the view that the man should be the breadwinner.[106] Another resource that has been found to influence division of housework is workplace authority. When women have more power on the job than their husbands and more power than most women, they tend to do less housework.[107] It should be noted, however, that even when women's resources exceed their husbands', women still do more of the household tasks than do their husbands.

Not surprisingly, women feel deeply resentful and stressed by the inequality in the home. Most believe more of the daily tasks should be shared, and two-thirds feel men are not doing their fair share of the household chores. One-half of all women indicated they feel resentful often or from time to time about the amount of work their mate does around the house. Moreover, nearly half of all women feel some level of resentment about not having enough free time.[108] Some social scientists believe that the failure of most husbands to take an equal role not only fuels resentment from their wives but also contributes to a lack of marital contentment and an increase in divorce.

Aside from the sharing of household tasks, is the rest of the marriage relationship becoming more equal? One area of consideration is power over family decisions. As we noted earlier, most reports from the past century find that husbands dominated family decision making. As recently as the 1950s, just before the dawn of the current women's rights movement, wives indicated the balance of power favored the male head of the household, with the husband making most of the important economic decisions and wives' decision making tending to be limited to areas closely connected with their roles as mothers and housewives.[109] The locus of authority in the era of the feminine mystique can perhaps be best seen in the contrast between two areas of family decisions: what job a husband should take and whether the wife should work. With respect to the first, 90 percent of women said it was the husband's decision alone to make. By contrast, in a third of the families the husband also determined whether the wife should seek paid employment.[110]

Although views about the appropriate division of authority in the family have changed since the 1950s, there is still a tendency to give men the final say. In one poll, 44 percent of men sampled reported that ultimately they were the main decision makers when it came to what the family could or could not afford. Nearly a third of all women in the poll agreed with that assessment.[111] In 1994, however, a majority of men and women claimed that investment decisions and planning family vacations were jointly shared in their home.[112]

Research by scholars on family leadership and decision making still reports that men have an edge. This is because social scientists continue to discover that it is a husband's superior financial resources that give him greater authority.[113] Although in gender-egalitarian families the relationship is weaker, generally, the more a husband makes the more power he has in family decisions and the more leadership he exercises. Wives' power on both measures is also affected by their income levels, but generally women need to earn many more dollars than their husbands to obtain an equal increment in authority.

Blumstein and Schwartz find that a key intervening variable is the relative income dependency of the wife. More specifically, as the gap in what the two spouses earn increases, so too does the tendency of men to dominate family decision making.[114] Thus, contributing to women's increased power is their movement into the work force and the narrowing wage gap. However, Blumstein and Schwartz find the most important asset men have in determining family policy is their greater assertiveness.[115] As this may be tied to more immutable role socialization, men's authority in the family may not be easily eliminated by women's movement into well-paying jobs.

The overall test of marital quality, however, may not be how much roles are shared or decision making is equalized. Rather, it may be how happy or satisfied a couple is with their marriage. Social scientists have begun to examine this in great detail, and their research suggests a number of factors contribute to marital success. The results show that some of the indicators we have identified indeed do contribute to a decline in marital quality. More specifically, the presence of children and stepchildren affects marital happiness negatively, in part because they lower satisfaction with role sharing and companionship.[116] This finding is not surprising given the extra burden young children place on women. A key factor may also be whether each spouse perceives the other as doing a fair share.[117] A wife working does not necessarily lower marital happiness, but differences in views about appropriate roles of husbands and wives or men and women do depress marital quality. This is especially true for couples where the husband holds traditional views about sex roles and the wife has more modern notions.

Research by Norval D. Glenn on marital quality in the 1980s finds that because of the strain brought about by the attempt to share roles in marriages, marital happiness has deteriorated, both for long-term and relatively recent marriages.[118] He attributes the decline to changed expectations about marriage, as well as to a waning of the ideal of marriage permanence. He argues that rising divorce rates are not only a function of growing acceptance of divorce but also of a decline in marital quality.[119] Media depictions of relationships reinforce romantic expectations that many do not find in their own relationships.

Divorce. As Glenn anticipated, even when women and men do marry today, they are less likely to stay married than they were in previous eras. Since the mid-nineteenth century, the divorce rate has risen almost tenfold. The 1970s saw the fastest increase in divorce, with the rate in the 1980s and 1990s remaining at a rather stable high. Today, the chance of a marriage ending in divorce is triple the rate of the 1920s and 1930s, and double the rate of 1950 to 1965. (See Table 6–7 for a comparison of marital status from 1950 to 1995.)

Seen another way, in the late 1800s, only one in ten marriages ended in divorce; in the 1950s, the rate was one in three; and today, four in ten marriages are not expected to survive. Arguing that the divorce rate ignores those who separate permanently without formally divorcing, at least some scientists think two-thirds of all marriages may fail.[120]

Lynn K. White, in a review of the literature on the reasons for the high marital instability in the United States (higher than in Europe since records have been kept), finds several factors to be important.[121] Among the most significant may be the notion that a marriage should be based on love and, in the twentieth century, sexual attraction. This has come to mean that when a marriage does not live up to the ideal of a companionship union giving a couple emotional and/or sexual fulfillment, it is seen as failed. In addition, as we have noted, in the past two decades women's and men's notions of marriage have changed to include the concept of "role-shared" unions. The

TABLE 6–7 Marital Status, by Race, 1950 to 1995

	1950[a]	1960[a]	1970	1980	1995
All Races					
% Married	66.6	67.6	64.2	61.0	57.6
% Divorced	2.2	2.3	2.9	5.8	8.7
% Never married	23.1	22.0	25.0	25.9	27.1
% Widowed	8.1	8.3	8.0	7.4	6.6
White					
% Married	67.0	68.4	65.3	62.8	60.0
% Divorced	2.2	2.2	2.8	6.2	8.1
% Never married	23.0	21.5	24.1	24.4	24.7
% Widowed	7.8	8.0	7.8	7.3	6.7
Black					
% Married	63.2	60.3	55.4	46.5	40.0
% Divorced	2.3	3.2	3.8	7.6	9.9
% Never married	24.4	26.7	31.4	37.0	43.0
% Widowed	10.1	9.8	9.5	8.8	7.1

[a]1950 and 1960 data are for the population 14 years old and over. All other years are for 15 and older.

Source: U.S. Bureau of the Census, Current Population Reports, Series P20, no. 484, "Marital Status and Living Arrangements: March 1995" (Washington, D.C.: http://www.census.gov)

inability of most marriages to achieve this sharing, especially as it relates to housework and child care, may also result in more people being convinced their marriage has not achieved the goals they have set for it. Paralleling these views on marital expectations has been a growing emphasis on individualism. No longer is the question what is good for the marriage, but what is good for me. Both women and men may have been making this calculation in the "me" decades of the 1970s and 1980s. In the 1990s, the divorce rate leveled off as boomers enter the age when they are less likely to divorce (their forties and fifties).[122]

Also contributing to the rising divorce rate has been the movement of women into the marketplace. The ability to achieve a measure of economic resources, and thus independence, may have allowed women in unhappy marriages to leave. Data also suggest, however, that work per se may not be as important as women's autonomy from her spouse or her commitment to the work force. Indeed, there is some evidence that more equitable marriages in which the wife's share of the income is high may actually be more stable unions, perhaps because they more closely approach the kind of "role-sharing" marriage that is seen as desirable.

Some researchers, notably Lenore Weitzman, believe that the advent of no-fault divorce may have expedited the exit of men and women from unhappy marriages.[123] At the least, it has detracted from the notion that a man is obligated to support his wife for life. As with the decline in marriage rates, the oversupply of women of marriageable age and status in comparison to men may also be a factor in the increase of divorce. Men who have many "wife options" may be less interested in maintaining their current marriage. Support for this proposition can be found in the higher divorce rates of African Americans, where the numbers of marriageable women far exceed those of marriageable men.

Fueling these trends, or resulting from them, has been the growing acceptance of divorce as an answer to failed marriage. There is at least some indication, however, that attitudes toward divorce may be changing, with large segments of the public wanting to make divorce more difficult to obtain, especially when there are children in the family.[124] It should also be noted that most divorced persons remarry, although rates for remarriage declined 40 percent between 1970 and 1988.[125] In large part, this seems to be a function of women not wanting to remarry. Barbara Foley Wilson of the National Center for Health Statistics claims, "It's hard for men to remarry when women aren't interested."[126]

The sources of marital instability are not completely understood, but most observers agree that the impact of divorce on the American family has been overwhelming. For example, the cultural stereotype that the responsibility for child care should remain with the mother means that in most divorces where there are children the mother gets custody. Even in the large number of states that encourage joint custody, the mother remains the primary parent.[127] The result of such practices has been the burgeoning number of single-parent families headed by women. In 1995, in families with children under eighteen, 22.2 percent were headed by the mother only, compared to 6.2 percent in 1950.[128] The largest proportion of these households were the result of divorce or separation; a growing number were the product of never-married women having children.[129] The remainder of such families, 10 percent, are headed by widows. Because of the complementary trends of divorce and childbirth without marriage, it is estimated that somewhere between one-half and three-quarters of all children will spend part of their youth in a family headed by a woman.[130] Among African Americans, where both trends are more pronounced, more than 80 percent of all children will live in a single-parent household at some time during their youth.[131] However, in any one year, the majority of children live in two-parent families. In 1995, for instance, almost 69 percent of children under eighteen were living in a household with two parents.[132]

Divorce not only alters the family structure but also often brings dramatic income inequalities between the women and men who experience the dissolution of their marriages. Under old divorce laws, husbands were assumed responsible for the support of their wives and their children. Since the adoption of no-fault laws, this has changed. Today, when marriages dissolve, both spouses are assumed to be able to "make it on their own." One result of this change is the virtual elimination of most permanent alimony awards. Today when alimony is awarded (only in about 15 percent of divorces) it is usually for a short duration, generally two years or less.[133] Moreover, no matter how limited a woman's preparation for employment, judges assume women are able to support themselves. Rarely is there an awareness of the wage discrepancies between working women and men noted in Chapter 4. The difficulty in finding a good job is particularly hard on women who have been full-time homemakers, especially if they are older and have spent most of their adult years raising children. Few can ever make up for the time they were out of the job market, losing experience and work-related skills.

Most people assume that women with children get child support. The reality is that less than 60 percent are awarded child support, and even fewer receive it (see Table 6–8). Studies by the U.S. Census Bureau in 1992 found child support was conferred by the court to only 56 percent of all women with children. (The figure is far lower for African American and Hispanic women, only 36 and 35 percent of whom, respectively, are awarded child support.)[134] Because more stringent enforcement has been shown to increase compliance, it is likely that stricter prosecution of dead-beat dads should result in more full and partial payment of awards. A key factor in the lack of awards to African American women, however, is out-of-wedlock births. The welfare reform, however, includes more stringent efforts to identify birth fathers and may result in more awards to women of color, although negative attitudes toward the legal system and the low income of minority fathers will continue to keep awards and payment of awards to women of color low.[135]

Only 52 percent of the women awarded child support actually receive full payment, a quarter receive partial payment, and the remainder receive no money at all. (Again the figures are far lower for women of color.)[136] Though the lack of compliance is often tied to fathers' inability to pay child support, research suggests fathers could be paying almost twice as much.[137]

TABLE 6–8 Child Support Payments, 1991

	All (%)	White[a] (%)	African American[a] (%)	Hispanic[a] (%)
Women awarded child support	56	69	36	35
Women receiving full amount	52	54	43	43
Women receiving partial amount	24	23	27	25
Women receiving nothing	24	22	30	32
Women not awarded child support	44	31	64	65

[a]Numbers may not add to 100 percent due to rounding error.

Source: U.S. Bureau of the Census, Current Population Reports, Series P60–187, "Child Support for Custodial Mothers and Fathers: 1991" (Washington, D.C.: Author, 1995), 7 and 14.

Most awards take less than 30 percent of a father's income, and for wealthy men only 20 percent.[138]

In part because men pay so little support, the standard of living for most divorced women and their children falls dramatically after divorce. In a review of fifteen studies of the effect of divorce on women's economic status, measured by varying standards, Karen C. Holden and Pamela J. Smock found declines ranging from a low of 7 percent to a high of 73 percent. Most of the studies found a drop of around 25 percent.[139] Many women remarry, which generally raises their standard of living to predivorce levels. Failing this, most women can expect a lower living standard for many years if not for the rest of their lives.[140]

Research shows men's economic status after divorce either declines marginally for a short time, does not change at all, or improves.[141] Three factors explain the difference between women's and men's economic status. First, mothers get custody of children, which raises their cost of living. Second, men earn more than women, especially if the wife has been a full-time homemaker and/or has young children. Third, few men pay "fair" child support and some pay none. As a result, one-fourth of divorced women and their children are living in poverty.[142]

The Feminization of Poverty and Welfare Reform

During the 1980s, scholars and the media began to focus on the growing trend of poverty among women. This development was soon labeled the feminization of poverty. It is estimated that among female-headed families (which include divorced, separated, and never-married women and their children), 27 percent of white families, 45 percent of African American families, and 49 percent of Hispanic families are living below the poverty level.[a] Collectively, more than one-half of all persons falling below the officially defined poverty level were living in families headed by women. Reports indicated that if those trends continued, nearly all persons in poverty by the year 2000 would be women and children.

Many scholars who have charted the growth of poverty among women and their children have identified several causes. First is the growing number of female-headed families. Second are the relatively low wages earned by women. Third is the absence of support facilities (day care, paid parental leave) to help women balance a job and a family. Fourth is the phenomenon of fathers failing to support their children and the inability of government, to date, to force them to do so. In combination, these several factors make female-headed families very susceptible to poverty.

As the need for two wage earners to keep a family from poverty has grown, the focus of much of the research on the causes of poverty among women and children has been the growing numbers of female-headed families. Divorce and out-of-wedlock births do correlate with poverty. Among families headed by divorced women, a quarter live in poverty; whereas among families headed by women who have never married, more than half are poor.

Conservatives argue that the welfare system—notably Aid to Families with Dependent Children (AFDC)—is to blame for the rising numbers of out-of-wedlock births. Even though the evidence does not support their theory (out-of-wedlock births rose while AFDC payments in constant dollars declined, and many women who have children out of wedlock are poor before the pregnancy), conservatives were able to successfully convince the public of the need to reform welfare. In 1994, for instance, a majority of the public agreed that most recipients of welfare were taking advantage of the system and that poor women have babies to collect welfare.[b]

In 1996, President Clinton and the Republican-led Congress responded to the public's desire for reform by eliminating the federal AFDC program and shifting welfare to the states in the form of block grants set at 1994 expenditure levels. The result will be fifty different welfare programs, although all must meet certain guidelines. These guidelines state that recipients may not receive aid if they do not work after two years of aid, they have received aid for more than five years in total once the program is in place, and they do not cooperate in assisting the government in establishing paternity. States may also deny aid to unwed mothers who do not live at home and attend school and to children born to women already on welfare.[c]

Even though the guidelines make some provisions for additional money for child care and job training, most proponents of legislation to protect poor women think the results for these women and their children (almost all former AFDC recipients are women and children) will be disastrous. Opponents of the legislation reason that there will not be enough well-paying jobs for poor women to support their families, nor will there be sufficient help in terms of child care and transportation to work for mothers who are able to secure a position. Concurrent changes in Medicaid and the food stamp program will make it even harder for poor women to secure needed medical care and food for their children. Kathleen Mullan Harris, who has studied poor women, writes of welfare recipients, "Eliminating welfare without improving the pay and benefits or the jobs they can get—or improving their ability to get better jobs—can only have one result: an increase in poverty among women and children."[d]

Susan L. Thomas argues convincingly that the whole logic behind welfare reform is based on faulty reasoning as to why women are in poverty, including the erroneous assumption that welfare recipients do not want to work and that they become pregnant in order to receive government money. The research, however, finds most women on welfare want to work and half do work, but they need the government assistance in order to support their families. Likewise, the birthrate among women on welfare is lower than among women who do not receive public assistance. Thomas argues it is not the women who are at fault but the system of sex and race discrimination that is responsible for their poverty. Noting that most women in poverty were poor before divorce or an out-of-wedlock birth, she cites many of the barriers we identified in Chapter 4, namely inadequate preparation for the job market, the lack of family-friendly policies, and wages too low to support a family, as the real reasons for women's poverty.[e]

[a]1995 Census figures from http://www.census.gov

[b]"A Devastating Critique of the System for Teaching the Wrong Values," *Public Perspective* 6, no. 2 (1995): 40.

[c]Jeffrey L. Katz, "Welfare Showdown Looms as GOP Readies Plan," *Congressional Quarterly Weekly Report* 54, no. 30 (1996): 2115–19.

[d]Kathleen Mullan Harris, "The Reforms Will Hurt, Not Help, Poor Women and Children," *Chronicle of Higher Education* (October 4, 1996): B7. See also the entire issue of *The Future of Children*, 7, no. 1 (1997), which is devoted to the question of the impact of welfare reform on women and children.

[e]Susan L. Thomas, *Gender and Poverty* (New York: Garland, 1994).

Motherhood. More pressing demands on single mothers are not the only sign of changes in the maternal role. Although, in the past, one of the most defining characteristics of women has been the enduring cultural stereotype of the importance of motherhood in women's lives, this is increasingly less true.

One indication of change can be found in birthrates, which have steadily declined. The one exception to this trend occurred in the late 1940s through the early 1960s. Because of the delayed births brought about by World War II and the emphasis on women's maternal role that characterized the era of the feminine mystique, the United States experienced a baby boom from 1946 to roughly 1965. Correspondingly, the number of births per 1,000 for women of childbearing age was 121 in 1921, 89 in 1930, rising again to a peak of 123 in 1957, and declining from that point to a nearly stable rate of 65 to 68 since the early 1970s.[143]

Of course, a critical factor in the probability of a woman having a child has been access to birth control. In the latter part of the nineteenth century, with the decrease in infant mortality and the increased emphasis on the mother in shaping a child's development, women began to limit their pregnancies. However, this was difficult because of changes in the medical profession (male doctors increasingly replaced women doctors and midwives) and Victorian attitudes toward women's sexuality, which resulted in the illegality of both abortion and the dissemination of birth control information. With abstinence as the only acceptable method, it is probable that the real birthrate far exceeded the desired birthrate. The renewed realization of female sexuality in the early twentieth century, as we saw in the last chapter, led to more widespread access to birth control and a corresponding decline in the birthrate, with the baby-boom period as an aberration in the trend.

In the early 1960s, however, the birth control revolution began. New forms and methods of limiting pregnancy, including the pill and abortion, were critical to a renewed downward trend in fertility. Joan Huber and Glenna Spitze even attribute the move toward equality for women to their being able to control the timing and number of children.[144] The 1988 Survey of Family Growth found that among women age fifteen to forty-four, 60 percent were using some method of birth control, with the fastest-growing method being sterilization. Limiting the focus to sexually active women who were not sterile, pregnant, or trying to conceive found only 6.7 percent of women not using some form of birth control.[145] Moreover, about half of all unintended pregnancies ended in abortion, with unmarried women making up the largest number (about 80 percent) of those obtaining them.[146] Indeed, almost half of all pregnancies of women under age nineteen and more than half of all pregnancies of unmarried women resulted in abortion.[147] Thus, any restrictions in access to this procedure would have the greatest impact on the lives of young women.

As Table 6–9 shows, the largest percentage of abortions involve non-teenage women, white women, and unmarried women. Stanley K. Henshaw and Katherine Kost, who calculated the rate of abortion for different groups, found abortions were most likely to be obtained by women under thirty, never-married women, women without a religious affiliation, and poor women. African American women were twice as likely to have an abortion as white women, even though attitudes toward abortion are more negative in this sector of the population.[148] Some have suggested this anomaly may be a function of more negative attitudes toward abortion among African American

TABLE 6–9 Who Has Abortions?

Percentage of abortions in the United
States, by category, 1991

Age	
19 or younger	21
20 to 24	34
25 to 29	22
30 and over	23
Race	
Nonwhite	37
White	63
Marital Status	
Never married	83
Married	17

Source: U.S. Bureau of the Census, *Statistical Abstract of the United States: 1996,* 116th ed. (Washington, D.C.: Author, 1996), 86.

men, but not among African American women once factors such as education and income are controlled.[149] The precarious economic status of many African American families may also be a reason.

Roe v. Wade (1973) had a dramatic effect on the number of legal abortions obtained. In 1973, there were 745,000 abortions. By 1980, this number had climbed to 1,554,000, a number that remained relatively constant throughout the 1980s.[150] However, birth control information is still not available to all women who want such information, nor is abortion accessible to all women. Indeed, in part because of the aging of the population and in part because of restrictive state legislation, the abortion ratio per one thousand live births has actually fallen slightly in recent years.[151] Few states provide funding for Medicaid recipients, whereas a growing list of other states require parental notification or consent, spousal notification or consent, counseling or informed consent, a waiting period, or tests to determine fetal viability.[152] The Clinton administration, however, is committed to opening up access to poor women. Were birth control information and abortion more widely available, the birthrate might fall even more.

Another indicator of changes in attitudes toward childbearing that have accompanied the women's rights movement is the practice of delaying the birth of the first child (see Table 6–10). Unlike the women of the 1950s and 1960s, women today are likely to remain child-free until well into their late twenties or even their thirties and forties. Birthrates among women over age thirty increased 73 percent from 1975 to 1980.[153] The birthrate for women age thirty to thirty-four climbed from sixty per one thousand in 1980 to eighty per one thousand in 1990.[154] Indeed, women in their thirties were the only group of women whose fertility increased in the decade. Although there are several reasons for the delay in childbearing, perhaps one of the most significant is the practice of many women to postpone childbirth to concentrate on the development of their careers. Research suggests that women who have

TABLE 6–10 First Births per 1,000 Women, by Age

Age	1980	1985	1988	1990	1994[a]
18 to 24	46.8	47.1	47.7	43.2	
15 to 19					36.3
20 to 24					58.4
25 to 29	NA	38.7	35.2	46.2	43.9
30 to 34	NA	15.8	20.3	21.9	23.0
35 to 39	NA	5.2	5.1	6.5	7.3
40 to 44	NA	0.8	0.5	1.2	1.8

NA = Not available.
[a]Age groupings were changed for 1994.

Source: U.S. Bureau of the Census, *Statistical Abstract of the U.S.: 1996,* 116th ed. (Washington, D.C.: Author, 1996), 81.

babies later in life are better educated, have higher-status jobs, are more likely to have planned the birth, will have fewer children, and are more likely to return to work soon after the baby is born.[155] As a result, during the 1990s, there was much talk and often heated debate about the ticking of women's "biological time clocks."

For some women, there may be a growing realization that they have waited too long or that they do not want a family after all. Caroline Bird quotes a reporter as saying:

> When I was growing up, I never questioned that I would one day have a child. But now I'm not so sure. I've found a job that I really like and I now can see what children really mean—a lot of time, a lot of expense, a lot of frustration— and I am sure, too, a lot of satisfaction. But I can't see myself quitting my job and staying home with the kids.[156]

Delayed childbearing may eventually mean no children for some women. For example, in 1994, 44 percent of women age twenty-five to twenty-nine were childless, as were 26 percent of women age thirty to thirty-four, 20 percent of women thirty-five to thirty-nine, and 18 percent of women forty to forty-four. The corresponding figures for 1976 were 31 percent, 16 percent, 11 percent, and 10 percent.[157]

Rather than have no children at all, others, especially working women, are choosing to limit their families to one or two children. The total fertility rate, which measures the number of children a woman can expect to have in her lifetime, has fallen from 3.7 children in 1957, the height of the baby boom, to 1.3 in the early 1990s. The current figure is below the replacement level for the population.[158] In 1945, 49 percent of those polled believed four or more children to be the "ideal"; in 1997, 54 percent said their ideal was zero to two children.[159] Researchers at the Joint Center for Urban Studies predict that as many as 40 percent of women born in the 1950s will have no children or only one child.[160]

An apparent trend contrary to the declining emphasis on motherhood has been the rising percentage of babies being born to women who are not married. In 1960, if a woman became pregnant while not married, she generally married the father. Thus, only 14.5 percent of all women having their first child in 1960 were unmarried. With changing attitudes toward marriage and premarital sex, this figure had risen to 22.3 percent in the late 1970s, climbing to 25.9 percent in 1994.[161] Part of the explanation for this phenomenon is the rising percentage of young women who engage in premarital sexual intercourse, up nearly 100 percent from 1978, although 1996 saw the first decline in this figure.[162] This trend is not occurring only among teenagers. Indeed, four out of five women having children without a husband are age twenty or older.[163] Among African American women, more than 70 percent of first births are to women who are unmarried; among Hispanics, one in three; and among white women, one in five.[164]

Most observers note that unmarried women who are having babies are not really countering the trends in motherhood that we have discussed. If anything, the number of children born to individual unwed mothers is declining in a parallel trend to the declining number born to married women.[165] What has changed is the desire and the opportunity to marry. Larry Bumpass, a professor at the University of Wisconsin, claims, "This is more a change in marriage behavior than a change in child-bearing behavior."[166] Jane Mattes, the founder of Mothers by Choice, agrees. She notes, "I decided I couldn't go through life without a child, and I put the child first, marriage later."[167] For many women who have children without a husband, however, the resultant economic hardship of not being in a dual-income family can be devastating for the woman and her children. As we noted, a very large proportion of these women and their families have incomes that place them below the poverty level.

One of the results of today's smaller families and decisions to remain childless is that both married and unmarried women are devoting less time to motherhood. Unless there is a complete reversal of these trends, the data suggest that motherhood in the future will loom as even less of an important role for women. If the proportion of one's life devoted to a particular pursuit determines its importance, the worker role may replace the mother role in the value hierarchy of at least some women. The growing practice of returning to work shortly after the birth of a child, especially for professional women, may indicate this reversal has already occurred for some. A more likely scenario for most women is that the two roles will have equal importance. For this to occur, however, either men will have to share family responsibilities more than they do now or the government will have to adopt policies to make the executions of joint mother-worker roles more manageable. We turn now to see whether fathers' role changes have kept pace with mothers'.

Fatherhood. Often in the public discussions about changing motherhood practices, little is said about the changing role of fathers. Social scientists have attempted to fill this void with research on the "other parent." What they find is often a paradox. On the one hand, there is some still very limited evidence that men are taking their job as parent more seriously. On the other hand, there is disturbing evidence that some men are "abandoning the good provider role."[168]

On the positive side, many married men now take an active part in their wives' pregnancies, go to childbirth classes, and are in delivery rooms. Many men now help their wives with child care, although the bulk of the work and the responsibility to see that the work gets done still generally stay with the mother. Fathers' "help" is often limited to taking care of the children while the wife is engaged in some other household chore or at work. Even fathers in delayed families (where the first child was born to a mother after age twenty-eight), who are better educated, older, and more egalitarian in their views, contribute only marginally more to household tasks than all fathers in two-parent families with children under age eighteen. Thus, whereas more than 50 percent of men with children under eighteen in a national sample claim that child care is equally shared, only 24 percent of the women think that in their families there is sharing. Most women (68 percent) say they do most of the care.[169] Correspondingly, almost half of all women with children and a spouse are resentful about the way child-care-related duties are shared in their households.[170]

If this relatively modest change is the "good dad" side of the equation, the "bad dad" side is even more disturbing.[171] Several authors present convincing evidence that men are, in many ways, abandoning their parental role. One indicator of this is the declining proportion of time that men spend with their children, down 43 percent between 1960 and 1980.[172] If we focus on divorced dads and fathers of children born to unmarried mothers, the evidence of declining notions of fatherhood become even more convincing. Few divorced dads, as we already noted, make a very serious effort to take care of the financial needs of their children, often ignoring court orders to pay child support. In a similar vein, Frank F. Furstenberg Jr.'s research found divorced fathers maintain only minimal contact with their children from a former marriage. Among children whose parents had been divorced two to nine years, more than 20 percent of the children had not seen their father in five years; this percentage rose to nearly 50 percent for children of parents who were divorced for ten years or more. As Furstenberg notes, "Men often sever ties with their children in the course of establishing distance from their former wives."[173] Remarriage appears to hasten the exit, with fathers often apparently too busy with the responsibilities of their new family to maintain contact with the children from a former marriage.[174]

Fathers of children from unions where there was no marriage are even less attached to their children. Few give any child support. Moreover, many seem to "forget" the child completely, not even recalling their existence when asked to list or name their children on social surveys.[175]

The failure of fathers to assume an equal parenting role seems traceable to the same problems we have identified as limiting the movement to an equitable marital or parental relationship. First, society does not encourage, and may discourage, especially in the workplace, role sharing by men. Few fathers can take time off to stay home with sick children, whereas women are more likely to find they can do this, although not without damage to their careers. Research on the implementation of the Family and Medical Leave Act of 1993, for example, finds far higher numbers of women than men took advantage of its provisions. Second, men are inadequately trained to assume the parental role. Fathers of babies and young children seem to be the least prepared to assume an equal role. Third, men are not motivated to change.[176] Fourth, some men may find that economic conditions make it financially difficult or impossible to live up to the culturally defined provider role assigned to men. Young white men and African American men more generally may find they are unable to support their children.

Changes in African American Family Patterns: Cause or Effect?

In 1965 Daniel Patrick Moynihan wrote a controversial book, *The Negro Family: The Case for National Action.* His main argument was that "at the heart of the deterioration of the fabric of Negro society is the deterioration of the Negro family."[a] Moynihan reasoned that the higher marital instability in African American families (higher divorce and abandonment rates, higher illegitimacy, and single parenthood) was directly responsible for the decline in the economic status of members. Moynihan traced the deterioration of the family to declining support for traditional family values among African Americans. He reasoned that improper gender socialization was at the heart of the problem, producing overly strong women (black matriarchy) and too weak men. Patricia Hill Collins has pointed out that the Moynihan thesis is alive and well today although the villain has shifted from black matriarchy to the welfare system. Both supposedly undermine traditional family values, encouraging women to go it alone (or with minimal government support) and men to abandon their provider role.[b]

The Moynihan report stimulated numerous studies on the African American family in the 1970s and 1980s. Most studies quickly discounted major parts of his argument, finding that African Americans and whites of all classes hold nearly identical values regarding the family, and if anything African Americans are more supportive of the institution. Moreover, there was little evidence that African American men were too weak or African American women too strong, although the data does suggest that both are more egalitarian in their ideas about women's role than are whites, especially white men.[c]

Because most research showed that the African American family was not deteriorating because of lower commitment to family values, researchers turned to an examination of other possible causes for the apparent changing patterns in family life. Indeed, in the years since the Moynihan report was issued, the trends in family change evidenced in the 1960s have continued.

Some reasoned the greater marital instability was a legacy of slavery or the movement of African Americans out of the South to the North and its urban environments. Others sought an explanation in cultural practices imported from Africa. Research found, however, that the disparity in the marital practices of African Americans and whites is relatively recent (until 1950, only minor differences in divorce, abandonment, and illegitimacy were observable [see Table 6–7]), suggesting the changes were a product of recent events.[d] In searching for an answer to the apparent paradox, researchers began to turn Moynihan's thesis on its head. They reasoned it is not the African American family that was causing the race economic difficulties, but economic difficulties that were causing the institution of marriage to weaken among members of the race. More specifically, the effects of discrimination and economic change (in the form of deindustrialization) have considerably reduced the ability of African American men to find well-paying jobs. African American women, on the other hand, have seen their economic opportunities rise with the growth of the service economy, although their unemployment rate is increasing in the 1990s. The diverging patterns in employment are thus encouraging women to reconsider the institution of marriage and lowering the ability of men to fulfill the breadwinner role.[e]

A related explanation for the higher instability has focused on the high ratio of African American women to men. The high mortality and incarceration rates of young African American men, both products of a society that has ignored the devastating effects of racism and the postindustrial economy on the African American community, are other reasons why fewer African American women are married and more are choosing to have children without a husband.[f] The African American family is adapting to these trends by relying more on extended families to help raise children and to support mothers who find themselves without permanent mates.[g]

[a]Quoted in Patricia Hill Collins, "A Comparison of Two Works on Black Family Life," *Signs* 14, no. 4 (1989): 877.

[b]Ibid., 878–82.

[c]Robert Joseph Taylor et al., "Developments in Research on Black Families: A Decade Review," *Journal of Marriage and the Family* 52, no. 4 (1990): 995–96.

[d]Henry A. Walker, "Black-White Differences in Marriage and Family Patterns," in *Feminism, Children, and the New Families,* ed. Stanford M. Dornbusch and Myra H. Strober (New York: Guilford Press, 1988), 89–99.

[e]Ibid., 105–7; Collins, "A Comparison of Two Works," 882–84; and Robert Staples and Leanor Boulin Johnson, *Black Families at the Crossroads* (San Francisco: Jossey-Bass, 1993), 221–41.

[f]Scott J. South and Kim M. Lloyd, "Marriage Opportunities and Family Formation: Further Implications of Imbalanced Sex Ratios," *Journal of Marriage and the Family* 54, no. 2 (1992): 440–51.

[g]Taylor et al., "Developments in Research on Black Families," 997.

The New Families

The intersection of the trends we have been discussing in marriage, divorce, and parenthood has produced a radical alteration in what we might call the typical family. As Table 6–11 makes clear, the typical family is no longer a married couple with children. Moreover, if we were to divide this latter group into families where only the father works, we would find less than 21 percent of all families meet the historically defined "traditional" family.[177] The implications for women's status in the family are far reaching. For many women living alone, their status is solely a function of their own self-determined lifestyle and their earning power. For women who head single-parent families, they are both parent and breadwinner. Their ability to share family responsibilities may depend on the number and ages of their children and the support from their extended family, but for most important decisions they alone are responsible. Women living with a spouse find their status depends on whether they work, what their earning capacity is relative to

TABLE 6–11 **Household Composition, 1960 to 2010, Compared (in percentages)**

	1960	1990	1995	2010[a]
Married couples with children	44.2	26.3	25.2	20.1
Married couples without children	30.3	29.8	29.5	31.5
Other families with children	4.4	8.3	8.2	7.9
Other families without children	6.4	6.5	7.1	8.3
Living alone	13.0	24.6	24.9	26.8
Other nonfamily households	1.7	4.6	5.2	5.4

[a]Projected

Source: Jennifer Classen Day, "Projection of Number of Households and Families in the U.S., 1995–2010," *Current Population Reports* P25–1129 (Washington, D.C.: Department of Commerce, 1996).

their spouse's, whether they have children, and the willingness of their spouse to "role-share."

A very important variable in the status of women is the relative economic position of the family in which the woman lives. Figures from the U.S. Bureau of the Census indicate that families of married couples where both partners work have the highest earnings, followed by families where only the husband works and then families headed by a woman.[178]

Thus, women's status in the family is variable and can expect to become even more so in the decades to come as the trends we have been describing continue to affect even more women. How the women's movement and the government react to this growing diversity may be critical to all women's futures.

CONCLUSION

Although there has been considerable progress in the direction of creating a more equitable institution of marriage, many of the traditional practices remain. This lack of equality of men and women in marriage is of considerable consequence for the position of women, not only within but outside the family. Women cannot achieve an equal position in politics or the marketplace as long as they have the primary responsibility for housework and child care. For equity in these areas, women need what men have: "a wife." The situation, of course, is even more precarious for the women who head families alone. They lack even the "help" that husbands and fathers provide. Perhaps more importantly, they lack the second, and still generally primary, income that comes from a man's paid employment.

Many feminists argue that the institution of the family may be particularly resistant to change because it signifies and creates our understanding of gender roles. The same could be said of motherhood. A person's sense of self-identity and society's definition of woman and man may be intimately linked to what happens in the family. Relatedly, as we saw in Chapter 4, what transpires at work may also seek to create gender. Thus, women are not merely socialized to become wives and homemakers; rather, the social structures in which they live act to reinforce the notions of what women must or should do if they are "to be a woman." The same argument can be made perhaps even more forcefully for men, who seem particularly concerned about confirming "their manhood." Thus, in making any prognosis about further change in the institution of the family, not only do we need to look at the barriers we have identified, but also we must be sensitive to how altering the family is seen as threatening to many people's very sense of gendered self.

With respect to the first of our three barriers, cultural attitudes about the family, we expect that further change can be predicted. Even during the 1980s, when the political leadership in Washington emphasized traditional family values, an evolution in the desired family structure continued. By the 1990s, more men and women wanted a role-shared relationship. While both political parties now seem generally concerned that the trends we have identified have not always been beneficial, especially for children, there seems to be little public policy can do to alter public opinion or social practices.[179]

It is likely that the conflict between feminists and conservative women will continue, each claiming the other's proposals will not solve the decline of the family. Correspondingly, the divisions between women who stay at home and those who work full time about what impact the women's rights movement has had on women's status in the family will also not go away. Feminists will continue to push for policy changes in an attempt to give women greater independence and to allow them to blend their marital and work roles. Homemakers, however, may increasingly resist what they see as changes undermining their way of life.

With respect to the other two barriers (differential resources of men and women and discrimination or reluctance to change by men), women, especially young women, seem increasingly better equipped to demand equal role sharing. They are more likely to work and to work at well-paying jobs. Men, however, seem only marginally inclined to adopt the practices that would produce equitable unions. The resultant resentment by women may contribute to marital dissolution and to women's increasing reluctance to marry and to have children. Men's "flight from commitment" may symbolize their own reluctance to save the institution.

Betty Friedan's comments about the restructuring of the institution of home and work several years ago still seem applicable. She claims, "We will never bring about these changes unless fathers demand them too."[180] Because the pressure on the traditional institution of marriage is not likely to diminish, we may expect men to soon join the chorus of voices calling for change.

NOTES

1. Linda Gordon, *Woman's Body, Woman's Right: A Social History of Birth Control in America* (New York: Viking Press, 1976), 18, 48–49.
2. Carl N. Degler, *At Odds: Women and the Family in America from the Revolution to the Present* (New York: Oxford University Press, 1980), 73.
3. John Demos, "Husbands and Wives," in *Our American Sisters: Women in American Life and Thought*, ed. Jean E. Friedman and William G. Shade (Boston: Allyn & Bacon, 1973), 36–41.
4. Quoted in ibid., 31.
5. Robert Staples and Leanor Boulin Johnson, *Black Families at the Crossroads* (San Francisco: Jossey-Bass, 1993), 7.
6. Herbert G. Gutman, "Marital and Sexual Norms among Slave Women," in *A Heritage of Her Own*, ed. Nancy F. Cott and Elizabeth H. Pleck (New York: Simon & Schuster, 1979), 305–6.
7. Susan A. Mann, "Slavery, Sharecropping, and Sexual Inequality," *Signs* 14, no. 4: 779–81, 786–87.
8. Staples and Johnson, *Black Families at the Crossroads*, 7–8; Gutman, "Marital and Sexual Norms," 306–7.
9. Michael Gordon, *The American Family: Past, Present, and Future* (New York: Random House, 1978), 201–9, 203–9; Carroll Smith-Rosenberg, "Sex as Symbol in Victorian Purity: An Ethnohistorical Analysis of Jacksonian America," in *Turning Points: Historical and Sociological Essays on the Family*, ed. John Demos and Sarane Spence Boocock (Chicago: University of Chicago Press, 1978), 212–47.
10. Mary Frances Berry, *The Politics of Parenthood* (New York: Viking, 1993); Barbara Welter, "The Cult of True Womanhood: 1820–1860," in *Our American Sisters*, ed. Friedman and Shade, 102–3.
11. Gordon, *Women's Body, Women's Right*, 320.
12. Myra Marx Ferree, "Beyond Separate Spheres: Feminism and Family Research," *Journal of Marriage & the Family* 52, no. 4 (1990): 872.
13. Ibid.
14. Ibid.
15. Helena Znaniecki Lapata, *Occupation Housewife* (New York: Oxford Press, 1991), 48–53.
16. Arland Thornton and Deborah Freedman, "Changes in the Sex Role Attitudes of Women, 1962–1977," *American Sociological Review* 44, no. 4 (1979): 833.
17. Ibid., 833–35.
18. The 1985 Virginia Slims Poll found 70 percent of women believed they could have a happy and complete life without marriage. Data made available by the Roper Center for Public Opinion Research, Storrs, Conn. A 1989 poll found the proportion of women who felt they could be happy without marriage had risen to 90 percent. Cited in Susan Faludi, *Backlash: The Undeclared War against American Women* (New York: Crown, 1991), 15.
19. James Allan Davis and Tom W. Smith, *General Social Surveys, 1972–1996*. Principal Investigator, James A. Davis; Director and Co-Principal Investigator, Tom W. Smith. NORC ed. Chicago: National Opinion Research Center, producer, 1996; Storrs, Conn.: The Roper Center for Public Opinion Research, University of Connecticut, distributor.
20. A 1987 survey found 81.5 percent of all men age eighteen to twenty-four agreed (strongly agree, agree) that they would like to get married someday. For young women the desire to be married was equally strong, although women were more likely to strongly agree they would like to marry. Bruce A. Chadwick and Tim B. Heaton, *Statistical Handbook on the American Family* (Phoenix, Ariz.: Oryx Press, 1992), 22.
21. The Virginia Slims Polls: 1970, 1974, 1979, 1985, 1990, 1995. Data made available by the Roper Center, Storrs, Conn.
22. Chadwick and Heaton, *Statistical Handbook*, 224; 1996 General Social Survey. Data made available by the Roper Center, Storrs, Conn.
23. Thornton and Freedman, "Changes in the Sex Role Attitudes of Women," 833, 837–38.
24. The 1995 Virginia Slims Poll.
25. The 1994 General Social Survey.
26. Ibid.
27. The 1990 Virginia Slims Poll.
28. Ibid.

29. The 1994 General Social Survey.
30. Chadwick and Heaton, *Statistical Handbook,* 94.
31. In the 1996 General Social Survey, 52.1 percent of those who had an opinion favored making divorce more difficult, 28.6 percent favored making it easier, and 19.4 percent did not want any change.
32. The 1990 Virginia Slims Poll.
33. The 1995 Virginia Slims Poll.
34. Sixty percent of the public thought there had been strong/moderate decline in family life when polled in 1996. "Our Country's Main Challenges Are in the Moral Dimension, Not in Economics or Power," *Public Perspective* 8, no. 2 (1997): 10.
35. "Family Values," *Public Perspective* 3, no. 6 (1992): 85.
36. The 1980 Virginia Slims Poll.
37. The 1994 General Social Survey.
38. Ibid.; Chadwick and Heaton, *Statistical Handbook,* 129.
39. "Nearly 6 in 10 Said Four or More Children Is the Ideal in 1959; 1 in 10 Say that Today," *Public Perspective* 8, no. 2, (1997): 24.
40. Ibid.
41. "The Solutions We Identify Match Our Definition of the Problems," *Public Perspective* 8, no. 2 (1997): 12.
42. "An Overview of Attitudes," *Public Perspective* 3, no. 4 (1992): 99; George Gallup Jr., "Public Generally Supports a Woman's Right to Abortion." http://www.gallup.com
43. Gallup, "Public Generally Supports a Woman's Right to Abortion."
44. Ibid.
45. Elaine J. Hall and Myra Marx Ferree, "Race Differences in Abortion Attitudes," *Public Opinion Quarterly* 50, no. 1 (1986): 197–99.
46. Ibid., 199–204.
47. Gallup, "Public Generally Supports a Woman's Right to Abortion."
48. Debra L. Dodson, "Abortion Politics in State Elections: Comparisons Across States" (New Brunswick, N.J.: Center for the American Woman and Politics, 1991).
49. Ibid.
50. Alan I. Abramowitz, "It's Abortion Stupid: Policy Voting in the 1992 Presidential Election" (paper prepared for delivery at the annual meeting of the American Political Science Association, Washington, D.C., 1992); Mark J. Wattier, Byron W. Daynes, and Raymond Tatalovich, "Abortion Attitudes, Gender, and Candidate Choice in Presidential Elections: 1972 to 1992," *Women and Politics* 17, no. 1 (1997): 55–72.
51. Chadwick and Heaton, *Statistical Handbook,* 145.
52. In 1965, 69 percent of women under age thirty thought premarital sex was always or almost always wrong. In 1985, only 22 percent felt premarital sex was always or almost always wrong. Reported in David Popenoe, "Flight from the Nuclear Family: Trends of the Past Three Decades," *Public Perspective* 2, no. 3 (1991): 19.
53. The 1990 Virginia Slims Poll. Seventy-eight percent of both women and men agreed with the statement.
54. Ibid. Only 37 percent of men and 29 percent of women thought a trial marriage would make for a better marriage.
55. Ibid.; Mary Geraghty, "Finances Are Becoming More Crucial in Students' College Choice, Survey Finds," *Chronicle of Higher Education* 43, no. 19 (1997): A43.
56. "Attitudes and Characteristics of Freshmen, Fall 1991," *Chronicle of Higher Education Almanac* (Washington, D.C.: Chronicle of Higher Education, 1992), 13.
57. "What's OK on a Date," *Public Perspective* 3, no. 2 (1992): 102.
58. Ibid. Only 40 percent of men over age fifty think it is rape when a husband has sex with his wife even if she does not want to; among young men, 69 percent think it is rape. In general, young men seem much more sensitive to the fact that sex must be by mutual agreement.
59. Susan Estrich, *Real Rape* (Cambridge, Mass.: Harvard University Press, 1987).
60. The 1990 Virginia Slims Poll.
61. Chadwick and Heaton, *Statistical Handbook,* 146.
62. Geraghty, "Finances Are Becoming More Crucial," A43.
63. Sixty-nine percent of women think homosexuality is always wrong, while 74 percent of men think it is always wrong. "Views about Homosexuality," *Public Perspective* 4, no. 3 (1993): 82. The percentage of men and women, respectively, calling each of the following a

family are as follows: lesbian couple (19 percent/22 percent); gay men couple (15 percent/24 percent); lesbian couple raising a child (23 percent/31 percent); and two gay men raising a child (24 percent/28 percent). "What Constitutes a Family?" *Public Perspective* 3, no. 5 (1992): 101.

64. Susan Cohen and Mary Fainsod Katzenstein, *Feminism, Children, and the New Families* (New York: Guilford Press, 1988), 25–46. See also Jeanne J. Flemming, "Public Opinion on Change in Women's Rights and Roles," in *Feminism, Children, and the New Families,* ed. Stanford M. Dornbush and Myra H. Strober (New York: Guilford Press, 1988), 47–66.

65. Jennifer Glass, "Housewives and Employed Wives: Demographic and Attitudinal Change, 1972–1986," *Journal of Marriage & the Family* 54, no. 3 (1992): 559–69.

66. Ibid., 568.

67. The 1996 General Social Survey.

68. Caroline Bird, *The Two-Paycheck Marriage* (New York: Rawson, Wade, 1979), 43.

69. Laurie Wermuth, Jennifer Ham, and Rebecca L. Robbins, "Women Don't Wear Condoms: AIDS Risk Among Sexual Partners of IV Drug Users," in *The Social Context of AIDS,* ed. Joan Huber and Beth E. Schneider (Newbury Park, Calif.: Sage, 1992), 83.

70. Ibid., 78–79.

71. Constantina Safilios-Rothschild, *Sex Role Socialization and Sex Discrimination: A Synthesis and Critique of the Literature* (Washington, D.C.: The National Institute of Education, 1979), 35.

72. Donna Fisher-Thompson, "Adult Sex Typing of Children's Toys," *Sex Roles* 23, no. 5 (1990): 291–303; P. N. Lackey, "Adults' Attitudes about Assignment of Household Chores to Male and Female Children," *Sex Roles* 20, nos. 5/6 (1989): 271–81; R. Lytton and D. M. Romney, "Parents' Differential Socialization of Boys and Girls: A Meta-analysis," *Psychological Bulletin* 109, no. 2 (1991): 267–96.

73. *The General Mills American Family Report, 1980–1981: Family Strengths and Strains at Work* (Minneapolis, Minn.: General Mills, n.d.), 75.

74. Geraghty, "Finances Are Becoming More Crucial," A43.

75. The 1974 and 1979 Virginia Slims Polls both questioned women about whether boys should do laundry and mend clothes. In the earlier survey only three out of five mothers thought a boy should do laundry and four out of ten thought he should sew. By 1979, these figures were four out of five and nearly six out of ten, respectively.

76. *The General Mills American Family Report,* 41. The report found that while 72 percent of all men and 77 percent of all women reported they take their families into consideration in deciding the amount of on-the-job travel they will accept, interviews with executives in large corporations found only 34 percent believed this was a consideration for men. Sixty-four percent said it was important for women.

77. Degler, *At Odds,* 7–8.

78. Ibid., 152.

79. "Demographics of Marriage," *Public Perspective* 2, no. 4 (1991): 101; U.S. Bureau of the Census, "Marital Status and Living Arrangements," *Current Population Reports,* Series P20, no. 484.

80. "Demographics of Marriage," 101.

81. Barbara Vobejda, "Divorce Remains an American Way of Life, Study Finds" *Buffalo News,* December 9, 1992, A15.

82. Scott J. South and Kim M. Lloyd, "Marriage Opportunities and Family Formation: Further Implications of Imbalanced Sex Ratios," *Journal of Marriage & the Family* 54, no. 2 (1990): 440–51. They find, however, that availability of men is only a partial explanation for the lower marriage rates among African Americans. See also Maxine Baca Zinn, "Family, Race, and Poverty in the Eighties," *Signs* 14, no. 4 (1989): 867–68.

83. For a general discussion of the influence of sex ratios on social and sexual behavior, see Marcia Guttentag and Paul F. Secord, *Too Many Women?* (Beverly Hills, Calif.: Sage, 1983).

84. Quoted in Jane Gross, "Divorced, Middle-Aged, and Happy: Women, Especially, Adjusted to the '90s," *New York Times,* December 7, 1992, A14.

85. Ibid.

86. Andrew Cherlin, "Women and the Family," in *The American Woman: 1987–1988,* ed. Sara E. Rix (New York: Norton, 1987), 75.

87. The 1990 Virginia Slims Poll.

88. Jean Seligmann et al., "The Art of Flying Solo," *Newsweek,* March 1, 1993, 70–71, 73.

89. James R. Wetzel, "American Families: 75 Years of Change," *Monthly Labor Review* 113, no. 3 (1990): 12; Katrine Ames et al., "Domesticated Bliss," *Newsweek*, March 23, 1992, 62–63.
90. Ibid.
91. Joann Vanek, "Housewives as Workers," in *Women Working: Theories and Facts in Perspective*, ed. Ann H. Stromberg and Shirley Harkess (Palo Alto, Calif.: Mayfield, 1978), 402.
92. John P. Robinson, "Who's Doing the Housework?" *American Demographics*, December 1988, 24–28, 63.
93. Chadwick and Heaton, *Statistical Handbook*, 225.
94. Ibid., 69.
95. The 1994 General Social Survey and the 1995 Virginia Slims Poll.
96. Study by Work/Family Directions of 60,000 employees of fifteen major corporations. Reported in Pat Swift, "Men Fail to Pull Weight at Home," *Buffalo News*, January 1, 1992, B2.
97. Robinson, "Housework," 28. Some research using a broader definition found full-time housewives worked fifty-five hours per week. See Vanek, "Housewives as Workers," 401.
98. In one study, husbands of working wives did 7.33 hours of housework compared to 5.28 hours contributed by husbands whose wives were not employed outside the home. Philip Blumstein and Pepper Schwartz, "Money and Ideology: Their Impact on Power and the Division of Household Labor," in *Gender, Family, and Economy: The Triple Overlap*, ed. Rae Lesser Blumberg (Newbury Park, Calif.: Sage, 1991), 272.
99. Scott Coltrane and Masako Ishii-Kuntz, "Men's Housework: A Life Course Perspective," *Journal of Marriage & the Family* 54, no. 1 (1992): 46, 52–53; Blumstein and Schwartz, "Money and Ideology," 268–70; Theodore N. Greenstein, "Husbands' Participation in Domestic Labor: Interactive Effects of Wives and Husbands' Gender Ideologies," *Journal of Marriage & the Family* 55, no. 3: 585–95.
100. Robert Joseph Taylor, Linda M. Chatters, M. Belinda Tucker, and Edith Lewis, "Developments in Research on Black Families: A Decade Review," *Journal of Marriage & the Family* 52, no. 4 (1990): 995.
101. Blumstein and Schwartz, "Money and Ideology," 272.
102. Chadwick and Heaton, *Statistical Handbook*, 69. See April A. Brayfield, "Employment Resources and Housework in Canada," *Journal of Marriage & the Family* 54, no. 1 (1992): 28, for a discussion of ethnic group differences in Canada.
103. Coltrane and Ishii-Kuntz, "Men's Housework," 44.
104. Sara Fenstermaker, Candace West, and Don H. Zimmerman, "Gender Inequality: New Conceptual Train," in *Gender, Family, and Economy: The Triple Overlap*, ed. Rae Lesser Blumberg (Newbury Park, Calif.: Sage, 1991), 301. See also Feree, "Beyond Separate Spheres," 866–85.
105. Blumstein and Schwartz, "Money and Ideology," 265–68; Coltrane and Ishii-Kuntz, "Men's Housework," 45–46, 52.
106. Blumstein and Schwartz, "Money and Ideology," 265–68.
107. Brayfield, "Employment Resources," 25.
108. The 1989 and 1994 Virginia Slims Polls.
109. Robert O. Blood and Donald M. Wolfe, *Husbands and Wives: The Dynamics of Married Living* (Glencoe, Ill.: Free Press, 1960), 2–23.
110. Ibid., 21.
111. *The General Mills American Family Report*, 46.
112. The 1994 Virginia Slims Poll.
113. Blood and Wolfe, *Husbands and Wives*, 40; Stephen J. Bahr, "Effects on Power and Division of Labor in the Family," in *Working Mothers*, ed. Lois Wladis Hoffman and F. Ivan Nye (San Francisco: Jossey-Bass, 1974), 173–77; Cynthia Fuchs Epstein, "Toward a Family Policy: Changes in Mothers' Lives," in *The Changing American Family and Public Policy*, ed. Andrew J. Cherlin (Washington, D.C.: The Urban Institute, 1988), 169–70; Blumstein and Schwartz, "Money and Ideology," 273–76.
114. Blumstein and Schwartz, "Money and Ideology," 276–77.
115. Ibid., 277–78.
116. Norval D. Glenn, "Quantitative Research on Marital Quality in the 1980s: A Critical Review," *Journal of Marriage & the Family* 52, no. 4 (1990): 818–32.
117. Ibid., 826–27.
118. Norval D. Glenn, "The Recent Trend in Marital Success in the United States," *Journal of Marriage & the Family* 53, no. 2 (1991): 261–70.
119. Ibid., 269–70.

120. Frank F. Furstenberg Jr., "Divorce and the American Family," *Annual Review of Sociology* 16 (1990): 381–82.
121. The following discussion draws heavily on Lynn K. White, "Determinants of Divorce: A Review of Research in the Eighties," *Journal of Marriage & the Family* 52, no. 4 (1990): 904–12. See also Furstenberg, "Divorce and the American Family," 379–81.
122. "Families Led by 2 Parents Post Increase," *Buffalo News,* November 16, 1995, C1.
123. Lenore J. Weitzman, "Women and Children Last: The Social and Economic Consequences of Divorce Law Reforms," in *Feminism, Children, and the New Families,* ed. Sanford M. Dornbusch and Myra H. Strober (New York: Guilford Press, 1988), 241–43.
124. Democrats and the Clinton administration have also begun to talk about developing a set of social policies designed to "save the family."
125. Karen C. Holden and Pamela J. Smock, "The Economic Costs of Marital Dissolution: Why Do Women Bear a Disproportionate Cost?" *Annual Review of Sociology* 17 (1991): 59–60; Gross, "Divorced," A14.
126. Quoted in Gross, "Divorced," A14.
127. Furstenberg, "Divorce and the American Family," 384–85; Leslie A. Morgan, "The Multiple Consequences of Divorce: A Decade Review," *Journal of Marriage & the Family* 52, no. 4 (1990): 917.
128. U.S. Bureau of the Census, "Marital Status and Living Arrangements: March 1994," *Current Population Reports,* Series P20, no. 484.
129. Andrew J. Cherlin, ed., *The Changing American Family and Public Policy* (Washington, D.C.: The Urban Institute, 1988), 12.
130. Furstenberg, "Divorce and the American Family," 383.
131. Ibid.
132. U.S. Bureau of the Census, "Marital Status and Living Arrangements: March 1994," *Current Population Reports,* Series P20, no. 484.
133. Lenore J. Weitzman, "Women and Children Last," 224–25; Chadwick and Heaton, *Statistical Handbook,* 104.
134. Holden and Smock, "Marital Dissolution," 71–72; U.S. Department of Commerce, "Child Support for Custodial Mothers and Fathers: 1991," P60–187 (Washington, D.C.: Author, 1996).
135. Daniel R. Meyers and Judi Bartfeld, "Compliance with Child Support Orders in Divorce Cases," *Journal of Marriage & the Family* 58, no. 1 (1996): 210–212; John W. Graham and Andrea H. Beller, "Child Support in Black and White: Racial Differentials in the Award and Receipt of Child Support in the 1980s," *Social Science Quarterly* 77, no. 3 (1996): 528–42.
136. Ibid.; Steven Waldman, "Deadbeat Dads," *Newsweek,* May 4, 1992, 46, 48–50, 51.
137. Morgan, "Multiple Consequences," 914; Meyer and Bartfeld, "Compliance with Child Support Orders," 201–12.
138. Holden and Smock, "Marital Dissolution," 72; Weitzman, "Women and Children Last," 230.
139. Holden and Smock, "Marital Dissolution," 54–55.
140. Ibid., 58–59.
141. Ibid., 57–58.
142. Furstenberg, "Divorce and the American Family," 386.
143. Wetzel, "American Families," 8.
144. Joan Huber and Glenna Spitze, *Sex Stratification: Children, Housework, and Jobs* (New York: Academic Press, 1983).
145. Chadwick and Heaton, *Statistical Handbook,* 162.
146. Rachel Benson Gold and Cory L. Richards, "Women and Reproduction," in *The American Woman, 1987–1988,* ed. Sara E. Rix (New York: Norton, 1987), 254.
147. U.S. Department of Commerce, "Abortions, by Selected Characteristics, 1973 to 1988," *Statistical Abstract of the United States* (Washington, D.C.: Author, 1992), 74.
148. Stanley K. Henshaw and Kathryn Kost, "Abortion Patients in 1994–5: Characteristics of Contraceptive Use," *Family Planning Perspective* 28 (1996): 140–47. Catholic and Jewish women were more likely to get an abortion than Protestant women, although the abortion rate for all religious groups was one-quarter that for women without a religious affiliation.
149. Barbara Hinkson Craig and David M. O'Brien, *Abortion and American Politics* (Chatham, N.J.: Chatham House Publishers, 1993), 254–56.

150. U.S. Department of Commerce, "Abortions," 74.
151. Ibid.
152. Craig and O'Brien, *Abortion and American Politics,* 351–53.
153. "At Long Last Motherhood," *Newsweek,* March 16, 1981, 86.
154. Margaret L. Usdansky, "A Baby Doesn't Mean Marriage Anymore," *USA Today,* December 4, 1991, 8A.
155. Ibid.; Coltrane and Ishii-Kuntz, "Men's Housework," 44.
156. Quoted in Bird, *The Two Pay-Check Marriage,* 158–59.
157. U.S. Department of Commerce, Bureau of the Census, "Fertility of American Women," *Current Population Reports,* series P20, no. 470.
158. Coltrane and Ishii-Kuntz, "Men's Housework," 8–9.
159. "Life on the Homefront," *USA Today,* March 11, 1997, 6D.
160. George Masnick and Mary Jo Bane, *The Nation's Families: 1960–1990* (Cambridge, Mass.: Joint Center for Urban Studies of MIT and Harvard University, 1980), 143.
161. U.S. Bureau of the Census, "June Population Survey 1994" (Washington, D.C.: Department of Commerce, 1995).
162. Popenoe, "Flight from the Nuclear Family," 19.
163. Ibid.
164. Ibid.
165. Mary Jo Bane and Paul A. Jargowsky, "The Links Between Government Policy and Family Structure: What Matters and What Doesn't," in Cherlin, ed., *The Changing American Family,* 223.
166. Quoted in Usdansky, "A Baby," 8A.
167. Ibid.
168. Jessie Bernard introduced this idea. Jessie Bernard, "The Good Provider Role: Its Rise and Fall," *American Psychologist* 36, no. 1 (1981): 1–12. See also Barbara Ehreneich, *The Hearts of Men: American Dreams and the Flight from Commitment* (New York: Anchor Press, 1983); Frank F. Furstenberg Jr., "Good Dads–Bad Dads: Two Faces of Fatherhood," in Cherlin, ed., *The Changing American Family,* 193–218.
169. "Women's Lives: A Scoreboard of Change," *New York Times,* August 20, 21, 22, 1989. Data made available through the paper.
170. The 1989 Virginia Slims Poll.
171. Furstenberg, "Good Dads–Bad Dads."
172. Ibid., 201.
173. Ibid., 388.
174. Ibid., 203–4.
175. Ibid., 201–2.
176. Ibid., 209–10.
177. Howard V. Hayghe, "Family Members in the Work Force," *Monthly Labor Review* 113, no. 3 (1990): 18.
178. In white married couple families in 1993 the median income was $43,659; for white females heading families, median income was $19,962. The figures for African American families were $35,181 and $11,905, respectively; and for Hispanic families, $28,454 and $12,047. Cynthia Costello and Barbara Kivinae Krimgold, *The American Woman, 1996–97: Where We Stand* (New York: Norton, 1996), 309.
179. Bane and Jargowsky, "Government Policy and Family Structure," 227–47.
180. Quoted in "The Superwoman Squeeze," *Newsweek,* May 19, 1980, 78. See also Betty Friedan, *The Second Stage* (New York: Summit Books, 1981), especially chaps. 3, 6, and 8.

The Future
of the Movement

Our discussion of the various women's movements' attempts to gain greater political, employment, educational, and personal rights has revealed both periods of progress and periods of stagnation and even retrenchment. To evaluate the advances of women and these respective movements, we use as our standard the goals movements set for themselves. Table 7–1 highlights the demands made by women at Seneca Falls and then again at the next woman's rights meeting, which was held in Rochester, New York, on August 2, 1848, just two weeks after the Seneca Falls Convention. The Declaration of Sentiments and the Resolutions issued in Seneca Falls were a bit vague; the Rochester Resolutions were an effort by Elizabeth Cady Stanton to make lofty goals more concrete. The early goals for the current women's movement are derived from the National Organization for Women's Bill of Rights, which was drafted in 1967. Look closely at the demands made by women in 1848. Although women got the right to vote in 1920, they are underrepresented at all levels of lawmaking. Clearly, they have yet to gain an equal standing with men in social, political, or religious life.

The Married Women's Property Acts that were passed in the states in the 1800s, were a first step on the long road to equality within marriage. Women are far more equal within the institution of marriage today than they were in 1848, yet, as we saw in Chapter 6, many women often now have not one, but two places where they suffer from inequality—in their homes and in the workplace. Divorce laws, however, even after no-fault reforms, still often result in the unequal treatment of women, and child custody laws and child support enforcement lag behind the goals of most women's organizations today.

Employment opportunities for women are also limited and alone are insufficient to bring equity to women in the workplace. And, although women attend college in greater numbers than men, Title IX has yet to be

TABLE 7–1 Goals of the Women's Movements

Woman's Movement	Women's Rights Movement
The Declaration of Sentiments/ Rochester Resolutions[a]	*NOW Bill of Rights[b]*
The right to vote	Passage of an ERA
Equal representation in the government	
Equal standing in social, political, and religious life	
—an end to the double standard	
Equal rights for women in marriage including:	
• estate law	
• control of her own wages and services	
• reform of the marriage contract including coverture (civil death) and obedience	
Equal educational opportunities for women	Equal educational opportunities
Fairer wages for women	Equal job training opportunities for women in poverty
	Enforcement of laws banning discrimination in employment
	Maternity leave rights in employment and in social security benefits
	Tax deductions for home and child-care expenses
	Government creation of child-care centers
	Right of women to control their reproductive lives

[a]For the full text of the Declaration of Sentiments see http://www.rochester.edu/SBA/declare.html

[b]For an explanation and excerpts of the NOW Bill of Rights see http://www.feminist.org/research/chronicles/early2.html

implemented fully. A chilly climate for girls and women continues to exist in many schools, colleges, and universities.

Women at the Seneca Falls Convention also demanded greater participation in church affairs. Today, many major religions still prevent women from becoming ministers or priests. In medicine and law, women's opportunities are also far from equal. The double moral standard, while weakened, continues to limit women's progress. Women's "sphere of action" is still more confined than men's to the home and to "women's" jobs, and the public continues to harbor doubts about women's ability to manage in certain fields and to lead independent lives.

NOW's goals, as well as those of the larger women's rights movement, too, have only been partially achieved. There is no equal rights amendment (ERA). In spite of passage of the Pregnancy Discrimination Act and the Family and Medical Leave Act, maternity leave is limited and adequate child care is unavailable for most working women. Poverty among women continues to grow, and access to job training was curtailed during the Reagan-Bush years. New welfare reforms may, in fact, make it more difficult for many women to raise their children and be employed outside the home. And while secure for the moment, the right to control one's reproductive life is restricted by the limited availability of abortion and birth control. Moreover, for the first time, Congress appears ready to restrict certain abortion procedures, and even a supposedly pro-choice Democratic president is apparently willing to do so under certain conditions.

In previous chapters, we identified public attitudes, role conflict, women's lack of preparation, and male resistance and discrimination as some of the barriers to full equality and securing women's demands. These hindrances have been considerably weakened since 1848 (and even since 1967). Many of the most dramatic changes that have occurred during the past three decades were a result of pressure from the women's rights movement. But whether the roadblocks to women's full equality will continue to fall is an open question.

Some commentators argue that women's progress is only partially dependent on the existence of a women's movement. Anne N. Costain, for example, argues that the government often took the lead in passing policy proposals beneficial to women.[1] Our review suggests that without the prodding and pressure of organized women, not only will many advances not occur, but also gains won can quickly become gains lost. The decades of the 1920s and 1930s are particularly instructive. Split into two camps divided over whether working women needed differential (protective) or equal treatment, women witnessed few gains and, more ominously, were unable to prevent their economic opportunities from being undermined during the depression. Differences in tactics and goals also hindered the progress of the first woman's movement. The current movement, too, seemed to have taken a dramatic hit from the "backlash" described by Susan Faludi.[2] During the Reagan-Bush years, the continued onslaught of government attacks on women's programs and policies not only hurt women, but women's rights groups seemed unable to counter those actions until abortion rights truly seemed threatened in the late 1980s. This threat, when coupled with the Senate's treatment of Anita Hill during the Clarence Thomas confirmation hearings, seemed to energize the movement and produced considerable results in the 1992 elections. Women were united on two fronts—the need to keep abortion safe and legal and the clear need for more women in elected positions. This seemed to happen with the election of the first pro-choice president, record numbers of women in the House and Senate, and the appointment of a female, pro-choice justice to the Supreme Court. These

1992–1993 successes, however, appeared to lull some women into thinking that the fight was over. As detailed in Chapter 2, women stayed home from the polls in droves in 1994, and the most antifemale Congress ever was elected.

The efforts of several groups including EMILY's List, the League of Women Voters, and NOW to turn out the women's vote in 1996 were discussed in Chapter 1. Still, in spite of those efforts, many women stayed home from the polls and the Republican Congress continued its efforts to roll back many gains made by women in the political, employment, educational, familial, and reproductive spheres discussed throughout this volume. The question then remains, what is necessary to reenergize the women's rights movement and get it back on the solid road to equality?

PREREQUISITES FOR A REENERGIZED WOMEN'S RIGHTS MOVEMENT

In our introduction to this volume, we outlined the prerequisites for a women's movement. We argue that unless many of these factors are present, the kind of sustained activity for women's rights displayed in the 1970s will not occur. Instead, sporadic events may energize some women for short periods of time to act for easily identifiable goals, but this activity will be insufficient to bring about the kind of dramatic changes in women's status that occurred in the 1960s and 1970s.

Organizational Base and Organizational Support

The first prerequisite for a revitalized movement is an organizational base. Although the membership of many feminist and traditional women's rights groups wavered or declined in the 1980s, women's organizations continue to proliferate. In the wake of the Clarence Thomas hearings, many groups reported sharp increases in membership.[3] Mary Fainsod Katzenstein, moreover, argues that the unobtrusive mobilization by women in women's caucuses and within existing organizations long dominated by men "drives second-wave feminism ahead into the 1990s."[4] Still, these groups, while undoubtedly changing existing traditionally male-dominated organizations, have yet to form a sufficient base necessary to reenergize the movement.

As Nancy F. Cott's analysis of women's activity in the 1920s found, women's associations proliferated in the decade after suffrage, but their growth drew potential membership from the more clearly defined pro-women's groups like the national League of Women Voters.[5] Much of the same sort of phenomena may have happened in the 1970s and 1980s. Women's caucuses in the professions and new women's groups that organized around new or reinvigorated issues such as abortion, peace, nuclear disarmament, or domestic violence siphoned off members from NOW, the National Federation of Business and Professional Women's Clubs, the League of Women Voters, and other pro-women's rights groups.

Even earlier, the younger branch of the women's movement witnessed most of its constituent organizations' fading or their transformation into local associations with more narrow focuses. Flora Davis notes that between 1972 and 1975, a "metamorphosis" occurred in the women's movement. As original women's liberation groups died, what she terms *liberal feminism* became the mainstream of the movement.[6] This growing mainstream, however, was soon affected by the proliferation of women's groups in the 1980s, which often meant, as it did in the 1920s, a dispersal of women's energies and a resultant lack of focus on a single agenda at the same time that there was outside pressure from the government and even the media *against* the women's rights movement and its goals.

Countering this trend somewhat has been the development of "permanent flexible alliances" of women's groups that agree to work together on a common agenda.[7] Perhaps the most notable of these are the National Women's Conference Committee and the Council of Presidents. The former has established coalitions of women's groups in almost all the states. These state coalitions have agreed to work together on the twenty-five-point National Plan of Action for Women adopted at the 1977 National Women's Conference held in Houston, Texas. Growing out of and usually working in concert with the remaining state commissions on the status of women, these alliances are based on the premise that groups will work together to reform state laws. Like the Women's Joint Congressional Committee (WJCC), which was national in scope, members do not have to work on all issues, but affiliated organizations must agree not to work in opposition to items on the common agenda. Success in changing state laws involving marital property reform, domestic abuse, pay equity, child support, and gender discrimination in insurance rates can be partially attributed to these coalitional efforts.

Whereas the National Conference Committee works for state law reform, the Council of Presidents works on the national level. It is composed of women representatives from more than one hundred national women's groups. Since it was organized in 1985, it annually adopts a set of legislative priorities, called the Women's Agenda. Like the WJCC, its member organizations agree to jointly lobby the Congress and executive branch on agenda items.

In conjunction with these coalitions, national and state governments, as they have in the past, may also play an important role in providing organizational support for the women's rights movement. With both President Clinton and Hillary Rodham Clinton committed to women's rights, women's groups have had a more responsive ear in the White House, and many more feminists were appointed to positions of authority and power within the administration. With more cabinet-level jobs than in any previous administration, women are more strategically placed to push the women's agenda. A good example of this phenomenon is Secretary of State Madeleine Albright. She has been able to push the goal of more equitable treatment for women in all nations to the forefront of national foreign policy. President Clinton's appointment of Ruth Bader Ginsburg, a pioneer in women's rights litigation and an advocate of stricter constitutional protections for women, also has already affected the Supreme Court's decision making on women's rights issues, as witnessed by her majority opinion in *United States v. Virginia Military Institute,* discussed in Chapter 3. Although the collective impact of women in these high-ranking government slots helps to push the women's agenda forward, the election of a Republican Congress in 1994 and Clinton's own increased conservatism has had the effect of slowing or reversing women's progress. Welfare reform, most notably, is likely to have a disastrous impact on poor women, as is the administration's support of abortion restrictions after viability. The lesson is clear. Women cannot rely on others to be as committed to their agenda.

Leaders and Organizers

The second criterion for a successful movement is the availability of leaders and organizers. There is a pressing need for a second generation of feminist spokespersons. Most of the foremothers of the current movement are ready to retire or have moved on to other issues. Those who will shepherd the movement into the twenty-first century may well be found among the many newly elected and appointed women public officials who have already begun to parlay their positions in Washington and in state capitals into a platform from which to champion women's issues. The power of elected women at the national level was best exemplified after their gains in the 1992 election, but even in the post-1994 Congress, women such as Senator Barbara Boxer (D-Calif.), who took the lead in the abortion restriction debate in 1997, continue to fight for the women's agenda.

In 1997, NOW held a Young Feminist Summit, which attracted more than twelve hundred participants from all over the nation. NOW and several other women's rights groups including the National Women's Political Caucus realize how important it is to attract young, energetic women to the cause as organizers and potential leaders. Still, a cadre of nationally known young organizers of the same renown as those women who came to the forefront in the 1960s has yet to emerge.

Communications Networks

Communications networks are also a third key to a reenergized women's movement. Although women's networks and coalitions continue to play an important role in getting the message of the movement to supporters, a question remains about the willingness of the media to provide favorable coverage. Although the national media are not the kind of communications network historically discussed by social movement theorists, the impact of the news media as a way of conveying information about the women's rights movement cannot be ignored. In her best seller, *Backlash: The Undeclared War Against American Women,* Susan Faludi argued persuasively that the media in the 1980s was a critical coplayer with the New Right in a tacit alliance to undermine the movement. She cited several examples of the media backlash, including coverage of the "marriage crunch," the problem of getting pregnant when over the age of thirty (the ticking biological clock), and other (often mythical) miseries besetting professional women.

Just as most magazine editors after World War II urged women to adopt the feminine mystique, leave their jobs, and return to homes in the suburbs, the hidden message in the media in the 1980s was that the women's rights movement was responsible for the problems supposedly besetting women who followed its philosophy. Faludi is quick to point out that she does not believe the backlash was an overt conspiracy, but the results were the same. She writes:

> The force and furor of the backlash churn beneath the surface, largely invisible to the public eye. On occasion in the last decade, they have burst into view. We have seen New Right politicians condemn women's independence, anti-abortion protesters firebomb women's clinics. . . . The ascendancy of virulently misogynist comics like Andrew Dice Clay—who called women pigs and sluts and strutted in films in which women were beaten, tortured, and blown up—or radio hosts like Rush Limbaugh, whose broadsides against "femi-Nazi" feminists made his syndicated program the most popular radio talk show in the nation. . . . Taken as a whole, however, these codes and cajolings, these whispers and threats and myths, move overwhelmingly in one direction: they try to push women back into their "acceptable" roles—whether as Daddy's girl or fluttery romantic, active nester or passive love object.[8]

Not all reviewers have seen a media backlash against feminism. Surely, the coverage of the Year of the Woman in 1992 helped to fuel the success of women candidates. Perhaps it is best to note that the media can be both friend and foe of the movement, but that it cannot always be relied on to motivate women to support the movement.

One new avenue that has yet to be fully explored in terms of reaching women is the Internet. Hundreds of women's rights and feminist home pages, chat rooms, and lists abound, facilitating communications among women, some of them probably previously unorganized. The women regularly logging on to the Internet may prove to be the critical mass yet to be mobilized. Still, women's movement leaders will have to develop more effective strategies to organize this untapped force.

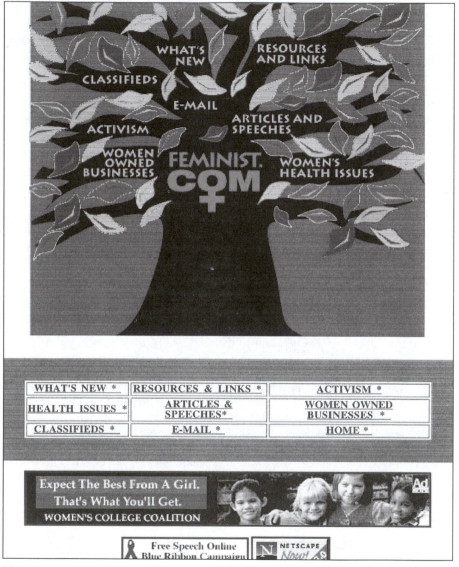

The women's movement on the Internet. (Reprinted with the permission of the Women's College Coalition)

Critical Mobilizing Events

Communication networks often serve as signals to participants that the time has come to act. In the 1980s, there were few events that roused women to action. Indeed, the defeat of the ERA in 1982 seemed to have the opposite affect, warning movement activists that it was not an auspicious time to seek major change. Other critical demobilizing events were the election and reelection of Ronald Reagan, an avowed foe of many items on the women's agenda, particularly the ERA and freedom of choice. George Bush's victory in 1988 reinforced the message that the 1980s was not a time to advance the agenda of the women's movement.

In 1989 and into the 1990s, however, a few critical events served notice to women that they must act. The first was the U.S. Supreme Court's decision in *Webster v. Reproductive Health Services* (1989), which sent a strong signal to women that the right to control their bodies might soon be lost. In reaction, women by the thousands took to the streets, contributed money, or joined women's rights organizations. This behavior was quite understandable. Research suggests that threats to public goods (in this case, freedom of choice) are more powerful motivators of action than are attempts to mobilize for new or yet-to-be-won public goods.

Fear about the loss of abortion rights also played a role in the next critical event, the Clarence Thomas hearings. When Anita Hill testified that Thomas (a conservative expected to provide the critical vote to overturn *Roe v. Wade*) had subjected her to sexual harassment, the "treatment" she received by the all-male Senate Judiciary Committee served as another critical mobilizing event. Again, many women vowed to work to put more women in the Senate and House, and millions of dollars were raised and votes secured for women candidates.

The election of Bill Clinton to the White House in 1992 activated women elected to the 103rd Congress to push a women's agenda. But the sudden political shift in 1994 cut short some major gains and reversed others. The battle over late-term abortions and abortion rights after fetal viability is just one signal that the rear-guard action to protect gains won in the 1970s is not yet over.

Political Mobilization

The factors discussed previously are critical to forging a movement, but no movement can succeed unless it can mobilize the potential beneficiaries, in this case, women. Surveys among women find generally strong and growing support for the movement. For instance, as illustrated in Table 7–2, in 1970, when the movement was just gaining visibility, only 40 percent of women favored efforts to "strengthen and change women's status in society." By 1994, this percentage had climbed to more than three-quarters of all women, with young, educated women being even more approving.

The future of the women's rights movement depends very much on mobilizing this support. The need to do so is particularly critical for women of color, who in the twenty-first century will become the majority of American women. Polls reveal that African American and Hispanic women are very strong proponents of the movement. However, the movement has not

TABLE 7–2 Support for Efforts to Strengthen and Change Women's Status, 1970–1994[a]

	1970 (%)	1972 (%)	1974 (%)	1979 (%)	1985 (%)	1989 (%)	1994 (%)
Women who favor efforts	40	48	57	63	73	77	78
Women who oppose efforts	42	36	25	27	17	12	10
Women who don't know	18	16	18	11	10	11	12

[a]Survey question: "There has been much talk recently about changing women's status in society today. On the whole, do you favor or oppose most of the efforts to strengthen and change women's status in society today?"

Source: Virginia Slims Polls, made available by the Roper Center for Public Opinion Research, Storrs, Conn.

always embraced these women. Both the early woman's movement and even more so the suffrage movement were flawed by racism that drove women of color out of mainstream women's organizations. In the modern era, the issue has been less one of overt racism than an inability of white women leaders to recognize the biases built into their structures and the movement's focus on issues that have not always been a high priority to women of color. Abortion, for instance, is less strongly supported by both Hispanics and African Americans than whites. The women's movement, moreover, has not placed racism, an issue of extreme importance to women of color, very high on its agenda. Likewise, even though welfare reform was in many ways a targeted attack on poor African American women, mainstream women's groups lined up uneasily to be sure behind President Clinton's efforts to change the system. The key to a reenergized women's movement, therefore, depends on a set of goals that will strengthen the resolve of the traditional core of the movement while attracting a much broader and more diverse constituency. The foundation for such an agenda can be seen in Table 7–3, which gives women's responses to a series of questions about areas where changes are needed to make women's lives better.

GOALS FOR THE WOMEN'S RIGHTS MOVEMENT

What is notable about Table 7–3 is the widespread support among women for changes in all of the three spheres that have been the focus of women's movements: politics, economics, and the family. There is nearly unanimous support among women for change in government and the marketplace. Only with respect to family roles is there some hesitancy expressed about the need for change. With respect to the goals of a reenergized women's movement, the unmet goals of 1848 or 1967 can and still do serve, with some minor modification, to set a possible platform for the movement.

TABLE 7–3 Support for Changing Women's Roles, 1994[a]

	Major Changes Needed		Some Changes Needed		No Changes Needed	
	Women (%)	Men (%)	Women (%)	Men (%)	Women (%)	Men (%)
Opportunities for leadership positions in government	38	22	49	54	10	19
Salaries of women compared to men	44	27	50	56	4	14
Kinds of jobs open to women	36	23	53	56	10	19
Opportunities for leadership positions in business	39	24	48	53	10	19
Day-care options for working mothers	35	26	48	50	11	17
Flexibility at work, job sharing, flexible hours, work at home	35	23	52	54	9	16
Women's roles as homemakers	24	19	49	47	24	29
Kinds of marriages women have	30	22	45	45	20	25
Women's roles as mothers	26	20	48	48	22	27

[a]Survey question: "Regardless of how much things have changed over the past ten to twenty years, how much do you feel each of these things needs to change over the next ten years to make women's lives better?[a]

Source: 1995 Virginia Slims Poll, made available by the Roper Center for Public Opinion Research, Storrs, Conn.

A 1996 U.S. Department of Labor Women's Bureau survey of 250,000 working women supports this. It found that women were very concerned with improving their pay and career advancement opportunities. Finding affordable child care and securing paid sick and family leave also topped the list of needs for working women.[9] Considerable consensus exists among women about the need to focus on three problems of particular concern to working women: (1) combining work and family, (2) discrimination in hiring, and (3) low pay. Women of color were particularly likely to identify these issues as important.[10] Interviews with women in focus groups found "real anger about equal pay and not getting a decent wage for working all day long."[11] Women in the study complained not only about the lack of money but also the lack of time, with middle-class women more concerned about the latter, and poor and working-class women the former. Pay equity, family leave, and flextime were seen as solutions to the dual demands on women to provide for, and take care of, their families. Also high on women's list of concerns was national health care. Further down in the rankings of priorities, however, were crime, child support, and abortion rights.

The message to the movement is clear. Women are suffering under their dual roles as worker and homemaker-mother, and they need help. The problem for women's organizations is framing a solution that will mobilize women—who are already stressed from combining roles with little actual time to spare—to act in concert for change. Suffrage served in that capacity during the early years of this century, and the ERA filled the role during the 1970s. Throughout most of the 1980s, however, the movement remained adrift with no central or core issue around which to mobilize women. In the late 1980s and early 1990s—at least until the Clinton victory—abortion rights appeared immediately threatened, and women did mobilize women to march on Washington, D.C., *and* to go to the voting booth. Similarly, the Clarence Thomas hearings encouraged a national debate about sexual harassment. Sexual harassment, however, is not perceived by most women as one of the major problems facing them.

The issue of political underrepresentation of women might provide a unifying issue. Certainly, to obtain the legislation necessary to meet women's goals for change, it will be critical to have women in the national and state legislatures. If women in the United States can be made to believe that political representation is the key to policy success, in the same manner that they were convinced that the right to vote itself was key to obtaining a wide range of goals, the movement may have its mobilizing issue.

Women continue to vote in larger numbers than men and to cast their votes more frequently for women, Democrats, or pro-choice female Republicans. This political clout may help elect more women legislators who will be more likely to advance and secure the wide array of issues that make up the women's agenda. If the movement wants to attract the diverse constituency it needs to survive, however, it must tie the election of women to the need to work for issues that will ease the burden of the average working woman.

NOTES

1. Anne N. Costain, *Inviting Women's Rebellion: A Political Process Interpretation of the Women's Movement* (Baltimore: Johns Hopkins University Press, 1992), chap. 6. See also Georgia Duerst-Lahti, "The Government's Role in Building the Women's Movement," *Political Science Quarterly* 104 (1989): 249–68.
2. Susan Faludi, *Backlash: The Undeclared War Against American Women* (New York: Crown Publishers, 1991).
3. See Sarah Slavin, *Women's Issues Interest Groups* (Westport, Conn.: Greenwood Press, 1995).
4. Mary Fainsod Katzenstein, "Feminism within American Institutions: Unobtrusive Mobilization in the 1980s," *Signs* 16 (1990): 28.
5. Nancy F. Cott, *The Grounding of Modern Feminism* (New Haven, Conn.: Yale University Press, 1987), chap. 3.
6. Flora Davis, *Moving the Mountain: The Women's Movement in America since 1960* (New York: Simon & Schuster, 1991).
7. Sarah Harder, "Flourishing in the Mainstream: The U.S. Women's Movement Today," in *The American Woman, 1990–1991*, ed. Sara E. Rix (New York: Norton, 1990), 278.

8. Faludi, *Backlash,* xxi–xxii.

9. U.S. Department of Labor, Women's Bureau, *The Working Women Count Honor Roll Report* (Washington, D.C.: Author, 1996), 1–2. See also Women's Voices Project, commissioned by the Ms. Foundation and the Center for Policy Alternatives.

10. Linda Tarr-Whelan, quoted in Marcia Eldredge, "Women's Voices: An Agenda for Change," *National Business Woman,* Winter 1992, 14.

11. Ibid., 14–15.

Index